D0411481

THE CONSTITUTIONAL HISTORY
OF
THE UNITED STATES

1826–1876

THE MACMILLAN COMPANY
NEW YORK · CHICAGO
DALLAS · ATLANTA · SAN FRANCISCO
LONDON · MANILA

IN CANADA
BRETT-MACMILLAN LTD.
GALT, ONTARIO

THE
CONSTITUTIONAL
HISTORY OF THE
UNITED STATES
1826–1876

A More Perfect Union

by HOMER CAREY HOCKETT

Professor of History in The Ohio State University

NEW YORK

THE MACMILLAN COMPANY

Published November, 1939
Third Printing, 1959

We the People of the United States, in Order to form *a More Perfect Union,* . . . do ordain and establish this Constitution for the United States of America.

　　　—*Preamble of the Constitution.*

PREFACE

T HE "apology" which the writer of a book in the good old days felt obliged to offer to the "gentle reader" has in our times degenerated into a "preface." An author, however conscious of the defects in his work, can safely trust the reviewer to point out shortcomings which might otherwise escape attention. Nevertheless the preface may be useful in explaining a writer's purpose and viewpoint.

The present volume, according to title, covers the half-century from 1826 to 1876. In fact, owing to a treatment which is partly topical, there is some lapping back into the years nominally assigned to the preceding volume.

The theme of this work, and space limitations, require that the currents of thought dealt with be confined strictly to those bearing on constitutional history, and, moreover, that these currents be indicated by discussion of the views and acts of a few only of the major participants in events. Many an interesting secondary character is passed by without notice, and important themes are often necessarily alluded to so briefly that readers will merely be made aware of their existence. These points, especially in the case of college students, may well be made the termini from which to embark on profitable topical investigations.

Much space in the present volume is perforce given to the slavery controversy and the sectional war to which it led. No part of our history has been more studied and more often retold. For that reason if no other it is difficult to give the subject a fresh or original treatment. To minimize the boredom of readers who are familiar with the story, the author has avoided narrative and restricted himself severely to the constitutional phases of the matter.

There are other topics in this middle period which, in the perspective of the present, are of perhaps greater interest. The democratization of the federal government, the rise of capitalistic industry, the adoption of the corporate form of organization, and the territorial expansion of the United States are developments of these years which affected our constitutional system, in the long run, quite as profoundly as the slavery issue.

The literature pertinent to the topics covered by this volume is abundant, but many readers may not have access to adequate libraries. For this class of readers, as well as for college students who desire to make an intensive study of fundamental documents, attention is called to the fact that many of these documents have been collected in readily available books. Of particular value is Allen Johnson's *Readings in American Constitutional History, 1776–1876* (Houghton Mifflin Company). Of more general character but of great utility are William MacDonald's *Select Documents of United States History, 1776–1861*, and *Select Statutes of United States History, 1861–1898* (The Macmillan Company). A recent work of similar character is Henry S. Commager's *Documents of American History* (Crofts & Co.). For the guidance of those who wish to make use of these documents, references to these several books have been made freely in the footnotes on the following pages.

Readers of the first volume in this series may have felt that the subtitle—The Blessings of Liberty—was used ironically, so largely was the story one of strife and discord. The subtitle of the present volume—A More Perfect Union—drawn likewise from the preamble of the Constitution, may arouse a similar reaction, since the book is in large part the story of a continuous sectional struggle which culminated in an effort to sever the Union. Nevertheless the phrase is appropriate for the period, for the close of the first century of independence found the Union more firmly cemented than it had ever been before. This phrase set forth, of course, the immediate purpose of the framers of the Constitution, to improve upon the union under the Articles of Confederation. More than once in the years which followed the permanence of the Union which they formed was in doubt. Not, indeed, until the great attempt to dismember it had been thwarted was the success of their effort assured.

HOMER CAREY HOCKETT

COLUMBUS, OHIO
August 23, 1939

CONTENTS

PART ONE

THE REACTION AGAINST NATIONALISM

I

THE SUPREME COURT UNDER FIRE

CRITICISM OF THE McCULLOCH AND COHENS DECISIONS

A PRECEDING volume has shown that the Supreme Court consistently upheld federal legislation in the years following the War of 1812–1815. On the contrary, state legislation was more than once set aside. The decisions of the period confirmed the apprehensions which had led Thomas Jefferson, in 1798, to formulate the doctrine advanced in the Virginia and Kentucky Resolutions. At that time it had seemed to him inevitable that the court as part of the federal government would side with the legislative branch of that same government in any dispute with the states over their respective powers. The acceptance of the view that the court was the judge of the allocation of powers under the scheme of distribution embodied in the Constitution, he believed, would place the reserved rights of the states completely at the mercy of the central government. In 1819, the decision in the case of McCulloch v. Maryland illustrated all of the dangers to the states which he had foreseen.[1]

The McCulloch decision was followed by nationwide discussion, but many of the critics of the court took offense for a very different reason from that which had disturbed them in 1802 and 1803. At the earlier date they asserted with Breckinridge that the court was bound to give effect to the laws of Congress and denounced the ruling in the Marbury case which held a part of the Judiciary Act of 1789 unconstitutional.[2] Now they objected to the court's posi-

---

[1] See Hockett, *Constitutional History of the United States, 1776–1826*, p. 287 *et seq.*, and 358–362. Hereafter this book will be referred to as *Con. Hist.*, I.

In the footnotes throughout this volume the titles of books are printed in *italics*, while the titles of articles and essays in magazines and composite books are placed in quotation marks. To save repetition the place and date of publication of books and the volume and pages of magazines, etc., in which articles and essays are to be found, as well as full titles, are given only in the List of References at the back of the volume. All entries in this List are arranged alphabetically under the name of authors or editors.

[2] *Ibid.*, 305 *et seq.*

tion for exactly the opposite reason—because it upheld an act of Congress which they disliked. Even Madison was dismayed by the latitude which the court seemed disposed to allow to the legislature. Since as President he had signed the very act which came before the justices in the Maryland case (the act incorporating the Second United States Bank), it is not to be supposed that he doubted its constitutionality, or that he desired the court to hold it void.[3] It was Marshall's broad endorsement of the doctrine of implied powers to which he now took exception; and the announcement of the decision hastened his return to the view that in doubtful cases the amending process should be resorted to. The court's ruling [4] seemed to him "to break down the landmarks intended by a specification of the powers of Congress, and to substitute, for a definite connection between means and ends, a legislative discretion as to the former, to which no practical limit can be assigned." [5] Such a rule of construction, if announced at the time of the ratification of the Constitution, would, he believed, have defeated it. "It has been the misfortune, if not the reproach, of other nations," he wrote, "that their governments have not been freely and deliberately established by themselves. It is the boast of ours that such has been its source, and that it can be altered by the same authority only which established it. It is a further boast, that a regular mode of making proper alterations has been providently inserted in the Constitution itself. It is anxiously to be wished, therefore, that no innovations may take place in other modes, one of which would be a constructive assumption of powers never meant to be granted." [6]

Jefferson refused to accept the decision in the bank case as conclusive, at least for his own state. Clinging to the view that questions involving the respective powers of state and nation do not fall within the jurisdiction of the court, and that the Constitution does not provide an impartial umpire in such disputes, he wrote to his

[3] *Ibid.*, 343.
[4] *Ibid.*, 360–361. See W. E. Dodd, "Chief Justice Marshall and Virginia, 1813–1821."
[5] Letter to Judge Spencer Roane, Sept. 2, 1819. Madison's *Letters and Other Writings*, III, 143 *et seq.*
[6] *Ibid.*

friend of former days, John Adams, eight months after Marshall's pronouncement, saying that the branches of the bank in Virginia would "probably conform voluntarily to such regulations as the Legislature may prescribe. . . . If they do not, we must shut their doors, and join the other States which deny the right of Congress to establish banks, and solicit them to agree to some mode of settling this constitutional question." [7]

Soon afterwards (Dec. 22, 1819), Andrew Stevenson presented in the Virginia House of Delegates resolutions reviving the Pennsylvania proposal of an "impartial tribunal" which Virginia had rejected a few years previously.[8] The resolutions instructed the senators of the state at Washington to seek an amendment to the Constitution "creating a tribunal for the decision of all questions, in which the powers and authorities of the general government and those of the states, where they are in conflict, shall be decided," and to resist all legislation by Congress not expressly included within its powers, unless "necessary and proper," in the strict Jeffersonian sense,[9] for carrying into effect the powers expressly given. The resolution was not adopted.

Marshall's summons to Virginia to appear in the Cohens case revived the agitation which had followed the decision in the case of McCulloch v. Maryland. The Virginia House of Delegates adopted by a large majority a report which asserted that "if the federal legislature cannot abrogate state laws, the federal judiciary cannot abrogate state judgments." [10] Resolutions were also adopted denying the appellate jurisdiction of the Supreme Court in any case decided by a state court, and asserting that, even if appellate jurisdiction did exist, it could not include a suit to reverse a judgment obtained in a state court.[11]

The next winter, a few months after the decision in the Cohens case, resolutions to amend the Constitution were defeated by a small majority in the same chamber. These resolutions proposed:

[7] Nov. 7, 1819. Paul L. Ford, ed., *Writings of Jefferson*, X, 147.

[8] *Niles Weekly Register*, XVII, 311. For the Pennsylvania proposal see Hockett, *Con. Hist.*, I, 328–329.

[9] See *ibid.*, 271.

[10] January 9, 1821. *Niles Register*, XX, 118 *et seq.* For the Cohens case see Hockett, *Con. Hist.*, I, 369 *et seq.*

[11] Herman V. Ames, *State Documents on Federal Relations*, 104.

"That the legislative authority of the United States should not be construed to embrace any power not expressly granted by the Constitution, or absolutely necessary and proper for carrying same into execution.

"That no department of the national government should be construed to have power to bind conclusively the claims of the states where their rights and those of the General Government are in contest.

"That the judicial power of the United States should not be construed to extend to any case in which a state was a party, except in controversies between two or more states, nor to any other controversy to which a state should claim to be a party.

"That no appeal shall lie to any court of the United States from any decision rendered in a state court.

"That no law made for the District of Columbia should have force within any state." [12]

ROANE AND TAYLOR

In taking this position the House was following the lead of Spencer Roane, of the Virginia appellate court, who wrote for the *Richmond Enquirer* during 1821 a series of articles attempting to refute Marshall's reasoning.[13] Roane seized upon the words of the supreme law clause of the Constitution, which lays upon *state* courts the obligation to recognize the binding effect of federal law as supreme law, and pointed out that the Constitution contains no express grant of authority to the central government to be the

[12] *Niles Register*, XXI, 404.

[13] Ames, *State Docs.*, 103. Roane's cousin, Thomas Ritchie, was editor of the *Enquirer*. Other articles appeared in the same paper from March to August by other writers on the same subject. Roane wrote under the pseudonyms "Algernon Sidney," "Amphictyon," and "Hampden."

Judge Roane was Patrick Henry's son-in-law. He was thought of by the Republicans as a possible successor of Marshall, during their attack upon the federal courts while Jefferson was President. See Hockett, *Con. Hist.*, I, 314. A biographical sketch by Edwin Smith, together with reprints of his articles and some of his correspondence, are to be found in the *John P. Branch Historical Papers* for 1904–1906. There is another sketch by T. R. B. Wright, entitled "Judge Spencer Roane," in the *Virginia Law Register*. A meritorious study of his views is that by Jeannette Elder, *The Constitutional Views of Judge Spencer Roane*. Additional correspondence is published in New York Public Library *Bulletin*, X. There is a study of Ritchie by Charles H. Ambler.

judge of the extent of its own powers. The twenty-fifth section of the Judiciary Act of 1789, therefore, providing for the appeal of cases arising under federal law to the Supreme Court as the tribunal of last resort, he now maintained was unconstitutional.[14] His view was the more plausible because clearly the Constitution did not contemplate a consolidated union, but a system of distributed powers.[15] The state courts were bound by the Constitution to uphold the paramount authority of federal law, but it seemed to Roane equally necessary that they should guard that portion of "sovereignty" which the state retained. He accepted the doctrine of divided sovereignty, reaffirmed the position which he had taken in Martin v. Hunter's Lessee,[16] and supported Jefferson's doctrine of 1798. It was the old question as to where was vested the right to judge of the allocation of powers under the scheme of distribution. Roane gave it to the state judiciary.

The preceding autumn John Taylor had published his book entitled *Construction Construed*, taking his text from the recent decisions of the Supreme Court, especially in the case of McCulloch v. Maryland.[17]

JEFFERSON AND MADISON

Of Taylor's book Jefferson wrote: "It is the most logical retraction of our governments to the original and true principles of the constitution creating them, which has appeared since the adoption of that instrument. . . . It should be put into the hands of all our functionaries, authoritatively, as a standing instruction, and true exposition of our Constitution, as understood at the time we agreed to it." [18] Jefferson indeed, was almost in panic for fear of his old adversary Marshall and his colleagues on the supreme bench. He referred to them as "the subtle corps of sappers and miners constantly working under ground to undermine the foundations of our confederated fabric . . . construing our constitution

[14] See Hockett, *Con. Hist.*, I, 238–239 and note.
[15] On the distribution of powers see *ibid.*, 229.
[16] *Ibid.*, 367.
[17] There is a sketch of Taylor by W. E. Dodd,—"John Taylor of 'Caroline.' " The chief biography is that by Henry H. Simms. It contains a bibliography. See also W. E. Dodd, ed., "John Taylor, Prophet of Secession."
[18] June, 1821. H. A. Washington, ed., *Writings of Jefferson*, VII, 213.

from a coordination of a general and special government to a general and supreme one alone." [19]   Again he declared that, like gravity, they were "ever acting, with noiseless foot, and unalarming advance, gaining ground step by step, and holding what is gained . . . ingulphing insidiously the special governments." [20]

In this state of mind he hailed Judge Roane's articles with delight: "I . . . confess that they appeared to me to pulverize every word which had been delivered by Judge Marshall, of the extra-judicial part of his opinion [in the Cohens case]; and all was extra-judicial, except the decision that the act of Congress had not purported to give to the corporation of Washington the authority claimed by their lottery law, of controlling the laws of the States within the States themselves.   But unable to claim that case, he could not let it go entirely, but went on gratuitously to prove, that notwithstanding the eleventh amendment . . ., a state *could* be brought as a defendant, to the bar of his court; and again, that Congress might authorize a corporation of its territory to exercise legislation within a State, and paramount to the laws of that State. . . .   This doctrine was so completely refuted by Roane, that if he can be answered, I surrender human reason as a vain and useless faculty, given to bewilder, and not to guide us." [21]

Jefferson denied not only the right of the court to act as final judge of the powers of the federal government, but also those of its several departments.   To Roane he wrote: "In denying the right they usurp, of exclusively explaining the constitution, I go further than you do, if I understand rightly your quotation, from the Federalist, of an opinion that 'the judiciary is the last resort in relation *to the other departments* of the government, but not in relation to the rights of the parties to the compact under which the judiciary is derived.'   If this opinion be sound, then indeed is our constitution a complete *felo de se*.   For intending to establish three departments, coordinate and independent, that they might check and balance one another, it has given according to this [McCulloch] opinion, to one of them alone, the right to prescribe rules for the

[19] Letter to Thomas Ritchie, Dec. 25, 1820. *Ibid.*, 192.
[20] To Roane, Mar. 9, 1821. *Ibid.*, 212. *Cf.* letter to N. Macon, Nov. 23, 1821. *Ibid.*, 223.
[21] To Judge Johnson, June 12, 1823. *Ibid.*, 294.

government of the others, and to that one too, which is unelected by, and independent of the nation. . . .

"My construction of the constitution is very different from that you quote. It is that each department is truly independent of the others, and has an equal right to decide for itself what is the meaning of the constitution in the cases submitted to its action; and especially, where it is to act ultimately and without appeal." [22]

Jefferson believed that much of the trouble with the court was due to Marshall's dominating personality and his methods. He condemned the practice of making up opinions in secret "conclave, perhaps by a majority of one, delivered as if unanimous and with the silent acquiescence of lazy or timid associates, by a crafty Chief Judge, who sophisticates the law to his mind, by the turn of his own reasoning." He would have required every judge to deliver a separate opinion, which he thought would make impossible the "cooking up of a decision and delivering it by one of their members as the opinion of the Court without the possibility of our knowing how many, who, or for what reasons each member concurred." The practice defeated "the possibility of impeachment by smothering evidence." [23]

Jefferson thought that Marshall was responsible for this practice, but it had been followed before his accession. His own plan was that after the judges had announced their individual opinions on constitutional questions, Congress should denounce those which it thought erroneous. Then if any judge failed to accept the reasoning of the legislators, he should be subject to impeachment. In this way he hoped that the "unconstitutional invasions of State Rights" might be checked. Jefferson also favored a constitutional amendment fixing definite terms of office for the judges, with a provision for reappointment by Congress. He naively overlooked the possibilities of intrigue and corruption involved in the suggestion.[24]

[22] September 6, 1819. Ford, *Writings of Jefferson*, X, 140.
[23] See the discussion of all these criticisms of the court in Charles Warren, *Supreme Court in United States History*, Chap. XVII. See also the same author's *Supreme Court and the Sovereign States*, and *Congress, the Constitution, and the Supreme Court*.
[24] Warren, *Sup. Court*, I, 655–656. On June 15, 1821, Marshall wrote to Story: "For Mr. Jefferson's opinion as respects this department, it is not difficult to assign

Madison was by no means a mere echo of Jefferson on constitutional questions. He took a more liberal view of the functions of the court. While agreeing with Jefferson that the justices were given to the regrettable "practice of mingling with their judgments pronounced comments and reasonings of a scope beyond them," he thought, referring to the McCulloch case, that there was less danger to be apprehended from the court's stretches of power than from the latitude which it had assigned to Congress. "The Judicial power of the United States over cases arising under the Constitution," he insisted, "must be admitted to be a vital part of the system." [25] "I have never yielded my original opinion indicated in the 'Federalist,' No. 39, to the ingenious reasonings of Col. Taylor against this construction of the Constitution." [26]

In this number of the Federalist Madison had written: "In controversies relating to the Boundary between the two jurisdictions [state and federal], the tribunal which is ultimately to decide is to be established under the general government." Thus he seems to admit that the federal court is the judge of the allocation of powers between the state and federal governments, although it is difficult to reconcile his resolutions of 1798 with this view. As to the right of the court to judge of the powers of the coordinate branches of the federal government, however, he was much nearer to Jefferson's opinion. In the First Congress he had declared: "I acknowledge, in the ordinary course of Government, that the exposition of the laws and constitution devolves upon the Judiciary. But, I beg to know, upon what principle it can be contended, that any one department draws from the constitution greater powers than another, in marking out the limits of the powers of the several departments? . . . If the constitutional boundary of either be brought into question, I do not see that any one of these inde-

the cause. He is among the most unforgiving of men. . . . He looks, of course, with ill will at an independent Judiciary. That in a free country with a written Constitution any intelligent man should wish a dependent Judiciary, or should think that the Constitution is not a law for the Court as well as the Legislature would astonish me if I had not learned from observation that with many men the judgment is completely controlled by the passions." See this and other letters in Mass. Hist. Soc. *Proc.*, 2d ser., XIV, 324–360.

[25] To Roane, May 6, 1821. *Letters and Other Writings*, III, 221.
[26] To Jefferson, June 27, 1823. *Ibid.*, 325 *et seq.*

pendent departments has more right than another to declare their sentiments on that point." [27]

CONGRESS AND THE COURT ISSUE

The Virginia dissidents were reinforced during the winter of 1821–1822 by the Kentuckians who felt themselves aggrieved over the decision against the claimant laws.[28] In December of 1821 Senator Richard M. Johnson of Kentucky introduced an amendment giving to the Senate appellate jurisdiction in all cases under laws of the United States where a state should be a party or where state laws were brought into question.[29] Barbour of Virginia seconded Johnson's motion, mentioning "other decisions" which had led to the opinion that "an evil exists in the collisions between the constituent members of our Union and the Federal authority, as to the sphere of the powers of the latter."

This alliance of Kentucky and Virginia in support of an amendment to deprive the court of powers which it was exercising may be regarded as the climax of the attack upon it, and Johnson's

[27] *Annals of Congress,* 1 Cong., 1 sess., 501. June 17, 1789. It must be borne in mind that both Madison and Jefferson thought of the people as holding the ultimate power to decide disputes over the distribution of powers between states and federation, and between departments of the federal government, a function to be exercised presumably by interpretative amendments of the Constitution. Madison's later explanations of the resolutions of 1798 are to this effect. See Edward McNall Burns, *James Madison, Philosopher of the Constitution,* Chap. V, especially pp. 154–161.

[28] When Kentucky severed her connection with Virginia and became a separate state, she agreed to respect the titles to lands under grants already made. Later, disputes arose between occupants and absentees who claimed the same tracts under Virginia grants, and the Kentucky legislature passed several acts providing for certain payments to be made to evicted occupants. The United States Supreme Court held (in Green *v.* Biddle, 1823) that the Kentucky acts were unconstitutional, because they violated the contract with Virginia, under which the new state was bound to decide conflicting claims by the laws of Virginia in force at the time the agreement was made. See John Bach McMaster, *History of the People of the United States,* V, 414 *et seq.*

A preliminary decision in March, 1821, indicated the probable outcome of the proceedings, and in October the legislature passed resolutions to the effect that they considered an adjudication holding the laws in question void would be incompatible with the constitutional powers of the state and injurious to the best interests of its people. They therefore remonstrated against any such judgment and instructed commissioners of the state to attend the next term of the Supreme Court to oppose any such decision. See *Niles Register,* XXI, 404–405, and references in Ames, *State Docs.,* 105.

[29] December 12. *Ann. of Cong.,* 17 Cong., 1 sess., I, 23.

speech in support of his resolution may be taken as a summary of the views of the anti-nationalizing party:

"When the parties are not agreed upon the line which divides their powers, the question is, which shall preponderate, and which shall concede. The States claim authority which the Federal judiciary denies, and the Federal judiciary exercises powers which the States do not acknowledge to be legitimate. There is no umpire to decide between them; and the difficulty is, to determine which shall submit. . . .

"At this time there is, unfortunately, a want of confidence in the Federal Judiciary, in cases that involve political power. . . . It is the opinion of many eminent statesmen that there is a manifest disposition, on the part of the Federal Judiciary, to enlarge, to the utmost stretch of Constitutional construction, the powers of the General Government, at least in that branch, and by consequence to abridge the jurisdiction of State tribunals." [30]

Complaining that the trouble lay in the lack of responsibility of the Supreme Court to the people, since judges have the frailties common to mankind, he urged that the evil would be reduced "if their powers are confined to the proper object of their office . . . that of defining questions of law; but when they transcend those limits and bring to their bar every other department, both of the Federal Government and the States, it becomes necessary to ordain some tribunal that may guard against an abuse of their power. . . . From what source is the power which they exercise derived? From the Constitution? No; that is as silent as death upon the subject; and it is doubtful whether one man of a thousand in the nation would vote so to amend the Constitution as to confer this power. Is it in the theory of our Government? No; it is in direct hostility to the theory of our Government.

"The support of federal authority must, from the very nature of their situation, be a point for them to maintain rather than abandon. The Supreme Court has even decided that Congress is the sole judge of the measures necessary to carry into effect the specific powers delegated by the Constitution. Had the same delicacy been observed by that tribunal when State laws have been the subject of

[30] January 14, 1822. *Ann. of Cong.*, 17 Cong., 1 sess., I, 68.

construction it is probable the examination of judicial encroachment upon their sovereignties might never have been commenced." [31]

At some length the cases where the United States courts had set
aside state laws were now reviewed,[32] after which Johnson concluded:

"We owe it more to the patriotic forbearance of the States, that
intestine commotions have not been the result, than to a conviction in the minds of those States that these proceedings were
sanctioned by justice or by the spirit of the Constitution. A
remedy is necessary . . . a tribunal, responsible to all the States,
should be constituted with appellate jurisdiction, and in its decisions
all will acquiesce." [33]

Johnson's amendment went as far as its second reading and consideration in committee of the whole, after which, like all its predecessors, it was tabled and heard from no more.[34] The attack on
the court continued, however, in other forms. In September, 1821,
Marshall predicted that an attempt would be made to repeal the
twenty-fifth section of the Judiciary Act of 1789.[35] A bill for this
purpose was introduced in the House by Andrew Stevenson of
Virginia, in April, 1822.[36] Following its failure, a new attempt
was made by C. A. Wickliffe, of Kentucky, in 1824.[37] Finally a
determined effort was made to effect the repeal, in 1831, but the
proposal was defeated on its second reading by a vote of 158 to 51.[38]

When in 1823 the decision was handed down in Green v. Biddle,
in which it was rumored only three judges concurred, bills were
introduced in both houses requiring, for a decision in any case

[31] *Ibid.*

[32] Under Marshall laws of thirteen states were declared unconstitutional in nineteen different cases.—Blaine F. Moore, *The Supreme Court and Unconstitutional
Legislation*, 151.

[33] *Ann. of Cong., loc. cit.*

[34] In 1867 Senator Davis, of Kentucky, proposed a tribunal composed of one
member from each state to decide questions concerning the constitutional powers
of the United States, and questions where the jurisdiction of the states and the
federal government conflicted.—Herman V. Ames, *Proposed Amendments to the
Constitution*, 163.

[35] To Story, Sept. 18. Mass. Hist. Soc. *Proc.*, 2d ser., XIV, 329–331.

[36] *Ann. of Cong.*, 17 Cong., 1 sess., 1681–1682.

[37] *Ibid.*, 18 Cong., 1 sess., 915.

[38] *Congressional Debates*, 21 Cong., 2 sess., 532, 535, 542.

involving the validity of a state law, the concurrence of more than a bare majority of the judges sitting. Johnson in the Senate proposed to require the concurrence of seven judges in any decision involving the validity of either state or congressional legislation. Another bill, providing for the assent of five justices, was reported by Van Buren, from the committee on the judiciary. No action was taken on either. In the House a committee reported that no change was advisable.[39]

During the agitation in Congress Daniel Webster was willing to enact that no judgment should be rendered until a majority of the entire bench concurred—a rule which the court presently adopted without legislation.[40] In spite of all these proposals to restrict the court, the tribunal escaped discipline at the hands of the legislative branch of the government. If it felt any chastening influence under adverse criticism, the effects were hardly apparent. However, its temper changed when, through the filling of vacancies, new men came to the bench whose views were more in harmony with those of the critics of Marshall and his associates.

CONSTITUTIONAL THEORY IN THE EIGHTEEN TWENTIES

On certain points the court and its critics were in agreement. One was that the Constitution created a system of distributed powers. Tacitly and theoretically at least, there was agreement also on the right of the enfranchised portion of the people to overrule the acts of all governmental agencies, whether state or federal, by amending the Constitution.

As to the first, Chief Justice Marshall explained the distribution of powers in the following terms: "The genius and character of the [federal] government seem to be, that its action is to be applied to all the external concerns of the nation, and to those internal concerns which affect the states generally; but not to those which are completely within a particular state, which do not affect other states, and with which it is not necessary to interfere, for the purpose of executing some of the general powers of the government." [41]

---

[39] *Ann. of Cong.*, 18 Cong., 1 sess., I, 27, 31, 38, 335, 419, 1291.
[40] Warren, *Sup. Court*, I, 664.
[41] From the opinion in Gibbons *v.* Ogden. See Hockett, *Con. Hist.*, I, 371 *et seq.*

Beside this may be placed Jefferson's exposition: "The whole field of government is divided into two departments, domestic and foreign, (the States in their mutual relations being of the latter,) . . . the former department is reserved exclusively to the respective States within their limits, and the latter assigned to a separate set of functionaries, constituting what may be called the foreign branch, which, instead of a federal basis, is established as a distinct government *quoad hoc*, acting as the domestic branch does on the citizens directly and coercively; . . . these departments are distinct, coordinate, and equally independent and supreme, each within its own sphere of action." [42]

In praise of this duality of government Monroe wrote: "It is impossible to speak too highly of this system taken in its twofold character and in all its great principles of two governments, completely distinct from and independent of each other, each constitutional, founded by and acting directly on the people, each competent to all its purposes. . . . A system capable of expansion over a vast territory not only without weakening either government but enjoying the peculiar advantage of adding thereby new strength and vigor to the faculties of both. . . ." [43]

The strict constructionists in the Republican Party placed great emphasis on the amending process, while the liberals—Clay and his group—flouted it. Monroe as President, like Jefferson and Madison, urged the importance of the amending provisions to preserve the constitutional system in its original intent. The words just quoted were used in a message to Congress in which he sought the enlargement of the powers of the federal government by amendment. Jefferson in these years was explaining and qualifying his doctrine of 1798 by maintaining that the ultimate interpreter of the Constitution is a convention representing the people of the Union, assembled at the call of Congress or of the legislatures of three fourths of the states; that is, a constitutional convention such as the

[42] To Edward Livingston, April 4, 1824. Ford, *Writings of Jefferson*, X, 300 *et seq.*
[43] "Views of the President of the United States on the Subject of Internal Improvements." Document accompanying message vetoing the Cumberland Road Bill, 1822. James D. Richardson, comp., *A Compilation of the Messages of the Presidents*, II, 144–183.

Constitution itself provides for.[44]   Short of an appeal to this ultimate authority, however, he was still of the opinion that states, as parties to the constitutional compact, were as much entitled to judge of its meaning as any branch of the federal government.

No defender of the nationalist interpretation came forward as yet to offer as clear-cut a statement of the views of the Hamilton-Marshall group as Jefferson had made of the compact theory in the Kentucky resolutions.[45]   Marshall's attempt to show how the authority of the Constitution was derived from the people was not happily phrased.   The people "acted upon it in the only manner in which they can act safely, and wisely, on such a subject. . . . They assembled in their several states,—and where else should they have assembled?   No political dreamer was ever wild enough to think of breaking down the lines which separate the states, and of compounding the American people into one common mass.   Of consequence, when they act, they act in their states.   But the measures they adopt do not, on that account, cease to be the measures of the people themselves, or become the measures of the state governments.

"From these conventions the constitution derives its whole authority.   The government proceeds directly from the people . . . the assent of the states, in their sovereign capacity, is implied in calling a convention, and thus submitting that instrument to the people.   But the people were at perfect liberty to accept or reject; and their act was final.   It required not the affirmance, and could not be negatived, by the state governments.   The constitution, when thus adopted, was of complete obligation, and bound the state sovereignties."[46]

All that Marshall makes clear in this passage is that it was not the governments of the states that established the Constitution.   Beyond that, in ambiguous terms he seems to regard "the people," in the act of establishing the Constitution, as composing several sovereignties rather than a single community.   Jefferson would not have dissented from either of these views.

[44] See, for example, letter of June 12, 1823, to Associate Justice Johnson. Washington, *Writings of Jefferson*, VII, 422.
[45] See, however, McDuffie's argument, *infra*, Chap. II.
[46] From the opinion in McCulloch *v*. Maryland.

Strangely enough it was Monroe, co-leader with Jefferson and Madison of the Virginia school, who approached nearest in these years to an adequate statement of the nationalist theory of the origin of the Constitution. "The Constitution of the United States," he wrote, "being ratified by the people of the several states, became of necessity to the extent of its powers the paramount authority of the Union. . . . The people, the highest authority known to our system, from whom all our institutions spring and on whom they depend, formed it. . . .

"In the institution of the Government of the United States by the citizens of every State a compact was formed between the whole American people which has the same force and partakes of all the qualities to the extent of its powers as a compact between the citizens of a State in the formation of their own constitution." [47] Not even Webster in his famous reply to Hayne in 1830 [48] was able to match this statement of the view that the Constitution was a "compact between the whole American people."

We are forced once more [49] to face the fact that the words of the Constitution did not themselves prove whether it was an agreement of the individuals of one great community, or of several communities each acting in its corporate capacity. The language of the great document did not command uniformity of opinion, nor indicate unmistakably how conflicts arising from this lack of agreement were to be decided, short of resort to the amending process by which the decision in Chisholm v. Georgia had been overruled. [50]

The strict school criticised the court for its principles of constitutional interpretation. In defense of the court, Marshall gave the following exposition:

The Constitution "contains an enumeration of powers expressly granted by the people to their government. It has been said that these powers ought to be construed strictly. But why ought they to be so construed? Is there one sentence in the constitution which gives countenance to this rule? . . . What do gentlemen mean by a strict construction? If they contend only against that en-

[47] Document accompanying veto message of 1822.
[48] See infra, Chap. III.
[49] Cf. Hockett, Con. Hist., I, 260.
[50] Ibid., 287.

larged construction which would extend words beyond their natural and obvious import, we . . . should not controvert the principle. If they contend for that narrow construction which, in support of some theory not to be found in the constitution, would deny to the government those powers which the words of the grant, as usually understood, import, and which are consistent with the general views and objects of the instrument; for that narrow construction, which would cripple the government and render it unequal to the objects for which it is declared to be instituted, and to which the powers given, as fairly understood, render it competent, then we cannot perceive the propriety of this strict construction, nor adopt it as the rule by which the constitution is to be expounded. As men, whose intentions require no concealment, generally employ the words which most directly and aptly express the ideas they intend to convey, the enlightened patriots who framed our constitution, and the people who adopted it, must be understood to have employed words in their natural sense, and to have intended what they said. If, from the imperfection of human language, there should be serious doubts respecting the extent of any given power, it is a well settled rule that the objects for which it was given, especially when those objects are expressed in the instrument itself, should have great influence in the construction." [51]

Marshall assumed the air of one who stands on firm ground, and stigmatizes his critics as mere theorists. With more apparent deference to a coordinate branch of the federal government he defined the relations of the judiciary to Congress. For the court, he said, to inquire into the *wisdom* or *necessity* of legislation "would be to pass the line which circumscribes the judicial department, and to tread on legislative ground." Only in case Congress should "adopt measures which are prohibited by the constitution" or "under the pretext of executing its powers, pass laws for the accomplishment of objects not entrusted to the government," would it "become the painful duty of this tribunal . . . to say that such an act was not the law of the land." [52]

This last pronouncement marks a base line, so to speak, from

[51] From the decision in Gibbons *v.* Ogden.
[52] From the opinion in McCulloch *v.* Maryland.

which one may measure the later advances of the judiciary; for the boundary which Marshall defined as separating judicial from legislative ground has hardly been respected by the court in recent decades.

Apart from the writings of John Taylor and perhaps of Judge Roane, one finds little theorizing about the nature of the Union in the decade following the peace with England. The writers mentioned do little more than expand the theory which Jefferson had propounded in 1798.[53] Yet Calhoun probably found in the discussions of these years stimuli which set him on the path leading to the theory of nullification. Among the suggestions which may have influenced him were Marshall's reference to the state conventions as expressing the will of the sovereign people of a state, and the general recognition of the amending power—or as Jefferson put it, a convention of the states—as the final judge of the meaning of the Constitution. The practical difficulties of his section supplied fertile soil for the growth of these germs.

[53] Taylor's most significant book was *An Inquiry into the Principles and Policy of the Government of the United States,* printed at Fredericksburg in 1814. It was not so much an argument on the nature of the Constitution or the Union as an exposition of the agrarian philosophy which Taylor shared with Jefferson, as an opponent of capitalism. For critiques see Charles A. Beard, *Economic Origins of Jeffersonian Democracy,* 197–211; Bernard Drell, "John Taylor of Caroline and the Preservation of an Old Social Order"; Vernon L. Parrington, *Main Currents in American Thought,* II, 14–19; H. H. Simms, *John Taylor,* 134–140.

II

THE GROWTH OF SOUTHERN
DISCONTENT

VIRGINIA ON INTERNAL IMPROVEMENTS AND THE TARIFF

THE reaction against the nationalism of the majority group among the Republicans in the period following the War of 1812 showed itself first in opposition to the United States Bank, then in criticism of the Supreme Court and the legislation in behalf of internal improvements and the protective tariff. For a decade, perhaps, the South directed its fire against internal improvement measures even more vigorously than against the tariff, although opposition to the two was often united. Then the impost came to be felt as the greater grievance, and the opposition to it culminated in the theory of nullification and the attempt of South Carolina to put it into practice.

Madison was disposed to acquiesce in the adjustment between Monroe and Congress which led to the general survey bill,[1] and in correspondence with Jefferson applied the doctrine of *res judicata*[2] which he had previously accepted as a solution of the problem of the constitutionality of the United States Bank. "I consider the question as to canals, etc., as decided, . . . because sanctioned by the nation under the permanent influence of benefit to the major portion of it; and if not carried into practice, will owe its failure to other than Constitutional obstacles."[3]

Jefferson was less easily satisfied. When President John Quincy Adams's first message advocated a liberal policy of internal improvements, he drafted a statement which he entitled "The Solemn Declaration and Protest of the Commonwealth of Virginia, on the principles of the Constitution of the United States of America, and on the violation of them." This he sent to Madison proposing that

---

[1] See Hockett, *Con. Hist.*, I, 355.
[2] *Ibid.*, 347–348.
[3] February 17, 1825. *Letters and Other Writings*, III, 483.

it be adopted by the state legislature.[4] Holding the views he did at that time, Madison advised against this course. Nevertheless, the failure of renewed efforts to obtain an amendment to the Constitution led to the passage by the Virginia legislature, in March, 1826, of a set of resolutions reaffirming the doctrines of 1798 and directing them specifically against legislation for internal improvements and a protective tariff. A year later a still more elaborate set of resolutions to the same effect was adopted.[5]

From 1816 on the maritime and planting states protested against the unequal operation of the protective system, and their remonstrances set forth clearly and accurately the economic interests which were adversely affected.[6] During the first few years the economic argument is relied on, and protective legislation is denounced as an abuse of power but not as unconstitutional. By 1820 the opponents of protection are appealing to the Constitution, and have soon thereafter developed the argument that customs duties may be imposed constitutionally only for revenue or regulation of trade, but not for the promotion of manufactures.[7]

SOUTH CAROLINA AND THE TARIFF

The leadership which South Carolina assumed by the end of the twenties, in the anti-tariff crusade, makes the development of opinion in that state a matter of especial interest and consequence. Despite the leadership of Calhoun and Lowndes in pushing through the bill of 1816, sentiment in South Carolina was never predominantly in favor of such legislation. Two other members of the delegation voted for the tariff of 1816, while three voted Nay and two did not vote.[8] Calhoun was censured for his conduct, and some of his constituents charged that he had sold his state for the hope of the presidency.[9] Lowndes became an opponent of the tariff by 1820.

[4] Ames, *State Docs.*, 140, gives references.
[5] *Ibid.*, 141–144.
[6] See H. C. Hockett, *Western Influences on Political Parties*, 119–122, and references in footnote, p. 119.
[7] See, for example, memorial from Petersburg, Va. *Ann. of Cong.*, 18 Cong., 1 sess., App., II, 3141.
[8] *Ibid.*, 14 Cong., 1 sess., 1352.
[9] D. F. Houston, *Critical Study of Nullification in South Carolina*, 5.

An elaborate memorial containing the same type of economic argument which was being advanced by other memorials of the time was drawn up at a meeting of citizens of Charleston and communicated to the Senate on Dec. 8, 1820.[10] This document concluded with words which are quite typical of the remonstrances in general: "Against a system . . . designed to elevate one interest in society to an undue influence and importance; against a system intended to benefit one description of citizens at the expense of every other class; against a system calculated to aggrandize and enrich some States to the injury of others; against a system, under every aspect, partial, unequal, and unjust, we most solemnly protest."

There was in this memorial no challenge of the constitutionality of protection; nor was there in the report adopted the same month by the House of Representatives of South Carolina. In fact, while deprecating the protective system, the House deprecated also the custom of memorializing Congress, because the necessity of regulating commerce on uniform principles had been a chief motive in framing the Constitution, which had expressly vested that power in Congress; and because of the unfortunate consequences which are likely to result "from the practice, unfortunately become too common, of arraying upon the questions of national policy, the states as *distinct and independent sovereignties* in opposition to, or, (what is much the same thing) with a view to exercise control *over* the general government." [11]

Other South Carolina statesmen besides Calhoun were prominent in the era of nationalism as leaders of the New School, and the tone of the above report reflects this temper. Eldred Simkins of that state had said on the floor of the House of Representatives in 1818, that he was not afraid of "a consolidation of state sovereignties, or a destruction of state rights, by men coming from and identified with the people of the States." [12] Simkins was succeeded in Congress by George McDuffie, who was even more pronounced in his nationalism. In reply to a series of press articles which had attacked

[10] *Ann. of Cong.*, 16 Cong., 2 sess., 1505.
[11] Ames, *State Docs.*, 134–135.
[12] Houston, *Nullification*, 8, quoting *Ann. of Cong.*, 15 Cong., 1 sess., 1920–1921.

Monroe's administration as unrepublican, judged by the Jeffersonian canons of 1801, he had written a "Defense of a Liberal Construction of the Powers of Congress." [13]

In this essay McDuffie maintained that the general government is as much the government of the people as are the state governments, and that responsibility for abuses of power by it is not to the state *governments* but to the people. "The state governments . . . have no political powers not delegated to them by their respective constitutions. . . . We have more cause of apprehension from the states, than from the general government; . . . there is in our system a greater tendency to disunion than to consolidation. . . .

"He must have read the lessons of history to little purpose, who does not perceive that the people of particular states are liable to fall, occasionally, into a dangerous and morbid excitement upon particular subjects; and that under this excitement, they will impel their rulers into the adoption of measures in their tendency destructive of the Union. . . .

"If, after the National Judiciary have solemnly affirmed the constitutionality of a law, it is still to be resisted by the state rulers, the constitution is literally at an end; a revolution of the government is already accomplished, and anarchy waves his horrid scepter over the broken altars of this happy union! . . .

"Without implied and incidental powers, almost the entire mass of means by which the machine of government is kept in motion, could not be wielded a single moment, but would fall from the hands of the administration. . . . A government never did exist, nor never can exist, for a single year, without such [discretionary] power. . . . Its first act would be an act of usurpation, founded upon necessity."

In view of the attitude which the state leaders were to take within a few years, McDuffie's criticism of the Jeffersonian dogma that each party (state) has a right to judge for itself of infractions of the Constitution, and of the mode and measure of redress, is

[13] Between July, 1820, and July, 1821, McDuffie published a series of articles in the newspapers in answer to the critics of Monroe. These articles were later collected and published as a pamphlet signed "One of the People." In 1831 the contents were republished under the title given in text, with the evident intent of showing that McDuffie had forsworn his earlier nationalism.

particularly significant: "No climax of political heresies can be imagined, in which this might not fairly claim the most prominent place. It resolves the government, at once into the elements of physical force; and introduces us directly into a scene of anarchy and blood. There is not a single power delegated to the general government, which it would not be in the power of every state government to destroy, under the authority of this licentious principle. . . . To suppose that the general government have a constitutional right to exercise certain powers, which must operate upon the people of the states, and yet that the government of each state has a right to fix and determine its own relative powers, and by necessary consequence to limit the powers of the general government, is to suppose the existence of two contradictory and inconsistent rights. In all governments there must be one supreme power; in other words, every question that can arise as to the constitutional extent of the powers of different classes of functionaries, must be susceptible of a legal and peaceable determination by some tribunal of acknowledged authority, or force must be the inevitable consequence. And where force begins, government ends."

McDuffie took a prominent part in the discussion of the bill which became the tariff of 1824, and while vigorously opposing it as economically unjust, still protested his readiness to acquiesce in the will of the majority: "There is a portion of this country, . . . a portion which I have the honor to represent, that, modify it as you will, must sustain from the passage of this bill vast and heavy pecuniary loss. But regarding the general interests of the Union, if it can be shown that the proposed duties are connected with the independence, the power of the country, this consideration will always with them have great weight; and a system of protection of manufactures, tending to these objects, although it may bear heavier on them than on any others, will not be disapproved. But a system of a combination of particular interests, for the particular benefit of each, is one which will never receive their sanction. . . ." [14]

[14] Speech of Feb. 12, 1824. *Ann. of Cong.*, 18 Cong., 1 sess., I, 1497. McDuffie delivered a speech in Congress on February 5, 1824 on the subject of the distribution of powers in which he said: "The Convention did not regard the State Governments as sentinels upon the watchtowers of freedom."—Ames, *State Documents*, 138, note, citing *Ann. of Cong.*, 18 Cong., 1 sess., 1372.

"It would be some consolation to me, sir, if I could believe that the heavy impositions, which must operate so oppressively upon the part of the Union I have the honor to represent, would produce an equivalent benefit to other portions of the Union. . . . But even this humble consolation is denied us. . . . I do beseech its advocates, as they regard the principles of justice, the interests of the Republic, or the mutual good will of its members, to pause before they give this bill the irrevocable sanction of their final vote. If, however, they should pass it, even with a majority of a single vote, I shall, as bound by my allegiance, submit to it as one of the laws of my country." [15]

In this debate, however, other members of the South Carolina delegation urged that Congress was without power to lay duties for the protection of manufactures. In reply to their talk of a confederation and the principles of construction of the Constitution, Henry C. Martindale of New York, said: "Gentlemen talk of a Confederation—of a Confederated Government. Sir, this language is new to me. I have not read it in the Constitution. It sounds foreign in my ears, and it is foreign to my feelings, and I am confident it is foreign to the feelings of my countrymen generally. . . . Let us be Americans, sir, and feel and act as Americans. Let us feel that we have a country, and let those feelings embrace the whole of it. . . . I know these are feelings which prevail in this country, and govern this Committee. We are tempted occasionally, sir, in the warmth of debate to forget these feelings, and to assume the character of sectional advocates. We will then, sometimes, sir, speak of this Government as a confederation of independent States, and about the inhabitants of such and such a State not submitting to the operation of such and such a measure. By this I presume gentlemen mean that they will remonstrate against it, and endeavor to convince this Government that they ought to repeal it. If more than this is meant; if by this gentlemen mean, 'peaceably if we can, forcibly if we must,' [16] I would remind gentlemen that there is one sacred, invariable, enduring principle

[15] Speech of April 15, 1824. *Ibid.*, II, 2424. See John L. Conger, "South Carolina and the Early Tariffs."

[16] A quotation from Quincy's speech against the admission of Louisiana to statehood. See Hockett, *Con. Hist.*, I, 331.

of our Government, which no portion of our country can ever violate with impunity, and that is, as the majority must govern, their decision must prevail, and the minority must submit. . . . If they [the cotton states] think this measure wrong, gentlemen may talk with propriety of appealing to the sovereignty of the people. They have full scope and perfect right to obtain that sovereign majesty —to do what? To secede from the Union; to dissolve this Government? No, it is impossible; but simply in a quiet, pacific, Constitutional way, to change the Administration, to dismiss their public servants, and substitute others more honest, or more intelligent, who will understand and consult their interests better." [17]

However sound Martindale's views concerning the Constitution may have been, there was little in them to bring contentment to a section of the country which believed itself to be confronted by a permanent majority bent upon promoting its selfish interests. State sovereignty and state interposition seemed to be the only means of defending minority rights, and to these doctrines South Carolina gradually turned. In December of 1824, Governor Wilson, in his message to the legislature, led the way: "Every friend of our present constitution, in its original purity, cannot but have witnessed the alarming extent to which the Federal Judiciary and Congress have gone toward establishing a great and consolidated government, subversive of the rights of the States and contravening the letter and spirit of the Constitution of the Union. The act of the last session of Congress appropriating money to make surveys," he continued, alluding to the general survey bill, "is but an entering wedge which will be followed, no doubt by the expenditure of millions. Unless the People apply the proper corrective, the day, I fear, is not far distant, when South Carolina shall be grievously assessed, to pay for the cutting of a canal across Cape Cod. None of the friends to the assumed powers of the General Government pretend to derive them from any specific grant of power in the Constitution, but claim them as implied, resulting or necessary to the common defence and general welfare. The construction contended for by them is an open violation of that which has heretofore universally been admitted the true rule for expounding all

[17] Speech of Feb. 24, 1824. *Ann. of Cong.*, 18 Cong., 1 sess., I, 1831.

grants"—a reference to the common-law rule that corporate charters are to be strictly construed. To such a charter Wilson likened the Constitution. "It never for a moment entered into the imagination of the members of the convention that formed the union that they were surrendering the sovereignty and independence of the states. On the contrary, there was a universal sensitiveness on that point, which produced the section [tenth amendment] which declared all power not expressly granted to be reserved to the people or the states. Whenever we become a great consolidated nation, the day will soon arrive when we shall crumble into as many parts as there are cardinal points of the compass. It is our duty as public sentinels to give the alarm, in order that those who are friendly to the present constitution may preserve it in its original purity." [18]

By these sentiments Governor Wilson proved himself to be a true disciple of Jefferson, and the state senate was prepared to support him. Although the governor did not mention the tariff of 1824 in his message, the senate passed a series of resolves, by a vote of 30 to 13, denouncing as unconstitutional both the internal improvement and protective legislation of Congress. The House of Representatives was still of the temper of that of 1820, however (and of McDuffie), and substituted for the senate resolves a series of its own, of which the following are representative: "3. *Resolved*, That the people have conferred no power upon their State Legislature to impugn the Acts of the Federal Government or the decisions of the Supreme Court of the United States. . . . 5. *Resolved*, That the Representatives of the People in Congress are only responsible under God to the People themselves. 6. *Resolved*, That the People of this State are quite competent to the superintendence and control of the conduct of their Representatives in Congress as well as their Representatives in this Legislature. . . . 8. *Resolved*, That the liberty of the People of this country will be seriously

[18] Ames, *State Docs.*, 137. Governor Wilson recognized that "every citizen of these United States owes a double allegiance; namely to the government of the United States, and to the government of the individual State to which he may belong."—Andrew C. McLaughlin, *Constitutional History of the United States*, 434. In saying that the tenth amendment contains the word "expressly" he committed an error common in his day and since.

endangered, whenever they permit their servants in this Legislature or in Congress to use any power not delegated to them." [19]

By December, 1825, the lower house was ready to join the senate in passing resolutions which asserted that "among those rights retained in this constitution to the people, is, the unalienable right of remonstrating against any encroachments upon that constitution by the Congress of the United States, or any other officer belonging or acting under the General Government." [20] As to internal improvements and protective duties, the resolutions maintained that Congress does not possess the power to adopt a general system of internal improvements as a national measure; that the right to tax does not authorize Congress to lay a tax "for any other purpose than such as are necessarily embraced in the specific grants of power, and those necessarily implied therein"; that it is an unconstitutional exercise of power to tax the citizens of one state to make roads and canals for those of another state; and that it is an unconstitutional use of power to lay duties to protect domestic manufactures.[21]

The alarm of Carolina increased as the tariff movement progressed with no sign of abatement. The protectionist propaganda of the Harrisburg convention, which followed the failure of the woollens bill of 1827, aroused such leaders as Dr. Thomas Cooper, of sedition trial fame, who was now a prominent citizen of the state, and the popular excitement began to threaten extreme measures.[22] The attitude of the legislature reflected the temper of the people, and its utterances became distinctly Jeffersonian. In December, 1827, a special committee, combatting Marshall's pronouncement in McCulloch v. Maryland, presented a report and resolutions; in the report the view that the federal Constitution emanated from the people is characterized as "one of the most dangerous doctrines that can be promulgated," adding "that collisions

[19] Ames, *State Docs.*, 138–139.
[20] *Ibid.*, 139.
[21] *Ibid.* For the early discussion of internal improvements see Hockett, *Con. Hist.*, I, 345 *et seq.*
[22] See Dumas Malone, "Thomas Cooper and the State Rights Movement in South Carolina, 1823–1830"; also, by the same author, *The Public Life of Thomas Cooper.*

will sometimes arise between the States and Congress, when it would not only be unwise, but even unsafe, to submit questions of disputed sovereignty to any judicial tribunal"; "least of all ought the States to consent to make the Supreme Court of the United States the arbiter finally to decide points of vital importance to the States." [23]

The resolutions declare that the Constitution is a compact between the people of the different states as separate, independent sovereignties, that it is the right of the legislatures as well as of the people to remonstrate against violations of the compact, and that the protective tariff, internal improvements, and appropriations for the Colonization Society are unconstitutional.[24]

Other southern states joined in the protests of South Carolina, and in justification of their course entered into more or less lengthy examinations of the nature of the Union and the Constitution. Thus Georgia took the ground that "the proper constituents of the General Government are the states, and the States are to that Government what the People are to the States." [25] She developed the view, hardly stated with clarity up to this time, that the powers of the general government "were delegated, not by the People of the United States at *large*, but by the People of the *respective States*"; and that, therefore, the Constitution is a compact not between state legislatures, but bodies politic. She reasserted the doctrine of sentinelship, holding that the legislature is the guardian of the rights of the people from encroachments by the general government. The powers of the latter are to be determined by a strict construction of the Constitution.[26]

CALHOUN AND THE NULLIFICATION THEORY

While the policies of the federal government were being combatted along these lines, a new departure was being prepared through the thinking of John C. Calhoun. Soon after making his speeches on the tariff and internal improvements in the closing

[23] Ames, *State Docs.*, 145, note.
[24] *Ibid.*, 144–145.
[25] *Ibid.*, 146–148.
[26] *Ibid.* For the origin of the doctrine of sentinelship see Hockett, *Con. Hist.*, I, 267.

years of Madison's administration,[27] he had entered Monroe's cabinet, where for eight years he was an observer rather than an actor in current events.   During these years, while he witnessed the reaction against nationalism which we have traced, the progress of his own views is difficult to follow.   Soon after leaving the cabinet he took occasion, in a speech at Abbeville, N. C., to state his principles in terms which seemed to indicate that he was a confirmed nationalist.   He favored, he said, "a due protection of those manufactures which had taken root during the period of war and restriction, and . . . a system of connecting the various portions of the country by a judicious system of internal improvement." [28] Such, he said, were his principles at the close of the war and since.

After two more years of silence, while Vice-President under Adams, events revealed him as the enemy of the protective system; for in 1827 the woollens bill encountered a tie vote in the Senate, and it became necessary for him to determine its fate by his casting vote.   His decision, which killed the measure, Van Buren predicted would also kill him politically.

Calhoun watched developments from that moment with great solicitude.   He had become convinced that the protective system, which he had advocated as a means of putting American industries on their feet as a measure of national safety in case of war, had ceased to possess national value and had become the instrument for the advancement of the selfish interests of particular groups and sections.   The combination of these groups had come to form a majority strong enough to control Congress and there seemed but slight possibility of breaking the alliance.   Calhoun therefore became more and more engrossed in the problem of protecting the minority against the tyranny of the majority.   Loving the Union, he sought the solution of this problem in some interpretation of the Constitution, and found it, as he believed, in the doctrine of Jefferson, that a state as a party to the constitutional compact had the

[27] *Ibid.*, 346 *et seq.*
[28] Houston, *Nullification*, 6, 7. *Cf.* Chauncey S. Boucher, *The Nullification Controversy in South Carolina.* Gaillard Hunt, *John C. Calhoun*, is of interest in connection with the nullification episode. Especially important is Frederic Bancroft, *Calhoun and the South Carolina Nullification Movement.* See also C. E. Merriam, "The Political Philosophy of John C. Calhoun."

right to judge for itself of the infraction of that compact and of the mode and measure of redress.

From the germ for which Jefferson was responsible Calhoun evolved the theory of nullification. From hints in letters to friends, it seems that he began this task about the time of the passage of the tariff of 1828,[29] and when the South Carolina legislature met in the autumn of that year, he was ready with the theory which was set out in the so-called "South Carolina Exposition." His authorship was concealed, like Jefferson's when he wrote the Kentucky Resolutions of 1798, and upon the advice of Governor Tayler the legislature published the Exposition on December 19, 1828, in the form of a committee report.[30]

The main portion of this report was a review of the economic effects of the tariff upon the industry of the South and of the state in particular, but the significant part, of course, is that in which the author deals with the right of the state, under the Constitution, to protect its interests from injury at the hands of the general government. Calhoun saw more clearly than most of his contemporaries that governments are not sovereign, and that sovereignty is not divisible: [31] "There is, in our system, a striking distinction

[29] Lamenting the burden which the tariff laid upon the South, Calhoun wrote to Monroe on July 10, 1828, saying: "It seems to me that we have no other check against abuses, but such as grow out of responsibility, or elections, and while this is an effective check, where the law acts equally on all, it is none in the case of the unequal action to which I refer."—J. F. Jameson, ed., *Correspondence of John C. Calhoun*, 266–267. The letter indicates that Calhoun was pondering the problem of an adequate check.

[30] The Exposition is to be found in Richard Crallé, ed., *Works of John C. Calhoun*, VI, 36–51 *et passim*. The important portions are reprinted in Allen Johnson, *Readings in American Constitutional History*, 317–322. Calhoun prepared the statement at the request of Colonel William C. Preston, of the committee. As published it was not in the exact form in which Calhoun drew it, and the original has been lost. In a letter dated October 25, 1854, Robert Barnwell Rhett wrote to Richard Crallé, who was then engaged in editing Calhoun's works, saying that the Exposition "was greatly altered by the Committee who reported it to the Legislature of which I was one. Mr. Calhoun had nothing to do with these corrections and I know disapproved of them." Rhett gives no clue to the alterations. His letter is published in the *Am. Hist. Rev.*, XIII, 311 (Jan., 1908). On July 26, 1831, Calhoun published in the *Pendleton Messenger* a long public letter restating the Exposition and revealing his relation to it. The revelation made him the leader of the State's Rights party.

[31] Madison, for example, did not agree with Calhoun as to the indivisibility of sovereignty. "Of late," he wrote, "doctrine . . . supposes that sovereignty is in its nature indivisible." He continued to believe "that the supreme power, that is, the

between Government and Sovereignty. The separate governments of the several States are vested in their Legislative, Executive, and Judicial Departments; while the sovereignty resides in the people of the States respectively. The powers of the General Government are also vested in its Legislative, Executive, and Judicial Departments, while the sovereignty resides in the people of the several States who created it."

This assertion of the nature of state sovereignty is apparently weakened by the next statement: "But, by an express provision of the Constitution, it may be amended or changed by three fourths of the States; and thus each State, by assenting to the Constitution with this provision, has modified its original right as a sovereign, of making its individual consent necessary to any change in its political condition; and, by becoming a member of the Union, has placed this important power in the hands of three fourths of the States,—in whom the highest power known to the Constitution actually resides."

If this is true, one may object that sovereignty resides not in the state as a political community, but in the three fourths of the states, or the people thereof, who possess "the highest power known to the Constitution." Such, indeed, is in the United States the modern doctrine of sovereignty—it resides in that portion of the people who can change the Constitution; that is, by the terms of the instrument itself, a majority of the voters in three fourths of the states acting through representative legislatures or conventions.[32]

The Exposition continues: "Not the least portion of this high sovereign authority resides in Congress, or any of the departments of the General Government. They are but the creatures of the

sovereignty of the people of the United States, was in its nature divisible, and was, in fact, divided . . .; that as the States, in their highest sovereign character, were competent to surrender the whole sovereignty and form themselves into a consolidated State, so they might surrender a part and retain, as they have done, the other part. . . ."—*Letters and Other Writings*, IV, 390–391, *et passim*.

[32] In recent years, under state regulations establishing the referendum, amendments are in some states passed upon by the voters directly. But even if state laws require a referendum, ratification by the legislature alone has been held to be valid. Calhoun would have met the objection stated in the text by saying that while a state, as a member of the Union, was bound by the decision of this "highest power," its sovereignty permitted its resort to the alternative of withdrawal from the Union if unwilling to accept the decision.

Constitution, and are appointed but to execute its provisions; and, therefore, any attempt by all, or any of these departments, to exercise any power which, in its consequences, may alter the nature of the instrument, or change the condition of the parties to it, would be an act of usurpation."

Proceeding: To prevent the states from encroaching on the authority delegated to the general government, the Judiciary Act of 1789 provides for an appeal from the state courts to the Supreme Court of the United States in all cases involving federal law, "thus giving to that high tribunal the right of final interpretation, and the power, in reality, of nullifying the acts of the State Legislatures whenever, in their opinion, they may conflict with the powers delegated to the General Government. . . . But by a strange misconception . . . it has been regarded as the ultimate power, not only of protecting the General Government against the encroachments of the States, but also of the encroachments of the former on the latter;—and as being, in fact, the only means provided by the Constitution of confining all the powers of the system to their proper constitutional spheres. . . . Such a construction of its powers would, in fact, raise one of the departments of the General Government above the parties who created the constitutional compact, and virtually invest it with the authority to alter, at its pleasure, the relative powers of the General and State Governments, on the distribution of which, as established by the Constitution, our whole system rests;—and which, by an express provision of the instrument, can only be altered by three fourths of the States. . . . In fact, to divide power, and to give to one of the parties the exclusive right of judging of the portion allotted to each, is, in reality, not to divide it at all; and to reserve such exclusive right to the General Government . . . is to convert it, in fact, into a great consolidated government."

The author holds therefore that the states must have a reciprocal right of judging of encroachments upon their reserved authority on the part of the general government, and believes that such a right is an essential attribute of sovereignty "of which the States cannot be divested without losing their sovereignty itself," as the above argument, indeed, proves.   "But the existence of the right of judging of their powers, so clearly established from the sovereignty of States, as clearly implies a veto or control, within its limits, on the action of the General Government, on contested points of authority; and this very control is the remedy which the Constitution has provided to prevent the encroachments of the General Government on the reserved rights of the States; and by which the distribution of power, between the General and State Governments, may be preserved forever inviolable, on the basis established by the Constitution. It is thus effectual protection is afforded to the minority, against the oppression of the majority."

Save for the substitution of indivisible for divided sovereignty, the thought of the Exposition thus far was substantially a restatement of the ideas previously promulgated by Jefferson, Roane, and Taylor. But from this point there is a divergence.[33] The next step is to inquire how the remedy may be applied by a state, and the decision is that the proper organ through which the sovereignty of a state should act is not the legislature or courts, but a convention chosen by the voters of the state for the express purpose of passing upon the questionable acts of Congress.[34] "It will belong to the Convention . . . to determine, authoritatively, whether the acts of which we complain be unconstitutional; and, if so, whether they constitute a violation so deliberate, palpable, and dangerous, as to justify the interposition of the State to protect its rights. If this question be decided in the affirmative, the Convention will

[33] Calhoun, in fact, believed that he was following Jefferson's doctrines of 1798. In 1823 the latter had said that the ultimate arbiter in judging of infractions of the Constitution is the people of the Union assembled in convention at the call of Congress or of the legislatures of three fourths of the states; *i.e.,* a constitutional convention is the ultimate judge when two branches of the government come into conflict in interpreting the Constitution.—Letter to Justice Johnson, June 12, 1823, in Washington, *Writings of Jefferson,* VII, 422. Madison denied that the principles of the nullifiers were identical with those of the resolutions of 1798. "The error . . . has arisen from a failure to distinguish between what is declaratory of opinion and what is *ipso facto* executory; between the rights of the parties [states] and of a single party [state]; and between resorts within the purview of the Constitution and the *ultima ratio* which appeals from a Constitution, cancelled by its abuses, to original rights, paramount to all Constitutions."—To Livingston, May 30, 1830 (Madison's *Letters and Other Writings,* IV, 80). See also letters to Edward Everett, August 28, 1830 (Hunt, *Writings of Madison,* IX, 383 *et seq.*), and Andrew Stevenson, February 4, 1833 (*Letters,* etc., IV, 269 *et seq.*). See Kentucky's explanation of the resolutions of 1798, *infra,* Chap. III.
[34] *Cf.* Marshall, *supra,* Chap. I.

then determine in what manner they ought to be declared null and void within the limits of the State; which solemn declaration, based on her rights as a member of the Union, would be obligatory, not only on her own citizens, but on the General Government itself; and thus place the violated rights of the State under the shield of the Constitution."

This, however, is not the end of the matter, for the negative of the state is only a suspensive veto, subject to the overruling authority of the higher power: "As high as this right of interposition on the part of a state may be regarded in relation to the General Government, the constitutional compact provides a remedy against its abuse. There is a higher power,—placed above all by the consent of all,—the creating and preserving power of the system,—to be exercised by three-fourths of the States,—and which, under the character of the amending power, can modify the whole system at pleasure,—and to the acts of which none can object. . . .

"If, on an appeal . . . the decision be favorable to the General Government, a disputed power will be converted into an expressly granted power;—but, on the other hand, if it be adverse, the refusal to grant will be tantamount to an inhibition of its exercise: and thus, in either case, the controversy will be determined."

Here, then, is Calhoun's answer to the long quest for an "impartial tribunal." The practical fruit of such procedure, it was urged, would be to give vitality to the amending power. So long as there is no means of forcing an appeal to that power, the general government will assume power by construction, and the amending power will in time become atrophied. No proposal of an amendment on the part of an aggrieved state can avail, when it requires the ratification of three fourths of the states and the proposing state is in the minority at the outset. "On the contrary, giving the right to a State to compel the General Government to abandon its pretensions to a constructive power, or to obtain a positive grant of it, by an amendment to the Constitution, would call efficiently into action, on all important disputed questions, this highest power of the system. . . . It is thus that the *creating* becomes the *preserving* power. . . . Such will be the operation and effect of State interposition."

III

NULLIFICATION ATTEMPTED

DISCUSSION OF THE EXPOSITION

THE South Carolina legislature promulgated the Exposition as a statement of principles and a possible program in case of persistence by the federal government in its obnoxious policy. In resolutions the legislature reaffirmed its opinion on the tariff, adding that it was "restrained from the assertion of the sovereign rights of the state by the hope that the magnanimity and justice of the good people of the Union will effect the abandonment of a system, partial in its nature, unjust in its operation, and not within the powers delegated to Congress," and "that the measures to be pursued consequent on the perseverance in this system are purely questions of expediency, and not of allegiance."[1] A copy of the resolutions was sent to each state.

Other southern states joined in the denunciation of the tariff of 1828, but none of them went beyond the conventional protests and remonstrances. Some of the northern states adopted pro-tariff resolutions in reply to these anti-tariff manifestoes from the cotton states, and Kentucky, on the border between the two sections, threw in her lot on the side where her interest at the time seemed to lie. The report adopted by her legislature on January 27, 1830, is an answer to South Carolina, an argument designed to refute the errors of the nullification theory.

Ignoring the possibility of an appeal from the nullifying action of a state to the higher authority of three fourths of the states, Kentucky objected that "the consequences of such a principle, if practically enforced, would be alarming in the extreme. Scarcely any important measure of the general government is ever adopted, to which one or more of the States are not opposed. If one State have a right to obstruct and defeat the execution of a law of Congress because it deems it unconstitutional, then every State has a

[1] Ames, *State Docs.*, 153.

similar right. When the dissatisfied State opposes to the Act of Congress its measures of obstruction, the alternative is presented, shall the act be enforced within the particular State, or be abandoned by Congress? If enforced, there is a civil war; if abandoned, without being repealed, a virtual dissolution of the Union. As the successful exercise of the power of resisting an act of Congress by one State, would naturally stimulate other States, disapproving other acts of that body, to similar resistance, the practical result would be, that Congress could adopt and enforce no measure whatever, to which any one of the twenty-four States might be opposed . . . there is, there can be, there ought to be, but one rule, which is, that the majority must govern." [2]

Realizing that the Kentucky Resolutions of 1798 had furnished the basis of the South Carolina Exposition, the authors of the Kentucky report took pains to deny that the earlier resolutions embodied the doctrine now contended for: "From the principles now advanced, there has been no deviation on the part of the General Assembly of Kentucky. At a former epoch, when certain acts [were] passed by Congress, called the alien and sedition laws, which were believed to be unconstitutional by the General Assembly, it neither interposed nor threatened the adoption of any measures to defeat or obstruct their operation within the jurisdiction of Kentucky. It expressed, and expressed in very strong language, its disapprobation of them and its firm conviction that they were unconstitutional, and therefore void. There it stopped, and that is the limit which no state should pass, until it has formed the deliberate resolution of lighting up the torch of civil war. Every state, as well as every individual, has the incontestible right freely to form and to publish to the world, its opinion of any and of every act of the federal government. It may appeal to the reason of the people, enlighten their judgments, alarm their fears, and conciliate their support, to change federal rulers, or federal measures. But neither a state nor an individual can rightfully resist, by force, the execution of a law passed by Congress." [3]

[2] *Ibid.*, 158–161.
[3] *Ibid.* *Cf.* Madison, *supra*, Chap. II, note 33.

THE WEBSTER-HAYNE DEBATE

In January, 1830, occurred the great debate between Hayne and Webster which called forth a restatement of the nullification theory by the former and led to the famous reply in which Webster attempted to refute it. The occasion of the discussion was the resolution offered by Senator Foote proposing to limit the sale of western lands. Viewing this as, like the protective tariff, a move to promote the selfish interests of New England at the expense of the other portions of the Union, Senator Hayne joined Benton of Missouri in opposing its adoption. In the course of his argument Hayne referred to the power of a state to check the general government in case it adopted unfair and oppressive measures, and Webster challenged him to explain his meaning. He thereupon expounded the nullification theory. Webster in his reply said: "The proposition, that, in case of a supposed violation of the constitution by Congress, the States have a constitutional right to interfere, and annul the law of Congress, is the proposition of the gentleman: I do not admit it. . . . I admit that there is an ultimate violent remedy, above the constitution, and in defiance of the constitution, which may be resorted to, when a revolution is to be justified. But I do not admit that, under the constitution, and in conformity with it, there is any mode in which a State Government, as a member of the Union, can interfere and stop the progress of the General Government, by force of her own laws, under any circumstances whatever." [4]

To refute the fallacy of the nullifiers, Webster examined the origin of the government:

"If the Government of the United States be the agent of the State Governments, then they may control it, provided they can agree in the manner of controlling it; if it be the agent of the people, then the people alone can control it, restrain it, modify or reform it." The former alternative leads to absurdity, for the federal government becomes "the servant of four and twenty masters, of dif-

[4] *Cong. Debates*, 21 Cong., 1 sess., VI, 58–80. Extract containing chief portions in Johnson, *Readings*, 337–343. For Hayne see Theodore D. Jervey, *Robert Y. Hayne and His Times*. The most thorough modern study of Webster's public career is by Claude M. Fuess.

ferent wills and purposes, and yet bound to obey all. This absurdity . . . arises from a misconception as to the origin of this Government in its true character. It is, sir, the people's constitution, the people's government; made for the people; made by the people; and answerable to the people. The people of the United States have declared that this constitution shall be the supreme law." [5]

Like Marshall, Webster thinks in the language of divided sovereignty, and in speaking of the people fails to use terms with entire clarity. "The States are, unquestionably, sovereign, so far as their sovereignty is not affected by this supreme law. But the State Legislatures, as political bodies, however sovereign, are yet not superior to the people. So far as the people have given power to the General Government, so far the grant is unquestionably good, and the Government holds of the people, and not of the State Governments. We are all agents of the same supreme power, the people. The General Government and the State Governments derive their authority from the same source. . . . The National Government possesses those powers which it can be shown the people have conferred on it, and no more. All the rest belong to the State Governments or to the people themselves. So far as the people have restrained State sovereignty, by the expression of their will, in the constitution of the United States, so far it must be admitted, State sovereignty is effectually controlled. . . .

"Who then shall construe this grant of the people? . . . They have left it with the Government itself, in its appropriate branches. . . . The very chief end . . . for which the whole constitution was framed and adopted was, to establish a Government that should not be obliged to act through State agency, or depend on State opinion and State discretion. The people had had quite enough of that kind of government, under the Confederacy. . . . The people have wisely provided, in the constitution itself, a proper, suitable mode and tribunal for settling questions of constitutional law . . . by declaring . . . that 'the constitution and laws of the United States, made in pursuance thereof, shall be the supreme law of the land, anything in the constitution or laws of any State to the contrary notwithstanding. . . .'

[5] *Cong. Debates, loc. cit.*

"But who shall decide this question of interference? . . . This, sir, the constitution itself decides also, by declaring 'that the judicial power shall extend to all cases arising under the constitution and laws of the United States. These two provisions . . . cover the whole ground. . . .'

"Gentlemen do not seem to recollect that the people have any power to do anything for themselves; they imagine there is no safety for them any longer than they are under the close guardianship of the State Legislatures. Sir, the people have not trusted their safety, in regard to the general constitution, to these hands. They have required other security, and taken other bonds. They have chosen to trust themselves, first, to the plain words of the instrument, and to such a construction as the Government itself, in doubtful cases, should put on its own powers, under their oaths of office, and subject to their responsibility to them: just as the people of a State trust their own State Governments with a similar power Secondly, they have reposed their trust in the efficacy of frequent elections, and in their own power to remove their own servants and agents, whenever they see cause. Thirdly, they have reposed trust in the Judicial power, which, in order that it might be trustworthy, they have made as respectable, as disinterested, and as independent as was practicable. Fourthly, they have seen fit to rely, in case of necessity, or high expediency, on their known and admitted power to alter and amend the constitution, peaceably and quietly, whenever experience shall point out defects or imperfections. And, finally, the people of the United States have, at no time, in no way, directly or indirectly, authorized any State Legislature to construe or interpret their high instrument of Government; much less to interfere, by their own power, to arrest its course and operation." [6]

The strength of Webster's argument lay in its refutation of the doctrine that a single state could constitutionally halt the operation of federal law within its bounds. But the speech was not above criticism. Its chief weakness lies in the assumption that the nullifiers regarded the state *governments* as the parties to the constitutional compact, whereas in fact they distinguished between the people as political communities and their governments. And it is

[6] *Ibid.*

none too clear that Webster thinks of the Constitution as established by the people of the United States in the aggregate. That this was his belief he made evident later, however, first in his final speech in the Hayne debate, on January 27, 1830, and again, replying to Calhoun, on February 16, 1833. Quoting the words of New Hampshire and Massachusetts in ratifying the Constitution —"They recognize the Divine goodness 'in affording the people of the United States an opportunity of entering into an explicit and solemn compact with each other, by assenting to and ratifying a new Constitution,' "—he said: "You will observe, Sir, that it is the people, and not the States, who have entered into this compact; and it is the people of all the United States." [7]

CALHOUN AND THE NULLIFICATION ORDINANCE

After Calhoun's breach with Jackson he became the open and avowed leader of the nullifying party in his native state, and as the election of 1832 approached, the issue between this party and the so-called "Unionists" became definitely the question whether nullification should be put into operation. The passage of the tariff of 1832, which was clearly a perpetuation of the protective system, drew the issue sharply. As leader of the party of nullification, Calhoun wrote a number of comments and explanations of the theory first advanced in the Exposition, among which were the Address to the People of South Carolina, issued from his home at Fort Hill, in 1831, and the Fort Hill letter to Governor Hamilton. In the latter he pointed out that the people of the United States had from the beginning lived in distinct communities, which became independent as the result of the Revolution, and as such formed the old Confederation. Moreover, when it was decided to form a new Constitution, "they met in convention as States, acted and voted as States; and the Constitution, when formed, was submitted for ratification to the people of the several States; it was ratified by them as States, each State for itself; each by its ratification binding its own citizens. . . . The conclusion is inevitable, that the Constitution is the work of the people of the States, considered as separate and independent political communities . . . that

[7] Edward Everett, ed., *Works of Daniel Webster*, III, 476.

the government formed is, in reality, their agent; and that the Union, of which the Constitution is the bond, is a union of States, and not of individuals."

In this same letter he refutes the charge that the nullifiers aim at secession by pointing out the difference between nullification and secession: "Secession is a *withdrawal from the Union;* a separation from *partners.* . . . Nullification, on the contrary, *presupposes the relation of principal and agent:* the one granting a power to be executed,—the other, appointed by him with authority to execute it; *and is simply a declaration on the part of the principal, made in due form, that an act of the agent transcending his power is null and void.* . . . The object of secession is to *free* the withdrawing member from the obligation of the association or union, and is applicable to cases where the object of the association or union has *failed,* either by an abuse of power on the part of *its members,* or other causes. . . . On the contrary, the object of nullification is to confine the agent within the limits of his powers, by arresting his acts transcending them, *not with the view of destroying the delegated or trust power, but to preserve it, by compelling the agent to fulfil the object for which the agency or trust was created."* [8]

The campaign of 1832 in South Carolina resulted in the triumph of the nullification party. The new legislature was assembled in special session in October and Governor Hamilton recommended that it provide for a convention. It promptly complied, and the

---

[8] *Works,* VI, 147–169 *et passim.* Extract in Johnson, *Readings,* 323–325. Compare report of legislative committee likening the Union to a partnership, *ibid.,* 322–323. If there is some doubt as to whether the Exposition correctly presents Calhoun's ideas, a check may be found in later writings. In "A Disquisition on Government" (*Works,* I, 35), he developed the theory of the concurrent majority; that is, that no legislation affecting sectional interests should become operative without the assent of the minority section as well as the majority region. This negative power, he thought, was the essence of the Constitution. The union formed by the Constitution, he held, "is as strictly and as purely a confederation, as the one which it superseded."—*Works,* VI, 158. Calhoun's theory of the concurrent majority may be regarded as an extension of the theory of checks and balances. In it may be found, moreover, a foreshadowing of the modern theory of pluralism, for he sought to make the government the result of the consent and cooperation of distinct interests rather than of a numerical majority.

As no reliable record of the proceedings of the Constitutional Convention was yet published, Calhoun's theories as formulated before 1832 do not rest on any knowledge of what the delegates intended.

convention was in session at Columbia from the 19th to the 24th of November. Its most important action, of course, was the passing of the ordinance of nullification on the last day of the session. The enacting clause of the ordinance reads: "We . . . the People of the State of South Carolina, in Convention assembled, do Declare and Ordain. . . ." [9]

The ordinance declared that the tariff acts of 1828 and 1832 were "unauthorized by the Constitution of the United States . . . and null, void and no law, nor binding upon this State, its officers, or citizens; and all promises, contracts and obligations, made or entered into, or to be made or entered into, with purpose to secure the duties imposed by said acts, and all judicial proceedings which shall be hereafter had in affirmance thereof, are, and shall be held, utterly null and void."

It was declared unlawful for federal or state authorities to attempt to enforce the acts, and made the duty of the legislature to adopt measures to give effect to the ordinance and prevent the operation of the nullified acts within the state after the first day of February, 1833. No case arising from the tariff acts or the ordinance of nullification was to be appealed from any state court to the Supreme Court of the United States; all officials of the state were required to take an oath, to be prescribed by the legislature, to obey and enforce the ordinance and acts of the legislature pursuant to it; and it was declared that "we will consider the passage, by Congress, of any act authorizing the employment of a military or naval force against the State of South Carolina, her constituted authorities or citizens, or any act abolishing or closing the ports of this State, or any of them, or otherwise obstructing the free ingress and egress of vessels to and from the said ports, or any other act, on the part of the Federal Government, to coerce the State, shut up her ports, destroy or harass her commerce, or to enforce the acts hereby declared to be null and void, otherwise than through the civil tribunals of the country, as inconsistent with the longer continuance of South Carolina in the Union; and that the People of this State will thenceforth hold themselves absolved from all

[9] Ames, *State Docs.*, 170–173. Also in William MacDonald, *Select Documents*, 268–271. and Henry S. Commager, *Documents of American History*, 261–262.

further obligation to maintain or preserve their political connexion with the people of the other States, and will forthwith proceed to organize a separate Government, and to do all other acts and things which sovereign and independent States may of right do."

PRESIDENT JACKSON'S PROCLAMATION

Reconvening a few days after the adjournment of the convention, the legislature passed a series of acts to give effect to the ordinance. Hayne being elected governor, left the Senate, and Calhoun, resigning the Vice-Presidency, was sent, by prearrangement, to champion the state in the national forum. President Jackson, who had kept close track of events in South Carolina, met the situation created by the passage of the ordinance by issuing on December 10, a proclamation addressed to the people of South Carolina.

This document, the ablest paper of Jackson's administration, was the President's conception, but it came probably from the pen of Livingston, the secretary of state. In its nationalism it is on a par with the utterance of Webster. It refutes the theory on which the South Carolina ordinance is founded, and ends in a warning to the people of the state of the consequences which must follow persistence in their ill-advised course:

"The Constitution of the United States . . . forms a *government*, not a league. . . . It is a government in which all the people are represented, which operates directly on the people individually, not upon the States. . . . Each State having expressly parted with so many powers as to constitute, jointly with the other States, a single nation, cannot, from that period, possess any right to secede, because such secession does not break a league, but destroys the unity of a nation. . . . Secession, like any other revolutionary act, may be morally justified by the extremity of oppression; but to call it a constitutional right, is confounding the meaning of terms. . . .

"A league between independent nations, generally, has no sanction other than a moral one. . . . A government, on the contrary, always has a sanction, express or implied; and, in our case, it is both necessarily implied and expressly given. An attempt, by force of arms, to destroy a government, is an offence by whatever means the constitutional compact may have been formed, and such government has the right, by the law of self-defence, to pass acts for punishing the offender. . . .

"The States severally have not retained their entire sovereignty. . . . The allegiance of their citizens was transferred, in the first instance, to the Government of the United States: they became American citizens, and owed obedience to the Constitution of the United States, and to laws made in conformity with the powers it vested in Congress. This last position has not been, and cannot be denied. How, then, can that State be said to be sovereign and independent whose citizens owe obedience to laws not made by it, and whose magistrates are sworn to disregard those laws when they come in conflict with those passed by another? What shows conclusively that the States cannot be said to have reserved an un-divided sovereignty, is, that they expressly ceded the right to pun-ish treason, not treason against their separate power, but treason against the United States. Treason is an offence against *sov-ereignty*, and sovereignty must reside with the power to punish it. . . .

"The ordinance [of nullification] is founded, not on the inde-feasible right of resisting acts which are plainly unconstitutional, and too oppressive to be endured; but on the strange position that any one State may not only declare an act of Congress void, but prohibit its execution—that they may do this consistently with the Constitution—that the true construction of that instrument per-mits a State to retain its place in the Union, and yet be bound by no other of its laws than those it may choose to consider as con-stitutional. It is true, they add, that to justify this abrogation of a law, it must be palpably contrary to the Constitution; but it is evident, that, to give the right of resisting laws of that description, coupled with the uncontrolled right to decide what laws deserve that character, is to give the power of resisting all laws. . . . There are two appeals from an unconstitutional act passed by Congress—one to the Judiciary, the other to the people, and the States. There is no appeal from the State decision in theory, and the practical illustration shows that the courts are closed against an application to review it, both judges and jurors being sworn to decide in its favor. But reasoning on this subject is superfluous, when our social compact, in express terms, declares that the laws of the United States, its Constitution, and treaties made under it, are the supreme law of the land; and, for greater caution, adds 'that the judges in every State shall be bound thereby, anything in the Constitution or laws of any State to the contrary notwithstanding. . . .'

"If South Carolina considers the revenue laws unconstitutional, and has a right to prevent their execution in the port of Charleston, there would be a clear constitutional objection to their collection in every other port, and no revenue could be collected anywhere; for all imposts must be equal. . . .

"I consider, then, the power to annul a law of the United States, assumed by one State, incompatible with the existence of the Union, contradicted expressly by the letter of the Constitution, unauthorized by its spirit, inconsistent with every principle on which it was founded, and destructive of the great object for which it was formed."

Advancing from general principles to the application made by South Carolina, Jackson notes that the nullification of the tariff acts rests on the argument that while the laws purport to be revenue laws, they are in reality intended for the protection of manufactures. These laws, then, he comments, were passed by virtue of a power expressly given to lay and collect imposts, and their constitutionality is denied from the *motives* attributed to those who passed them. "However apparent this purpose may be in the present case, nothing can be more dangerous than to admit . . . that an unconstitutional purpose, entertained by the members who assent to a law enacted under a constitutional power, shall make that law void: for how is that purpose to be ascertained?"

The next objection, he continues, that the laws operate unequally, might be urged against every law that could be passed. The position of South Carolina presents the federal government with two alternatives: to repeal all acts for raising revenue on imports, or to acquiesce in the dissolution of the Union by the secession of one member. The former course Congress could not pursue without involving itself in disgrace and the country in ruin, while the attempt to enforce the laws is declared by the state to be the signal for leaving the Union. As to the profession of the Governor that the people of South Carolina "sincerely and anxiously seek and desire" the submission of their grievances to a convention of the states, the proclamation points out that neither Congress nor any functionary of the general government has authority to call such a convention, unless demanded by two thirds of the states.

In conclusion the President announced that "it is the intent of this instrument to proclaim, not only that the duty imposed on me by the Constitution 'to take care that the laws be faithfully executed,' shall be performed to the extent of the powers already vested in me by law, or of such others as the wisdom of Congress shall devise and entrust to me for that purpose, but to warn the citizens of South Carolina who have been deluded into an opposition to the laws, of the danger they will incur by obedience to the illegal and disorganizing ordinance of the Convention; to exhort those who have refused to support it to persevere in their determination to uphold the Constitution and laws of their country; and to point out to all the perilous situation into which the good people of that State have been led, and that the course they are urged to pursue is one of ruin and disgrace to the very State whose rights they affect to support." [10]

The legislature promptly replied to Jackson's proclamation in a series of resolutions denying his constitutional right to use his proclamation as a mode of interfering "whenever he may think fit, in the affairs of the respective states, or . . . as a means of promulgating executive expositions of the Constitution"; condemning his opinions as "erroneous and dangerous," and inconsistent with the stand taken when Georgia acted upon principles "identical with those now denounced by him in South Carolina"; [11] declaring that each state has the right to secede peaceably from the Union, and "that there is no constitutional power in the general government, much less in the executive department . . . to retain by force such state in the Union"; and asserting that "the primary and

[10] Richardson, *Messages*, II, 641–652 *et passim*. Reprint in Johnson, *Readings*, 329–337, MacDonald, *Sel. Docs.*, 273–283, and Commager, *Docs.*, 262–268.

[11] A reference to the Georgia Indian controversy. See McMaster, *History*, V, 175–181, and citations in Ames, *State Docs.*, 114.

paramount allegiance of the citizens of this state, native or adopted, is of right due to this state." The last resolution expressed indignation at "the menaces which are directed against it," and declared "that the state will repel force with force, and relying upon the blessings of God, will maintain its liberty at all hazards." [12]

CONGRESS AND THE FORCE ACT

On January 16, 1833, Jackson reported to Congress the situation in South Carolina, submitting copies of all the documents, and asked for additional authority to enforce the tariff laws. The bill with which Congress responded, known as the force bill, led to a debate in which Calhoun stood almost unsupported against the field. In his speech he reviewed his whole career and tried to justify his course; Webster was the chief speaker on the other side. The bill became a law on March 2, receiving the vote of three

[12] Ames, *State Docs.*, 174–176; also Commager, *Docs.*, 268–269. Calhoun thought that there would be no opportunity for the government to use force in South Carolina. He wrote to Gov. Hamilton on August 28, 1832: "I pass over the fact that the General Government has no right to resort to force against a State. . . . Let it, however, be determined to use force, and the difficulty would be insurmountable, unless, indeed, it be also determined to set aside the Constitution, and to subvert the system to its foundations. Against whom would it be applied? Congress has, it is true, the right to call forth the militia 'to execute the laws and suppress insurrection' but there would be no law resisted, unless, indeed, it be called resistance for the juries to refuse to find, and the courts to render judgment, in conformity with the wishes of the General Government; no insurrection to suppress; no armed force to reduce; not a sword unsheathed; not a bayonet raised; none, absolutely none, on whom force could be used, except it be on the unarmed citizens engaged peaceably and quietly in their daily occupations."—*Works*, VI, 163–164.

Van Buren says that Jackson "had at this time . . . one feeling which approached to a passion and that was an inclination to go himself with a sufficient force, which he felt assured he could raise in Virginia and Tennessee, as 'a *posse comitatus*' of the Marshal and arrest Messrs. Calhoun, Hayne, Hamilton and McDuffie in the midst of the force of 12,000 men which the Legislature of South Carolina had authorized to be raised and deliver them to the Judicial power of the United States to be dealt with according to law. The reader will find this project more than once stated in his letters to me. . . ."—*Autobiography*, 544.

Jackson wrote to Joel Poinsett, January 24, 1833, that if Congress did not pass the force bill, and he was informed of any "illegal assemblage" to oppose the revenue acts, he would issue warning to disperse, and if the assemblage did not comply would call out a force sufficient to "overawe resistance, put treason and rebellion down without blood, and arrest and hand over to the judiciary for trial and punishment, the leaders, exciters and promoters of this rebellion and treason."—Poinsett MSS., quoted by McMaster, VI, 163, note.

members from South Carolina, four of the delegation of nine being Unionists.

The force act of 1833, which formed another in the succession of acts beginning with the one passed by Congress during Washington's administration relating to the use of the militia to enforce the laws of the United States,[13] reads as follows in the most important section:

"Sec. 5. *And be it further enacted,* That whenever the President of the United States shall be officially informed, by the authorities of any state, or by a judge of any circuit or district court of the United States, in the state, that, within the limits of such state, any law or laws of the United States, or the execution thereof, or any process from the courts of the United States, is obstructed by the employment of military force, or by any other unlawful means, too great to be overcome by the ordinary course of judicial proceeding, or by the powers vested in the marshal by existing laws, it shall be lawful for him, the President of the United States, forthwith to issue his proclamation, declaring such fact or information, and requiring all such military and other force forthwith to disperse; and if at any time after issuing such proclamation, any such opposition or obstruction shall be made, in the manner or by the means aforesaid, the President shall be, and hereby is, authorized, promptly to employ such means to suppress the same, and to cause the said laws or process to be duly executed, as are authorized and provided in the cases therein mentioned by the act of the twenty-eighth of February, one thousand seven hundred and ninety-five, entitled 'An act to provide for calling forth the militia to execute the laws of the Union, suppress insurrections, repel invasions, and to repeal the act now in force for that purpose' "; and also the act of March, 1807, authorizing the use of the land and naval forces in cases of insurrection.[14]

[13] See Hockett, *Con. Hist.,* I, 275.

[14] *U. S. Statutes at Large,* IV, 632. The act of 1807 made lawful the use of the regular forces wherever existing laws permitted the use of militia. *Ibid.,* II, 443. The force bill was entitled "An Act further to provide for the collection of duties on imports." It became a law on February 26, the compromise tariff following on March 1, 1833. The Senate vote on the force bill stood 32 to 1. Fifteen senators did not vote. The negative vote was cast by John Tyler. Among the affirmative were one from Virginia, one from Georgia, two from Louisiana. The House vote

THE CLOSE OF THE EPISODE

The story of the settlement of the contest need not be repeated here. It need only be noted that South Carolina found herself unsupported by her sister states, who repudiated the theory of nullification as emphatically as they had denounced the tariff laws against which it was directed. Just before replying to Jackson's proclamation, the South Carolina legislature had adopted resolutions to the effect that it was expedient to hold a convention of the states at as early a date as practicable, "to determine and consider" such questions of disputed power as were at issue between Congress and the states. This proposal was a departure from the procedure provided by the Constitution when amendments thereto were in contemplation, and reminded the public of the irregular method pursued by the New England states in calling the Hartford Convention. Delaware replied that "the Constitution of the United States . . . does not recognize any such tribunal or political assemblage as a Convention of the States, but has expressly provided for modes of amendment"; that such a convention, when called by Congress, must be a convention of the people, and that no such political assemblage as a Convention of the *States* could have power to "*consider* and *determine*" questions of disputed power.[15]

Georgia was not hostile to the idea of a southern convention to consider the tariff and devise and recommend the most effectual

stood 149 to 47. See *Cong. Deb.*, 22 Cong., 2 sess., App. 1; Senate Journal, 198–199; House Journal, 453–454. Twenty-seven representatives of states which seceded in 1861 voted for the force bill, showing the belief in the right of the government to enforce its laws in the face of the opposition of a state as expressed by the action of a delegate convention.

Concerning the act, Calhoun wrote later that it rested on a theory of nationalism which was dangerous to southern interests. So long as the Union was viewed as a federation, with a government of limited powers, he thought, belief in the "sinfulness of slavery" did not lead to interference with it on the part of the North. But the force act of 1833 openly proclaimed that the government had the right to judge of the extent of its own powers, and to use the military and naval forces of the Union to carry its decisions into execution. Calhoun believed that this act inspired the Abolitionists to agitate the question of slavery and to flood the South with documents designed to inspire discontent among slaves—also to petition Congress to abolish slavery in the District of Columbia. See "Discourse," written in 1850, in *Works*, I, 373. Cf. speech of March 4, 1850, *ibid.*, IV, 552–553. The act formed an important precedent for Lincoln's course in 1861.

[15] Ames, *State Docs.*, 176–177.

means of obtaining relief from the evils of that system, but by resolution declared "that we abhor the doctrine of Nullification as
neither a peaceful, nor a constitutional remedy, but, on the contrary, as tending to civil commotion and disunion; and while we
deplore the rash and revolutionary measures, recently adopted by
a Convention of the people of South Carolina, we deem it our paramount duty to warn our fellow citizens against the danger of
adopting her mischievous policy." [16]

Alabama passed resolutions denouncing the tariff and proposing
to the co-states a "federal convention," but, like Georgia, rejecting
nullification: "Nullification, which some of our southern brethren
recommend as the constitutional remedy for the evils under which
we labor, is unsound in theory and dangerous in practice; . . . as
a remedy, it is unconstitutional and essentially revolutionary, leading in its consequences to anarchy and civil discord, and finally to
the dissolution of the Union." [17]

North Carolina, Mississippi, and Virginia took a similar position,
leaving South Carolina no choice but to face the might of the
federal government alone or to retreat.[18] The conciliatory disposition of the administration, the persuasions of Virginia and North
Carolina, and the disposition of the protectionists themselves to pass
a compromise tariff, offered an opportunity for retreat from a
position of danger without abandoning the principles for which
she contended. Hence, accepting the compromise tariff of 1833,
a new session of the state convention repealed the former ordinance
of nullification, but as a gesture of defiance, nullified the force act
which there was no danger would be put to the test.[19]

[16] *Ibid.*, 179–180.

[17] *Ibid.*, 180–182. For resolutions of other states, see *ibid.*, 183–188.

[18] Virginians "believe that when all the departments of the general government
have affirmed the constitutionality of an act of Congress, no state has a right to
oppose it by penal laws any more than certain other states had a right to oppose,
positively or negatively, the late war with Great Britain; whereas, South Carolinians contend that a state, being sovereign, has a right to decide for herself
whether the general government has exceeded its power or not, and to refuse to
yield obedience to its laws accordingly."—*Southern Patriot and Commercial Advertiser*, 1822, quoted by Hunt, *John C. Calhoun*, 75. The accuracy of this comparison is quite doubtful.

[19] Ames, *State Docs.*, 188–189; Commager, *Docs.*, 269–270. The feeling in South
Carolina following the nullification episode is illustrated by the following newspaper paragraph: "This little State has defied the swaggering giant of the Union.

The chief significance of the nullification controversy was that it brought into prominence in the public mind two rival theories of the Constitution which were to continue in conflict until one went down in the blood of civil war. Neither the theory of state sovereignty nor of national sovereignty was new in 1832. Men had been seeking some satisfactory and consistent theory from the beginning, and had provided most of the materials used by Calhoun and Webster in the formulation of their respective views. Calhoun's particular application of the state sovereignty theory did not, indeed, survive, but the discussions of the period gave the belief in state sovereignty itself even greater vitality than it had possessed before. Webster uttered no idea which Marshall and others had not held before his speech of January, 1830; but never before had a great orator proclaimed these doctrines under circumstances which broadcast them to the entire country. The battle of the giants in the era of nullification was a forerunner of the greater contest which arrayed the sections in arms a generation later.

Thirteen thousand Carolinians have not only awed the wild West into respect, compelled Pennsylvania stolidity into something like sense, New York corruption into something like decency, Yankee rapacity into a sort of image of honesty, but they have done all this loftily and steadily and in the face of seventeen thousand betrayers of the liberty of their own State."—*Columbia Telescope* of March 12, 1833, quoted by McMaster, *History*, VI, 169.

Marshall almost despaired during the nullification episode. He wrote to Story on September 22, 1832, saying: "If the prospects of our country inspire you with gloom, how do you think a man must be affected who partakes of all your opinions and whose geographic position enables him to see a great deal that is concealed from you? I yield slowly and reluctantly to the conviction that our Constitution cannot last. I had supposed that north of the Potomack a firm and solid government competent to the security of rational liberty might be preserved. Even that now seems doubtfull. The case of the South now seems to me to be desperate. Our opinions are incompatible with a united government even among ourselves. The Union has been prolonged thus far by miracles. I fear they can not endure." Mass. Hist. Soc. *Proc.*, 2d ser., XIV, 351–352.

PART TWO

THE DEMOCRATIZATION OF THE FEDERAL GOVERNMENT

IV

THE PROCEEDINGS OF THE CONSTITU-
TIONAL CONVENTION COME TO LIGHT

MEAGERNESS OF INFORMATION IN THE EARLY YEARS

THE intense interest in the constitutional aspects of the public questions which arose in such numbers during the years following the second war with England led Congress to pass a resolution, on March 27, 1818, directing that the journal of the Convention of 1787, together with all acts and proceedings of the Convention in the possession of the government, should be published under the direction of the President. Previous to this action trustworthy information concerning the formation of the Constitution had been but meager. The delegates had sat behind closed doors, depriving the public as far as possible of knowledge of their doings. Before adjournment they had even considered the propriety of destroying the minutes of the debates, lest publication permit a "bad use" to be made of them by those who desired to prevent a favorable decision on the Constitution. This proposal had been rejected on the ground that it would be unwise to make it impossible to contradict falsehoods, and in response to Washington's inquiry, the secretary had been directed to deposit the records in his hands, as presiding officer, to be held "subject to the order of Congress, if ever formed under the Constitution."[1] A generation elapsed before these or any other authentic records of the discussions were published.[2]

[1] The material on which this chapter is based is found almost wholly in Max Farrand, *Records of the Federal Convention*, and few specific citations seem to be required. For the narrative account of the framing and adoption of the Constitution, see Hockett, *Con. Hist.*, I, Chap. XI.

[2] The rule of secrecy was enforced very rigidly. Sentries guarded the approaches to the chamber in which the sessions were held. On one occasion, a copy of the Virginia plan having been picked up from the floor, Washington reminded the delegates so sharply of the necessity of greater care lest documents fall into the hands of outsiders that the owner of the paper never dared, by claiming it, to admit his dereliction.

Opinions as to the wisdom of the rule of secrecy varied. Madison believed that it gave general satisfaction. Hamilton wrote in 1792: "Had the deliberations been

That outsiders had some inkling of developments, during the sessions of the Convention, however, is shown, for example, by contemporary correspondence of which the following is a sample: "It seems to be agreed here [Massachusetts] that the Virginia plan was admitted to come upon the floor of investigation by way of experiment and with a few yieldings on this point & that it keeps its ground at present. The contents of this plan was known to some, I believe, before the Convention met." [3] Another indication is found in the professions of the French minister that he was in touch with the proceedings. In reports to his superior he alluded to communications made to him by delegates, and gave a somewhat detailed analysis of the proposals pending before their body. The total knowledge that sifted through to the public must have been slight.[4]

With the return of the delegates to their homes interest shifted from the Philadelphia proceedings to the exciting question of adopting or rejecting the plan of government which had come out of the convention hall. In some of the states delegates made oral

open while going on, the clamours of faction would have prevented any satisfactory result." (Farrand, *Records*, III, 368.) On the other hand, Jefferson deplored the rule as "an abominable precedent" (*ibid.*, 76), and Luther Martin complained that it deprived him of the coveted right to seek the advice of leaders in his state, and even restricted the privilege of members in copying documents which were essential in following the discussions (*ibid.*, 151).

[3] Nathan Dane to Rufus King, July 5, 1787. Farrand, III, 55.

[4] "Les plans de réforme qui m'ont été communiqués . . . me mettent en état de vous informer plus amplement des innovations que les députés se proposent d'introduire. . . . Les députés . . . qui m'ont communiqué ces différens projets, sont determinés à les soutenir avec vigueur." M. Otto to Montmorin, June 10, 1787.—Farrand, III, 39.

How much information leaked out it is impossible to determine. In spite of all care, delegates undoubtedly forgot themselves now and then long enough to betray some of the details. One who visited New York about the middle of June is known to have talked too freely. Nicholas Gilman, a New Hampshire delegate who arrived late, understanding that "secrecy is enjoined only as prudence might dictate to each individual," sent to his brother a "hint respecting the general principles of the plan of National Government" that was likely to be adopted. This memorandum has been lost. Even Franklin, most prudent of men, was on a certain occasion about to refer to an incident in the Convention, when reminded that such references were forbidden.

There is at least a suggestion of clandestine revelations in Otto's repeated statements that he has had communication with delegates. The alleged knowledge which he imparts is difficult to correlate with the occurrences in the Convention, however, and seems to bear out the conclusion that the total leakage was not of great consequence.

or written reports to the legislatures. In one such report Gerry told the Massachusetts assembly the story of the controversy between the large and small states which eventuated in the great compromise. In Maryland the delegates presented explanations of the proceedings at Philadelphia by request of the House of Representatives. In compliance with this request, McHenry prepared a statement from the notes which he had taken, but having been absent during June and July, his report was chiefly a commentary upon the completed instrument. His colleague Martin went much further, presenting on November 29, 1787, the substance of a statement which in the printed form given to it a little later has ever since been known as the *Genuine Information*.

In the fifty pages of Martin's report an account was given of the contest between the large and small states over representation, and in connection with many of the provisions of the completed instrument, a summary of the arguments which had been urged both for and against them. While candid, the *Genuine Information* was not unbiassed, as it reflected the judgment of a man under emotional stress which rendered him incapable of dealing fairly with the views of the triumphant majority whose work he disapproved. Charles Pinckney referred to it as a "long mischievous detail of the opinions and proceedings of the late general convention," and a correspondent wrote to Jefferson from London: "I blush'd in my own bed-chamber when I read his speech on this side of the Atlantic."

Martin's statement was nevertheless revealing, and while most of the delegates spoke with some reserve of proceedings the record of which had been withheld from publication, the criticism accorded Martin was less due to any betrayal of secrets than to his Antifederalism. The discussions of the period of ratification were bound to show a relaxation of the former reticence, and publicity was both inevitable and desirable. Washington wrote, three weeks after leaving Philadelphia: "Much will depend . . . upon literary abilities, and the recommendation of [the Constitution] by good pens should be openly, I mean publickly afforded in the Gazettes." There was little need of Washington's exhortation, for friends and foes of the proposed government were alike eager to seize their pens; and during the fall, winter, and spring, while the state ratifying conventions, one after another, were in session, they poured forth a considerable volume of controversial literature.

Although incidental to this major discussion bits of Convention history thus came to light. Much more comprehensive statements were made semi-confidentially by delegates during these same months to friends and acquaintances. In private communications they wrote and spoke quite freely; and in some cases these expositions amounted to rather elaborate outlines of the history of the Convention. Such, for example were Madison's letter to Jefferson written in October, and Baldwin's conversation in December with Ezra Stiles, president of Yale College.

The public obtained bits of information, moreover, through the utterances of delegates who became members of the state ratifying conventions, and who, in the course of debate, found it expedient to make allusions to what had occurred at Philadelphia. These were in no case systematic reviews of the whole proceedings, but in sum they contributed a good deal of detail to the outlines afforded by such reports as the *Genuine Information* and Gerry's letter to the Massachusetts legislature.

After the establishment of the new government the process of gradual diffusion of knowledge went on. In interpreting the Constitution and applying it to actual conditions it was natural that legislators and administrative officials should seek light as to the intent of the framers. At least six times during the First Congress Sherman of Connecticut enlightened the House of Representatives on the transactions or views of the Convention, on topics ranging from the appointing power, the apportionment of representation in the House, and the powers of Congress over the time, place, and manner of holding congressional elections, to naturalization and a national university. In connection with representation he informed his hearers that the ratio had been changed in the Convention at the request of Washington. Baldwin and Gerry, in these early sessions, were also prominent expounders of the Convention's point of view, and Madison was drawn into statements concerning its action on the questions of the assumption of state debts and the power of incorporation.

In literally dozens of instances, during the early years under the Constitution, ex-delegates volunteered information, or responded to the requests of colleagues in Congress, concerning the attitude of the Convention; and as time passed, unusual prestige even came to be attached to the enactments of the First Congress, because it contained sixteen ex-delegates, and therefore presumably acted in close conformity with the intent of the framers of the organic law. For several decades, indeed, questions of great public concern continued to elicit explanatory comment from delegates. During the discussion of the twelfth amendment and the Louisiana purchase treaty, letters of Gouverneur Morris to various correspondents contained many illuminating comments. In the former instance he elucidated the relation of the small states to the original plan of choosing the President and Vice-President, and in the latter, explained the powers of Congress in acquiring and governing dependent territory. During the Chase impeachment trial, in 1804, Luther Martin, as one of the attorneys for the defense, described the process by which the Convention came to invest the trial of impeachments in the Senate; and in the same year Madison, in a letter to Noah Webster, told the story of the part taken by the Virginia delegates in framing the Randolph resolutions. In 1815 Morris explained the intent of the Convention with regard to the militia, the federal control of which had been a vexed question during the war just terminated. Illustrations might be multiplied. Surviving members of the Convention, so long as there were any, were regarded as a source of information concerning the intent of the framers in relation to almost every clause of the Constitution which became a matter of controversy.

Within a few years after the establishment of the government persons who had not been in the Philadelphia gathering began to refer to its transactions in support of their positions on current issues. Public men were evidently diligent in collecting information. Jefferson made note of several matters of interest after conversations with Baldwin and Mason, and at an early date was allowed to make confidential use of Madison's notes of the debates.[5]

[5] The date when Madison took Jefferson into his confidence and allowed him to inspect his notes is not ascertainable. It may have been as early as 1791, when

Before the first veto, he had learned, through conversation with the President, that the apportionment bill (the first occasion for its use) was "contrary . . . to what was understood at the time by the makers" of the Constitution. In February, 1791, he was able, in his famous opinion on the United States Bank, to assert: "It is known that the very power now proposed *as a means* was rejected as *an end* by the Convention which formed the Constitution." In June, 1798, Albert Gallatin, in the House, alluded to the effort of a member of the Convention (Gouverneur Morris) to throw the "general welfare" clause into a distinct paragraph. As late as 1820, Walter Lowrie of Pennsylvania explained in the Senate, on the authority of a statement by Wilson, the purpose of the "migration" clause.

MISINFORMATION AND MYTHS

In reply to Jefferson's appeal in his bank opinion to the Convention's discussion concerning incorporation, Hamilton had written: "What was the precise nature or extent of this proposition, or what the reasons for refusing it, is not ascertained by any authentic document, or even by accurate recollection." Hamilton may have had in mind the fact that in the spring of the previous year Gerry and Madison had differed in their recollections on this very point. Before the close of 1791 Gerry was again involved in a difference of memory with a member from North Carolina who was also an ex-delegate.

Such differences were the inevitable result of the want of authentic documents. Madison soon learned to deprecate citations of Convention views. In 1796, in reply to a question concerning them, he reminded the House that nine years had elapsed since its sittings, and that, with no notes at hand to assist his memory, there was liability of error. Besides, there was some indelicacy, he thought, in presuming to give the opinion of a body in which opinions were often divided. Then, too, views of delegates and the

the secretary of state wrote his opinion on the unconstitutionality of the United States Bank. It is certain that as early as April, 1796, Jefferson had these notes in his possession, and some time before he left Philadelphia, with the author's permission, a transcript was made for his confidential use by John W. Eppes, his son-in-law.

decisions of the whole body were without authority. Since their powers were merely recommendatory, and the Constitution derived its force from the ratifying conventions, it was to these that one must go for light on the meaning of provisions.

The habit of citing the Convention was not at all checked by these wise words of Madison, and led, in June, 1798, to an unseemly controversy between Abraham Baldwin and Jonathan Dayton, ex-delegates from Georgia and New Jersey. The latter was at the time the speaker of the House. Even worse evils appeared in the form of malicious misrepresentation. In 1792 Hamilton was the victim of a story in the *National Gazette* charging him with having advocated government of the United States by king, lords and commons. The authorship was anonymous, but the truth of the story was alleged to have been confirmed by the talkative Baldwin. The unsigned refutation, easily recognized as Hamilton's work, cited documentary evidence (his draft plan of a constitution), but did not effectively counteract the slander.[6]

Madison became in his turn a sufferer from the misuse of Convention history by designing politicians. The episode in which he was involved was as follows: Mr. Edmund C. Genêt, the notorious minister of France during Washington's presidency, instead of returning to his own country, settled in New York, as is well known, and married a daughter of Governor George Clinton. In the year 1808 Clinton and Madison became rivals for the presidential nomination, and Genêt interested himself in the promotion of his father-in-law's political fortunes by the common method of exposing his competitor's record. He had in some way come into possession of the notes on the debates in the Convention taken by Robert Yates,

[6] Oddly enough, Hamilton's statement contained an error on the very point at issue. He admitted that he had originally favored a tenure of office by the President during good behavior, but stated that on maturer thought he had come to prefer a limited term as his plan of a constitution would show. The original of this plan, he said, was in his possession, and a copy in Madison's. Madison had, in fact, made a copy at Hamilton's instance, at the time the plan was presented in the Convention, and this copy comparison shows to be exact. Long after Hamilton's death examination of both original and copy showed that the plan proposed presidential tenure during good behavior. Madison attributed Hamilton's misstatement to lapse of memory, as, the means of disproving it being in Madison's power, he thought Hamilton could never have intentionally misrepresented its contents.

one of the New York delegates. In these were entries which he found might be twisted in such a way as to indicate that Madison had favored the abolition of the state governments and the substitution of one centralized system. Advocacy of a plan so contrary to the ideas of his party in 1808 could hardly fail to damage Madison's reputation if revealed to the public. Genêt therefore addressed an open *Letter to the Electors of President and Vice-President of the United States*, signed "By a Citizen of New York," and accompanied by an alleged "extract of the secret debates of the Federal Convention" taken by Judge Yates.

In the notes as Yates took them, there occurs, under date of June 6, the following entry:

"Mr. Read is of opinion, that the state governments must sooner or later be at an end, and that therefore we must make the present national government as perfect as possible.

"Mr. Madison is of opinion, that when we agreed to the first resolve of having a national government, consisting of a supreme executive, judicial and legislative power, it was then intended to operate to the exclusion of a federal government,[7] and the more extensive we made the basis, the greater probability of duration, happiness and good order."

The question before the body when this statement was made related to the method of choosing the members of the first branch of the legislature, later denominated the House of Representatives. Some delegates wished to have the choice made by the state legislatures. Madison's speech was intended as an argument for election by the people. In the "Extract" published by Genêt the old device was employed of taking words out of their context:

"The 2d of June, 1787, Mr. Randolph displayed the views of the plan of Virginia, with respect to the executive branch of the union."

So reads the "Extract." Then, passing over the debates of the days intervening between June 2 and 6, and continuing as if Madison's speech followed Randolph's at once, it proceeds:

"Mr. Madison, from Virginia, endeavoured to support the plan of that state in all its branches, and after a speech pronounced by

[7] In the original sense of the word "federal."

Mr. Reed, to prove that the state-governments must sooner or later be at an end, and that therefore it was the duty of the convention to make the new national government as perfect as possible; he gave it as his opinion that when the Convention agreed to the first resolve of having a national government it was then intended to *operate to the exclusion of federal government*, and that the more extensive the basis was made the greater would be the probability of duration, happiness and good order."

Madison was thus made to appear to be in sympathy with Read's suggestion that the states should be set aside and a consolidated republic substituted. By pursuing such methods throughout the "Extract," paraphrasing, rearranging, and garbling the text of Yates's notes, Genêt was able to make a plausible case against Madison as a consolidationist.

Such publications made the state of knowledge worse rather than better. Yet, perhaps because the effect upon the political campaign was not great, the episode seems not to have produced the logical consequence, that is, a demand for publication of the full record.

While partisan malice distorted the truth to the detriment of individual reputations, ignorance, forgetfulness, and hero-worship gave rise to myths and legends. The Washington legend began early to take form. Gouverneur Morris contributed to it by his oration upon the death of General Washington. Morris made no contemporaneous notes on the Convention, finding his "faculties . . . on the stretch to further our business"; but as an eye-witness of events he was looked upon by the public as unimpeachable authority. After the blurring of memory by the lapse of a dozen years, under stress of the strong emotions evoked by Washington's demise and the temptation to seek rhetorical effects, he allowed himself, in referring to a critical moment just previous to the first meeting of the Convention, to indulge in the following flight:

"*Americans!*—let the opinion then delivered by the greatest and best of men, be ever present to your remembrance. He was collected within himself. His countenance had more than usual solemnity—His eye was fixed, and seemed to look into futurity. 'It is (said he) too probable that no plan we propose will be adopted. Perhaps another dreadful conflict is to be sustained. If to please the people, we offer what we ourselves disapprove, how can we afterwards defend our work? Let us raise a standard to which the wise and the honest can repair. The event is in the hand of God.' "

The central idea here attributed to Washington is not improbably correct although Morris's statement lacks confirmation; but the descriptive touches and the quoted words, giving the vividly realistic effect, are clearly due to the orator's art. With such utterances current, it is small wonder that within a few years after Washington's death, newspaper eulogists ascribed to him the founding of the American government, in terms which inculcated the belief that his work in the Convention had been active to the utmost degree. This only the surviving delegates knew to be an exaggeration, but they left their dissent unvoiced except to confidants.

The growth of legend touched others of the "Fathers" in varying measure. By 1825 one story represented General Dayton as announcing on behalf of the small states that they would secede from the Convention unless the vote for proportional representation in the Senate were rescinded; introduced an apochryphal speech of conciliation by Franklin, concluding with his proposal (which was in truth made but rejected) of daily prayers; described Washington's face as Franklin sat down—" at once so dignified and delighted"; represented Hamilton as opposing Franklin's proposal on the ground that he saw no necessity of calling in "foreign aid," while Washington gazed at him "with a mixture of surprise and indignation"; and pictured the Convention as adopting Franklin's proposal instantly and unanimously, barring the solitary negative or silent disapprobation—it was uncertain which—of Hamilton. The time came when Madison found himself compelled, in the interest of truth, to repudiate the title of writer of the Constitution, and to advise the historian Jared Sparks that Gouverneur Morris was not entitled to as much credit for conciliating the anger of delegates at the crisis of the Convention as popular stories attributed to him.

PUBLICATION OF THE RECORDS

It will be recalled that the decision to preserve the records of the Convention was taken in order to make possible the refutation of misstatements. It appears strange, at first thought, that the mischievous gossip about individuals and the prevalence of apochryphal stories did not sooner prove the necessity of publishing the authentic records and critically studying them. In fact so few persons were in position to recognize falsehood that there was little to nourish a public demand for the documents. Moreover, many ex-delegates doubted the propriety of publishing them during the life of any of the framers. At the very moment when Hamilton was engaged in self-defense, he argued that disclosure of the deliberations was not to be desired, because "propositions, made without due reflection, and perhaps abandoned by the proposers themselves on more mature reflection, would have been handles for a profusion of illnatured accusation."

The most important of the records deposited in Washington's hands was the journal which had been kept by Major Jackson as official secretary. Jackson owed his appointment more to political influence than to any marked qualifications for the task, and the journal, intended primarily to assist the delegates in keeping track of their progress from day to day, turned out to be "no better than the daily minutes from which the regular Journal ought to have been, but never was, made out." In addition to this barren document, which Jared Sparks once called "dry bones," Jackson made extensive minutes of the debates, intending to profit by their publication. Absorption in this private enterprise, which he strangely conceived to be consistent with his official duty, may account in a measure for the unsatisfactory character of his journal.

Fortunately for the cause of history, the secretary's notes were supplemented by unofficial documents. The rule of secrecy did not forbid the delegates to take notes for their own use, and a number of them did so, induced in part perhaps by the need of supplementing the slight minutes with which the limited competence of the secretary supplied them. These notes were retained by the takers as personal papers, instead of being deposited with the official records in Washington's keeping; and while most of them are more or less fragmentary, they formed, with the journal, the basis for the work of the historian who should one day seek to trace the steps in the framing of the Constitution.

At least one of the members who took notes had the future student definitely in mind. As delegate-elect from Virginia, James
Madison prepared for the Philadelphia meeting by elaborate study
of historic confederacies, and the difficulties he experienced in the
quest for reliable information suggested to him the importance of
preserving a full and accurate report. As he tells us himself, he
was not unaware "of the value of such a contribution to the fund
of materials for the History of a Constitution on which should be
Staked the happiness of a people great even in its infancy, and
possibly the cause of liberty throughout the world." [8]

To accomplish this self-appointed task, he chose a seat directly
in front of the presiding officer's desk, and as nearly as possible
equally distant from the extremities of the room, in order that
nothing of importance might escape his sight or hearing. Thus
advantageously placed, by attending the sessions diligently, every
day, and every hour in the day, using an abbreviated longhand and
expanding his notes each evening, and collecting and keeping copies
of the written documents presented on the floor, he was able to
preserve an account of the debates which has proved to be of far
more value than all other sources of information.

As has already been noted, Jefferson early became confidentially
familiar with Madison's notes. In conformity with his political
principles he had deplored the secrecy of the Convention, and was
one of the first to advocate the publication of the materials relating
to it. Following the sharp contention in Congress over the constitutional aspects of the war measures of 1798, he urged Madison to
consider the publication of his notes for the sake of the aid they
would afford in interpreting the Constitution in such times of controversy. After describing the preparations for hostilities, he
added:

"In a society of members, between whom & yourself is great
mutual esteem and respect, a most anxious desire is expressed that

---

[8] Before turning over the journal to Washington, Jackson burned all the "loose
scraps" of paper in his possession. What valuable documents may have been thus
destroyed can only be conjectured. Jackson told John Quincy Adams in 1818
that he had refrained from publishing his own notes at the request of Washington,
at a loss to himself, he supposed, of many thousands of dollars. Jackson's notes
have never been found.

you would publish your debates of the Convention. That these measures of the army, navy & direct tax will bring about a revulsion of public sentiment is thought certain, & that the constitution will then receive a different explanation. Could those debates be ready to appear critically [i.e., at the critical moment], their effect would be decisive. I beg of you to turn this subject in your mind. The arguments against it will be personal; those in favor of it moral; and something is required from you as a set off against the sin of your retirement."

Jefferson, although ever a partisan, evidently believed that the truth would promote national as well as party welfare; and as the years passed and the body of misinformation accumulated, he must have regretted more than once the rejection of his advice. That he looked forward hopefully to the day when the true history of the Convention would be written may be inferred from a letter to his old friend John Adams, in 1815. Adams had raised the question of a history of the Revolution, inquiring who might be considered a fit person to undertake it. Jefferson in reply said that no one would ever be able to write of anything but its external facts, because Congress had done everything with doors closed and no member had made notes of the proceedings as a whole. Then, as if it suddenly occurred to him that for the history of the Convention the case was very different, he added:

"Do you know that there exists in manuscript the ablest work of this kind ever yet executed, of the debates of the constitutional convention of Philadelphia in 1788 [sic]? The whole of everything said and done there was taken down by Mr. Madison, with a labor and exactness beyond comprehension."

Madison's judgment as to publicity was quite at variance with Jefferson's. Although it was always his intention that his notes should some day be put in print, he leaned more and more to the opinion that their appearance should be posthumous. Madison was in full accord, in this respect, with Hamilton. Neither seems ever to have been convinced that the malicious use of the records would not be productive of greater evils than ill-natured gossip based on ignorance. Madison, moreover, felt bound by the action of the Convention in subjecting the official records to the discretion of

Congress.   When Washington declined the request of the House
of Representatives, in 1796, for the papers relating to Jay's negotiations in England, justifying his action by citing the "Journals of
the General Convention, deposited in the office of the Department
of State," [9] in which it would appear, he alleged, "that a proposition
was made, 'that no Treaty should be binding on the United States
which was not ratified by a law,' and that the proposition was
explicitly rejected," the message brought forth from Madison a
criticism of the President's action.   By citing the journal which had
been committed to him for safe-keeping but not for public use,
Madison thought the President had transgressed the proprieties.
Commenting privately, he queried:
    "According to my memory & that of others, the Journal of the
Convention was, by a vote deposited with the P., to be kept sacred
until called for by some competent authority.   How can this be
reconciled with the use he has made of it?"
    To Jefferson's suggestion, in 1799, that his own notes be pub-
lished, Madison responded that the idea ought to be well weighed
before a decision.   "The whole volume ought to be examined with
an eye to the use of which every part is susceptible. . . .   It is a
problem what turn might be given to the impression on the public
mind."   Madison had no desire to promote Jefferson's partisan purpose by publication, and with a suggestion that Jefferson examine
the notes attentively before finally making up his own mind, he
dismissed the matter.   It is safe to conclude that his answer was
intended as a courteous non-compliance, and that he already
thought substantially as he did when he wrote, nearly thirty years
later: "I have not yet ceased to think, that publications [sic] of
them, posthumous as to others as well as myself, may be most
delicate and most useful. . . .   As no personal or party views can
then be imputed, they will be read with less of personal or party
feelings, and consequently, with whatever profit, may be promised
by them."
    Following the War of 1812–1815 the direction of the wind of

---

[9] Washington kept the journal in his own possession until 1796, when he deposited it in the state department.   There it remains to this day, in the bureau of
rolls and library.

interest in the origins of the Constitution is betrayed by the plan conceived by William Plumer, Jr., of preparing the official journal for publication. He enlisted the aid of his father, who was an ex-senator and at the time governor of New Hampshire, and both addressed John Quincy Adams, the secretary of state, requesting a copy of the journal to be used for this purpose. Adams forwarded the letters to Madison, at the suggestion of President Monroe, who thought that compliance with the request should depend upon Madison's opinion as to whether publication would be detrimental to the public interest. In reply, Madison commented that the work conceived by the younger Plumer, and the manner in which he had outlined the project, indicated talents which merited cultivation and encouragement. He evaded a direct expression of opinion on the question of publication, citing once more the action of the Convention in making the ultimate disposition of the records a matter for congressional determination, and suggested that Secretary Adams was better able than himself to decide, upon perusal of the journal, whether publication would be of use.

Whether the resolution of Congress, approved by Monroe on March 27, 1818, was inspired by the administration in consequence of this episode, does not appear. Some time later Adams informed Plumer of this resolution, by way of explaining his non-compliance with the latter's request. President Monroe asked Adams to assume the task of preparing the records for publication, and the secretary was soon engaged in the quest for information and missing documents. Among the papers in his department were those of George Read, delegate from Delaware, placed there following his death. From these Adams seems to have obtained a copy of the Randolph resolutions. Finding none of the plan which the minutes showed had been presented to the Convention by Charles Pinckney, Adams wrote to the author asking for one. Pinckney replied that he found several similar documents among his papers, and could not positively identify the one desired; he transmitted a copy of the one which he believed to be the plan submitted by him in 1787. Recent criticism has proved that this document was one of the preliminary drafts of the Constitution prepared by the committee of detail; but Adams, who was having editorial difficulties without end, inserted the document at the proper place in the journal and thus introduced a spurious source into the first collection ever printed of material relating to the formation of the Constitution.[10]

Adams's edition of the *Journal, Acts and Proceedings of the Convention . . . which formed the Constitution of the United States,* with most of the defects due to Secretary Jackson's carelessness, and with others due to his own editorial errors, appeared in 1819. The action of Congress in ordering its publication was generally regarded as a lifting of any ban on publicity which had existed previously, and it was not long before the full text of the notes of Judge Yates was issued.[11]   Those of William Pierce, a Georgia delegate, came next, appearing in the *Savannah Georgian* in 1828; and at about the same time Jonathan Elliot, a journalist, collected, largely from contemporary newspapers and pamphlets, the matter for the first edition of his *Debates, Resolutions, and other Proceedings, in Convention, on the adoption of the Federal Constitution, as recommended by the General Convention at Philadelphia. . . .*[12]

During the last years of his life Madison went through his notes preparatory to their publication after his demise. He now had before him the materials described in the preceding paragraph, and attempted to utilize them in revising and correcting his own notes. Especially did he have recourse to the Adams edition of the *Journal* for this purpose, and the unfortunate result was that he introduced corruptions in many places where his notes had been correct.   Upon his death in 1836 Congress purchased his papers and provided for their publication.[13]

[10] A restoration of the Pinckney plan, by J. F. Jameson and A. C. McLaughlin, is printed in Gaillard Hunt and James B. Scott, *Debates in the Federal Convention of 1787,* 596–598.

[11] *Secret Proceedings and Debates of the Convention Assembled at Philadelphia, in the Year 1787, for the purpose of forming the Constitution of the United States of America. From Notes taken by the late Robert Yates, Esq., Chief Justice of New York, and copied by John Lansing, Jun., Esq. . . .* (Albany, 1821).

[12] The first edition of Elliot's *Debates* was published at Washington, 1827–1830. It bore the title given above. The later editions were given the more accurately descriptive title, *The Debates in the Several State Conventions, on the adoption of the Federal Constitution.* Revised editions and supplementary volumes issued in 1836 and 1845 contained additional documents, such as a reprint of the Yates notes, some official and private letters, and the Madison notes. Many reprints of the edition of 1845 have been issued.

[13] H. D. Gilpin, ed., *The Papers of James Madison* (3 vols., Washington, 1840). More than half of the space in the three volumes is devoted to the notes of the

By 1840 the chief sources for the history of the conventions, both federal and state, had been made available. Nevertheless the story of the publication of records runs on through the whole of the nineteenth century and into the twentieth, although after the appearance of the Madison *Papers* the work was largely a matter of reprinting and critical editing, with occasional additions of bits of material supplementary to the early collections. The essays of Madison, Hamilton and Jay, known as *The Federalist*, which had appeared in serial form in various newspapers during the ratification contest, had been collected in a volume as early as 1788. Thereafter they were frequently reprinted, but many other controversial essays of the same period long lay buried in the files of obscure news sheets. In 1888 and 1889 Paul Leicester Ford issued two volumes in which were resurrected a number of the most important of these papers, both for and against the adoption of the Constitution.[14] Six years earlier, in the first edition of George Bancroft's *History of the Formation of the Constitution*, there had been included a collection of letters and papers not previously published.

From time to time during the later decades of the nineteenth century, letters written by members of the Convention while it was in session were printed in various places—in the lives of statesmen, publications of state historical societies, magazines, and elsewhere.[15] The notes of another delegate were put in print in 1894, when Charles R. King brought out *The Life and Correspondence of Rufus King*,[16] and within the next dozen years those taken by several others were ferreted out and put in type. The original manuscript of Pierce's notes was the basis of a reprint which appeared in the *American Historical Review* for January, 1898. In January, 1904, the same journal published the Paterson notes, and in October of the same year those of Hamilton (which had first

debates in Convention. Gilpin made no effort to eliminate corruptions of text. Madison's interpolations are incorporated into his original text without any type changes to indicate them.

[14] See Hockett, *Con. Hist.*, I, 221, note 19.

[15] A list of these is given in J. F. Jameson, "Studies in the History of the Federal Convention of 1787," 100–103.

[16] Vol. I, Appendix.

appeared the previous June in the *Proceedings* of the Massachusetts Historical Society). The series was concluded by the publication of McHenry's notes in the *Review* for April, 1906.

Meantime the government had once more taken a hand in the
business, and in 1893 had begun to issue the *Documentary History
of the Constitution*.[17] An attempt was made in these volumes to
indicate by variations of type and otherwise the actual appearance
of the manuscripts, so that changes might be distinguished from the
original reading.

The crowning work of critical scholarship, in the field of source
materials for the study of the Convention, was that of Max Farrand, under the title *The Records of the Federal Convention of
1787*.[18] Previous to its appearance, a century and a quarter after
the Fathers had finished their task, the historian was not really in
position to give a critically exact account of what was said and done
in Independence Hall during the summer of 1787.

It has been suggested that constitutional theory might have developed differently if statesmen of the twenties had had access to
the records of the Convention. It is a striking fact that of all the
prominent men whose opinions entered into the discussions of that
decade only Madison and Rufus King had been members of the
body which framed the Constitution; the others had only such
knowledge as could be gained in the ways indicated in this chapter;
and of the sources of information the imperfect *Journal* was the
chief. Calhoun, for example, could hardly have learned why the
framers decided against the coercion of a state as a corporate body,
and was led to infer that its immunity was due to the recognition
of its sovereignty.

If the records of the Convention period had been published immediately and in full, they would doubtless have proved serviceable
as guides to the lawmakers. But it may be questioned whether the
growth of constitutional theory would have been greatly altered.
Jefferson's early opportunity to study Madison's notes did not prevent him from concluding that the Constitution was a compact to

[17] The first form of this undertaking was as a series of appendices to bulletins
of the bureau of rolls and library, but in final form (1894–1905) it consists of five
volumes of documents of both official and private character.
[18] 3 vols. Yale University Press, 1911.

be construed by the states which as separate sovereignties had formed it. The record did not prove to his mind that the Fathers designed to centralize authority as Hamilton, Marshall, and other nationalists insisted that the Constitution did centralize it. Opinion in the Convention was diverse, and besides, the Constitution was admitted on all sides to derive its authority from the people for whom the ratifying conventions acted. It was not practicable to get at the intent of the people except through their acceptance of the words of the Constitution itself, and the words of the great document did not compel agreement on fundamental points.

V

THE COMING OF POLITICAL DEMOCRACY

THE IDEALS OF THE FOUNDERS

IN THE first volume of this series an attempt was made to ana-
lyze the political and social philosophy of the English middle
class which became dominant in the course of the seventeenth
century. It was attempted also to show that this philosophy was inherited in all its essential features by the class in America which
became responsible for the constitutional movement and for the
content of the Constitution itself.[1] As the product of the efforts of
this class, the Constitution was not intentionally designed to become
the basis of a democratic system, although its provisions were so
worded that a democratic interpretation and development were
possible.[2] If the framers of the instrument had been able to control
events in accordance with the philosophy which most of them held,
the constitutional system of the country at the end of its first half-
century would have been quite different from what it had actually
become. By Jackson's presidency it was a resultant of contending
forces of which, on the one side, those making for popular government had been conspicuously successful. On the other hand, the
conservatism of the founders had been by no means without influence.

The class which framed the Constitution as a more or less conscious expression of its ideals cherished the concept of an ordered
liberty, a society in which the disciplined and capable, even if they
formed only a minority of the population, should regulate the
commonwealth with due regard to the well-being and good behavior of every one. Its members gloried in the "principles of the
Revolution," by which they meant particularly the freedom from
oppressive restraint by government, and the guarantees of the liberties of individuals as set down in the bills of rights, such as freedom

[1] Hockett, *Con. Hist.*, I, 13–17, 21, 70–71, 121, 207–208. *Cf.* Vernon L. Parrington, *Main Currents of American Thought*, I, 267–291.
[2] Hockett, *Con. Hist.*, I, 218–220, 260 *et seq.*

of worship, freedom of speech, and jury trial. The right to participate in government was not one of these liberties, although the "equality" of men entitled all to the benefits of government. The right to direct one's own economic life, an unwritten corollary of the "new freedom," was especially prized. In a new country, the challenge of undeveloped resources seemed to promise independence and plenty for every man of thrift and initiative. America was the synonym of Opportunity. Every man's fortune was in his own hands. It seemed, then, that by a process of natural selection the deserving would come to the top.

Amid such conditions as America afforded, the upper-class American, even more than the middle-class Englishman for whom Locke spoke, was likely to regard poverty as proof of an indolent or vicious disposition which disqualified the propertyless man for political life.[3] Long experience, moreover, seemed to prove that most men were incapable of responding to the stimulus even of such a favorable environment as the New World afforded. The privileged class as a class was not sensitive to the inequities of the traditional social order. The handicaps under which the great majority of the people existed were of such long standing that "the poor ye have always with you" seemed to be a principle of nature itself.

Nevertheless the founders of the Republic and their spiritual successors were not sordidly indifferent to human welfare. The early American governments of states and nation were probably devoted to the common good to a degree which was unusual in that age. Franklin testified to "the glorious public virtue . . . predominant in our rising country," in contrast with "the extreme corruption prevalent among all orders of men in [the] rotten old state [of England]"; [4] and this type of self-approval is revealing.

[3] This view, which is by no means extinct today, was set forth in a book by the Reverend Thomas P. Hunt, published in 1836 under the title *Book of Wealth*. "The main design of this work," wrote the author, "is to prove that it is the duty of all men, as the general rule, to become rich. That riches are blessings which may promote our present and eternal welfare." "One thing is certain; no man can be obedient to God's will as revealed in the Bible, without . . . becoming wealthy." The sentiment is exactly in line with middle-class philosophy as expressed by Locke. See Hockett, *Con. Hist.*, I, 21, and *cf.* the philosophy of the early Protestants as interpreted by R. H. Tawney in *Religion and the Rise of Capitalism*, and Max Weber, *Protestant Ethic and the Spirit of Capitalism*.
[4] John Bigelow, ed., *Works of Franklin*. V, 435.

It embraced the sort of idealism which is typified by the statue of liberty enlightening the world which stands at the entrance to New York harbor. The greatest of the patriot fathers dreamed dreams of human betterment and were not averse to social experimentation. The satisfaction with which they regarded the provision for amending the Constitution exhibits the hopefulness with which they contemplated the future.[5]

In the second generation, especially, the intellectuals showed a disposition to experiment with new forms of social organization. The Brook Farm venture of Emerson and his transcendentalist friends is only one example of the many projects of the Jacksonian era. Some of these undertakings found their inspiration in the radicalism of French and English socialists and social reformers. American idealism was, however, bound up in large measure with the great experiment in government which the United States was making. Orators like Webster swayed men marvelously with impassioned appeals on behalf of "Liberty *and* Union, now and forever, one and inseparable!" while the poets no less than the orators fostered the tradition of the sacredness of the Constitution.[6]

The idealism of the founders did not take the form of enthusiasm for the extension of the suffrage to persons of the lower order. Many of them agreed with the historian Francis Parkman that white manhood suffrage—which is what Americans usually mean when they speak of political democracy—would result in "organized ignorance, led by unscrupulous craft, and marching, amid the applause of fools, under the banner of equal rights."[7] Parkman found his dislike of democracy still undissipated near the end of his life. Writing in 1875, after the observations and reflection of a half-century, he declared that his political faith lay "between two

---

[5] Hockett, *Con. Hist.*, I, 217, 222.

[6] For example, take such lines as these from Longfellow's Building of the Ship:

> "Thou, too, sail on, O Ship of State!
> Sail on, O UNION, strong and great!
> Humanity with all its fears,
> With all the hopes of future years
> Is hanging breathless on thy fate!"

[7] Henry Dwight Sedgwick, *Francis Parkman*, 308. *Cf.* views of Chancellor Kent in New York convention of 1821. Johnson, *Readings*, 356–360.

vicious extremes, democracy and absolute authority, each of which" he detested "the more because it tends to react into the other. I . . . prefer a conservative republic, where intelligence and character, and not numbers, hold the rein of power." [8]

Parkman may be taken as the spokesman for his class. It was not selfishness or inertia so much as fear that gave form to the conservatism of the intelligentsia—fear not merely that democracy might deprive them of a privileged status, but that it would cause the miscarriage of social order and justice.

THE DEMOCRATIZING PROCESSES

Competing from the beginning with this ideal of a conservative republic was that of a democracy. The inconsistency between Locke's theory that governments derive their authority from the agreement of the people, and the practice of his followers in reserving political privileges to a few had struck James Otis. When he asserted that "no good reason . . . can be given . . . why every man of a sound mind should not have his vote in the election of a representative," and that "if a man has but little property to protect and defend, yet his life and liberty are things of some importance," [9] he stated only what Locke's theory logically implied. Just as the English middle class appealed to Locke's philosophy to justify their attack upon the monarchy, and promptly forgot to be guided by it after they had gained power, so the American aristocrats, after utilizing Locke against the British mercantilists, contented themselves with lip service to the popular phases of his teachings. [10]

The masses took the situation more seriously. Although because of conditions, the people in rural districts and on the frontier enjoyed almost complete personal freedom, they chafed under numerous legal disabilities imposed upon them by the ruling class, and continually demanded equality of rights and privileges. Both during and after the Revolutionary War they were especially desirous of gaining the suffrage, as a means of electing legislators

[8] Letter to L'Abbé Casgrain, *ibid.*, 274–275.
[9] Hockett, *Con. Hist.*, I, 72.
[10] *Ibid.*, 121 *et seq.*

and other officers who would serve them instead of the old masters.[11]

Unfortunately, when governments in sympathy with popular demands gained control, as they did in some of the states in the years of the Confederation, they made blunders which aroused the conservatives and led to the formation of the Constitution partly as a means of checking the "excess of democracy."[12]

In spite of its conservative origin, Jefferson sought to make of the Constitution an instrument of popular government.[13] However, even he advocated manhood suffrage only when associated with land ownership; but conditions in America, with its vast extent of available lands, seemed to him to make a democracy possible. Throughout his career, therefore, save perhaps while he was in the presidency, he was the champion and promoter of the agrarian society of rural and frontier America.[14]

In spite of Jefferson's propaganda on behalf of agrarian equalitarian democracy, it is more than doubtful whether the federal government could ever have been democratized if the United States had been confined to the region east of the Appalachian Mountains. The real dynamics of the democratic movement were supplied by the new communities of the Mississippi Valley. Owing to the conditions under which the western lands had been ceded to Congress, the government found itself committed to the policy of carving the West into states to be admitted to the Union on terms of equality with the original members of the federation.[15] Confirming the pledge made in the Ordinance of 1787, the Constitution applied a uniform rule for apportioning representation among the states both new and old. Moreover, regarding the determination of the qualifications of voters as a function which each state should perform for itself, and considering the Union as a federation, the framers of the Constitution accepted whatever tests a state saw fit to impose upon its own voters as applying also in the election of members of the national House of Representatives. The result

[11] *Ibid.*, 168 *et seq.*
[12] *Ibid.*, 171, 199, 215.
[13] *Ibid.*, 259.
[14] *Ibid.*, 264–265; Parrington, *Main Currents*, II, 5–14; Beard, *Economic Origins*, *passim.*
[15] Hockett, *Con. Hist.*, I, 159.

was that the House was automatically made representative of the masses as manhood suffrage spread.[16]

If all states had continued to restrict the ballot under the rules which prevailed in 1789, the federal government would probably have remained what it was at the beginning, a government controlled by the "rich and well-born" followers of Alexander Hamilton. New states changed the situation. A large portion of the people who colonized the new regions and swelled their populations to statehood numbers came from the back country of the older states where they had felt the domination of the ruling class. By migrating they escaped from this domination and gained the opportunity to put into practice the philosophy which one pioneer described by saying "our community is an association of persons— of human beings—not a partnership founded on property."

By the time of Jackson's presidency men of this stamp had added ten new states to the original thirteen; and in all of these communities political institutions rested on the belief that political equality was the natural right of all white men. Their constitutions provided for white manhood suffrage, absolute or virtual, and office-holding was put on the same basis as voting. Judges as well as legislators, moreover, were generally elective.

Early in the nineteenth century the original states began likewise to revise their constitutions. Maryland and South Carolina led by bestowing the ballot on all adult white male citizens, by constitutional changes of 1810. Connecticut followed in 1818, replacing her old colonial charter with a liberal constitution. Three years later Massachusetts abolished all restrictions upon the right of adult white males to vote except a nominal tax payment. In 1826 New York adopted the liberal plan of Maryland and South Carolina. Virginia extended the franchise somewhat in 1830, but postponed for two more decades the adoption of full white manhood suffrage.

There is some difference of opinion concerning the motivating forces behind these changes,[17] but there is no doubt that the old

[16] *Ibid.*, 219–220.

[17] Frederick J. Turner first advanced the hypothesis that the adoption of manhood suffrage by the western states compelled the old states to follow suit. The idea is combatted by Benjamin F. Wright, Jr., in "Political Institutions and the Frontier." See documents illustrating changes in the states, in Johnson, *Readings*, 360–369.

states sought if possible to stem the tide of migration westward, which became for them a serious problem during the decade following the War of 1812–1815. In 1817 Governor Wolcott of Connecticut recommended a legislative investigation of the ravages of the "Ohio fever," which he regarded as by far the most important subject that could engage attention. Southern states also sought to counteract the attractions of the new country, proposing among other things to improve the facilities for marketing the produce of their own inland counties by improving the means of transportation. Privately, far-sighted men advised the younger generation to "go west."

The liberalizing movement in the old states may mean that the backwash of the frontier philosophy was undermining the very citadel of the old aristocratic system. Without regard to political theory, the original states could not afford to permit the continued drain of wage earners, and the extension of the suffrage may represent a part of the price paid, reluctantly, in the hope of checking it. In the Northeast, the owners of the rising factories were finding it necessary to pay high wages to keep workers at home, and the right to vote may well have been conceded as an added inducement. Both economic and political considerations dictated efforts to retain the population; in most of the old states it was almost stationary, while the West was growing by leaps and bounds.

The political consequence of the growth of the West was a shift in the relative weight of the sections in dealing with the affairs of the Union. When the Constitution went into effect the population of that part of the West which later became new states was practically nil. From the point of view of influence in national affairs it was negligible. Under the first census (1790) the transmontane inhabitants numbered only one in fifteen of the nation's population. The ensuing forty years brought a new western world into existence. The West of the Jacksonian era contained more than five million inhabitants, exceeding by more than twenty-five percent the numbers for the entire country in 1790. The comparison of areas at the two periods is even more striking: that settled after 1790 exceeded the area occupied at the time of the first census by two thirds. As in population and extent, so also in economic importance, the West of 1830 approximated the whole United States of 1790. In spite of the growth of the original states, the change in relative weight is indicated by a sixfold increase in the ratio of transmontane population to the total, and a corresponding movement westward of the center of population and of economic and political power. New states carved from what was wilderness when Washington was inaugurated elected more than one third of the members of the House of Representatives under Jackson—more than all of the South Atlantic states and nearly twice as many as the whole of New England.[18] The results were new issues, new intersectional relations, and new political alignments.

Thus was a vast weight thrown into the scales on the side of democracy. By 1828 the admission of new states and the enfranchisement of large sections of the population of the eastern states who had not previously voted had created a nation-wide body of electors who were able to elect the man of their choice. Through the clever work of Jackson's campaign managers, his cause was identified with that of the people, and on this issue he was triumphantly elected.

The significance of Jackson's election is that the masses had at last triumphed over the select class which had up to this time possessed the major influence in the government. The question was, what would the people be able to do with their new-found power.

JACKSONIAN DEMOCRACY

The political philosophy of the eighteenth century led men rather naively to believe that the powers of government could be accurately defined and permanently delimited in written constitutions. At the inception of the national government there were many who shared Jefferson's view of the Constitution as a charter of incorporation, setting forth precisely the powers to be exercised by the United States—powers which could be enlarged only by the further act of the grantors. This theory was emasculated almost at the beginning by resort to the doctrine of implied powers,

---

[18] This paragraph is reproduced almost verbatim from a former study by the author—*Western Influences on Political Parties*, 83–84.

and political realists came to recognize that constitutional provisions are but one of several factors which determine what may be called "government in its behavioristic aspect."

These considerations apply to all three branches of the federal government. In theory these branches are equal, independent, and coordinate. Nevertheless some scholars have held that in practice the legislature is, from the nature of its function, necessarily predominant, while others have discovered in the judiciary an irresponsible oligarchy. In fact, the pendulum has swung from one department to another. During the reconstruction era following the Civil War, for example, as will be noticed later, Congress dominated; at other times the judiciary has wielded the decisive influence; while in times of crisis such as the Civil War the executive has exercised almost dictatorial powers.

The historian must have regard not only for the letter of the Constitution, but must penetrate the personalities both of officials and of persons in their entourage. General political trends and the exigencies of daily events, moreover, provide the stimuli and condition the responses of the personalities who carry on government. The whole social complex must be understood, therefore, by any one who wishes to understand the workings of the constitutional system during any particular administration. The relations between leaders and people are one of the most important factors.

In the long rivalry of ideologies, the dynamics of the frontier had by 1828 given democracy an advantage over the aristocratic concepts inherited from the Old World. Without the change of a letter in the Constitution, a new spirit appeared in the federal government which makes the presidency of Andrew Jackson the most notable of the whole period between Jefferson and Lincoln. Once again the fact was demonstrated that the Constitution possesses a certain colorless cast which makes its actual words of comparatively little significance. Its provisions neither proscribed democracy nor prescribed it. Democracy having been achieved, the mind and will of the administrators became the matters of chief significance.

The circumstances under which Jackson came to the presidency made him the special guardian of the rights and interests of the people. Such a presidential function has no particular basis in the provisions of the Constitution; indeed, its framers could hardly have foreseen the development of such an idea. The delegates had not yet outgrown the colonial dread of the royal governor, and like their forebears trusted the legislature as the safest guardian of their liberties. A generation which had experienced the legislative excesses of the Confederation era had learned the difficulty of fixing responsibility for legislative conduct, however, and popular favor had swung from the legislature to the executive.

This swing is closely correlated with the rise of democracy through the admission of new states and the enfranchisement of the masses in the East. Distrust of high-brow statesmen was a natural corollary of the democratic movement; the new voters preferred men of their own class whom they knew and understood. As a "man of the people" Jackson appealed to them. He on his part believed in the plain citizens. Their thoughts and emotions were his thoughts and emotions too, although he thought more clearly than the rank and file. Hence mingled with his confidence in the people was the belief that the newly-enfranchised populace, un-used to the practice of politics and to judging of public questions, needed leadership. Even during the campaign which resulted in his election, Jackson and his advisers set out to supply this leader-ship. Professing to be the servants of the people, they were adept in interpreting the people's mind to the people themselves. Thus they succeeded in leading where they seemed to follow.

In such a situation there is a great incentive to employ the tricks of the demagogue. In the campaign of 1828 Jackson himself was undoubtedly animated by the desire to vindicate the right of the people to rule. Intricate economic issues faced the country, but of these the rank and file were incapable of forming wise judg-ments. Moreover, intelligent opinion in South and West did not agree on these issues, and unless these two sections united in support of Jackson he could not be elected. Appreciating these conditions, Jackson's managers cleverly manufactured an issue out of the whole cloth. Seizing upon Adams's appointment of Clay to the state department in 1825 as evidence of a political deal by which the people's choice for the presidency had been defeated, these managers loudly proclaimed that the vital issue was whether the people should come into their own or yield to the arts of corrupt politicians.

Thus Jackson was brought to office as the champion of the people. Once in power it was relatively easy to pursue the arts of management. Through the use of patronage, and especially by subsidizing the press through contracts for the public printing, the so-called "typographical crowd" was enlisted in disseminating the administration policies so cleverly that they seemed to be called forth by the people themselves.

One of the most successful and at the same time least objectionable of the means taken to identify the public interest with administration policies was the unique use which Jackson made of the veto power. As early as 1791 Jefferson had expounded his theory of the veto. It was intended to be used, he said, to defend the executive and judicial departments and the states against unconstitutional acts of legislation. In doubtful cases respect for the opinion of the legislature should incline the executive to refrain from its use.[19] Neither John Adams nor Jefferson himself found occasion for employing the veto, but Madison and Monroe resorted to it, in accordance with Jefferson's exposition, when they rejected the bonus bill and the Cumberland Road bill.[20]

This slight use of the veto by Jackson's predecessors may be accounted for in large part by the undeveloped state of political parties. When Jefferson discussed its use, parties had as yet hardly emerged from the void, and at no time previous to the term of the second Adams was there a well-formed opposition majority in Congress. The campaign of 1828 was a hard-fought party contest, and the capture of the presidency by the new democracy left a vigorous antiadministration group in the legislative branch. During part of Jackson's presidency the National Republicans controlled the Senate, and since the Democrats were by no means united in their views on current problems, it not infrequently happened that the will of the executive clashed with the desires of the congressional majority. In the inchoate state of party principles,

[19] Hockett, *Con. Hist.*, I, 248.
[20] *Ibid.*, 347–348, 353.

the opposing views of the two branches of government invited the President to seek the support of the electorate for his own policies as against those of Congress.

To this end Jackson applied the veto skilfully, especially in dealing with the Maysville Road bill and the bill for rechartering the Second United States Bank. In both cases the presidential message was much more than a compliance with the constitutional requirement that the reasons for rejecting bills should be laid before the house in which they originated. In both of these cases the President's argument was directed to the voters, with such plausibility as to lead them to believe that he was expressing their own half-formed thought. Many a voter, after reading these messages, exclaimed, in effect, "By gum, he's right!" Since these appeals to the voters were made conveniently near the election of 1832, the whole proceeding approximated the plebiscite, and the result was interpreted by Jackson as a mandate of the people to go ahead, assured of popular approval.

Moreover, Jackson's method stirred the people by its dramatic character. In his attack upon the United States Bank he appeared to stand single-handed as the people's champion against a "monster" which sought to devour them. Friends of the bank called him, in derision, "King Andrew I," although to the people he seemed to be playing rather the rôle of Jack the Giant Killer.

It was this popular support, at bottom, which determined the relations of Jackson as President with the other departments. In theory Jackson adhered to views long before set forth by Jefferson. The latter while President had felt affronted by the ruling of the Supreme Court in the Marbury case,[21] the delivery of whose commission lay, according to Jefferson, wholly within the discretion of the executive and outside of the purview of the judicial department, which was only an equal—not a superior—branch of government. However, as the court neither commanded nor forbade any action in the Marbury case, the discussion it elicited was purely academic. Jackson's opinion that the bank was unconstitutional, in spite of the decision of the Supreme Court in McCulloch v. Maryland, rested upon the same theory.[22] But practically it was

[21] *Ibid.*, 306 *et seq.*
[22] First annual message. Richardson. II, 462.

quite different, because the bank was a "going" institution, and Jackson's attitude meant that its days were numbered if he could make his will prevail. And, backed by the public, Jackson did carry out his purpose to destroy the bank, in spite both of the reasoning of the court and the desire of Congress to recharter. He overrode the legislative branch also in causing the withdrawal of the government deposits from the bank, in spite of the precautions Congress had taken to retain control over them by vesting the power of withdrawal in the secretary of the treasury subject to congressional approval.

In this affair Jackson demonstrated also the paramountcy of executive control over the acts of cabinet members, through the exercise of the appointing and removing power. Holding that the secretary of the treasury was his subordinate and therefore bound to carry out his policies, he assumed full responsibility for removing the deposits, and demonstrated his power to make his will effective by changing secretaries until he found one who was willing to act as he desired.[23] In spite of resolutions of censure and refusals of the Senate to confirm appointments, the President triumphed in the end, because the personnel of the two houses changed—a change which in its turn is traceable ultimately to the fact that the voters upheld the President.

Again, in the Cherokee Indian cases,[24] Jackson carried the theory of executive independence to a novel extreme. Differing from the judges in his opinion of the constitutional law covering those cases, he did not hesitate to render the decisions nugatory by his own inaction.

The Jacksonian Democracy came to power in the name of reform, but it soon brought machine politics to unprecedented efficiency. The Democrats not only adopted practices which they

[23] As to the relation of the secretary of the treasury to Congress see Hockett, Con. Hist., I, 236, 249. For Jackson's view of this relationship, see the Paper Read to the Cabinet, Niles Register, XLV, 73–77 (Sept. 18, 1833), reprinted in Johnson, Readings, 380–383. See the other documents in Johnson relating to the bank episode, pages 370 et seq. Jackson's final appointment of Roger B. Taney as secretary of the treasury and his compliance with the President's wishes in the matter of the bank deposits paved the way for Taney's elevation to the Supreme Bench.

[24] Cherokee Nation v. State of Georgia, 5 Peters 1–80 (1831); Worcester v. Georgia, 6 Peters 521–579 (1832). See narrative account in MacDonald, Jacksonian Democracy, Chap. X.

had condemned in their predecessors, such as the appointment of congressmen to office, but introduced others which the elder statesmen would have spurned. Nevertheless the spoils system seemed to enter the sheepfold by way of the door. Plausibly enough it was maintained that long tenure of office bred laxity and indifference. Rotation in office promised to preserve a keener sense of responsibility to the people. The promise of the Democrats to turn out rascals who held office as the result of bargain and corruption implied that they would be replaced with good men. But if the people were to hold the ground they had won, their champions must organize them for future battles. The dramatic appeals of the President had therefore to be supplemented by the quiet work of a corps of subordinates whose task it was to regiment the masses into an army which could be depended on to follow its leaders. How were these subordinate officers to be recruited and rewarded? Given the conditions—a crude, untutored electorate and two great competing parties—and the answer was inevitable: the appointing power of the President supplied the means through the gift of office to party workers. The assessment of such appointees to provide campaign funds was a natural corollary. Thus the President of the United States became the great dispenser of the patronage which was necessary to give his party cohesion and vitality as a militant organization designed to win elections. Printing contracts played their part in purchasing the aid of influential papers, and the nominating convention (invented by the Anti-Masons in 1830)[25] was seized upon as an excellent device for controlling nominations by utilizing office-holding delegates who knew their master's voice.

In the perspective of the twentieth century, Jackson's most important interpretation of presidential powers was in the field of federal law enforcement. In this regard his contribution ranks with that of Washington and Lincoln. It fell to the lot of the first President to demonstrate the ability of the government to enforce its enactments. The insurgents in the Whiskey Rebellion were easily distinguishable, however, from the people who as a body-politic bore the name of the State of Pennsylvania. They made no pretense of cloaking their violation of the federal excise under

[25] *Ibid.*, 193 *et seq.*

the plea that they constituted a sovereignty. Washington's resort
to force therefore provided no clear precedent for Jackson when
the latter was confronted by South Carolina's ordinance of nullification. The New England states had anticipated South Carolina's
stand more nearly; but the recalcitrancy of New England preceding
and during the War of 1812–1815 took the form of passive resistance. Active resistance was perhaps averted by the termination
of hostilities.[26] In the nullification episode Webster in his reply to
Hayne had reasoned convincingly against the constitutionality of
nullification. His argument was not, however, convincing to his
generation, or even to ours, as a refutation of the claim of state
sovereignty, and it was hardly to be expected that the conclusions
of this Whig would coincide with those of the head of the Democracy. De Tocqueville, studying the American government at
the very moment of the nullification incident, hailed the power of
the federal government to enforce its laws against individuals as a
great discovery in the political science of federations.[27] But De
Tocqueville said nothing of a power to coerce individuals when
they happened collectively to compose the population of a state
which claimed sovereignty even though a member of a federation.

Jackson's problem was, in fact, a new one. It is doubtful whether
any individual in his entourage would have dared to pursue the
course he chose. In many other matters it can be shown that Jackson modified his views or conduct under the influence of his advisers; in the nullification contest his course (barring only Livingston's aid in phrasing the proclamation against nullification) seems
to have been his own. If he did not expressly reject state sovereignty, he waived it as irrelevant by dealing with the inhabitants
of South Carolina merely as citizens of the United States, bound by
their allegiance to obey its laws. Such a procedure ignored the
corporate association of these citizens as a political entity possessing powers and rights above and beyond those claimed by the citizens individually.

As an exposition of the theory of the status of the states as
members of the Union Jackson's proclamation may have left much

[26] Hockett, *Con. Hist.*, I, 328 *et seq.*, 339–340.
[27] *Democracy in America*, I, 198 *et seq.* *Cf.* his comments on social conditions
and sovereignty of the people, in Johnson, *Readings*, 353–356.

to be desired. But in his determination to enforce the laws of Congress within the State of South Carolina, even if it took armies and navies to do so, he made history. His vigorous measures did much more than avert the crisis of 1833. Lincoln followed the precedent which he set, when he regarded the secessionists of 1861 as citizens in insurrection, and called their ordinances of secession "pretended acts, void and of no effect." If Jackson had supinely acquiesced in nullification, a chain of events would have followed which might have made the preservation of the Union impossible in 1861. Jackson, indeed, may be said to have made Lincoln's rôle possible.

THE PROGRESS OF CAPITALISM

The process of democratization had taken place so gradually that the conservative element had had time to adjust itself to changing conditions. There was no possibility of turning back to the old order. Hence many of those who theoretically opposed democracy accepted the people as their masters and played the game of politics as best they might, in the hope of leading them along the paths of sound policy. Others perceived the possibility of gaining their own ends by acquiring undue influence over officials who posed as agents of the people, and thus becoming the real but unseen government. In short, the situation invited shrewd and unscrupulous men to erect a plutocracy in a country which professed democracy.

The development of capitalism was in a sense the logical outcome of the middle-class philosophy which the American ruling class had taken over from the English mercantilists, and of which Hamilton was so striking an exponent.[28] There was in America, moreover, a liking on the part of all classes for rugged individualism and much admiration for the successful man. There was little disposition to place restraints upon any one who succeeded in fair and free competition with his fellows. In such matters the rule of *laissez faire* was generally acceptable. A partial exception appeared in the willingness to protect native industry by means of import duties, although Jefferson and his school deplored govern-

[28] See Hockett, *Con. Hist.*, I, 261 *et seq.*

ment patronage of industry in any form. Yet even Jefferson shared, at least for a time, the belief that the importance of national economic independence justified protectionism. Much to his disappointment, the West embraced the system, convinced that it would develop manufactures and thus create a home market for the products of the farm, as well as national internal improvements which it needed and was too poor to provide for itself.[29]

Jefferson's fear of the doctrine of implied powers was due largely to the fact that it was used to forward the projects of the industrial promoters. His insistence upon resort to the amending process where the exercise of doubtful powers was proposed, was undoubtedly a means in his mind of checking the inordinate growth of capitalistic enterprises. Failing in his efforts to vitalize the amending process, he sought to attain the same result by stressing the right of states to judge for themselves of their retained powers.

It should not be overlooked that Calhoun's motive in formulating the nullification theory was similar; that is, he desired to thwart the protectionists who sought to utilize the government for the advancement of their selfish interests by *compelling* the government to resort to the amending power when its acts were drawn into question by a state. Attention has been so concentrated on the weakness of the argument in support of the theory that its significance in relation to the growth of capitalism has been largely overlooked. Calhoun, like Jefferson and Madison, was an opponent of the program of current capitalism, but went beyond them in the attempt to mechanize the means of checking it.[30]

The Jacksonian democracy did not manifest hostility to industrialism *per se*, but was the avowed and implacable enemy of special privilege. As for the protective tariff, Jackson indeed took on the coloration of his western constituency; but he fought the policy of federal internal improvements because it fostered a class of contractors who he thought were exploiters of the public treasury.

[29] Letter to Thomas Ritchie. Charles H. Ambler, *Thomas Ritchie: A Study in Virginia Politics*, 102–103.

[30] Calhoun differed from Jefferson and Madison in rejecting equalitarianism and embracing economic realism—the defense of the interests of his section rather than those of the people at large. See Parrington's interpretation, *Main Currents*, II, 69–82.

The Democrats were the particular foes of corporate enterprise organized under charters conferring monopoly privileges. Of this type of organized capital the Second United States Bank was the most conspicuous and dangerous example, and it became the object of the chief attack. When Jackson appointed new judges of the Supreme Court, he naturally chose men who were of like mind on the question of corporate privileges.

The character of democracy as demonstrated under Jackson was not such as to encourage the belief that it could as yet deal successfully with the problems of capitalism and of corporations in particular. The close relations between the people and the President did not mean that the executive was guided by an intelligent public opinion. The public opinion of the time, if it may be called by that name, was evoked, or rather created, to a great extent by the leaders who decided what they wanted the people to think. The attitude of the President's followers of the rank and file was too nearly that expressed by the slang phrase, "Let George do it." The only check on government which the voter held was the ballot, and this was cast for the candidates whom he was persuaded to believe in.

Even under Jackson, then, the determining forces in government were the unseen manipulations of politicians. Jackson served the people faithfully, according to his honest judgment; but in the system as it then existed there was no guarantee that every future official would do likewise. Developments had, without change in the words of the Constitution, set the stage for a new struggle to realize the great ends of democracy in the face of the growing power of capitalism. The most important skirmishes of the era were not led, however, by President or Congress, but by the judiciary.

VI

THE NEW SUPREME COURT

CHANGES IN THE PERSONNEL OF THE COURT [1]

{THE reaction of the twenties had been accompanied by much criticism of the Supreme Court, and one of the most significant of the results of the rise of democracy was a changed attitude on the part of this tribunal. Since 1801, as chief justice, John Marshall had dominated the bench and had deeply marked national jurisprudence with his personality and views. So thoroughly were his associates imbued with his spirit that dissenting opinions were rare. Most of the great decisions of the court had been written by him, with the assent of his colleagues, and delivered as the judgments of the tribunal. This unanimity was achieved in part through the practice of conferring before the public announcement of decisions; in such conferences the chief justice's powerful mind produced the natural effect upon the thinking of his brethren of the ermine. The strictures of Jefferson and Madison on these and other practices of the court have been noted already.

Critics had proposed various remedies for the procedures of the court which they regarded as objectionable, but none of the proposals had won enough support to be adopted. Nevertheless the tribunal underwent a substantial transformation during Marshall's last years, partly in response to public sentiment, but chiefly in consequence of the gradual change in personnel which took place during the presidency of Andrew Jackson. These changes replaced Marshall's disciples with men whose views were more in harmony with democratic currents of thought.

When Jackson came to the presidency, the temper of the associate justices was still substantially that of Marshall. Foremost among these associates was Joseph Story, who from nature and close asso-

[1] On the topics discussed in this chapter and the one which follows Swisher's *Roger B. Taney* is especially valuable.

ciation with the chief justice had come to regard any deviation from his doctrines as akin to treason. Bushrod Washington of Virginia, appointed in 1798, had come into intimate relations with Marshall while the latter was engaged in writing the life of his illustrious uncle, the first President. Two other justices, William Johnson of South Carolina (appointed in 1804) and Smith Thompson of New York (1823), were also counted as intimates of the chief justice. Gabriel Duval of Maryland (1811) completed the roster of the bench. There was one vacancy, due to the death of Robert Trimble of Kentucky, late in 1828.

The first of Jackson's appointees was John McLean, of Ohio, whose selection (1829) as Trimble's successor was regarded in political circles as a reward for his zealous promotion of Jackson's campaign, while he was acting as postmaster-general under President John Quincy Adams, the rival candidate.[2] The next change came after Washington's death, in November, 1829; Henry Baldwin of Pennsylvania was designated as his successor. In 1834 Johnson died, and in his stead the President appointed James M. Wayne of Georgia (January, 1835). In the same month Duval, aged and deaf, resigned, and Jackson nominated Roger B. Taney of Maryland in his place. Whig senators, however, offended by Taney's recent action while secretary of the treasury, in withdrawing the government deposits from the United States Bank, prevented confirmation of the appointment. The vacancy remained unfilled until after Marshall's death, which occurred on July 6, 1835. Eventually (1836) Philip P. Barbour of Virginia was appointed and confirmed. Barbour will be remembered as one of those who, a few years before, had desired to give the Senate jurisdiction over cases involving state's rights.[3]

During Marshall's last days, then, there were upon the bench

[2] Biographers have rather neglected the individual justices of the Supreme Court. The most useful compilation is Hampton L. Carson's *History of the Supreme Court of the United States, with Biographies of All the Chief and Associate Justices, 1790–1902.* For the early period, Carson's work may be supplemented by George Van Santvoord, *Sketches of the Lives and Judicial Services of the Chief-Justices of the Supreme Court of the United States* (1854). Some biographical material is given in Charles Warren's *Supreme Court.* There are a few good lives of individual associate justices. For the early period see Story's *Story* and Weisenburger's *McLean.*

[3] *Supra,* Chap. I.

with him three justices of Jackson's choosing. In this changed complexion of the tribunal he himself read the doom of the court's unanimity and the passing of the old order. Evidences of the transformation had begun to appear. At the close of the term in 1834, for example, Marshall announced that "the practice of this Court is not (except in cases of absolute necessity) to deliver any judgment in cases where constitutional questions are involved unless four Judges concur in the opinion, thus making the decision that of a majority of the Court."

CHIEF JUSTICE TANEY

If Marshall could have chosen his successor he would undoubtedly have selected Story. No one else could have done so much to perpetuate the traditions of a great epoch in the development of the federal judiciary. Nor was there any other jurist whose qualifications were so evidently of the high character demanded by the post. Such a succession was impossible, of course, if for no other reason than that the Democratic party was in control of the administration. Story was personally obnoxious to Jackson, for he had supported Adams both in 1824 and 1828, had denounced the spoils system, had disapproved of the removal of the deposits in the United States Bank, and had upheld Marshall in his clash with the President over the Cherokee cases.

Moreover, it was but natural that upon the death of Marshall the Democrats should demand a new chief justice who would not, like him, pursue what they called "the policy of prostration of the States." A closer adherence to the letter of the Constitution and a greater sensitiveness to public opinion were regarded as essential qualifications of the jurist who should succeed him. Jackson accordingly turned again to the man whom the Senate had once rejected, and on December 28, 1835, official announcement was made of the nomination of Roger B. Taney for the headship of the court. On the 15th of the following March, despite the efforts of Webster and Clay in the Senate, that body confirmed the appointment by a vote of 29 to 15.

A contemporary description of the new chief justice presents a picture that is hardly engaging. Tall, square-shouldered, flat-breasted and stooped, with a face "without one good feature, a mouth unusually large, in which were discolored and irregular teeth, the gums of which were visible when he smiles"; dressed in black ill-fitting clothes; he could hardly have pleased at first sight. His voice was hollow like that of a consumptive. "Yet, when he began to speak, you never thought of his personal appearance, so clear, so simple, so admirably arranged were his low-voiced words. . . . There was an air of such sincerity in all he said, that it was next to impossible to believe he could be wrong." [4]

Taney was a Catholic, and had been for many years a prominent member of the bar of his native state. His friendly relations with the President were of several years' standing. In letters they had freely exchanged comments on public events of the early thirties, before Taney entered the cabinet. The Whigs regarded the elevation of the onetime secretary to the bench as a reward for partisan services, but the Democratic press appraised his abilities more justly, the *New York Evening Post*, which had been a prominent advocate of his selection, predicting that "his Republican notions, together with those of his democratic associates, will produce a revolution in some important particulars in the doctrines heretofore advanced by the tribunal, over which he is called to preside, highly favorable to the independence of the States, and the substantial freedom of the people." [5]

In his very first utterance from the bench Taney turned away from Marshall's questionable practice of giving extrajudicial opinions. "The Court deems it proper," he said, "to avoid volunteering any opinion on any question, involving the construction of the Constitution, where the case itself does not bring the question directly before them, and make it their duty to decide upon it." [6] Yet he proved to be no less zealous than his predecessor in upholding

---

[4] Warren, *Supreme Court*, I, 694–695, quoting John E. Semmes, *Life and Times of John H. B. Latrobe*. An able study of Taney has recently been made by Carl Brent Swisher, *Roger B. Taney*. Charles W. Smith studies his political theory in *Roger B. Taney, Jacksonian Jurist*. A somewhat older biography is that of Bernard C. Steiner, *Life of Roger B. Taney;* still older is Samuel Tyler, *Memoir of Roger Brooke Taney*. Swisher's book contains an excellent bibliography, with additional titles for Taney and other justices. With above description compare that quoted by Swisher, 359, and portrait *ibid.*, 358.

[5] Quoted by Warren, II, 33.

[6] Opinion in case of The Charles River Bridge Co. *v.* Warren Bridge Co.

the prerogatives of the court. Within a few years he asserted, in tones which remind one of Marshall, that "the high power has been conferred upon this Court, of passing judgment upon the acts of the State sovereignties and the legislative and executive branches of the Federal Government and of determining whether they are beyond the limits of power marked out for them respectively by the constitution of the United States." [7]

Taney was a more careful guardian of state powers than Marshall, due largely to the fact that they approached constitutional problems along different paths. While Marshall's chief interest was legal Taney's was economic and social. For Marshall, according to some critics, the heart of constitutional law was the doctrine of vested rights, and the protection of contracts was for him a considerable part of the duty of government. [8] Taney, on the contrary, approached cases from the human rather than the juristic standpoint, and was less attached to the doctrine of *stare decisis*. He was inclined to regard the state's power, which touched the daily life of the people more intimately than did that of the nation, as of greater significance and as deserving of wide exercise. The decisions of the court during the thirties, forties, and fifties developed the concept of the police power in a way which proved to be very gratifying to the friends of state's rights, since they exemplified the doctrine that it was not only the right but the duty of the state "to take such action as it saw fit, in the furtherance of the security, morality and general welfare of the community, save only as it was prevented from exercising its discretion by very specific restrictions in the written Constitution." [9] That Taney's contribution to American jurisprudence was timely and wholesome none but a prejudiced student would now deny. His sanity and impartiality, and his indifference to partisan vituperation, during a term of service almost as long as Marshall's, together with his contributions to our constitutional law, fairly entitle him to rank beside his illustrious predecessor in our national annals.

The membership of the court from the late thirties to the middle

---

[7] Opinion in case of Luther *v.* Borden.
[8] Edward S. Corwin, *National Supremacy*, 113–115.
[9] *Ibid.*

fifties centered about a core of Jackson's selection. Of the six justices whom he found in office only two, Story and Thompson, survived his presidency, and both of these were lost to the tribunal within a decade thereafter. Of his appointees, however, three, Taney, McLean, and Wayne, sat for many years, and while they did not always agree, they formed a semi-permanent element in the court of significant character and influence. Around them rotated, so to speak, other justices whose terms on the average were comparatively brief. Some of these other jurists deserve special mention, which will be given at the appropriate points.

NEW PROBLEMS FOR THE COURT

The court over which Taney presided confronted a country in which rapid social and economic changes were constantly creating new and perplexing problems of constitutional interpretation. The chief of the problems which it was required to pass upon may be stated in the form of the following questions: (1) where do the boundaries run between the power of the states and that of Congress in relation to commerce; (2) what principles of constitutional law are applicable to corporations doing an interstate business; (3) what is involved in the constitutional obligation of the United States to guarantee to every state a republican form of government; (4) what are the powers of the state in relation to bills of credit; (5) is the scope of the admiralty jurisdiction of the federal courts the same as that of the English admiralty courts; (6) what are the powers and limitations of the states and federal government respectively, in relation to the institution of slavery in its many ramifications?

These questions derived their constitutional importance very largely from the duality of the American system of government. The problems were unique because the American constitutional system was unique; European precedents, so far as there were any, were of little applicability because European conditions were not parallel. It was the duty of the judges to do justice in each particular cause, and at the same time, so far as possible, to set precedents which would be forward-looking. They had an unusual opportunity to employ that larger wisdom which applies old principles in such a way as to make for the sound development of a growing social organism.

POLICE POWER v. COMMERCE POWER

In a previous volume the origin of the problem of the relations between the police power of the state and the power of Congress to regulate interstate and foreign commerce has been noted.[10] The decision in Willson v. Blackbird Creek Marsh Company did little to clarify it;[11] in fact, it was followed by a series of perplexing cases with which the court wrestled for two decades before it discovered any approximately permanent and satisfactory principle which it could apply.

In 1837 there came before the court the case of the Mayor of the City of New York v. Miln.[12] Marshall was now gone, and along with Story and Thompson sat the new chief justice and associates McLean, Baldwin, Wayne, and Barbour. The Miln case was one of several in which the new judges were to exhibit a disposition to construe state powers liberally. This disposition was manifested by a distinctly generous interpretation of the police power, and a tendency to recognize the concurrent power of the states over commerce.

The new case grew out of the widespread alarm of the North Atlantic states over the immigration situation. A great wave of newcomers was bringing to their ports a large number of women, children, aged, and otherwise infirm persons who were unable to work and who landed almost penniless. Shipmasters encouraged this movement by offering low rates for passage, and public opinion in the states chiefly affected began to demand the enactment of laws to make these masters liable for the support or deportation of immigrants who might otherwise become a public charge. The legislatures of several states memorialized Congress urging regulatory legislation, and in the absence of congressional action New York passed a measure requiring the master of every vessel entering New York harbor to report within twenty-four hours to the mayor of the city, the name, nativity, age, and occupation of every passenger,

[10] See Hockett, Con. Hist., I, 371 et seq.
[11] Ibid., 377.
[12] 11 Peters 102. See Swisher, Taney, 394–396.

under penalty of a fine of $75 for each person not so reported or reported falsely.

The Miln case resulted from the refusal of a shipmaster to comply with the law, on the same ground urged by Willson's counsel in the Marsh Company suit, *viz.*, that it was an exercise of power to regulate commerce which the state did not possess. The argument on behalf of the plaintiff was two-fold. Oakley's argument in the Gibbons case [13] was repeated in support of the contention that even if viewed as a regulation of commerce, the act of the state was constitutional, so long as it did not contravene any regulation made by Congress. The claim of a concurrent power over commerce was not the main reliance in the present case, however, for the plaintiff denied that the measure in question was a regulation of commerce, and laid the chief emphasis upon the contention that it was a police regulation. The court was therefore compelled to determine the category in which the act belonged, and if it was held to be a commercial regulation, to pass upon the doctrine of concurrent powers.

The judgment of the majority of the court (Taney, Wayne, McLean, and Barbour) was read by Justice Barbour. Justices Thompson and Baldwin presented concurring opinions and Justice Story dissented. Barbour held that the act of New York was a police regulation, and that consequently it was not necessary to consider whether the power to regulate commerce was exclusive or concurrent. Following Marshall in Gibbons *v.* Ogden, he asserted that a state measure resting on the police power might be scarcely distinguishable in its effects from one of Congress resting on the commercial power, and yet be legitimate except in the event of a collision, in which case the state law must yield.[14] However, by an unfortunate use of words he beclouded the distinction between the two powers. "Even . . . if the . . . act in question could be considered as partaking of the nature of a commercial regulation," he declared, "the principle here laid down would save it from condemnation if no such collision exist." The words "partaking of the nature of a commercial regulation," considered apart

[13] Hockett, *Con. Hist.*, I, 371 *et seq.*
[14] *Ibid.*, 375.

from the rest of the opinion, seemed to endorse the doctrine of concurrency, and possibly did so, although the intention of the justice seems to have been to assert that even if the *police act* in question *produced effects* similar to those of a commercial regulation, the principle laid down would save it if there were no collision with federal law.

In this case, Barbour's opinion was not out of line with Marshall's thinking. It is possible, of course, that in this particular instance Marshall might have ruled that the New York law was an interference with commerce, as he had done in the case of the Maryland license law; [15] but it seems more likely, in view of the decision in Willson *v*. Blackbird Creek Marsh Company, that if he had been living in 1837 he would have agreed with Barbour.

Justice Thompson's concurring opinion rested upon the belief that the decision was in line with Marshall's. "The purposes intended to be answered by this law fall within the internal police of the State, which, throughout the whole case of Gibbons *v*. Ogden, is admitted to remain with the State. . . . Can anything fall more directly within the police power and internal regulation of a State than that which concerns the care and management of paupers or convicts or any other class or description of persons that may be thrown into the country?" "Even if this case be considered as legislating on a subject falling within the power to regulate Commerce, but which still remains dormant, Congress not having exercised any power conflicting with the law in this respect, no constitutional objection can in my judgment arise against it." [16]

Story, however, believed that the court was departing from Marshall's doctrines; hence his dissent. He protested that the decision as rendered by Barbour was opposed to the precedents set both in Gibbons *v*. Ogden and Brown *v*. Maryland. He saw in the New York law an interference with commerce, and devoted his

[15] Brown *v*. Maryland. See *ibid.*, 376.

[16] Thompson's opinion was prepared at Taney's request, but this somewhat ambiguous recognition of the state's concurrent power over commerce gained the assent of only two other justices. Barbour was thereupon directed to write the opinion of the court. His opinion was hardly an improvement, and did not have the wholehearted approval of the assenting justices. See Swisher, *Taney*, 395–396.

opinion to an argument upholding the exclusive nature of the congressional power of regulation. The full power to regulate, he urged, was the whole power. "The grant of the whole to one, is incompatible with the grant to another of a part."

The confusing character of the issue is well shown by Story's dissent. The real reason for it probably lies in the stress that Barbour placed upon the state police power. The latter's recognition of state's rights was not the grudging recognition of a nationalist. "It is," he said, "the bounden and solemn duty of the State to advance the safety, happiness, and prosperity of its people, and to provide for its general welfare . . . where the power over the particular subject is not surrendered or restrained. Those powers which . . . may . . . properly be called internal police, are not . . . surrendered . . . and . . . consequently, in relation to these, the authority of the State is complete. . . . It is difficult to define . . . a subject so diffuse. . . ." Story's dissent was really a protest against this new tenderness for the prerogatives of the states. He undoubtedly saw in the decision the thin edge of a wedge, in the guise of the police power, which would destroy the old nationalism of the court. As a prominent Whig paper put it, the decision made "a fatal breach . . . in the Constitution. . . . The Court has yielded up the exclusive nature of the grant, and let loose upon us the old Confederation claim of the States to interfere, and perplex, and burden and alter the Congressional regulation of commerce with foreign nations under pretexts (never wanting) that they were exercising only police authority for their own local interest and convenience." [17]

Barbour and Thompson seemed to many persons to uphold the concurrent power of the state to regulate commerce. A power to adopt police regulations which affected interstate or foreign commerce was, to many minds, indistinguishable from a concurrent power with that of Congress over commerce. There is nevertheless a valid distinction, but it was so easy to lose sight of it that the decision was, as Story feared, almost equivalent to a recognition of the doctrine of concurrent power. A lenient court could, by accepting state acts as police regulations, give to the states a con-

[17] *New York Review*, quoted by Warren, II, 32.

siderable degree of commercial control. In this manner, in fact, stress upon the police power led to an increased control by the states over commerce and finally to acceptance of a limited doctrine of concurrent power.

For nine years after the Miln case no other of this character came before the court. In the meantime, by an act of 1837, the membership of the tribunal was increased from seven to nine, and death again worked a considerable alteration in the personnel. As early as 1837 Story had resolved to resign. He had become professor of law at Harvard, and was depressed by the tendencies of the court. He had written to a friend, early in that year: "I am the last of the old race of judges. I stand their solitary representative, with a pained heart and a subdued confidence." [18] He postponed action, however, and the success of the Whigs in 1840 inspired him with the hope that the new President might send to the bench in his stead some one of the caliber and views of Webster or Sumner. Harrison's death dashed his hope for the time, and he held on, disliking to leave a vacancy until a Whig President should be elected, who would choose a man of congenial principles. Clay's candidacy in 1844 again raised his hopes, but Polk's election disappointed him, and failing health warned him that he could not continue to carry the double load of professor and judge. He finally sent in his resignation in 1845, but died before it took effect. He had written in that same year: "I have long been convinced that the doctrines and opinions of the old Court were daily losing ground, and especially those on great constitutional questions. New men and new opinions have succeeded. The doctrines of the Constitution, so vital to the country, which in former times received the support of the whole Court, no longer maintain their ascendancy. I am the last member now living of the old Court, and I cannot consent to remain where I can no longer hope to see those doctrines recognized and enforced." [19]

[18] To Harriet Martineau, April 7, 1837. Story, *Life of Story*, II, 275–277.
[19] To Ezekiel Bacon, April 12, 1845, *ibid.*, II, 527–529. As Story intimated, his old associate Thompson had died while he lingered on the bench. His successor was Samuel Nelson of New York (1845). John McKinley of Alabama (1837) and John Catron of Tennessee (1837) were the new appointees after the enlargement of the court in 1837. Barbour and Baldwin died before Story, and were replaced by Peter V. Daniel of Virginia (1841) and Levi Woodbury of New

Up to 1846 no justice (unless Thompson's opinion in the Miln case be so construed) had presented any opinion which indubitably accepted the doctrine of the concurrent power of the state over commerce. An approach to such an expression is to be found in the concurring opinion of Baldwin in the Miln case. Referring to the provision of the Constitution which forbids a state to lay any duty on imports or exports except what may be absolutely necessary for executing its inspection laws, he implied that such inspection laws, which the state clearly has the right to make, are regulations of commerce and must therefore rest upon a limited concurrent power of commercial regulation in the state.[20] Here is perhaps the germ from which developed the doctrines now to be studied. With the License Cases, at any rate, there appears at last a readiness of some of the justices to espouse openly the doctrine of concurrent power.

The License Cases so-called were three in number, and involved acts of Rhode Island, Massachusetts, and New Hampshire exacting licenses from sellers of spirituous liquor imported from abroad or brought in from other states of the Union.[21] The legal aspects of the cases were so similar that all were heard together. Nine opinions were given by the justices. McLean rendered one for each case, other justices covered all in one decision, and some concurred in the opinions of others without writing any of their own. In the Massachusetts and Rhode Island cases the original packages had been broken and the contents sold in small quantities without the license required by law. In the instance of New Hampshire, a barrel of gin, purchased in Boston, had been brought to Dover and sold in the original cask, in violation of the state law. For this the sellers were indicted and convicted. The question at issue therefore was whether the state regulations involved an unconstitutional exercise of control over interstate commerce.

Hampshire (1845) respectively. Story's death was followed by the appointment of Robert C. Grier of Pennsylvania (1846).

[20] For Baldwin's opinion see appendix between 11 Peters and 12 Peters. Apparently two justices were willing to join Thompson in upholding the New York act as a regulation of commerce. See Swisher, *Taney*, 395.

[21] Fletcher *v.* Rhode Island; Peirce *v.* New Hampshire; Thurlow *v.* Massachusetts. 5 Howard 504 *et seq.* (1847). See discussion in Swisher, *Taney*, 399 *et seq.*

Chief Justice Taney gave the first opinion, and others followed, the majority upholding the state license acts, but on varying grounds. In the Massachusetts and Rhode Island cases, he held that breaking the original packages marked the point at which state police regulations became applicable. On this ground he upheld the acts of those states. Even in the New Hampshire case Taney upheld the state law, finding a difference from the Brown *v.* Maryland case in the fact that the latter arose out of commerce with foreign nations, while the New Hampshire case related to interstate trade. Since in this case the original package doctrine did not apply, and there had been no congressional legislation on the subject, Taney rested his ruling upon acceptance of the concurrent power of states over commerce. He was evidently unwilling to abandon wholly the position he had taken in Brown *v.* Maryland.[22] "The controlling and supreme power over commerce with foreign nations and the several states is undoubtedly conferred upon Congress. Yet, in my judgment, the State may nevertheless, for the safety or convenience of trade, or for the protection of the health of its citizens, make regulations of commerce for its own ports and harbors, and for its own territories; and such regulations are valid unless they come into conflict with a law of Congress."

In this opinion, for the first time, a judge of the Supreme Court asserted that state measures affecting commerce might rest upon a concurrent power over that subject as well as upon the police power. This conclusion Taney reached by reasoning which is reminiscent of Oakley. "The language in which the grant of power to the general Government is made, certainly furnishes no warrant for" holding it to be exclusive. In other instances grants are followed by prohibitions in express terms of the exercise of the same power by the states. "If it was intended to forbid the States from making any regulations of commerce, it is difficult to account for the omission to prohibit it, when that prohibition has been so carefully and distinctly inserted in relation to other powers."

Justice Catron followed Taney in accepting this doctrine, hold-

[22] Taney's distinction was repudiated by the court in Leisy *v.* Hardin, 135 U. S. 100 (1890), in which it was said that his principle had been overthrown by numerous decisions. Even in Brown *v.* Maryland the court had said that the same principle would apply to interstate as to foreign trade.

ing "that the power to regulate commerce among the States may be exercised by Congress at pleasure, and the States cut off from regulating the same commerce at the same time it stands regulated by Congress, but that until such regulation is made by Congress, the States may exercise the power within their respective limits."

The other judges upheld the state legislation as based on the police power, but their opinions show that the concept of police power was still growing. Justice Daniel followed Marshall when he held that state police regulations which only remotely or incidentally affected commerce were not to be deemed void. "To render them so, they must be essentially and directly in conflict with some power clearly invested in Congress by the Constitution; and I would add, with some regulation actually established by Congress in virtue of that power." McLean asserted that neither the state police power nor the commercial power of Congress "can be so exercised as materially to affect the other. The sources and objects of these powers are exclusive, distinct, and independent, and are essential to both governments." He went so far as to hint that in some cases police regulations might even be paramount to federal acts. "When in the appropriate exercise of these Federal and State powers contingently and incidentally their lines of action run into each other, if the State power be necessary to the preservation of the morals, the health or safety of the community, it might be maintained. . . . But the exigency is not to be founded on any notions of commercial policy."

The most pregnant opinion rendered in these cases, if we regard influence on later judgments, was that given by Justice Woodbury. Taney and Catron frankly avowed belief in the concurrent power of the states; McLean and Daniel tended to extend the police power; Woodbury expressed views similar to those of McLean and Daniel, but going further sought also to find in the nature of commercial regulations some principle in accordance with which control of certain processes might be recognized as properly belonging to the state until Congress acted. "There is much in connection with foreign commerce," he suggested, "which is local within each State . . . to be acted upon by each till the power is abused or some course is taken by Congress conflicting with it. . . .

To hold the power of Congress as to such topics exclusive in every respect and prohibitory to the States though never exercised by Congress . . . would create infinite inconvenience and detract much from the cordial cooperation and consequent harmony between both governments, in their appropriate spheres."

Although Taney later referred to the decision in the License Cases as an endorsement of the doctrine of concurrent powers, this was not correct, since several of the justices based their opinions upon the police power. Nevertheless the extension given by their interpretations to the latter power was so great that it became less than ever distinguishable from a power over commerce.

Two years later (1849) came the Passenger Cases.[23] Twelve years had passed since the court in the Miln case had sustained the action of New York in dealing with immigration evils. Meantime the tide of undesirable immigration had increased, and the many paupers and petty criminals from abroad had alarmed the seaboard states. Even in colonial times some colonies had regulated immigration, and now several states enacted legislation imposing taxes upon alien passengers upon arrival at port, and requiring bonds from masters of vessels bringing them in. Massachusetts had passed a law of this kind, the fees collected to be used in maintaining a marine hospital; and New York had supplemented her earlier legislation by a similar act, the receipts under which were to be devoted to the support of foreign paupers.

Like the License Cases, the two so-called Passenger Cases were so similar that the court heard them together and rendered one judgment covering both. They differed from the case of New York v. Miln in that the law under which the latter arose had imposed, not a tax upon each incoming passenger, but a fine upon the shipmaster in case of failure to supply certain statistical information. Moreover, the Constitution restricts duties levied by the states, unless with the consent of Congress, to such as are necessary to defray the costs of executing their inspection laws, while the acts in question proposed to apply receipts to purposes not falling clearly within the category of inspection laws. Were these acts

[23] Smith v. Turner; Norris v. Boston. 7 Howard 392–752. See Swisher's discussion, *Taney*, 402–406.

to be regarded as inspection laws, warranted by the police power, or were they regulations of commerce? In the latter case, had the necessary consent of Congress been given? And were the funds legally applied?

The court was composed of the same judges who had heard the License Cases. As in so many of the great constitutional cases of the period, eminent counsel appeared on both sides. Daniel Webster was one of the attorneys, arguing against the validity of the acts. As defender of the New York regulation, appeared John Van Buren, an able young man noted for his wit, while Massachusetts was represented by John Davis.

While the cases were under discussion Webster wrote to his brother that in the days of Marshall and Story the Massachusetts law could not have stood for a moment, but "the present Judges, I fear, are quite too much inclined to find apologies for irregular and dangerous acts of State Legislatures." [24] Nevertheless he predicted that the law would not be sustained, and in this he was correct. Just before the decision was announced he wrote again that he thought it would "be more important to the country than any decision since that in the steamboat case [Gibbons v. Ogden]. That was one of my earliest arguments of a constitutional question. . . . I am willing to confess to the vanity of thinking that my efforts in these two cases have done something towards explaining and upholding the just powers of the government of the United States on the great subject of commerce." [25]

As in the License Cases, nine opinions were rendered. Justices McLean, Catron, Wayne, Grier, and McKinley concurred in declaring the state laws unconstitutional, while Taney, Daniel, Nelson, and Woodbury upheld them. All of the majority judges regarded the acts as regulations of commerce, and held expressly or impliedly that the power of regulation was vested exclusively in Congress. Said Wayne: "It seems to me . . . that the States have parted with all power over commerce, except the regulation of their internal trade." Catron, McKinley, and Grier, whose opinions are none too easy to interpret, seem to accept the view which Webster had

[24] Quoted by Warren, II, 176–177.
[25] Quoted ibid., 178.

held since the days of Gibbons *v.* Ogden, that what Congress had
not regulated was to be regarded as satisfactory to that body, and
to be left alone by the states.[26]

Taney's dissenting opinion does not clearly indicate whether he
considered the state acts to be police measures or regulations of
commerce. He held that in the Miln case the court had decided
that persons were not "subjects of commerce," which pointed to
the state acts as police measures.[27] He contended also that by an
act of 1819 Congress had dealt with certain aspects of the importation of passengers, and had thus tacitly consented to the application by the states of additional measures of inspection as to health
and condition. Hence, whether the laws of the states rested upon
the police power or the concurrent power over commerce did not
matter to Taney.[28] Nelson concurred with the chief justice, while
Daniel, pursuing the trend of his opinion in the License Cases,
found no such conflict between the state laws and federal measures
as to warrant holding the former void. His zeal to safeguard the
authority of the states appears clearly in his reference to the decision as a "trampling on some of the strongest defences of the
safety and independence of the States. . . . I am unable to suppress my alarm at the approach of power claimed to be uncontrollable and unlimited." [29]

Woodbury shared Daniel's fears. "A course of prohibitions and
nullifications as to their domestic policies in doubtful cases, and
this by mere implied power is a violation of sound principle and
will alienate and justly offend, and tend ultimately . . . to dissolve the bonds of that Union so useful and glorious to all concerned." His opinion, conceived in the spirit of these words, again

[26] As illustrating the freedom from political bias in this decision, it is to be
noted that Wayne, who was from the South, agreed with McLean, a northerner,
in maintaining the exclusiveness of the federal power, while, as a Washington
newspaper correspondent remarked, the deciding vote against the state laws was
given by McKinley, the most ardent state's rights member of the bench. *Cf.*
Warren, II, 178.

[27] Wayne's opinion held that the view that persons were not "subjects of commerce" was not concurred in by a majority of the court in the Miln case.

[28] Taney was less concerned with emphasis on the police power than with maintaining the "sovereignty" of states in matters over which they had not relin-
quished control. See Swisher, 408–411.

[29] Warren, II, 180.

foreshadowed the future stand of the court. He expressed the
belief that the federal government properly possessed the function
of regulating those commercial matters which were of national
scope or too general a nature for local regulation, and that the
states should deal with those matters which were purely local.
While essentially an effort to find the middle ground which would
satisfy all interests, Woodbury's view was evidently an attempt to
apply to the puzzling question of commerce the fundamental principle in accordance with which powers had been originally distributed between states and nation by the framers of the Constitution. The subjects dealt with by the laws involved in the Passenger
Cases were, he thought, of local character.

The practice of rendering separate opinions, as in the License and
Passenger Cases—a practice so ardently desired by Jefferson—
proved to be very confusing to the public. One reporter declared
that in the latter decision there was really no opinion of the court
as a court, and newspaper comment was to the same effect. Said
one sheet: "These seven or eight long opinions will greatly obscure
the points really decided, and impair the force of the decision,"
while another thought that the judges had "put the whole question
of constitutionality of such laws in doubt and mist. A slight change
in the composition of the Court of nine Judges will upset the decision. . . . These separate opinions are to be deprecated as a
great nuisance." The unanimity of the court under Marshall had
been deplored by Jefferson and his disciples, but now it appeared
that its prestige was menaced by the practice of giving seriatim
opinions. "In listening to the opinions of the eminent men who
were heard in Court today," commented the *Boston Advertiser's*
correspondent, "it was impossible not to be more impressed with
what are sometimes called 'the glorious uncertainties of the law'
than with the stability of the wisest of human judgments." [30]

As to the doctrine of concurrent power, however, the uncer-
tainty of nearly a generation was about to give place to definiteness.
The change came in the case of Cooley *v.* The Philadelphia Board
of Port Wardens,[31] involving a requirement of the wardens that

[30] *Ibid.*, II, 178.
[31] 12 Howard 299 (1852). See Swisher, *Taney*, 406–407.

incoming vessels pay a pilot fee whether they employed a pilot or not. The fee was to be placed in a fund for the care of disabled pilots and their families. By a decision of seven to two the court upheld the regulation of the wardens. McLean and Wayne, adhering to their view of the exclusiveness of the commercial power of Congress, composed the minority. Catron, Grier, and McKinley, who had joined McLean and Wayne in voiding the laws in the Passenger Cases on the ground of interference with the powers of Congress, changed their position in the Cooley case and accepted the theory of concurrent powers. Taney and Nelson, who had upheld the losing side in the Passenger Cases on this ground, consequently found themselves in the majority. Daniel stood with Taney and Nelson as before, but regarded the port regulation as a police act. Woodbury had died in 1851, but his successor, Benjamin R. Curtis, espoused his doctrine as set forth in the License and Passenger Cases and wrote the majority opinion.

The power to regulate commerce, Curtis wrote, embraced various subjects of diverse nature, "some imperatively demanding a single uniform rule, operating equally on the commerce of the United States in every port; and some . . . imperatively demanding that diversity which alone can meet the local necessities of navigation." "Whatever subjects of this power are in their nature national, or admit only of one uniform system or plan of regulation, may justly be said to be of such a nature as to require exclusive legislation by Congress." Although commerce includes navigation and the regulations of the qualifications of pilots are regulations of navigation and therefore of commerce, the subject of pilots and pilotage does not require one national, uniform plan of regulation. The act of Congress of 1789 relating to navigation, as understood by Curtis, rested upon just such a theory of the commercial powers of Congress and the states. As contemplated by this act, therefore, such local matters as pilotage regulations are "likely to be best provided for, not by one system, or plan of regulations, but by as many as the legislative discretion of the several States should deem applicable to the local peculiarities of the ports within their limits."

Thus at last, by an unambiguous decision, a majority of the court held that states have rights of local regulation of interstate and foreign commerce, not by virtue of the police power, but because they possess in such minor, local matters, a concurrent commercial power.[32] In a somewhat modified form this rule remains the law today.[33] Justice McLean, dissenting, predicted that "from this race of legislation between Congress and the States . . . will arise a conflict similar to that which existed before the adoption of the Constitution." Referring to this prediction, Judge Wayne, the other dissenter, admitted, fourteen years later, that none of the anticipated evils had appeared. "The stream of events has since flowed on without a ripple due to the influence of that adjudication."[34]

[32] Writing to George Ticknor, Curtis said: "I expect my opinion will excite surprise, because it is adverse to the exclusive authority of Congress. . . . It rests on grounds perfectly satisfactory to myself, and it has received the assent of five judges out of eight, although for twenty years no majority has ever rested their decision on either view of this question, nor was it ever directly decided before." Quoted by Warren, II, 237. The standard authority for Curtis is Benjamin R. Curtis, Jr., ed., *Memoir of Benjamin R. Curtis.*

[33] See State Freight Tax Cases, 15 Wall. 232 (1873). Also Bowman v. C. & N. W. R. R. Co., 125 U. S. 465 (1888).

[34] Quoted by Warren, II, 325, note. One of the best summaries by the Supreme Court of the doctrine of concurrent power is the following: "The adjudications of this court with respect to the power of the States over the general subject of commerce are divisible into three classes. First, those in which the State is exclusive; second, those in which the States may act in the absence of legislation by Congress; third, those in which the action of Congress is exclusive and the States cannot interfere at all. The first class . . . concern the strictly internal commerce of the State, and while the regulations of the State may affect interstate commerce indirectly, their bearing upon it is so remote that it cannot be termed in any just sense an interference. Within the second class of cases—those of what may be termed concurrent jurisdiction [note that the court abandons Marshall's distinction between power over commerce as a police power and as a concurrent power]—are embraced laws for the regulation of pilots; quarantine and inspection laws and the policing of harbors; the improvement of navigable channels; the regulation of wharves, piers, and docks; the construction of dams and bridges across navigable waters of a State; and the establishment of ferries. But whenever such laws, instead of being of a local nature and . . . affecting interstate commerce but incidentally, are national in their character, the non-action of Congress indicates its will that such commerce shall be free and untrammeled, and the case falls within the third class—of those laws wherein the jurisdiction of Congress is exclusive."—Covington, etc., Bridge Co. v. Kentucky, 154 U. S. 204 (1894).

W. W. Willoughby thinks that it was unfortunate that a distinction was ever made between the concurrent power over commerce and the effect of police regulations on commerce. He thinks that what has been called a concurrent power should have been recognized at all times as a phase of the police power.—*Constitutional Law of the United States,* II, 662.

At about the same time that the Cooley case was decided, another decision asserted the paramountcy of the commercial power of Congress over the police power of the state. Under authority of a Virginia statute a bridge had been constructed over the Ohio River at Wheeling, of which the State of Pennsylvania complained because it interrupted river navigation. The court held in 1852 [35] that the building of the bridge was an interference with the commerce on the river which Congress had power to regulate and had regulated. Chief Justice Taney did not accept this view, and he and Justice Daniel wrote dissenting opinions.

The influence of economic forces upon constitutional development is well illustrated by this Wheeling Bridge Case. Six months after the decision, Congress exercised its power of regulation by passing an act declaring that the bridge was a lawful structure, thus setting aside the verdict of the court. This act, of course, superseded the former statutes which the court had applied, and was upheld in its turn. The economic significance of the action of Congress lies in the fact that the bridge bore a railway, and Congress confronted the necessity of choosing whether it would exercise its power in favor of commerce by water or by rail. Its choice meant, as a contemporary newspaper remarked, that "the public convenience will require that the uninterrupted freedom of passing up and down a river should give way, in cases of conflict, to facilities for crossing it." [36]

[35] 13 Howard 234.
[36] Quoted by Warren, II, 236.

VII

THE DEVELOPMENT OF CONSTITU·
TIONAL LAW

CORPORATIONS AND CONSTITUTIONAL LAW

STUDENTS of American history first encounter corporations in the form of the chartered trading companies which
planted the colonies of Virginia and Massachusetts Bay, and
next in such "corporate" colonies as Connecticut and Rhode Island. These forms illustrate the political aspects of early corporations. Legally, the corporate colonies were akin to the incorporated
boroughs of medieval England, and to the gilds which were often
nearly identical with the borough corporations; and the British
government in pre-revolutionary days was never quite able to grasp
the claim of the corporate colonies for recognition as autonomous
political communities not subject to Parliament.[1]

Although the growth of these political communities out of commercial organizations is a tremendously significant feature of the
history of American corporations, the corporate form of association
for economic purposes never quite disappeared. Prior to the nineteenth century individual enterprise and simple partnerships suf-
ficed for most industrial and commercial undertakings, but certain
types of business called for a greater capital investment or involved
greater risks than individuals or partnerships could shoulder. The
commonest of these undertakings were turnpikes, canals, bridges,
ferries, and banks. Since both in England and America political
theory and practice limited quite strictly the activities of government, the corporation appeared, endowed with liberal powers, as
a form of association intermediate between people and government.
In the face of rapid internal development in America the corporation met the citizens' need of organization for functions which the
government was inhibited from performing.[2]

[1] On the early history of corporations see Hockett, *Con. Hist.*, I, *passim.*
[2] John P. Davis, *Corporations*, II, 264, 268.

113

England derived her earliest notions of corporations from the Roman law. By the end of the fifteenth century she had absorbed all of the older system that was applicable to her own experience, and during the sixteenth she began to develop the law of corporations along original lines. One of the chief concepts which she added was that such a body was an artificial person.[3] The Americans borrowed the English law in large part, but adoption of the federal form of government forced them to work out their own law along lines compatible with its distribution of powers.

The framers of the Constitution had no way of foreseeing the great expansion of corporate organization which was to set in a generation or so after their work was done. That great companies operating upon a national and international scale should within a century invade every branch of industry was to them an unrevealed vision. The regulation of the few small local corporations of their day seemed to fall almost wholly within the province of the state under its police power. It is true that they discussed the advisability of granting to Congress the power of incorporation, particularly with a view to making possible federal creation of interstate canal and turnpike companies; but the proposal was rejected, lest it prove a stumbling block to the ratification of the Constitution.

The states, from the beginning, maintained rather close supervision over the corporations which they chartered. Although public utility commissions are of recent origin, their functions were commonly provided for in one way or other. Charges were regulated, inspection of accounts was insisted upon, forfeiture of charters was stipulated for non-performance of specified obligations, and some effort was made to protect the public against unsound securities.[4]

Notwithstanding the silence of the Constitution on the question of corporations, it soon appeared that the federal government was not without power with regard to them. Congress promptly incorporated the United States Bank, justifying its action by Hamilton's doctrine of implied powers. A precedent was thus established for federal incorporation of companies for purposes falling

[3] *Ibid.*, II, 223.
[4] M. H. Hunter, "Early Regulation of Public Service Corporations."

within the scope of federal authority. It was discovered also that the same authority reached even, in some circumstances, to corporations created by the states, by virtue of the constitutional provision forbidding the latter to pass laws impairing the obligation of contracts. Since the Supreme Court was in practice the judge of violations of this clause by states, the federal authority could be invoked on occasion to restrain the states in their dealings with their own corporations.

This was the significance of the decision in the Dartmouth College case.[5] It delighted the capitalistic promoters of corporations, because of the security which it promised for vested interests; but it alarmed in equal measure the friends of state control, because it sharply circumscribed the police power. A corporation once chartered, it seemed, was guaranteed by the federal government a large degree of immunity from state supervision.

Nevertheless even under Marshall the court construed corporate charters strictly. In the case of Providence Bank v. Billings[6] it was ruled that a bank chartered by a state without any express stipulation exempting it from taxation, was subject to taxation. "As the whole community is interested in retaining" the power of taxation "undiminished, that community has a right to insist that abandonment ought not to be presumed, in a case in which the deliberate purpose of the State to abandon it does not appear." Under Taney it was to be expected that the court would go much further in redressing the balance in favor of the police power. This disposition was emphatically shown by the decision in the Charles River Bridge Company case.[7]

The Charles River Bridge Company was chartered by Massachusetts in 1785 for a term of fifty years. The bridge was opened in 1786, and six years later the legislature granted a thirty-year extension of the charter. In 1828, the legislature gave a charter of incorporation to a new company, which was to build a second

[5] See Hockett, Con. Hist., I, 370 et seq.
[6] 4 Peters 514 (1830).
[7] The Charles River Bridge Company v. Warren Bridge Company. 11 Peters 420 (1837). Reprinted in Commager, 285–287. Discussion in Swisher, Taney, 361–364, 368–374. On the whole question of the court's attitude towards corporations, see ibid., Chap. XVIII.

bridge over the Charles River, only a few rods distant from the first. This Warren bridge was to be turned over to the state as soon as the cost of construction had been collected in tolls, and in any event not later than six years from the opening of the bridge.

On the assumption that its charter granted it an exclusive right to maintain a bridge in the particular neighborhood, the Charles River Bridge Company sought an injunction to restrain the competing company from erecting its bridge. The Massachusetts courts ruled against the plaintiff, and the case came before the Supreme Court under the contract clause. It was argued in 1831 and came up for decision the next year, when Marshall, Story, and Thompson agreed that the decision of the state court should be reversed. But two of the justices were ill, Baldwin dissented, and McLean doubted the jurisdiction of the court. Under these circumstances a majority decision being impossible, the case was set for a rehearing. When it came up again in 1837, after Marshall's death, Story and Thompson held to their former opinion, but the other five justices upheld the Massachusetts court and the state law incorporating the Warren Bridge Company.

The essence of the decision as delivered by Chief Justice Taney was that no monopoly rights were to be derived by implication from any charter grant; that only express provisions could be construed as conveying such rights. "The object and end of all government is to promote the happiness and prosperity of the community by which it is established; and it can never be assumed, that the government intended to diminish the power of accomplishing the end for which it was created. . . . In a country like ours, free, active and enterprising, continually advancing in numbers and wealth; new channels of communication are daily found necessary, both for travel and trade, and are essential to the comfort, convenience, and prosperity of the people. A State ought never to be presumed to surrender this power, because, like the taxing power, the whole community have an interest in preserving it undiminished. . . . The continued existence of a government would be of no great value, if, by implications and presumptions, it was disarmed of the powers necessary to accomplish the ends of its creation, and the functions it was designed to perform, transferred to the hands of privileged corporations." "We cannot deal thus with the rights reserved to the States; and by legal intendments and mere technical reasoning, take away from them any portion of that power over their own internal police and improvement, which is so necessary to their well being and prosperity."

Such pronouncements reveal Taney as the champion not merely of state *rights* but of their *duties*. The principles which he laid down paved the way for later decisions, such as that of Stone *v.* Mississippi,[8] in which the court declared that the legislature of a state could not "bargain away the public health or the public morals" but must preserve its essential police powers for the welfare of the people.

For the historical background of this strict construction Taney turned to England, and asked why the courts of the United States should enlarge by implication the rights of corporations while England was "restraining, within the strictest limits the spirit of monopoly, and exclusive privileges in the nature of monopolies [,] and confining corporations to the privileges plainly given to them in their charters." Since we "adopted and adhere to the rules of construction known to the English Common Law, in every other case without exception," why should we make an exception of corporations?[9]

Nowhere does Taney more distinctly place the welfare of the community above the claims of individuals or groups to special privileges than in this decision. A recent writer has said: "It was this change of emphasis from vested individual property rights to the personal rights and welfare of the general community which characterized Chief Justice Taney's Court."[10] Equally well it illustrates the swing away from Marshall's position towards democratic principles. Conservative jurists and corporate interests were dismayed by the decision.

[8] 101 U. S. 814 (1880).

[9] During the dispute preceding the Revolution, Americans chafed under the treatment of the colonies by the British government as mere mercantile corporations, yet at the same time held their charters to be contracts the terms of which restricted the control of that government (*cf.* Hockett, *Con. Hist.*, I, 66, note, 94, *et passim*). Note the bearing of the latter view on Marshall's argument in the Dartmouth College case (*ibid.*, 370).

[10] Warren, II, 35.

Justice Story wrote an able dissenting opinion, and in a letter to Judge McLean showed disappointment and discouragement over the prospect.[11] Chancellor Kent, the head of the New York judiciary, thought that a "great principle of constitutional morality" had been abandoned or overthrown, and that the "moral sense of the community" was injured. To Story he wrote: "I abhor the doctrine that the Legislature is not bound by everything that is necessarily implied in a contract in order to give it effect and value."[12] As a result of this and other decisions he said: "I have lost my confidence and hopes in the constitutional guardianship and protection of the Supreme Court."[13]

The Whig press in general charged that the court was dominated by antifederal doctrines. In modern parlance it would be called anticapitalistic; in terms of Jacksonian democracy, it was anti-special privilege. The change in its tone was in harmony with the change in general social and economic conditions in the period, and with the advent of democracy as signalized by the general adoption of manhood suffrage. It was, moreover, in line with Jackson's attack on the Second United States Bank. Many Whigs saw in the decision evidence of too great subservience to the popular will, which would "be looked to as the leading star of the new dynasty and as the only exponent of the Constitution."[14]

Story, in dissenting, said that he could conceive of no surer plan to arrest improvements by private capital than by making investments uncertain. This, he thought, would be the effect of the decision. The mere agitation of the question was enough, he thought, to alarm the stockholders in every enterprise in the country.

The decision must stand in history as a fortunate corrective of the tendency imparted to corporate business at the expense of state control by the Dartmouth College judgment. That ruling had encouraged corporations at the expense of the power of control by states and public. The limitations and modifications placed upon them by the court under Taney relieved the public of some of the

[11] Story, *Life of Story*, II, 270.
[12] *Ibid.*
[13] Quoted by Warren, II, 29.
[14] *Ibid.*, II, 30.

dangers and freed the states from the grasp of great monopolies. "Even the most ardent advocates for Federal Supremacy can scarcely regret the decision." [15] Fifteen years after the decision, one of the justices declared that "no opinion of the Court more fully satisfied the legal judgment of the country, and consequently none has exerted more influence upon its legislation." The rigid principle of the Dartmouth College case which heretofore "had acted like a band of iron on legislative action" was modified by this decision in favor of the public interests.[16]

Moreover, the decision was soon recognized as favorable to the progress of enterprise, because it relieved men contemplating investments of the fear of monopoly claims concealed in ambiguous clauses of the charters of older corporations. It thus proved to be an important factor in the successful competition of new systems of transportation, for example, with antiquated ones. Taney, indeed, showed that he perceived this when he said that if charters gave monopoly by implication, the millions invested in railways and canals along lines already occupied by turnpikes would be jeopardized. Improvements would not be ventured until "old turnpike corporations consent to permit these States to avail themselves of the lights of modern science."

Having held that monopoly privileges could not be derived by implication, the court next decided that property rights acquired under a charter contract were subject to the power of eminent domain. Such was the decision in the case of West River Bridge Company v. Dix.[17] A toll bridge had been erected in 1795 over West River, in Brattleboro, Vermont, by a corporation whose charter gave it a monopoly for one hundred years over bridge rights within four miles of the junction of West River with the Connecticut. In 1839 an act of the legislature empowered the state courts

[15] Carson, *History of the Supreme Court* (edition of 1891), I, 280, 308. *Cf.* George W. Biddle, "Constitutional Development in the United States as Influenced by Chief-Justice Taney."

[16] Quoted by Warren, II, 24. For discussion of the influence of the Dartmouth College decision, and the later modification of Marshall's doctrine, see R. N. Denham, Jr., "An Historical Development of the Contract Theory in the Dartmouth College Case," and A. Russell, "Status and Tendencies of the Dartmouth College Case."

[17] 6 Howard 507 (1848).

to exercise the right of eminent domain against "any real estate, easement, or franchise of any turnpike or other corporation when in their judgment the public good requires a public highway." Three years later, on petition of Joseph Dix, commissioners recommended that the toll bridge be taken, with compensation to the corporation, in order that a free road and bridge might be provided for the public.

After the hearing before the Supreme Court Justice Daniel delivered the opinion. "Into all contracts," he said, "there enter conditions which arise not out of the literal terms of the contract itself: they are super-induced by the pre-existing and higher authority of the law of nature, of nations, or of the community to which the parties belong. Every contract is made in subordination to them. Such a condition is the right of eminent domain."

The exercise of the right of eminent domain does not conflict, the court held, with the inviolability of contracts, for a charter is like all other private rights. All property is held by tenure from the state, and corporation property stands on the same footing as that held by individuals.[18]

This decision, remarked one southern newspaper, "reverses some of the humbuggery which has hitherto been considered law. . . . The Court has triumphantly sustained the republican doctrine that a corporation can have no more rights than individuals. . . . It is a great triumph . . . over the absurd and venerable dogmas that have hitherto made charters too holy to be repealed or legislated on." Another commended it "to the particular notice of those who consider corporations too sacred to be made amenable to the laws." [19]

As corporations began to extend their activities beyond the states which chartered them, they ran against this principle of strict construction of their privileges, and for a time it seemed possible that their interstate activities might be entirely inhibited. This very

[18] Judge Catron did not sit in this case because of illness, and Chief Justice Taney did not sit because a near relative was interested in the outcome. Judge McLean was also absent. Judge Wayne dissented.

[19] Quoted by Warren, II, 165. For other decisions construing charters of corporations strictly see Perrine v. Chesapeake and Delaware Canal Co., 9 Howard 172 (1850); The Philadelphia, Wilmington and Baltimore R. R. Co. v. Maryland, 58 Maryland, 372; and Providence Bank v. Billings, already mentioned.

danger was revealed by the so-called "Comity Cases," in 1839.[20] The plaintiffs were banking corporations of Georgia, Pennsylvania, and Louisiana respectively, the second being the successor of the Second United States Bank, which, upon the expiration of its charter in 1836, had been granted a charter by Pennsylvania. All three concerns had agents in Alabama, through whom they purchased or discounted bills of exchange which the makers later refused to pay on the ground of want of power in the corporations to do business in Alabama, or, indeed, outside of their own states.

In the case of The Bank of Augusta v. Earle, Justice McKinley, in the circuit court for Alabama, gave judgment for the defendant on the ground that the laws of Alabama did not give foreign corporations the right to transact business within its limits. Many Democrats, as anti-corporation men, hailed the decision as an appropriate aftermath of Jackson's fight on the United States Bank. Supporters of the state banks hoped that the business of the United States Bank would now fall to them.[21] On the other hand, as Story said, the decision in the circuit court "frightened half the lawyers and all the corporations of the country out of their proprieties." [22] It opened the way for widespread repudiation of obligations by debtors, and coming hard on the heels of the panic of 1837, while business was still suffering under severe depression, corporations engaged in manufacturing, trading, or insurance curtailed their operations, hesitating to undertake activities outside of their own states.[23]

The decision of the circuit court was reviewed by the Supreme Court on writ of error. Webster was associated with D. B. Ogden in presenting the case of the corporations, and both men took pains to point out the social significance of the issue. Said Ogden: "The proposition in the Circuit Court . . . is the more injurious, as in the United States associated capital is essentially necessary to the operations of commerce and the creation and improvement of the

[20] Bank of Augusta v. Earle; Bank of the United States v. Primrose; New Orleans and Carrollton Rail Road v. Earle. 13 Peters 519. Discussion in Swisher, *Taney*, 380–386.
[21] Warren, II, 52.
[22] Quoted *ibid.*, 50.
[23] *Ibid.*, 51.

facilities of intercourse. . . . One of the most important objects and interests for the preservation of the Union is the establishment of Railroads. Cannot the railroad corporations of New York, Pennsylvania, or Maryland make a contract outside of the State for materials for the construction of a railroad?"[24] Webster declared: "I can see neither limit nor end to the calamitous consequences of such a decision. I do not know where it would not reach, what interests it would not disturb, or how any part of the commercial system of the country would be free from its influences. . . . The decision . . . is anti-commercial and anti-social."[25]

Jared Ingersoll defended the decision of the lower court on anti-monopoly grounds, portraying the evils which would follow forcing states to allow corporations to do business within their limits. Corporations should not become sovereign and states subjects, he urged. If they ought to be restricted to the specific purposes of their creation, the courts were bound to prevent their wandering from their place as much as from their purpose.[26]

The decision of the court was rendered by the chief justice. One of Taney's critics has said that he sometimes "decided what ought to be the law and then" wrote his opinions to justify his conclusions.[27] If the characterization was true in any case it would appear to be applicable to the one under discussion. Starting from strict construction premises he declared: "A corporation can make no contracts and do no acts either within or without the State which creates it except such as are authorized by its charter. If the law creating a charter does not give it the right to exercise its powers beyond the limits of the State, all contracts made by it in other States would be void." In the case in question, Georgia had clothed

[24] *Ibid.*, 54.

[25] *Ibid.*, 53.

[26] An article attributed to Amos Kendall, the postmaster general, praised this plea as "a conclusive argument against the right of these money-mongering monsters to stray from their spheres and invade the quiet regions of distant States, there to ravage, monopolize and *destroy*," and predicted that "vagabond banks are in a fair way to be chained up, to bite and bark only at their own houses. . . . What a blessing it would be if the Judiciary should interpose to administer law upon the wrong doers whose rapacity has so deeply encroached on the best interests and institutions of the country." Webster was reported to have denounced this last sentence as an attempt to dictate to the court. See Warren, II, 55, 56.

[27] William E. Mikell, "Roger Brooke Taney," 144.

the corporation with the right to make contracts outside the state; but such rights depended also upon the laws of the sovereignty in which they were exercised. The issue therefore turned upon the laws of the State of Alabama.

At this point Justice McKinley in the lower court had held that the corporation could not legally transact business in Alabama because the laws of that state did not authorize "foreign" corporations to operate within its jurisdiction. Permission was not to be implied by silence. Taney and the majority of the Supreme Court were unwilling to apply quite so rigid a rule of construction; they evidently felt the force of the arguments of Webster and Ogden, and were willing to allow the silence of the state to pass for consent. In the absence of clear evidence of prohibitory action by the state, a warrant for the operations of the foreign corporation was found in the principle of comity among nations. Courts of justice, said Taney, have always executed contracts made in a foreign country according to the law of the place in which they were made, provided that the law was not repugnant to the laws or policy of their own country.[28] It was well settled that by the law of comity among nations, a corporation created by one sovereignty is permitted to make contracts in another, and to sue in the courts. The same law of comity prevails among the several sovereignties of the Union. Since Alabama has declared the adoption of the law of international comity in the case of suits, the law of Alabama is not against suits of foreign corporations.[29]

The decision in the Comity Cases was one of the first indications that the court was inclined to recognize that corporations were not without some rights in interstate relations. Justice Story not only concurred but wrote to the chief justice: "Your opinion . . . has given very general satisfaction to the public, and I hope you will

[28] Thus a right established, for example, under Massachusetts law may be enforced in a court of France or any other civilized country. The same relation holds among the states of the Union, and is guaranteed by the "full faith and credit" clause of the Constitution (Art. IV, sec. 1). Where the parties are citizens of different states, they have the option of trying the cause in a federal court. In consequence the law of each of the several states becomes a part of the law which the federal judges may be called upon to apply, a fact which shows that they are dependent on the knowledge and arguments of counsel in no slight degree.

[29] McKinley, adhering to his decision in the lower court, dissented.

allow me to say that I think it does great honor to yourself, as
well as to the Court." [30]   The Whig papers hailed the judgment
with enthusiasm. They denounced the anti-monopoly sentiments
of the people in rather extravagant terms, as symptoms of a leveling
spirit, a "disposition to set the poor against the rich, the idle against
the industrious, the unruly against the law-abiding and finally the
State government against the government of the Union"; and re-
joiced that the progress of "Locofocoism," which had reached the
White House and the Capitol, had not brought it to the Supreme
Court. Taney came in for his share of praise. Fears for the "fabric
of constitutional law reared by the great Marshall" gave way to
assurance that the court was still sound.[31]

Both Whig and Democratic commentators overlooked the fact
that the decision allowed the states to exclude foreign corporations
if they so desired, for in spite of the comfort afforded to the friends
of the corporations, Taney had been careful to preserve the power
of the states intact. In the very next year, in the case of Runyan v.
The Lessee of Coster et al.,[32] the court again affirmed two principles
which were asserted, in a subordinate manner, in the Comity Cases:
viz., (1) that the law creating a corporation determines its right to
make contracts outside of the creating state; and (2) that every
power exercised in another state depends upon the laws of the
sovereignty in which it is exercized. This emphatic proclamation
of the power of a state, by express action, to repudiate the principle
of comity and refuse recognition to a foreign corporation lies at the
base of the great mass of state legislation regulating corporations
which has been since enacted. Alabama at once used the power
which the court thus emphasized, and expressly forbade the transaction within her borders of business by agents of foreign corporations, but the states generally pursued a more liberal course.

An exception to the principle of state control over corporations
not of their own creation must be recognized in the case of those
chartered by Congress, as agents of the federal government. This
exception had been emphasized by the case of McCulloch v. Mary-

[30] Quoted by Warren, II, 59.
[31] Ibid., II, 57–58.
[32] 14 Peters 122 (1840).

land. The decision that a state could not tax a branch of the United States Bank because it was an agency of the United States, and because the power to tax was equivalent to the power to destroy, logically pointed to the conclusion that a state could not by taxation or any other means restrict the privileges granted to such corporations by Congress. Thus arose the principle that a state cannot exclude a corporation chartered by Congress to perform any federal function—a principle which protects companies engaged in interstate commerce or the transmission of intelligence.[33] The Maryland decision, ranking with that in the Dartmouth College case in the history of the constitutional law of corporations, was quite in the temper of Marshall's court, and aroused much resentment. Both before and after it was announced, many friends of a vigorous federal government sympathized with the proposal to recognize the states' authority to the extent of seeking their consent to the establishment of branches of the bank within their bounds (and the same procedure was urged in the case of federal roads). Anger at the disregard of this alleged right of a state to exclude unwelcome corporations led Ohio, in the early twenties, to consider outlawing the branches of the United States Bank by withdrawing from them all protection under the laws of the state.[34]

It is difficult to see how the federal government could have met such a challenge save by itself shouldering the responsibility of protecting the bank, as it has come to do in the case of the mails. Indeed, the purpose of the state was to compel the government to assume this responsibility. But it was rightly judged that such an exercise of federal authority would hardly be risked. It was not until after the Civil War that an effective check was placed upon such a denial of protection by a state to corporations, created either

[33] In Philadelphia Fire Assn. v. New York (119 U. S. 110. 1886) the court held that insurance contracts were not interstate commerce and that a state could prescribe whatever conditions it saw fit for permitting a foreign insurance corporation to do business within its limits, even to total exclusion. But a corporation engaged in interstate commerce can not be excluded.—Pembina Con. Silver Mining Co. v. Pa., 125 U. S. 181 (1888).

[34] See Hockett, Con. Hist., I, 364. It will be recalled that a main issue in the contest between President Tyler and the Clay Whigs over the bank was this question of the right of Congress to authorize the bank to establish branches and transact business within the states without their consent.

by Congress or another state, by the provision of the fourteenth
amendment forbidding any state to deny to "any person within its
jurisdiction the equal protection of the laws." The word "person"
was sufficiently inclusive to embrace corporations, and twenty
years after the close of the war the Supreme Court recognized that
a corporation was a person within the meaning of the amendment.[35]
That a corporation was an artificial person had long before become
an accepted doctrine, inherited, indeed, from the English law, and
distinctly stated by Marshall in the Dartmouth College decision.
Said he: a corporation is "indeed a mere artificial being, invisible
and intangible. Yet it is a person for certain purposes, in contemplation of law."

The court under Taney was called upon to determine the standing of these artificial persons in the federal courts. One line of
approach had led the tribunal, as shown by the Comity Cases, to
recognize the validity of their contracts when not contrary to the
legislation of a "foreign" state. Another line of evolution during
the thirties and forties culminated in the recognition that, for the
purpose of suing and being sued in the federal courts, corporations
were to be regarded as citizens.

The Constitution gives to the federal courts jurisdiction, among
other classes of cases, over those between citizens of different states.
As corporations as such are unknown to the Constitution, their rise
inevitably raised the question of the power of the courts to entertain suits to which they were parties. If the Constitution had mentioned "persons" instead of "citizens," there would have been no
problem. Could corporations be considered as artificial citizens as
well as artificial persons? Justices Story and Washington urged
that this was the correct view to take, and Webster adopted it in
his argument of corporations cases.[36] Neither Marshall nor Taney,
however, was ever willing to admit that they were right. However, even though a corporation was not itself a citizen, its stockholders usually were, and in the early days it seemed safe to act
upon the theory that a suit involving such a body was the suit of

[35] Santa Clara County *v.* Southern Pacific Railroad, 118 U. S. 394 (1886). See
also Pembina etc. Mining Co. *v.* Pennsylvania, *loc. cit.* (1888).
[36] Story, *Life of Story*, II, 469.

the citizens composing it. The courts, that is, looked beyond the artificial person to the citizens behind it.

This apparently logical procedure was soon found to entail very serious difficulties. In Strawbridge v. Curtiss et al. and other cases[37] the court held that it had no jurisdiction where a corporation was a party unless all of the stockholders were citizens of a state other than that of the opposing party. Such a view of its jurisdiction was strictly justifiable by the letter of the Constitution, but the rule had never quite satisfied bar or bench, and Marshall himself had expressed regret that it had ever been laid down. In 1839 Congress passed an act intended to relieve the court of the embarrassing precedent. It declared that "where in any suit at law or in equity, commenced in any court of the United States, there shall be several defendants, any one or more of whom shall not be inhabitants of, or found within the district where the suit is brought, or shall not voluntarily appear thereto, it shall be lawful for the Court to entertain jurisdiction, and proceed to the trial and adjudication of . . . suit between the parties who may be properly before it." [38]

The intricacies of the situations to which the court was required to apply the Constitution are well illustrated by the case of The Louisville, Cincinnati, and Charleston Railroad Company v. Letson.[39] This railway company was a corporation organized under the laws of South Carolina. Its stockholders included two citizens of North Carolina, the State of South Carolina, and two corporations, each of which had members who were citizens of the State of New York. Letson, the defendant, was also a citizen of New York. It was impossible in such a situation to apply the original doctrine of diverse citizenship.

The tendency to substitute a new concept and to deal with corporations as entities distinct from the citizens who composed them had been shown in the Comity Cases. Taney had then remarked that "whenever a corporation makes a contract it is the contract of the legal entity; of the artificial being created by the charter,

[37] 3 Cranch 267 (1806). See also Hope Insurance Company v. Boardman, 5 Cranch 57 (1810); Bank of the United States v. Deveaux, 5 Cranch 61 (1809); Commercial and Rail Road Bank of Vicksburg v. Slocomb, 14 Peters 60 (1840).
[38] U. S. Stat. at Large, V, 321–323.
[39] 2 Howard 497 (1844).

and not the contract of the individual members. The only rights it can claim are the rights which are given to it in that character, and not the rights which belong to its members as citizens of a State." Such reasoning showed the doctrine of diverse citizenship to be untenable as well as impracticable in cases involving corporations. The alternatives were to obtain an amendment or new legislation, to abandon jurisdiction in corporation cases, or boldly to set aside precedent and deal with such cases as matters pertaining to the general welfare of the nation. Under these circumstances the court, encouraged and assisted by the act of 1839, abandoned the doctrine of *stare decisis* and took a long step in the shaping of our constitutional law in accordance with the demands of the expanding industrial system.

In arguing the Louisville railway case, objections to the jurisdiction of the court were raised on several grounds: (1) that citizens of one state cannot sue a corporation in the circuit court of the United States unless all the members of the corporation are citizens of the state in which the suit is brought; (2) that citizens of one state cannot sue a corporation if a state is a member of the corporation (because of the prohibition of the eleventh amendment); and (3) that citizens of one state cannot sue a corporation where one of the members of the corporation is another corporation whose members are citizens of the same state with the plaintiff.

Justice Wayne, delivering the opinion of the court, said that "after due deliberation we feel free to say that the cases of Strawbridge *v.* Curtiss and Bank of the United States *v.* Deveaux were carried too far." [40] Answering the objections to the jurisdiction, he said that the plea that the State of South Carolina as a member of the corporation could not be sued could not be sustained, for whenever a government becomes a partner in a trading concern, so far as the transaction is concerned it loses its sovereignty. As to the point of diversified citizenship of the corporation, a suit brought against a corporation by its corporate name in the state of its locality and where its business is done is a suit against citizens of the state where the suit is brought. It was unnecessary, in view of

[40] In Bank of U. S. *v.* Deveaux (1809) Marshall had said that the citizenship of the stockholders was the citizenship of the corporation.

these two rulings, to consider the other objections to the jurisdiction.

The gist of the decision was that "a corporation created by and transacting business in a state is to be deemed an inhabitant of the State, and capable of being treated as a citizen for all purposes of suing and being sued." A citizen of one state and a corporation of another state can be parties to a suit which may be tried either in the courts of the state where the contract was made or in a federal circuit court.[41] The decision was far from establishing the doctrine of Story and Webster, that corporations were citizens. After the Civil War it was definitely ruled that a corporation is not a citizen, and that it has no protection under the clause of the fourteenth amendment which guarantees the privileges and immunities of citizens of the United States against adverse state action.[42] Such is the law today, for the court has gone no further than to recognize corporations as *persons* with the rights belonging to them, plus *some* of the privileges of citizens.[43]

[41] Charles Warren regards the construction of the court in regard to the privilege of corporations to sue and to be sued in the federal courts as most unfortunate. By the "judicial legislation" in the Letson case and a series of decisions which followed, the court "decided, through the device of a conclusive presumption as to citizenship of the stockholders, to regard a corporation as a citizen of the State in which it was chartered." "This malignant decision has resulted in allowing a corporation sued in the State in which it actually does business, to remove the suit into a Federal Court on the ground of diverse citizenship, simply because it happens to be chartered in another State. No single factor has given rise to more friction and jealousy between State and Federal Courts, or to more State legislation conflicting with and repugnant to Federal jurisdiction, than has the doctrine of citizenship for corporations. And this diverse citizenship jurisdiction created by the Constitution and intended to allay friction and to afford equal and identical law to citizen and non-citizen in a State, has resulted in putting foreign corporations in a more favorable situation than domestic corporations, sued in a State. The failure to anticipate this corporation issue was one of the great defects of the [Judiciary Act of 1789]."—"New Light on . . . the Judiciary Act," 89–90. Quoted by permission of the *Harvard Law Review* and Mr. Warren.

[42] Paul *v.* Virginia, 8 Wallace 168 (1869); Minor *v.* Happersett, 21 Wallace 162 (1865); Pembina . . . Mining Co. *v.* Pennsylvania, 125 U. S. 181 (1888).

[43] See P. J. Altizer, "Jurisdiction of the Federal Courts Based upon Diversity of Citizenship"; and Jacob Treiber, "The Jurisdiction of Federal Courts in Actions in which Corporations are Parties."

THE GUARANTEE OF REPUBLICAN GOVERNMENT

The case of Luther *v.* Borden [44] is historically important as forming the chief precedent for the claims of the congressional party during the reconstruction period after the Civil War, that to Congress belongs the duty and power of determining whether the government of a state is republican in form.   In this case Luther was one of the insurrectionists during the Dorr Rebellion in Rhode Island in the early forties, and Borden was a militia officer.   Borden broke into Luther's house in the effort to find and arrest him, and Luther's suit was an action for trespass.   The design of the suit in reality was to test the legality of the Dorr government.   Borden had acted under authority of a declaration of martial law by the legislature of the old state government, and Luther's counsel argued that the declaration was void because the Dorr government was the legal one.   This contention was based on the doctrine that the people of a state are sovereign and may form a new government without the consent of their existing government.   The jurisdiction of the United States arose from the clause in the Constitution providing that the United States shall guarantee to each state a republican form of government.

The case was argued during a period of sharp controversy due to the Mexican War.   Many Democrats regarded it as involving the right of the people to alter or abolish their governments even by revolution, a right "that lies at the very foundation of our free institutions," as they said.   Webster was the chief attorney for Borden, and his argument was regarded by the Whigs as a masterful exposition "of the whole character of the Constitution, [and] the relations between the Federal and State Governments."   His chief contention was that the people were bound to change their government in the manner prescribed by existing law.   This opinion, the Democratic press denounced as "worthy of a monarchist." [45]

The decision was given by the chief justice in January, 1849. So far as the court was concerned, the only question was whether it had any duty to perform in connection with the guarantee clause,

[44] 7 Howard 1 (1848).
[45] Warren, *Sup. Court*, II, 186 *et seq.*

and its decision was that it had not. "It rests with Congress to decide what government is the established one in a State. For, as the United States guarantees to each State a republican government, Congress must necessarily decide what government is established in the State, before it can determine whether it is republican or not. And when Senators and Representatives of a State are admitted into the councils of the Union, the authority of the government, under which they are appointed, as well as its republican character, is recognized by the proper constitutional authority. And its decision is binding on every other department of the government, and could not be questioned by a judicial tribunal." [46]

This was the part of the decision on which the congressional party was to rely in struggling against presidential reconstruction in the sixties.[47] Taney went on to say that with Congress rested the determination of the means proper to quell domestic violence in fulfillment of the guarantee of a republican form of government, and from this statement also the congressional party was to derive authority for its stand. Taney declared that Congress might have placed it in the power of a court to decide when the contingency had arisen which required the intervention of the federal government; but instead of doing so, they had, by act of February 28, 1795, vested the power in the President.[48] In case of armed conflict, which is a clear case of "domestic violence," one party must be in insurrection against the lawful government, and the President must of necessity decide which is the government and which is the party unlawfully arrayed against it, before he can perform the duty imposed upon him by the act of Congress. The court may not inquire during nor after the insurrection as to whether the President's decision is right. The President, upon the application of the governor of Rhode Island claiming to act under the charter, had recognized him as the executive power of the state and was ready to call out the militia. A knowledge of this decision put an end to the armed opposition, and was "as effectual, as if the militia had been assembled under his orders."

[46] Johnson, *Readings*, 349.
[47] See *infra*, Chap. XVII.
[48] *Ibid.*, 350–352.

Of course, the chief justice continued, such a situation vested in the President a power which was dangerous to liberty, and might be abused. But all power may be abused, and it would be difficult to place this power in safer hands. "When citizens of the same State are in arms against each other, and the constituted authorities are unable to execute the laws, the interposition of the United States must be prompt, or it is of little value. The ordinary course of proceedings in courts of justice would be utterly unfit for the crisis." If the President invaded the rights of the people of a state, Congress would have power to apply the remedy. But the courts must administer the law as they find it. While the court "should always be ready to meet any question confided to it by the Constitution, it is equally its duty not to pass beyond its appropriate sphere of action and to take care not to involve itself in discussions which properly belong to other forums." The people of a state may alter their form of government at pleasure. "But whether they have changed it or not, by abolishing an old government and establishing a new one in its place, is a question to be settled by the political power." When that power has decided the courts must follow it.[49]

Many years earlier Jefferson had insisted that some cases could not properly come before the federal courts. Those touching the acts of the legislative and executive departments within their own proper spheres, he held to be of this kind, and also those in which the sovereign rights of the states were drawn into question. Marshall had in a very limited degree recognized that cases could arise which the court could not adjudicate on their merits. In Marbury v. Madison he had intimated that the courts had no power to issue a mandamus to an official of the executive department where discretionary action had been assigned to the department by the Constitution; and similarly, with respect to acts of Congress, he had acknowledged that the supreme tribunal could not inquire into the wisdom or policy of legislation so long as it did not transgress the bounds set by the fundamental law. Taney now gave clear expression to this doctrine, and christened the class of cases to which it referred by calling them "political." The recognition thus given

[49] Ibid.

of the existence of this class of cases was to become especially important during the Civil War and reconstruction. In effect it enabled the court to give Congress a free hand and to avoid a clash between the legislative and judicial departments at a critical juncture in national life.[50]

BILLS OF CREDIT

When the Supreme Court met for the first time under Taney, in 1837, three important constitutional cases were pending which had been argued before Marshall's death and assigned for rehearing for want of a majority decision. The first of these was the Charles River Bridge Company case, and the second that of Mayor of New York v. Miln. The third was Briscoe v. Bank of the Commonwealth of Kentucky.[51] It involved much the same questions as Craig v. Missouri, which had been decided in 1830.[52] Both were important to those who opposed the operation of the United States Bank and favored a currency issued by the states, or by state-chartered banks, and both involved the interpretation of the constitutional provision prohibiting states to emit bills of credit or to make anything but gold or silver legal tender.[53]

The Craig case came as the climax of a series of events which aroused in the states a sense of grievance against the Supreme Court. The decision was in direct line of succession from the judgments in McCulloch v. Maryland, Dartmouth College v. Woodward, Cohens v. Virginia, and Gibbons v. Ogden. In it was brought into question the power of the state to issue certain interest-bearing certificates, not declared to be legal tender, but receivable at the state treasury or any of the loan offices of the state in discharge of taxes or payment of debts due to the state. Certain property of the state was pledged for the redemption of these certificates, and the governor was authorized to negotiate

[50] On political questions see O. P. Field, "The Doctrine of Political Questions in the Federal Courts"; A. E. Gold, "Jurisdiction of the Supreme Court over Political Questions"; M. F. Weston, "Political Questions."
As early as 1796, in Ware v. Hylton, Justice Iredell had said that the issues involved were "political" and hence not within the court's jurisdiction.
[51] 11 Peters 257 (1837).
[52] 4 Peters 410. Reprinted in Commager, 252–253.
[53] Art. I, sec. 10.

a loan of silver or gold for the same purpose. These certificates, it was provided, might be loaned to the citizens of the state upon real or personal security.

The case was argued before the court on behalf of Missouri by Senator Thomas H. Benton, who interlarded his plea with indignant phrases alluding to the exercise by the court of its jurisdiction under the twenty-fifth section of the Judiciary Act of 1789, which section the critics of the court were finding so obnoxious just at that time. "The State of Missouri," said Benton, "has been 'summoned' by a writ from this Court under a 'penalty' to . . . appear. . . . Language of this kind does not seem proper when addressed to a sovereign State." [54]

The court's decision was made public while the debate on Foote's resolution, better known as the Webster-Hayne debate, was going on in the Senate, and Benton's words just quoted may be the better understood by recalling that, as a participant in this great debate, he was one of the senators who attacked the nationalizing tendencies of the federal government. The decision was characteristic of Marshall. The Missouri certificates were held to be bills of credit and therefore unconstitutional. In defining "bills of credit," Marshall said: "The term has acquired an appropriate meaning and Bills of Credit signify a paper medium, intended to circulate between individuals, and between governments and individuals, for the ordinary purposes of society. If the prohibition means anything, if the words are not empty sounds, it must comprehend the emission of any paper medium by a State government, for the purpose of common circulation."

Perhaps nothing connected with the court illustrates better the changing temper of the tribunal than this decision when taken in contrast with that in the Kentucky Bank case. In the Missouri case Marshall's view was sustained by a majority of only one of his associates, and the dissenting opinions indicated the probability of a reversal if the issue arose again after changes in the personnel. Marshall himself foresaw the event, and wrote to Story: "I have read the dissenting opinions of Judges Johnson, Thompson and McLean . . . and think it requires no prophet to predict that

[54] Warren, I, 725.

the Twenty-fifth Section is to be repealed or to use a more fashionable phrase, to be nullified by the Supreme Court."[55] That is, the states were to be allowed to have their way.

Justice Thompson, in his dissenting opinion, had held that a bill of credit was to be considered as one "drawn and resting merely upon the credit of the drawer; as contradistinguished from a fund constituted or pledged for the payment of the bill." This view, together with the democratized character of the court under Taney, gives the clue to the decision in Briscoe *v.* Bank of the Commonwealth. Kentucky had chartered a bank to issue notes, and the state itself was the owner of the entire stock of the bank. The bank was a mere agency of the state in emitting circulating notes; if they were bills of credit, could the state do through an agent what it was itself forbidden by the Constitution to do?

Justice McLean, giving the decision, held that Marshall's definition of a bill of credit had been too broad. It was "so general that it would embrace every description of paper which circulates as money." The constitutional prohibition he thought had a more restricted meaning. In the present case, while the state was the sole owner of the bank's stock, the bills were emitted by a corporation which could sue and be sued in the courts; and the courts could enforce payment of the bank's obligations, as ample funds were provided for the purpose. The conclusion was that the bills were not bills of credit within the meaning of the Constitution, and that the state law was valid.

Justices Thompson and Baldwin wrote concurring opinions. It was to be expected that Thompson would concur, for the new decision conformed to the views he had expressed in his dissenting opinion in 1830. Baldwin, however, had upheld the Craig decision, and now sought to show that there was a difference in the cases which enabled him to concur in the Briscoe judgment. In the first, he pointed out, the faith of the State of Missouri was pledged for the payment of the paper which she had emitted and given certain legal tender qualities, while in the second Kentucky had not pledged her faith to redeem the notes of the bank, nor made them legal tender. "Certificates emitted by a State, for circulation, payable

[55] Letter dated Oct. 15, 1830. Mass. Hist. Soc. *Proc.*, 2d ser. XIV.

in the future, on faith and funds of the State, which certificates were made a tender, were prohibited as bills of credit. On the same authority I now hold, that the notes in question are not such bills of credit, because not emitted by the State, nor made a tender in payment of any debts to individuals, nor [is] the faith or general funds of the States pledged for their redemption." [56]

Story wrote a dissenting opinion, based on the grounds on which he had agreed with Marshall in the Craig decision.

ADMIRALTY JURISDICTION

One of the constructive features of the work of the court during the middle period, one for which Taney was largely responsible, was the development of admiralty and maritime jurisdiction. The Constitution in describing the powers of the judiciary included admiralty and maritime jurisdiction but without defining its scope. Such jurisdiction being an inheritance from England, the early decisions of the federal courts followed the English rule and confined admiralty jurisdiction to such navigable waters as were affected by ebb and flow of the tides.

With the growth of commerce on the Great Lakes and navigable rivers of the western states, however, the conviction grew that the Constitution should not be understood to confine that type of jurisdiction within the limits of the English rule, and in Cutler v. Rae [57] Taney had regretted "that the jurisdiction of the Court of Admiralty in this country is not more clearly defined."

In May, 1847, the propeller *Genesee Chief* collided with the *Cuba*, on Lake Ontario. The *Cuba* sank, and under an act of Congress of 1845 the case was brought to the Supreme Court, where the main question was whether the law had unconstitutionally extended the jurisdiction of the federal courts. [58] The act was upheld, not as a regulation of commerce, but under the judicial power in admiralty and maritime cases.

[56] In Darrington v. Bank of Alabama, 13 Howard 12 (1851), the court decided that bank bills were not bills of credit even when the state was sole stockholder and its faith was pledged for redemption of the bills.

[57] 7 Howard 729 (1849).

[58] *Genesee Chief v.* Fitzhugh. 12 Howard 443 (1851). See discussion in Willoughby, *Con. Law*, II, 1108 *et seq.*

The court through the chief justice held that the Great Lakes were, in truth, inland seas, whereon commerce was "subject to all the incidents and hazards which attend commerce on the ocean." There is "nothing in the ebb and flow of the tide that makes waters peculiarly suitable for admiralty jurisdiction, nor anything in the absence of a tide" which makes them unfit. Although the distinction was sound in England, where "tide-water and navigable water are synonymous terms," it was arbitrary and unsuitable in America. Nothing like foreign commerce had been possible on the inland rivers of America with their unchanging currents until the steamboat had given the power to go upstream. This invention had altered the description of public navigable rivers which had been accepted in the case of the *Thomas Jefferson.*[59] Since there could be no reason for admiralty jurisdiction over a public tidewater which did not apply with equal force to any other public water used for commercial purposes and for trade, Taney reached the conclusion that such jurisdiction extended to the waters of the Great Lakes.[60]

Once more Taney and his court had not hesitated to break the rule of *stare decisis:*[61] "If we follow it, we follow an erroneous decision, into which the Court fell when the great importance of the question, as it now presents itself, could not be foreseen, and the subject did not, therefore, receive the deliberate consideration which at this time would have been given to it." The Judiciary Act of 1789, Taney thought, had more than tidal waters in contemplation, since it spoke of "waters which are navigable from the sea by vessels of 10 or more tons burden." Daniel, however, dissented, saying that the court had construed the Constitution by geographical considerations, and that if his view seemed antiquated,

[59] 10 Wheaton 28 (1825).

[60] This decision applied strictly only to the Lakes, but the admiralty jurisdiction was later expressly held to extend to river navigation beyond the tidal flow. See Steamboat *New World v. King*, 16 Howard 469 (1853).

[61] The court has been less inclined to be bound by the rule of *stare decisis* where constitutional decisions are involved than in ordinary law cases. Said Taney: "I . . . am quite willing that it be regarded hereafter as the law of this court that its opinion upon the construction of the Constitution is always open to discussion when it is supposed to be founded in error, and that its judicial authority should hereafter depend altogether on the force of the reasoning by which it is supported."—Opinion in Passenger Cases.

he had "the consolation of the support of Marshall, Kent, and Story." "Now, without there having been engrafted any new provision on the Constitution, without the alteration of one letter of that instrument . . ." the definition was changed.[62]

One biographer, commenting on this decision, said: "It is a remarkable instance of a thoroughly technical lawyer realizing that enlightened jurisprudence requires the judge to adapt our borrowed law to the conditions of our own country . . . a signal example of impartial wisdom." [63]   Another writer says that the argument was set forth so clearly and convincingly that it was incapable of being confuted.[64]   Here again, however, it seems that Taney may be suspected of having first decided what ought to be the law.

Anent this admiralty case Emerson wrote: "The commerce of rivers, the commerce of railroads, and who knows but the commerce of air balloons, must add an American extension to the pond-hole of admiralty." [65]   Although he confused the commercial and admiralty powers, his words curiously enough predicted an event which has come to pass in our own time.   To this development Taney's contribution was second only to Marshall's.

[62] Warren, II, 241.
[63] Tyler, *Life of Taney*, 303, quoted by Steiner, *Life of Taney*, 296.
[64] Biddle, quoted by Steiner, *ibid.*
[65] Essay on "Power," in *Conduct of Life,* quoted *ibid.,* 292.

PART THREE

THE CONSTITUTIONAL ASPECTS OF THE SLAVERY CONTROVERSY

VIII

ISSUES RAISED BY SLAVERY

GENERAL VIEW

ARTIN VAN BUREN, writing his autobiography at the mid-century, commented that even Mr. Jefferson's alarm at the tendencies of the court would have subsided if he had lived to be a witness of the changes which had come about. Notwithstanding the placid temper of the country, however, Van Buren did not face the future with entire confidence, for he foresaw that the state of affairs would last only until some strong interest divided the people and enlisted the majority of the judges on the side of one faction. Such an interest the slavery question was destined to become not long after his prophetic words were penned. After dealing with other social and economic questions so successfully that it reached the pinnacle of its prestige, the court failed in its attempt to settle the great problem of the period, the sectional problem of the black slave. In the middle fifties its reputation was all but wrecked by its decision in the Dred Scott case, and the odium incurred in consequence has hardly up to the present permitted an appreciation of its real greatness during the two decades preceding the Civil War.

To the framers of the Constitution the relationship between master and slave, like that between husband and wife or employer and employee, seemed to be wholly a matter of state internal police. Not the least doubt of the correctness of this view entered into the plans and purposes of the Convention; nor could such a doubt have been entertained without greatly endangering the continuance of the sessions. The people of the slave states not only assumed that slavery was a domestic institution which each state should regulate as it saw fit, but the Constitution contained two express provisions which promised aid to them in maintaining their peculiar labor system. The first of these was the clause which promised federal aid against domestic violence. In view of the fear of slave insurrection, which was always more or less present in those regions where there were large numbers of servile blacks, this clause gave a comforting assurance. Equally valued was the provision that "No Person held to Service or Labour in one State, under the Laws thereof, escaping into another, shall, in Consequence of any Law or Regulation therein, be discharged from such Service or Labour, but shall be delivered up on Claim of the Party to whom such Service or Labour may be due." [1]

In addition to these provisions, the interests of the slave states were protected by qualifications and compromises wherever it could be foreseen that they might be endangered by the powers to be given to Congress. Thus, since the foreign slave trade came within the scope of that commerce which Congress was to have power to regulate, the right to prohibit the migration or importation of such persons as any of the states existing in 1787 should think proper to admit, was withheld from the national legislature until 1808. Again: unless the Union were to continue to rest, as had the Confederation, upon a system of equal representation of states, slavery could not be ignored in apportioning the weight to be assigned to its several members in the matters of representation and taxation; hence the three-fifths compromise, under which part of the slaves were to be counted for both purposes.

These provisions were a part of the price paid for southern acceptance of the Constitution.[2] They were intended to effect an intersectional adjustment which would prevent disputes. And so plainly did the control of slavery in each state fall within its police power that the very first Congress under the Constitution admitted it could not interfere with it in any state where it existed. No prominent leader or group ever took any other stand. Nevertheless these clauses, so carefully worded by the Convention, did not prevent controversy. Some of them became themselves the cause of sectional irritation, and there were other clauses which proved unexpectedly to be the occasion of dispute because of unforeseen relations to issues involving slavery. Antislavery agitation led to

[1] Art. IV, sec. 2.
[2] One might reverse the statement and speak of the power to regulate commerce as the "price paid" for northern acceptance. See Royal B. Way, "Was the Fugitive Slave Clause of the Constitution Necessary?"

the discussion of the constitutional right of Congress to impose limitations upon the powers of new states as a condition of their admission to the Union, and raised other problems with regard to the power to acquire and govern territory, the mails and petitions, control over the District of Columbia, the rights of slave owners in international relations, and the regulation of the interstate slave trade. Many of these discussions brought up in new forms the question of the boundary between the state police powers and those of the federal government.

Although the federal guarantee of protection in case of servile insurrection seemed important in anticipation, in practice it was hardly needed. The second guarantee, that relating to fugitive slaves, became a fruitful source of trouble, because of the attempts of northern states to nullify it by "personal liberty laws." Almost from the beginning northerners chafed under the three-fifths compromise. In view of the rarity of resort to direct taxation, it seemed to them that the white inhabitants of the slave states enjoyed a disproportionate representation in Congress for which they actually gave no *quid pro quo*. At various times discontent over the provision was voiced in the form of proposals to amend the Constitution so as to base representation on white population, but no remedy was actually applied until the Civil War brought the emancipation of the Negro by the fourteenth amendment. Ever since the war, the measures by which the southern states have disfranchised the black man without sacrificing any portion of their representation in Congress have been, to party leaders in the North, a grievance which is the direct descendant of the old complaint about the three-fifths compromise.

The claim that Congress had the power to require the people of a proposed state to place prescribed provisions in the state constitution was equivalent to a claim that it could redraw the boundary between its own powers and those of the states, where the state in question was a new one. Although the champions of the doctrine that the rights of new and old states were identical had the better of the argument from the point of view of constitutional theory, northerners did not at the time admit it; and when, during the fifties, the antislavery movement became organized as the Repub-

lican Party, it took the position that Congress should not consent
to the admission of any more slave states. Without admitting that
a state might change its constitution after admission, the Republicans centered their efforts upon excluding slavery from the territories out of which new states would be created. And during the
era of reconstruction, they compelled the southern states to adopt
dictated constitutions in order to regain their representation in the
two houses.

The question of the authority of Congress over the territories
was debated when Louisiana was purchased and became critical
during the Missouri controversy. The passage of the compromise
of 1820 indicated that the majority of congressmen believed that
Congress possesssed the power to exclude slavery from the territories, but many southern members, notably those of the Virginia
delegation, denied it. A few years after the passage of the compromise, the Supreme Court, in American Insurance Company *v.*
Canter,[3] upheld the right of Congress to govern territory, basing
it upon Article IV, section 3, paragraph 2 of the Constitution, but
adding that it "may be the inevitable consequence of the right to
acquire." The great expansion which took place during Polk's
presidency brought the territorial issue to a head.

During the thirties the publication and distribution of abolitionist literature led to efforts to exclude such matter from the mails,
with a consequent discussion of the respective rights of the states
and the national government. During the same decade the presentation of petitions by those who desired to place restrictions of
various kinds upon slavery caused much disputation relating to the
government's powers over the District of Columbia and the territories, which merged with the agitation of the forties following
the acquisition of Texas and the Southwest. During the same years
the rights of slave owners became a controversial point in international relations.

The prohibition of the further importation of slaves from abroad
was accomplished in 1808 without a serious clash of opinion, but
the domestic interstate trade long presented a grave problem. This

[3] 1 Peters 511 (1828). Extract in Johnson, *Readings*, 241–243, and Commager,
Docs., 248–249.

aspect of the slavery question was a corollary of the controversy over the power of the states to control the incoming of undesirable persons. In the Passenger Cases, for example, public interest was due less to the immediate issue than to the fact that the validity of much legislation concerning Negroes was involved in the position which the court should take relative to the scope of the commerce clause. By 1850 the tendency to stress the police power, which we have traced in the decisions of the court, had gone so far that, on the principle of the right of a state by quarantine to protect itself against unwelcome incomers, many political leaders were willing to declare that the regulation of the interstate slave trade was not within the power of Congress.[4]

FEDERAL POWERS OVER TERRITORIES AND NEW STATES

While the Articles of Confederation were pending, Maryland withheld her ratification for some time after all the other states had assented to them, insisting that those states which claimed lands in the West must first cede their claims to Congress.[5] In order to bring about the adoption of the Articles, Congress repeatedly appealed to the claimant states to yield on the land question, and finally promised that all lands ceded should be "settled and formed into distinct republican states, which shall become members of the federal union, and have the same rights of sovereignty, freedom and independence, as the other states." [6]

This pledge of equality for new states to be erected in the West was not received cordially by the conservatives who were accustomed to dominate the political life of the old states, and in framing the Constitution they made an effort to abrogate it. After Gouverneur Morris, Rutledge, King, Gorham, and others had urged that the rule of representation ought to be so fixed as to secure a permanent majority in Congress for the original states, Elbridge Gerry moved that the number of representatives from new states should

---

[4] The following works are of value in studying the legal status of slavery in both its local and interstate aspects: Alice Dana Adams, *The Neglected Period of Anti-Slavery*; John Codman Hurd, *The Law of Freedom and Bondage*; George M. Straud, *A Sketch of the Laws Relating to Slavery*.

[5] See Hockett, *Con. Hist.*, I, 144 *et seq.*

[6] Worthington C. Ford and Gaillard Hunt, eds., *Journals of the Continental Congress*, XVIII, 915.

never exceed that from the old.[7] Mason, Madison, and Wilson championed the cause of equality, and Gerry's motion was lost by a vote of five states to four.[8] But when the committee of detail reported a clause providing for the admission of new states to equal status, the conservatives renewed their attack, and on motion of Morris, a substitute reading was adopted, which *permitted* Congress to admit new states and dropped the phrase promising equality. Morris later, as a member of the committee on style, formulated the final phraseology of the clause as it appears in the Constitution, *viz.*, "New States may be admitted by the Congress into this Union." [9]

Morris and his group seem to have hoped that this wording would make it possible for Congress, when admitting new states, to impose conditions upon them to protect the interests of the old states, which they regarded as paramount. The clause is, in fact, to be regarded as one of the compromises of the Constitution, since its ambiguity postponed the decision of a question on which there was little hope that the members of the Convention could agree. The jealousy of the eastern conservatives towards the West proved persistent, and showed itself in many ways. Especially can it be traced in their attitude towards the admission of new states and the acquisition of new territory, as seen in the matter of the Louisiana Purchase and the admission of the State of Louisiana.[10] The expansionist policy of the Republicans, and the consequent growth of a southern and western interest antagonistic to that of the Northeast, was one of the chief grievances of New England Federalists in the years preceding the War of 1812.[11]

The question of new states was entangled with that of slavery. As early as the Louisiana debate of 1803, the counting of three fifths of the slaves in apportioning representation was felt as a grievance by the free states, and led to several proposals to amend the Constitution. Thus the slavery question aggravated the sectional and party rivalry. Apart from the political evils of which

[7] Farrand, *Records*, I, 533–534, 540, 541, 560; II, 3.
[8] *Ibid.*, 578–579, 584, 605; II, 3.
[9] Art. IV, sec. 3.
[10] See Hockett, *Con. Hist.*, I, 317, 331–332.
[11] *Ibid.*

the North complained as bound up with the westward spread of slavery and slave representation, it may be questioned whether that part of the country was more keenly alive in this period to the iniquity of human bondage than the people of the slave states.

Three provisions of the Constitution touched slavery directly: (1) that which provided that direct taxes and representation in the lower house should be in proportion to the respective numbers of the states, including three fifths of the slaves; (2) that which forbade Congress to interfere with the importation of slaves before 1808; (3) that which provided for the rendition of fugitives from justice or service. The Ordinance of 1787, which included a prohibition of slavery in the Northwest Territory, had been passed before the adoption of the Constitution, but was promptly reenacted by the First Congress. This action indicated belief in the power of Congress to legislate on the subject for the territories, by virtue of the constitutional authority to "dispose of and make all needful Rules and Regulations respecting the Territory or other Property belonging to the United States." [12]

THE SLAVERY QUESTION IN CONGRESS

The question was first brought before Congress after the constitutional period opened by petitions presented, in 1790, by Pennsylvania Quakers and the Pennsylvania Society for the Abolition of Slavery. The latter, signed by Franklin as president, urged Congress to go to the very verge of its power in suppressing the institution. Some southerners betrayed much sensitiveness on the subject; Edanus Burke of South Carolina declared that reference of the petitions to a committee would "blow the trumpet of sedition," but Madison insisted upon discussion and reference, and such action was taken, by a vote of 43 to 11.

The committee reported several resolutions defining the powers of Congress with reference to slavery and indicating a disposition to use them to the utmost. The House, however, struck out all expressions of criticism of the institution and passed four resolutions, declaring that Congress had no power to prohibit the importation of slaves before 1808 nor to interfere with slavery within

[12] Art. IV, sec. 3.

any state, but asserting the power of regulating the foreign slave trade to a limited extent.[13]

These early actions indicate that slavery was regarded as a local or municipal institution which Congress might control in the territories but not in the states. The last land cessions in the old Southwest, however, had been made by the Carolinas and Georgia on condition that slavery should not be prohibited. Just as the North became more and more dissatisfied over the political evils attending the extension of the area of slavery the South grew increasingly conscious of its economic importance. An abundance of new soil was required for the production of cotton as the foreign demand increased. Even in the Northwest a movement arose for the repeal of the antislavery provision of the Ordinance of 1787, and although Congress would not consent, slavery continued, since those in bondage at the time the ordinance was passed were not freed by it, and other bondsmen were brought in under the guise of indented servants.

Congress had passed no antislavery legislation for the territory beyond the Mississippi after the purchase of Louisiana, but it seemed that it might do so, or even require any new states created there to adopt free constitutions. The danger of such a policy gave the South a political as well as an economic interest in the slave system. Due to its more rapid growth, the representation of the North outran that of the South in the House, and by 1819 it had become apparent that prevention of hostile legislation depended upon the admission of new slave states to preserve the balance of sections in the Senate.

THE MISSOURI CONTEST

Such considerations were in the back of men's minds when the legislature of the Territory of Missouri presented to Congress, during the session of 1817–1818, a petition for the admission of the territory as a state. The petition brought up the question of slavery in proposed new states, and precipitated one of the most dangerous constitutional contests in the history of the Republic.

The Missouri contest has three phases: (1) discussion of the ad-

[13] *Ann. of Cong.*, 1 Cong., 1182 *et passim.*

mission of the state under the restrictions proposed by the Tall-madge amendment, session of 1818–1819; (2) discussion of the ad-mission of the state under the restrictions proposed by the Taylor amendment, session of 1819–1820, and adoption of the first com-promise; (3) discussion of the question whether the constitution adopted by the state should be approved, session of 1820–1821, ended by a second compromise.

Following the petition from the territorial legislature a bill for the admission of the state had reached its second reading when Congress adjourned in 1818 for the summer. In November a sec-ond petition was presented by John Scott, the territorial delegate, in accordance with which an enabling act was reported on Feb-ruary 13, 1819. On the same day James Tallmadge, of New York, moved an amendment to the bill, forbidding the further introduc-tion of slavery into the state, and providing for its gradual extinc-tion there.[14] This amendment was adopted by the House but re-jected by the Senate, and the session ended in a deadlock.

The Tallmadge amendment squarely raised the question whether Congress may place any restriction upon a new state at the time of its admission to which the original states are not subject. After the lapse of almost a generation, Congress was now forced to interpret the clause which had enabled the framers of the Constitution to avoid a troublesome problem.

The ablest speech on the affirmative side of this question was that of Senator Rufus King, of New York, while the best on the nega-tive was delivered by Senator William Pinkney, of Maryland. Both men had had distinguished careers. Both had at different times represented the United States at the Court of St. James's. John Marshall regarded Pinkney as the greatest advocate he had ever seen before a court, and as an attorney it is doubtful whether even Webster outshone him. He acted as counsel in many of the most celebrated causes of his time, including the Dartmouth College case, McCulloch v. Maryland, Cohens v. Virginia, and Gibbons v. Ogden. In the Cohens case he upheld the right of the Supreme

[14] *Ibid.*, 15 Cong., 2 sess., 1170. Reprinted in MacDonald, *Select Docs.*, 221. A slightly different wording appears in the Journal of the House of Representatives, which is reproduced in Commager, *Docs.*, 225.

Court to hear appeals from the state courts. Without it, he thought, the Union would be "a mere league or confederacy."

In the Missouri controversy Pinkney came to the defense of the rights of the states, maintaining that the Union is "a confederation of States equal in sovereignty," and that the admission of new states can not change its character. Hence "you can prescribe no conditions which . . . would make the new State less a sovereign State" than the older ones. The admission of new states under restrictions to which the original members were not subject would destroy their equality and result in a new union. Such would be the effect of the Tallmadge amendment. If Congress has power to impose this condition upon Missouri, said Pinkney, "you may squeeze down a new-born sovereign State to the size of a pigmy, and then taking it between finger and thumb, stick it into some nitch of the Union, and still continue, by way of mockery, to call it a State." However, even if adopted the Tallmadge proviso could not bind Missouri, he urged, since the state could disregard the restriction and Congress would have no recourse.[15]

Aside from the unconstitutionality of the proposed condition, Pinkney objected to the injustice to the South of a restriction which would exclude the inhabitants of that section and their property from the territory which belonged to the states in common. In that case, he declared, they would not enjoy all of the rights of citizens of the United States. He held, moreover, that the Louisiana purchase treaty guaranteed to the inhabitants of the territory their property, and this guarantee an antislavery restriction would infringe.[16]

King, one of the men who in the Constitutional Convention had supported Gerry's motion, took the position of Morris and his group

---

[15] The Supreme Court has repeatedly upheld the correctness of Pinkney's contention. See, e.g., Escanaba Co. v. Chicago, 107 U. S. 678 et passim (1883), in which the court said, referring to the State of Illinois: "Whatever the limitation upon her powers as a government whilst in a territorial condition, whether from the ordinance of 1787 or the legislation of Congress, it ceased to have any binding force, except as voluntarily adopted by her, after she became a State of the Union." "She was admitted, and could be admitted, only on the same footing with the original states." Cf. decision in Strader v. Graham, discussed infra, Chap. XII. The doctrine is to be understood as referring to political rights and obligations. Conditions which can be met before admission are not of this class.

[16] Ann. of Cong., 16 Cong., 1 sess., I, 389 et seq.

at that time, and contended that the power to admit new states included that of prescribing the conditions of admission. Much of his speech was devoted to an effort to show the injustice of extending the three-fifths ratio of slave representation to states formed from acquired territory; in other words, the burden of the speech was the political evil of extending the system of slave representation. Whereas Pinkney held that the discretion of Congress was limited to unconditional admission or rejection, King showed that restrictions had been laid, for example, in the case of Louisiana, where it was required that the English language should be used in the courts. As to the exclusion of southerners, he pointed out that the framers of the Constitution had expected the gradual abolition of slavery, and that southerners had joined in passing the Ordinance of 1787 and the act abolishing the slave trade. The guarantee in the French treaty, that the inhabitants of the ceded territory should be admitted to all the rights of citizens of the United States, did not include the right to hold slaves, only those rights "common to the citizens of all the states" being federal. The guarantee of the enjoyment of liberty, property and religion "is expressly confined to the period of territorial government," as is shown by the words "in the meantime." Even if intended to include property in slaves, which was doubtful, "the stipulation is not only temporary, but extends no further than to the property actually possessed by the inhabitants of Missouri, when it was first occupied by the United States." Should the new state rescind the compact by which slavery is excluded, "the judiciary of the United States, on proper application, would immediately deliver from bondage any person detained as a slave in said state." [17]

At this session a bill was passed organizing a separate government for Arkansas Territory. In the debate on this bill the issue of restriction of slavery in the territories was raised, but the connection with the Missouri question prevented a decision on the merits of that controversy, and the bill as passed contained no restrictions.

[17] King's speech was delivered in February, 1819. It is printed in *Niles Register*, XVII, 216 *et seq.*, old ser. (Dec. 4, 1819), and in *Life and Correspondence of Rufus King*, VI, App., 696–703. It was not reported, but was written out later by King, from his notes, hence the versions cited probably do not give the exact words used on the floor.

PUBLIC DISCUSSION

The House vote on the Tallmadge amendment shows a rigid sectional cleavage, only one southern vote being cast for it. When the news of the failure of the bill reached Missouri, it aroused indignant protests from individuals and all kinds of public gatherings. The grand jury of Montgomery County denounced the restrictive amendment as "unlawful, unconstitutional, and oppressive," and declared that they could not admit "the right of any power whatever to impose restrictions on them in the form or substance of a state constitution."[18] A mass meeting at Ste. Genevieve resolved "That the people of Missouri Territory are under no obligation whatever to follow the dictates of congress in the adoption of their state constitution, provided, that constitution be a republican one."[19] In Howard County, delegates representing the Baptist church declared their belief that "the vote of a majority of the last congress, restricting the good people of this territory in the formation of their constitution for a state government" was in direct opposition to the provisions of the Constitution of the United States, and while regretting the existence of slavery and looking forward to the time when emancipation might be safely and justly effected, asserted that the question was one upon which the state possessed the exclusive right to decide.[20]

As the time drew near for the reassembling of Congress, the agitation increased, it being well understood that Missouri would renew her application. The election of members having taken place in the autumn of 1818, before the Missouri issue arose, there was no opportunity for the constituencies to decide the question at the polls, but the friends of restriction sought to arouse public opinion, and by holding mass meetings and passing resolutions to influence the action of Congress. At a meeting of the American Convention for Promoting the Abolition of Slavery, held in Philadelphia, a committee of the Delaware society submitted a report containing an elaborate arguement to prove that Congress possessed

[18] *Niles Register*, XVII, 71 (Oct. 2, 1819).
[19] *Ibid.*
[20] *Ibid.*, 200 (Nov. 27).

the power to impose conditions regarding slavery on new states.[21] A mass meeting at Trenton, N. J., resolved that the permission of slavery in new states would tend to perpetuate the evil, and that the principles of the Constitution and the honor and interests of the country demanded that its extension be prohibited. This meeting appointed a committee to correspond with other bodies engaged in supporting like principles.[22] Similar meetings were held and similar action taken at New York, Philadelphia, and Boston.[23] At the last Daniel Webster was one of the speakers, and served with Josiah Quincy on a committee appointed to send copies of the resolutions adopted to the delegates of the state in Congress. The report of the committee that drafted these resolutions affirmed that the opening of new territory to slaves from old states was contrary to the end sought by the enlightened men of the slave states, while the resolutions reaffirmed the constitutional power of Congress to prohibit the further extension of slavery in new states created beyond the limits of the original territory of the Union. Even at Baltimore a meeting at which the mayor presided passed resolutions, after a lively debate, in favor of congressional action against the further spread of slavery.[24] The geographical extent of the agitation was probably unprecedented.

During the session of Congress of 1819–1820, the subject was debated not only in Congress but in many of the state legislatures. The Virginia House of Delegates resolved that the "General Assembly of Virginia will support the good people of Missouri in their just rights . . . and will cooperate with them in resisting, with manly fortitude, any attempt which Congress may make to impose restraints or restrictions, as the price of their admission, not authorized by the great principles of the constitution, and in violation of their rights, liberties, or happiness." The upper house assumed a less threatening tone, and as finally adopted, the resolutions asserted the right of Missouri to admission without other restrictions than such as might be necessary to guarantee a republican form of government, and called upon the senators and repre-

[21] Ibid., 151 (Nov. 6).
[22] Ibid., 189 (Nov. 20).
[23] Ibid., 199 (Nov. 27); 241 (Dec. 11).
[24] Ibid., 304 (Jan. 1, 1820).

sentatives of the state to use their efforts to secure the admission of Missouri upon such principles.[25]

The legislature of Indiana censured Senator Waller Taylor for voting at the preceding session in favor of the continued admission of slaves into Arkansas Territory.[26]   Both houses of the Pennsylvania legislature voted unanimously that the bill to admit Missouri as a slave state was a measure tending to impair the political relations of the states, to mar the social happiness of the present and future generations, and perpetuate an odious stain, a measure which would be a covenant with crime, and against which duty to God and veneration for the founders of the Republic called for protest.[27]

The general assembly of Kentucky, professing to speak not as the friend or foe of slavery but as the advocate of state's rights, avowed its solemn conviction that the confederated states did not have the right to deprive new states of equal privileges with themselves.[28]   Maryland likewise protested against making the admission of Missouri conditional upon the prohibition of slavery.[29]   The lower house of the New York legislature adopted almost unanimously a declaration that the Constitution clearly gave Congress the right to require the prohibition of slavery as a condition of admission of states formed from territory not within the original bounds of the United States, and desired her senators and representatives to oppose the admission of any state unless the prohibition of slavery were made an indispensable condition.[30]   New Jersey, Delaware, and Ohio passed similar resolutions.[31]   However, in reply to Delaware's request that they vote accordingly, both senators and the one representative of the state expressed the opinion that restriction was unconstitutional.[32]   Public excitement was manifested by newspaper articles, pamphlets, and occasionally by the burning of effigies of congressmen whose votes displeased constituents.[33]

[25] *Ibid.*, 343–344 (Jan. 22); 416 (Feb. 12).
[26] *Ibid.*, 344 (Jan. 22).
[27] *Ibid.*, 296 (Jan. 1).
[28] *Ibid.*, 344 (Jan. 22).
[29] *Ibid.*, 395 (Feb. 5).
[30] *Ibid.*, 399.
[31] *Ibid.*, 343, 400.
[32] *Ibid.*, 434 (Feb. 19).
[33] *Ibid.*, 307 (Jan. 8); 441 (Feb. 26): *National Intelligencer*, March 23, 1820.

THE COMPROMISE

With such evidence of the support of their constituents, the advocates of restriction in the Sixteenth Congress took more advanced ground than at the preceding session. On December 28, 1819, John W. Taylor, of New York, who in the temporary absence of Tallmadge led the northern forces in the House, moved that slavery should be prohibited in the new state except in punishment for crime.[34] This radical temper of the House was met in the Senate by the device of coupling a bill for the unconditional admission of Missouri with one admitting Maine, which, still a part of the State of Massachusetts, was now seeking recognition as a separate state.[35]

Thus challenged, the program of the restrictionists was embodied in an amendment proposed by Taylor on January 26, 1820, which provided "that there shall be neither slavery nor involuntary servitude in the said state, otherwise than in the punishment of crimes," fugitive slaves from other states and persons already legally held to

[34] *Ann. of Cong.*, 16 Cong., 1 sess., 947. Reprinted in MacDonald, *Select Docs.*, 222, and Commager, *Docs.*, 225. See D. S. Alexander, "John W. Taylor, New York's Speaker of the House of Representatives."

The Missouri debate involved a new discussion of the meaning of the provision of the Louisiana Purchase treaty promising the incorporation of the territory into the United States and the admission of the inhabitants to the rights of citizens. See Hockett, *Con. Hist.*, I, 316 *et seq.* The opponents of restriction on Missouri said that the treaty involved the obligation to admit the populated areas as states when they contained a proper number of inhabitants. King thought the treaty lacked precision, but held that the provision constituted a stipulation for statehood. This promise, however, did not imply that the admission should be unconditional. Taylor said that "the object of the article doubtless was to provide for their admission to the rights of citizens, and their incorporation into the American family. The treaty made no provision for the erection of new States in the ceded territory." The treaty-making power could not "impose upon Congress an obligation to . . . admit acquired territory into the Union." Hence he held that the treaty had no bearing on the debate. *Ann. of Cong.*, 15 Cong., 2 sess., 1172–1173.

[35] Massachusetts had consented in June, 1819, to the separation of Maine on condition that she be admitted before March 4, 1820. Maine had framed a constitution and organized a state government before petitioning Congress for recognition, and a simple declaratory act would have admitted her to complete statehood. A bill for this purpose had actually passed the House when the Senate committee reported the Maine bill with the Missouri bill as a rider. The purpose was, of course, to compel northern congressmen to admit Missouri without condition, and in particular to coerce the Massachusetts members from the Maine district. See King, *Life and Correspondence*, VI, 255–258.

service in the territory being expressly excluded from the benefits of the provision.

The situation thus created was critical in the extreme. The dissolution of the Union was openly discussed, and to many seemed imminent.[36] Perhaps only to belief in the genuineness of this danger was due the final success of the efforts at compromise, based on the motion offered by Senator Jesse B. Thomas, of Illinois, on February 17, 1820, "that in all that territory ceded by France to the United States under the name of Louisiana, which lies north of 36° and 30′ north latitude, excepting only such part thereof as is included within the limits of the State contemplated by this act, slavery and involuntary servitude, otherwise than in punishment of crime whereof the party shall have been duly convicted, shall be and is hereby forever prohibited." [37]

When the Maine-Missouri bill with the Thomas amendment was sent to the House, it was rejected, and the House proceeded, on March 1, to pass its own Missouri bill with the Taylor amendment. In the meantime, however, it had agreed to the appointment of a joint committee, and on March 2 both houses, accepting the recommendations of the committee, passed the Senate Missouri bill with the Thomas amendment. Receiving the President's signature, the first Missouri compromise became law. A separate bill for the admission of Maine was passed on March 3.

The amendments of Tallmadge and Taylor had proposed to restrict slavery within the new state; the essence of the compromise was to transfer the restriction from the state to the remaining territory north of the southern boundary of Missouri and west of the Mississippi. The compromise is supposed to have originated with the moderate opponents of restriction, of whom Senator Thomas was the mouthpiece, but it was carried by northern votes. The plan may have been formed as early as the time of the union of the Maine and Missouri bills, and it is not unlikely that Monroe was in the secret as he surprised Adams on January 8 by his confidence that a compromise would be found which would satisfy all

[36] See *Memoirs* of John Quincy Adams, IV, 525; V, 13, and King, *Life and Correspondence*, VI, 286–287.

[37] *Ann. of Cong.*, 16 Cong., 1 sess., I, 427. Reprinted in MacDonald, 222, and Commager, 225.

parties.[38]   The line dividing slavery and freedom in the trans-mississippi region had been suggested by Louis McLane, of Dela-ware, in the course of the Arkansas debate in February, 1819.

The Thomas amendment was adopted by the Senate on February 17, 1820, by a vote of 34 to 10.   Every northern senator except those from Indiana voted Aye; the Southwest gave 9 affirmative votes and one negative, while the South voted 3 to 7 against the amendment.   The final vote in the House stood 134 to 42.   The extremists on both sides voted Nay, those in the North opposing any admission of slavery to the transmississippi region outside of the State of Louisiana, and those of the South opposing any restric-tion whatever.[39]   Only five northern votes were negative, while the southern vote was 38 to 37 for the measure.   The opposition centered around the Virginia state's rights and strict construction school, the delegation of that state voting 4 to 18 against the compromise.

VIRGINIA ON COMPROMISE

The strong sentiment in Virginia against all compromise for a time threatened Monroe's popularity and seemed likely even to influence his chances for reelection.   As stated above, Monroe ex-pected the success of compromise early in the year; and the situa-tion in Washington led him secretly to favor it.   Through a son-in-law, George Hay, he kept in touch with events at Richmond, and endeavored to influence public opinion in favor of compromise by sending to Hay an "Extract of a letter from a gentleman in Wash-ington to his friend in Richmond," in which the course of Rufus King was sharply attacked, and compromise recommended as the best means of defeating the designs of the northern politicians. Commenting on this "extract" the editor of the *Enquirer* wrote (Feb. 19): "The scheme of compromise has produced one general burst of reprobation." [40]

About the same time James Barbour, one of Virginia's senators, wrote confidentially to Charles Yancey, a member of the Virginia

[38] Adams, *Memoirs*, IV, 499.
[39] *Niles Register*, XVIII, 30 (March 11, 1820).
[40] See documents printed in *Congressional Globe*, 30 Cong., 2 sess., App., 63–67.

caucus for nominating a presidential electoral ticket, stating that the President and some members of the cabinet advised acceptance of the compromise. This information divulged by Yancey in the caucus led to adjournment without nominations, in order to await news of the fate of the Missouri question. Hay, writing to his wife, expressed the opinion that Monroe should let things take their own course, and reject any bill carrying restrictions on Missouri, or on the territories, if he thought Congress had no right to restrict them or should not exercise that right. H. St. George Tucker wrote Barbour on February 11, that Virginia was unwilling to purchase the election of Monroe at the price of compromise; that Monroe must choose between his southern and northern friends.

Yancey's letters indicate that the excitement soon subsided, although without any reaction in favor of compromise. On February 17 he wrote that he had seen a letter written by the President in which he said that he would not consent to restrictions in any manner. Evidently Monroe had caught the direction of the wind in his home state. The adjourned meeting of the caucus was to be held that evening, and Yancey expected no opposition to Monroe. The caucus, however, limited its action to the choice of an electoral ticket of "staunch" men, who were to act as circumstances dictated.[41]

THE PROPOSED VETO

In view of this sentiment in Virginia and his own constitutional scruples, Monroe drafted a veto message. One portion of this draft set forth the view that in providing for the admission of new states, the intention of the Constitution was that they should be admitted with all the rights and immunities of the original states; another portion maintained that restriction on territories is repugnant at least to the principles, if not the letter, of the Constitution, because intended to predetermine future policy of states, and because of operating unequally on the old states.

Apparently the draft was intended to sketch the principles on which the President's veto could be applied either to legislation

[41] For all of this correspondence, see *ibid.*, and *William and Mary College Quarterly*, First ser., X, 5–24 (July, 1901).

restricting Missouri or to a compromise affecting the territories. As the probability of the passage of the compromise increased, Monroe consulted his friends in regard to the constitutionality of restriction when applied to the territories.   Madison's reply was that restriction under the constitutional power to pass needful regulations would be an abuse of power because opposed to the great principle of self-government.[42]   Others of the Virginia school laid the stress on the equal rights of the states in relation to the territories.   Monroe writing to Judge Roane on February 16, showed sensitiveness at this point.   Said he: "As slavery is recognized by the constitution, it is very unjust to restrain the owner from carrying his slave into a Territory, and retaining his right to him there; but whether the power to do this has not been granted, is the point on which I have doubts, and on which I shall be glad to receive your opinion.   If I can be satisfied that the Constitution forbids the restraint, all further inquiry with me will be at an end." [43]

It is difficult to account for Monroe's vacillation but the opposition of his state to all compromise was doubtless one reason for it. Whether he became satisfied that acceptance of the compromise would not cost him its support, or whether he decided to take the risk, when the compromise bill came to him for signature he called the cabinet together and asked the members two questions: (1) had Congress the constitutional right to prohibit slavery in a territory? (2) did the compromise section apply to territories only while in the territorial state, or continue after they became states?

The cabinet, although Calhoun, Crawford, and Wirt were slave-holders, unanimously answered the first question in the affirmative.[44] In answer to the second, however, all but Adams held that the compromise would not bind the future states.   To avoid the embarrassment likely to result from this difference of opinion, Calhoun suggested that the second question be changed to an inquiry as to

[42] This opinion strongly suggests "squatter sovereignty."   An even more pronounced assertion of it had already been made during the Arkansas debate, by a North Carolina member, who objected to the proposed restriction on slavery in that territory on the ground that it would take away from the people of the territory "the natural and constitutional right of legislating for themselves."   See J. P. Gordy, *Political History*, II, 412.

[43] *Cong. Globe*, 30 Cong., 2 sess., App.

[44] Adams, *Memoirs*, V, 5–12.

whether the compromise section was constitutional. Put in this form, each cabinet member interpreting the word "forever" in his own way, all answered in the affirmative, and Monroe, accepting this opinion, signed the bill.

THE MISSOURI CONSTITUTION

The scene now shifted to Missouri, where a constitutional convention was to meet in June. After a sharp contest, the friends of slavery won complete control, and the first article considered was one taking from the legislature the right to manumit slaves without the consent of their owners or payment of full value therefor.[45] This provision was adopted, as well as one which made it the duty of the legislature to pass laws forbidding the immigration of free Negroes, and on July 17 the constitution with these provisions was adopted as a whole, without being submitted to the people for approval. In August Alexander McNair was elected governor, and John Scott, the territorial delegate, was chosen representative in Congress.[46]

Even before the meeting of the Missouri convention, there were indications that the fight against the admission of the state would be renewed when Congress met again, and in an editorial Niles had warned the Missourians against any indiscreet clauses which might give a pretext for a renewal of the contest in Congress.[47] The clauses just mentioned were well calculated to bring about such a renewal. The paragraph requiring legislation to prevent the incoming of free Negroes was especially open to attack, since it was easy to charge that it conflicted with the pledge in the federal Constitution that "the Citizens of each State shall be entitled to

[45] *Niles Register*, XVIII, 400 (July 27, 1820). Such action had been anticipated by the discussion before the convention met. One writer had advocated taking from the legislature the power to emancipate lest the popular will might sometime be disobeyed, under the influence of agitation by the "foreign enemy," whose "advance guard of preachers, voters, candidates, resolution-makers, writers in the Gazettes," has just arrived. *Ibid.*, XVIII, 258–259 (June 10, 1820). Senator Benton later claimed to have inspired the article in the constitution to prevent discussion of slavery. *Thirty Years View*, I, 8–9.
[46] *Niles Register*, XVIII, 448 (August 19). See *ibid.*, XIX, 112, 113 (Oct. 14 and 21). For the constitution see MacDonald, 225, or Commager, 226–227.
[47] *Ibid.*, XVIII, 258–259.

all Privileges and Immunities of Citizens in the several States." [48]
But the term "citizen" had not yet been defined, and there was a
general tendency to deny that title to free Negroes. A number of
the states already had laws similar to that contemplated in Missouri,
for the purpose of excluding them.[49] Nor was there any agreement
as to what constituted the privileges and immunities of citizens.[50]
Nevertheless this clause of the state constitution threatened for a

[48] Art. IV, sec. 2. When the Articles of Confederation were before it for adoption, the South Carolina legislature had proposed to substitute for the privileges
and immunities clause the specific provisions that the "free white inhabitants" of
each state should enjoy the privileges and immunities of free citizens in the several states "according to the law of such states respectively, for the government
of their own free white inhabitants," which should include "all the privileges of
trade and commerce, subject to the same duties, impositions and restrictions as
the inhabitants thereof." See Hockett, *Con. Hist.*, I, 144–145.

[49] Among these were Kentucky, Delaware and South Carolina. Within a few
years North Carolina followed their example, and even Illinois adopted similar
legislation in 1853. Missouri did not comply with the injunction in her constitution until 1847. See McLaughlin, *Con. Hist.*, 381, note 22. The Kentucky constitution is said to have supplied the model for Missouri. See Frank H. Hodder,
"Side Lights on the Missouri Compromises."

[50] In 1797, Judge Samuel Chase, in the Maryland case of Campbell *v.* Morris (3
Harr. and McHen., 535), held that the privileges and immunities clause merely
prohibits a state from discriminating against the citizens of other states in favor
of its own. Justice Bushrod Washington, in an *obiter dictum* pronounced in
1825, in the circuit court in the eastern district of Pennsylvania (Corfield *v.*
Coryell, *Federal Cases*, No. 3, 230, pp. 551–552), declared that the phrase referred
to the fundamental natural rights of citizens in all free governments—"protection
by the government; the enjoyment of life and liberty, with the right to acquire
and possess property of every kind, and to pursue and obtain happiness and safety;
subject nevertheless to such restraints as the government may justly prescribe for
the general good of the whole. The right of a citizen of one state to pass through,
or to reside in any other state, for purposes of trade, agriculture, professional pur-
suits, or otherwise; to claim the benefit of the writ of habeas corpus; to institute
and maintain actions of any kind in the courts of the state; to take, hold and
dispose of property, either real or personal; and an exemption from higher taxes
or impositions than are paid by the other citizens of the state; may be mentioned
as some of the particular privileges and immunities of citizens . . . to which may
be added the elective franchise, as regulated and established by the laws or constitution of the state in which it is to be exercised." The tests laid down by these
jurists did not determine whether free Negroes were or were not citizens, but
they made it apparent that if they were citizens they were in many states not
treated as such. Unfortunately they left the status of women and minors equally
uncertain. See *infra*, discussion of the Dred Scott case and the Slaughter House
cases. On the whole subject of the privileges and immunities of citizens see Roger
Howell, *The Privileges and Immunities of State Citizenship;* A. J. Lien, *Privileges
and Immunities of Citizens of the United States;* W. S. Meyers, "The Privileges
and Immunities of Citizens in the Several States"; Irving B. Richman, "Citizenship
in the United States"; Frederick Van Dyne, *Citizenship of the United States.*

time to prevent the consummation of the process of admission. Legislatures began to reaffirm their former declarations of principles, and to instruct their state delegations to oppose the admission of Missouri under the proposed constitution.[51]

This agitation raised the question of the status of Missouri. Having framed a constitution and instituted a state government under an act of Congress authorizing such a course, was her condition that of statehood, or was the acceptance of her constitution by Congress necessary to complete her admission? If not a state without further action of Congress, what would be her status if Congress failed to act? [52]

Some of the friends of Missouri advanced the doctrine that no further steps were necessary to make her a state. Upon the inauguration of the state government, the St. Louis *Enquirer* had said that Missouri would appear at the approaching session "as a sovereign state, according to the law of congress, and not as a territorial orphan," and would be able to defend her rights.[53] In his first message to the legislature, on September 19, Governor McNair wrote: "From the dependent condition of a territorial government, we have passed into a sovereign and independent state." He evidently thought that some further action on the part of Congress was necessary, however, for he added that the constitution adopted gave "every reason to expect that we shall without further difficulty, be admitted into the federal union." [54]

In some quarters there was a disposition to believe that the rights

[51] See *Niles Register*, XVIII, 337–339 (July 8, 1820), and XIX, 178–179 (Nov. 18, 1820), for examples of the agitation.

[52] When does a territory become a state? On the theory that "governments derive their just powers from the consent of the governed," it could be argued that the action of the people within the geographical area affected was the determining factor. However, this action is only one of several factors, since the people of the area are only a part of the population of the United States, associated in a federal union. It follows that to become a state in the Union the consent of the rest of the United States, given by action of Congress, is necessary to constitute a new state in the Union—and our constitutional system knows no such thing as a state *outside* of the Union and yet within the United States. See Scott *v.* Jones, 5 Howard 343 (1847), and compare Lincoln's discussion of secession in inaugural address and messages. *Cf.* theory underlying congressional reconstruction and decision of Supreme Court in Texas *v.* White, *infra*, Chap. XVII.

[53] *Niles Register*, XVIII, 451 (Aug. 26, 1820).

[54] *Ibid.*, XIX, 116 (Oct. 21).

of free Negroes should be left to the determination of the courts; that the constitution of Missouri should be accepted and the whole question of conformity to the federal Constitution be left to judicial determination. The editor of *Niles Register* dissented. In an editorial in the issue of October 21, 1820, he noted that several of the old states had passed laws for the exclusion of free blacks, which he declared would necessarily yield to the express letter of the Constitution whenever tested. Such laws were a question for the judiciary; but in the case of Missouri, to sanction her constitution would be to pass a law which was plainly unconstitutional. The status of the state was passed upon, however, by the circuit court for St. Louis County, in December, the opinion being that the state "was not only theoretically formed, but in full and constitutional operation, as regarded the Constitution of the United States and that of the State of Missouri." [55]

It was seriously proposed that at the opening of Congress the senators from Missouri should be seated without awaiting formal action on her constitution, but Monroe told Barbour that such action would be imprudent.[56] The predicament was an awkward one for the friends of Missouri, who for the most part agreed with the restrictionists that acceptance of her constitution was a preliminary essential to her admission. "The anti-restriction members, as well as others," wrote Niles, "regretted the existence of certain clauses in the constitution of Missouri, as unnecessary, and calculated only to create doubts and excite opposition." [57] Monroe wrote to Madison on November 16 that it was much to be regretted that Missouri had furnished a pretext for the revival of discussion,[58] and Madison replied on the 19th that it would make an awkward precedent to sanction the constitution, even with a declaration nullifying the objectionable clause, as the state might not accede to the annulment. He recommended a suspension of admission until the constitution was amended.[59]

The constitution was presented to the House of Representatives

---

[55] *Ibid.*, XIX, 372 (Feb. 3, 1821).
[56] King, *Life and Correspondence*, VI, 428.
[57] *Niles Register*, XIX, 266 (Dec. 23, 1820).
[58] *Cong. Globe*, 30 Cong., 2 sess., App., pp. 63–67.
[59] *Ibid.*

by Scott, the territorial delegate, on November 20, and referred to a committee of which William Lowndes of South Carolina was chairman. The committee reported a resolution declaring that Missouri was admitted to the Union as a state on an equal footing with the original states.

The old restrictionist majority, many of whom had voted for the compromise, refused to support any measure looking to the admission of the state. Some light on their attitude may be gained from King's correspondence. On November 21 he wrote to his son Charles that if the immigration clause had been omitted, the question of admission would have been taken without debate.[60] To Christopher Gore of Massachusetts he wrote a few days later: "We once thought of proposing to amend the Resolution to admit, by pointing out such provisions . . . as are repugnant to [the Constitution], and for this defect disapproving the Constitution, and sending it back to the People for revision and amendment." [61] This plan was abandoned under the feeling that those who fathered it would be bound to vote for the acceptance of the constitution when amended, which, as former restrictionists, they disliked to do.

"If to avoid this difficulty we propose to add the clause of restriction, we open the discussion of the last year. In these circumstances let those who have contributed to produce the actual embarrassment [s], take their own measures to get rid of them. We may act defensively, vote for what we approve, and against what we disapprove; in this course, come what may, we shall be free to act consistently, and without entanglement from former votes." [62]

The Lowndes resolution was killed on December 13, before its third reading, by a vote of 93 to 79. In January, the Senate proposed a resolution recognizing Missouri as a state, provided that the recognition should not be construed to give the assent of Congress to any provision in the Missouri constitution "if any such there be," which contravened the federal Constitution. Vain efforts were made to instruct the judiciary committee to report on the relation of the Union and Missouri; motions to insert the words "the State

[60] King, *Life and Correspondence*, VI, 356.
[61] *Ibid.*, 364.
[62] *Ibid.*

of" before Missouri in the records, and to insert the words "territory of," both failed. The effort to define the status of Missouri reached its climax in connection with the count of the electoral vote in February.[63] When the returns from Missouri were reached, Congress could not decide whether she was or was not a state, and consequently could not determine whether or not her vote should be included. Since the result of the election would not be affected in either case, it was finally decided that if any question was raised as to Missouri's vote, it should be announced that if it was counted, the result would be   votes for James Monroe; while if it was not counted, the result would be   votes for James Monroe; so that, in either case, he was reelected.

THE SECOND COMPROMISE

On February 2 Clay secured the appointment by the House of a committee, composed of members of all shades of opinion. The report of this committee on February 10 deprecated any effort to reopen the question of restriction, which had been settled by the compromise of the previous year, and recommended such an amendment of the Senate resolution as would admit Missouri upon condition that no law should ever be passed preventing citizens of any of the states from settling within her bounds. Upon the rejection of this report, *Niles Register* alleged that an excitement prevailed such as had never before been witnessed in the House of Representatives.[64]

At length William Brown of Kentucky moved the repeal of the compromise, on the ground that the condition agreed to, that is, the admission of Missouri, had not been complied with. The discussion eventuated in the appointment of a joint committee, at the solicitation of Clay, the report of which recommended the admission of Missouri on condition that the immigration clause should never be construed to authorize the passage of any laws by which any citizen of either of the states should be excluded from the enjoyment of any of the privileges and immunities guaranteed by the Constitution of the United States. Upon receipt of such

[63] James A. Woodburn, "Permanent Significance of the Missouri Compromise," 277, 291.
[64] Feb. 17, 1821, p. 401.

a promise from the legislature of Missouri, the President was authorized to proclaim the admission of the state into the Union.[65]

The joint committee was largely the work of Clay, whose effort won him the title of the Great Pacificator. Benton says that "it was well known that he drew up the list of names himself, and distributed it through the House to be voted." [66] The report was adopted on February 26, by a vote in the House of 87 to 81. This vote was as decidedly southern as the vote on the first compromise had been northern. Of the negative votes, only one was cast by a southern man, John Randolph voting to the last against all compromise. The North cast only 18 of the affirmative votes.

In accordance with this new compromise, the governor of Missouri convoked the legislature in June. Reviewing the struggle in his message, the governor said: "Although we had the best grounded hopes of immediate admission into the union, such has been the warm excitement produced by the Missouri question, both in and out of congress, that we have not only been disappointed in this our just expectation, but the nation itself has been brought to the verge of ruin." Since "better principles and a milder policy" had been adopted, however, the governor recommended the passage of such an act as the resolution of Congress required,[67] and accepting the suggestion, the legislature passed an act which, had President Monroe been less inclined to bring the issue to a speedy termination, might well have resulted in further controversy.

This act quoted the condition imposed by Congress, asserted that the people of Missouri virtually assented to the condition by applying for admission to the Union under the Constitution, declared that Congress had no constitutional power to annex any condition to the admission of Missouri, and that the legislature had no power to change the operation of the state constitution, but concluded that, since the promise of the legislature would not affect in any way the constitution of either state or nation, but might promote an earlier enjoyment by the people of Missouri of "their vested

---

[65] *U. S. Stat. at Large*, III, 645. Reprinted in MacDonald, 226, and Commager, 227.
[66] *Thirty Years View*, I, 10.
[67] *Niles Register*, XX, 300 (July 7, 1821).

federal rights," they consented to give the required assurance.[68] Monroe saw fit to accept this assurance and on August 10 issued the proclamation.

SUMMARY AND SIGNIFICANCE

The Missouri debates were far-reaching. Besides the questions of the power of Congress to impose conditions upon states when admitted, and of the extent of the power to regulate territories, many other issues were involved. Among them were: the binding effect of treaties; what is a "republican form of government"; the power of Congress or a legislature to bind its successors; the binding effect of the Ordinance of 1787 on the states created in the Northwest Territory; the meaning of the word "citizen"; the rights pertaining to United States and state citizenship; and the power of Congress over immigration, interstate migration, and slavery in the states.

The southerners interpreted the effort to restrict slavery in Missouri and the transmississippi territory as a part of the old-time hostility of New England Federalists to the purchase of Louisiana. The prominence of Rufus King and his frank avowal of hostility to the extension of the political power of slavery led the South also to the belief that he was seeking to utilize the slavery issue to resurrect the moribund Federalist Party. By creating a sectional alignment the old Federalist leaders might hope to dominate a party which would control not only the North but the Union.[69] Even John Quincy Adams believed that King had set on foot a "concert of measures" which was to form the basis for a new alignment of parties on sectional grounds.[70]

Jefferson shared this view, it seems, and nothing alarmed him more than such a possibility. The old division between Federalists

[68] *Ibid.*, 388–389 (Aug. 18, 1821).

[69] See editorial in *Louisiana Advertiser*, April 11, 1820; letters of Madison to Monroe, Feb. 10, 1820, and Monroe to Roane, Feb. 16, 1820; "Extract of a letter from a gentleman in Washington to his friend in Richmond;" editorial in *Richmond Enquirer*, Feb. 19, 1820; all in *Congressional Globe*, 30 Cong., 2 sess., App., 63–67. See also Ford's *Writings of Jefferson*, X, 161, 171, 175, 179, 279, and Benton's *Thirty Years View*, I, 10. Cf. Everett S. Brown, *The Missouri Compromises and Presidential Politics, 1820–1825*.

[70] *Memoirs*, IV, 529.

and Republicans had been bad enough, but he thought it "threatened nothing, because it existed in every State, and united them together by the fraternism of party." The revival of Federalism as a northern antislavery party, however, threatened the perpetuity of the Union. "The coincidence of a marked principle, moral and political, with a geographical line, once conceived, I feared would never more be obliterated from the mind; that it would be recurring on every occasion and renewing irritations, until it would kindle such mutual and mortal hatred, as to render separation preferable to eternal discord." [71]

There is no sufficient evidence that King had designs such as were attributed to him, but his influence was so widespread as to give plausibility to the conjecture. The ardor of some of the former Federalists, like Quincy, cooled measurably when they learned that the restriction movement was regarded by the South as a trick of political leaders. Apparently they did not desire, by pushing such a measure, to revive the stigma of being Hartford Conventionists. King himself referred to the southern interpretation of his course as "illiberal," which convicts him of hypocrisy if that interpretation was correct. [72]

By the compromise settlement the North won an apparent victory by securing the consent of the South to the exclusion of slavery from by far the greater portion of the territory acquired from France. To be sure, it was possible to maintain that the exclusion was limited to the territorial period; that the limitation was unconstitutional; and since it rested only upon an act of Congress, there was the possibility of repealing that act. All of these possibilities were to be realized, so that the compromise proved, as compromises usually do, only a temporary settlement. Moreover, the harmony of sectional relations was restored only on the surface, for, as Jefferson feared, the strife engendered a deep-seated mutual distrust, so that, in the end, the sectional cleavage was all the deeper on account of the Missouri struggle.

[71] To William Short, April 13, 1820, in *Writings* (Washington edn.), VII, 158. Parties, as it turned out, did not form along sectional lines until the 1850's; then Jefferson's words proved to be prophetic.

[72] The question of King's plans for a new party is more fully examined in H. C. Hockett, "Rufus King and the Missouri Compromise."

IX

ISSUES RAISED BY SLAVERY (*Continued*)

SLAVERY AND THE POWER OVER COMMERCE

EARLY in the nineteenth century, a number of states passed acts requiring that free Negroes entering their ports from other states or nations should be held in custody until the vessels on which they came were ready to depart. In arguing the Passenger Cases, Van Buren, supporting New York's act, cited laws of no less than fifteen of the states, both northern and southern, which forbade or regulated the incoming of free Negroes.[1] The right of states to pass such measures had been debated in 1819–1820, when northern members of Congress had attacked the clause in the proposed constitution of Missouri which required the legislature to exclude free Negroes coming from other states. They insisted that such exclusion would violate the constitutional guarantee to citizens of each state, of the privileges and immunities of citizens in the several states. The debate was inconclusive; it led to no agreement as to whether the free Negroes were to be regarded as citizens, or as to what constituted the privileges and immunities of citizens.[2]

As early as 1820 a discriminatory act of this type had come before a federal circuit court in the case of *The Brig Wilson*, but Marshall had not found it necessary to pronounce on the validity of the statute. In 1823, however, Justice Johnson, in circuit court for South Carolina, had held an act of that state to be unconstitutional on the ground that it violated the right to regulate commerce between the states and with foreign nations, which was "a paramount and exclusive right" of Congress.[3]

South Carolina disregarded Johnson's decision; but the case of Gibbons *v.* Ogden led to further discussion. Emmet, Oakley's associate, in attempting to show that the states possessed a power

---

[1] Warren, *Supreme Court*, II, 181.
[2] Jay W. McKee, *State Exclusion Laws*.
[3] *Warren*, I, 621–628.

concurrent with that of Congress in regulating commerce, cited an act of Congress of 1803 which penalized persons found guilty of importing slaves into states which prohibited their admission. This statutory recognition by Congress of the right of states to exclude slaves, he held, showed that they possessed concurrent power. Marshall's opinion, that this power in the states was derived from the clause forbidding Congress to exclude slaves prior to 1808, and formed an exception to the power of Congress for a limited period only, frightened the South because it intimated that after 1808 the states would no longer be able to control the immigration of slaves or other persons.[4]

During the thirties this issue became entangled with the question of fugitive slaves. Sometimes ships leaving southern ports carried off fugitives through connivance of officers or crew. Such acts were regarded by southerners as kidnapping or stealing, and under their laws the perpetrators were criminals. When they sought to extradite such persons, and bring them for trial to the states in which their crimes were alleged to have been committed, they encountered difficulties due to the unsympathetic attitude of northern officials. In 1837 and again in 1838 the governor of Maine declined to surrender persons indicted for violation of the criminal statutes of Georgia; and in 1839 Governor Seward of New York took a similar stand with reference to persons indicted in Virginia.

In this latter episode a vessel had left Norfolk carrying a slave who had been stolen by three members of the crew. The vessel took the slave to New York, and the governor of Virginia made a requisition upon Governor Seward for the rendition of the three men as fugitives from justice. Governor Seward, in refusing to give them up, declared that the Constitution required delivery only of persons who had committed offenses universally recognized as crimes. The laws of New York did not recognize that one man could be the property of another, and therefore did not recognize the crime of "man-stealing." The Virginia law making the theft of a slave a felony he held made an offense of an act which was not a crime within the meaning of the Constitution.

Thus the slavery struggle brought into question the interpreta-

[4] *Ibid.*

tion of the "fugitive from justice" provision of the Constitution. Governor Seward couched his reply in terms derived from international law rather than the Constitution.   Under the law of nations no country enforces the penal laws of another, and no right of extradition exists between countries except as it may be provided for by treaty; the rule made the United States an asylum for political refugees from the reactionary countries of Europe.   Even so, Governor Seward failed to regard the terms of the Constitution, which certainly required no less of the states of the Union in their reciprocal relations than a treaty between two nations.   Many years later the Supreme Court ruled that the obligation of the authorities of a state to surrender fugitives from justice rested merely on good faith, and could not be enforced by the federal authorities.[5]   If this decision had been made at the time of the New York-Virginia dispute, it would only have given the slave states additional cause for discontent, as showing the inadequacy of their supposed constitutional guarantees.   As it was, the Virginia legislature passed resolutions denouncing Governor Seward's refusal to surrender the kidnappers as a palpable and dangerous violation of the Constitution.   New York, on the other hand, passed an act granting jury trial to Negroes claimed as fugitives.[6]

Not content with mere words, the Virginia legislature enacted a measure to guard against the escape of slaves by water, and specifically denied to New York vessels some of the privileges accorded to boats from elsewhere.   South Carolina adopted a similar measure, and the southern papers predicted that it would "not be long before every State in the South . . . will array itself under the example of Virginia against the encroachments of New York on the Constitution and the dangers of these encroachments."[7]

There can be no doubt that these acts were unconstitutional. That they might be so declared by the Supreme Court was apprehended at the time, and the friends of state's rights who had hitherto feared the too liberal interpretation of the "necessary and proper" and "general welfare" clauses began to point out that the commerce

[5] Kentucky v. Dennison, 24 Howard 66 (1861).
[6] Ames, State Docs., 232–238.
[7] Warren, II, 169.

clause should be placed beside them as a source of danger. In 1841 one southern newspaper voiced its apprehensions in these words: "There have hitherto been said to be two 'sweeping clauses' in the Constitution, threatening to sweep off the rights of the States and the People; first the 'necessary and proper' clause; second the 'general welfare' clause. But a third sweeping clause has been sprung, which threatens to do as much mischief as its two predecessors. This is the power over commerce." [8] "In the name of Heaven," exclaimed this editor, "what power would the States have of protecting the lives and property of their own citizens, if this sweeping power of Commerce were admitted? What becomes of our quarantine laws, inspection laws, pilot laws—laws which would prevent the seeds of yellow fever from being imported from New Orleans? What becomes of the power to keep the citizens of New York from stealing our property and refusing to give it up or those who stole it, if we cannot pass such a bill as may authorize us to search their vessels, or to demand bond or security for the indemnity of masters, whose slaves may be stolen, by every kidnapper?" [9]

On the other side, the conservative northern press deplored the "war of commercial interdicts" which impended. "If every State may take the laws into its own hands, in regard to questions involving the regulation of commerce among the several States, and if the States are to be allowed to do what Congress cannot do, that is, to give preference by regulations of commerce to the vessels of one State over those of another, or to those of all other States over those of any one State—then has the Constitution failed in one among the most important of the purposes for which it was established." [10]

This issue was the same question of police power versus power to regulate commerce which was giving the Supreme Court so much trouble during these same years. The decision in New York v. Miln tended to reassure the friends of state power, but the License Cases had not yet come up, and the trend of the court to-

[8] *Richmond Enquirer*, March 4, 1841, quoted *ibid.*, II, 169–170.
[9] *Ibid.*
[10] *National Intelligencer*, Feb. 17, 1841, quoted *ibid.*

wards broad interpretation of the police power was not yet very apparent. In the early forties the state laws excluding free Negroes came under discussion once more. Disregarding the judgment of Justice Johnson in 1823, the right of the state to enact exclusion laws, indeed, the right of the state to control the whole matter of interstate commerce so far as it related to persons, was defended as an essential part of the police power. There appeared a disposition, moreover, to regard such police regulations as paramount law. Laws excluding free Negroes, it was said, like quarantine laws, were necessary as a "protection against what is infinitely worse than physical contagion—the introduction of free persons of color into a community where slavery exists, with the means of . . . deluding them into insurrection. . . . On the very same principle by which a State may prevent the introduction of infected persons or goods and articles dangerous to the person and property of its citizens, it may exclude paupers, incendiaries, vicious, dishonest and corrupt persons such as may endanger the morals, health or property of the people. The whole subject is necessarily connected with the internal police of a State, no item of which has to any extent been delegated to Congress." [11]

Such was the argument of Senator John H. Lumpkin of Georgia, in 1840. It was presently extended to the interstate slave trade. The next year the Supreme Court gave a judgment in Groves v. Slaughter [12] which encouraged the South to believe that that tribunal would never hold that the congressional power over interstate commerce extended to the slave trade. The case involved a provision of the Mississippi constitution of 1832, which declared that the introduction of slaves as merchandise should be prohibited on and after the first day of May, 1833. The question before the court was whether a note given for the purchase of slaves from without the state, after that date, was valid. Collaterally the issue was raised whether the clause in the constitution was invalid as conflicting with the power of Congress over interstate commerce. As a majority of the judges agreed that the constitutional provision contemplated legislation before it could become operative, and

[11] Quoted *ibid.*, 171–172.
[12] 15 Peters 449 (1841).

therefore held that the note was valid, it was not necessary to determine the compatibility of the provision with the power of Congress. Judge McLean, however, gave an opinion, which was frankly *obiter*, on the right of a state to regulate the slave trade. Although he did not accept the concurrent power of the state to regulate interstate commerce, he chose to regard slaves not as objects of commerce but as persons, over whose incoming the state had control by virtue of the police power. This he intimated was paramount to the commercial power of Congress—an opinion which is quite in harmony with the view which he was presently to express in the License Cases.[13] This right of the state, he held, was higher and deeper than the Constitution, because it rested on the law of self-preservation.

By this *obiter* opinion the laws of South Carolina, Georgia, Louisiana, and other states excluding free Negroes seemed to be vindicated, and one Mississippi paper predicted that "all the abolitionists . . . will now abandon so much of their petitions as call on Congress to regulate or prohibit the transportation of slaves."[14]

In 1845 the Territory of Florida applied for admission to statehood with a constitution which expressly empowered its legislature to prohibit the immigration of free Negroes. A debate ensued in Congress which echoed the arguments against the similar provision in the constitution framed by Missouri a quarter of a century earlier. Again the men of the North contended that free Negroes were citizens who could not be excluded from any state without violating the privileges and immunities clause, and George Evans of Maine offered a proviso to the bill for admitting Florida denying the power of the proposed state to prevent their entrance. The southern argument struck the note which McLean had sounded in his dictum. "Each State," said Berrien of Georgia, "has the power to protect itself—a power which would never be surrendered. It

---

[13] See *supra*, Chap. VI. McLean declared that Congress had exclusive control over interstate commerce, and seemed to think that the court had so decided. Taney corrected his erroneous statement. Although it was not yet known by the public, Taney already believed in the concurrent commercial power of the states. He agreed with McLean that each state might decide for itself whether it would admit slaves, but based his opinion on different grounds.—Swisher, *Taney*, 397–399, 418–419; Weisenburger, *Life of McLean*, 166.

[14] Quoted by Warren, II, 73.

is, therefore, useless for the other States to attempt to deprive any one of them of the right . . . to suppress a moral pestilence within her borders. I shall rejoice to see this question carried to the Supreme Court for its decision. I have not the slightest doubt that the power of the States to pass police laws for their own protection will be recognized." [15]

When Berrien delivered this speech the Passenger Cases were already on the docket of the Supreme Court, and their decision promised to involve the very issue on which he desired the court's opinion. "Everything may be said of them" (the Massachusetts laws out of which the Passenger Cases grew), wrote Webster, "that Massachusetts says against South Carolina." [16] The supporters of these northern laws were forced to the same reliance upon the police power which underlay the southern arguments, but inconsistency did not cause them to hesitate. In this as in previous cases the court prudently made every effort to avoid any broad definition of the scope of the commerce power; it confined its decision to the particular statutes drawn into question, well knowing that the laws of the southern states were also involved. But the decision was certain to arouse the fear and defiance of the South. The *Charleston Mercury* said that the points decided "sweep away our inspection laws enacted to prevent the abduction of our slaves in Northern vessels. They sweep away also all our laws enacted to prevent free colored persons—citizens from Massachusetts—or whatever abolition region, from entering our ports and cities. Thus it seems as if the Union is to be so administered as to strip the South of all power of self-protection and to make submission to its rule equivalent to ruin and degradation." [17]

The *Mercury* derived what consolation it could from the reflection that "the intellectual, as well as judicial, weight of the Court is clearly against the decision, but numbers prevailed." Another leading paper, less easily satisfied, voiced the hope that the states of Massachusetts and New York would continue to collect their taxes until the decision was repudiated by the sober judgment of

[15] Quoted *ibid.*, II, 171–173.
[16] Quoted *ibid.*, II, 174.
[17] Quoted *ibid.*, II, 182.

public opinion, "as so many other decisions of the Supreme Court on constitutional questions have been before. . . . If ever the Court should be again filled with such men as formerly occupied its seats, . . . this and other crudities of the present majority of little men would be swept away like chaff before the wind. . . . There are some States in the confederacy, which, if we are not mistaken, would exercise their sovereign rights, in spite of Mr. Justice Wayne and his Associates." [18]

The hope of a reversal of the position of the court in the Passenger Cases was encouraged by the dissenting opinions. Those of Daniel and Woodbury have already been studied. Even more to the point, for the slave states, was Taney's assertion that it must "rest with the State to determine whether any particular class or description of persons are likely to produce discontent or insurrection in its territory or to taint the morals of its citizens, or to bring among them contagious diseases, or the evils and burdens of a numerous pauper population . . . and to remove from among their people and to prevent from entering the State, any person or class or description of persons, whom it may deem dangerous or injurious to the interests and welfare of its citizens." [19] Even Wayne, who rendered the decision of the court against the tax laws of New York and Massachusetts, held that "the States where slaves are have a constitutional right to exclude all such as are, from a common ancestry and country, of the same class of men." [20]

It is not surprising, in the light of these discussions, that during the debates induced by the Mexican War, the slavery men in Congress cited McLean's dictum in support of their contention that Congress could not control the interstate slave trade. Said Thomas H. Bayley of Virginia, on August 3, 1848: "In that case was discussed the extent of the power of Congress over what is familiarly called the internal slave trade. . . . The decision has tended greatly to put an end to the agitation." [21] Even the advocates of

[18] *Southern Quarterly Review,* XVI, 444 (Jan., 1850), quoted *ibid.*
[19] Quoted *ibid.,* II, 181.
[20] Quoted *ibid.*
[21] 30 Cong., 1 sess. Quoted *ibid.,* 67. See also speeches in second session of 29 Cong., by Burt of South Carolina (Jan. 14, 1847), and Bowden of Alabama (on same date).

"popular sovereignty" found support for their doctrine in the argument derived from the right of self-defense. The Supreme Court never gave a majority opinion upholding the view that Congress could not regulate the interstate traffic in slaves, and efforts to make it a part of the compromise of 1850 failed, yet it appeared in Clay's preliminary resolutions concerning compromise, and some of the states asserted the doctrine.[22] It was in harmony with the currents of thought which produced the decision in Cooley *v.* Philadelphia Board of Port Wardens.

ABOLITION LITERATURE AND THE MAILS [23]

Under such moderate leaders as Benjamin Lundy, the early movement for the abolition of slavery found its support largely in the South. Unfortunately the more radical Garrisonian movement began at about the time of the Nat Turner insurrection in Virginia (1831), following which the people of the slave states became extremely sensitive lest abolitionist propaganda reach their slaves and render them restless and discontented if not actually rebellious. The plans of the American Antislavery Society were therefore regarded with detestation when, in 1835, that organization embarked upon an ambitious program of publication.

In the summer of 1835 a mail steamer carried copies of its publications from New York to Charleston, South Carolina. There a crowd of citizens, apprized of their coming, broke into the post office, carried off the papers, and burned them. The Charleston postmaster reported the incident to Postmaster General Amos Kendall adding that he would not deliver such literature in future unless ordered to do so. To this Kendall replied that he had no authority to exclude papers from the mails, but added "I cannot sanction and will not condemn, the steps you have taken." [24] In

---

[22] See Clay's eighth resolution. Senate Journal, 31 Cong., 1 sess., 118. Reprinted in Commager, 319–320. In October, 1849, a convention in the State of Mississippi declared that Congress had no power to prohibit the slave trade between the states. There were other declarations to the same effect from various southern sources. See Cleo Hearon, "Struggle in Mississippi over Compromise of 1850."

[23] W. Sherman Savage, *The Controversy over the Distribution of Abolition Literature.*

[24] See narrative accounts *ibid.,* 15 *et seq.,* and McMaster, *History,* VI, 272 *et seq.; cf. Niles Register,* XLVIII, 478; XLIX, 8, 9.

his report to the President, Kendall suggested that a copy of this letter be sent to each postmaster who asked for instructions as to how to deal with abolition literature, and that each should be allowed to interpret the letter for himself. Orally he advised the postmaster at Washington to hand out none of the papers save to persons who claimed them as subscribers. The New York postmaster refused to transmit such papers unless Kendall would order him to do so, but this the postmaster general would not do. On the contrary he told him that the postmaster who had stopped "these inflammatory papers will, I have no doubt, stand justified . . . before [the] country and all mankind."

Excitement ran high as news of these events spread, and there were many acts of violence against Negroes in the South and antislavery leaders in the North. Some public meetings in the North passed resolutions upholding the right of private judgment and the freedom of discussion of all questions, but denouncing the abolitionists and their methods, especially the practice of mailing papers to others than subscribers. In defense of its activities the American Antislavery Society published an address in which it conceded that Congress had no authority to abolish slavery, deplored servile insurrections, and declared that its publications were never sent to slaves and were not intended for them. But the address admitted that single copies of the papers were sent to public men who were not subscribers, and asserted that American citizens had the right to express and publish their opinions on the Constitution, laws, and institutions of any state under heaven.

In the fall the legislatures began to meet. Those of the southern states, in several instances, discussed the policy of commercial coercion of the northern states, and called on legislatures in the North to suppress incendiary agitation and to enact penal laws against it. Governors Marcy of New York and Everett of Massachusetts actually complied with southern demands and recommended to their legislatures the passage of regulatory laws.[25]

When Congress met in December, President Jackson recommended legislation to prohibit the circulation through the mails of

[25] Ames, *State Docs.*, 214–219. On the local aspects of the controversy, both North and South, see Savage, *op. cit.*, Chaps. II–IV.

incendiary publications, tending to instigate the slaves to insurrection.[26] Seeing in this recommendation a dangerous move in the direction of control by the general government of a matter pertaining to slavery in the states, Calhoun moved to refer the message to a select committee instead of to the standing committee on the post office, which contained only one member from the South. The motion caused considerable debate, some senators believing that the recommendations of the regular committee would carry more weight than those of a special committee. The motion prevailed, however, and in addition to Calhoun himself, two southerners and two northerners were selected.[27] The report was presented on February 4, 1836, but only one member of the committee concurred with Calhoun in making it. One of the members was altogether opposed and the other two preferred a bill which differed from the one advocated by the chairman.

In making the report Calhoun held that such a law as the President suggested would violate the Constitution and infringe upon the reserved powers of the states, since Congress was prohibited to pass any law abridging the liberty of the press. The President's proposal implied the right of Congress to decide what papers are incendiary, a power which is reserved to the states by the first amendment. He therefore reported a bill providing that no deputy postmaster should knowingly receive and put into the mails for transmission anything directed to a post office or person in any state, territory, or district, the laws of which forbade the circulation of such matter, or knowingly deliver such mail except to such persons as might be authorized by state law to receive it.[28]

In the ensuing debate those who favored the bill urged that the right to prohibit the circulation of incendiary matter or documents belonged to the states, and that the United States could do nothing more than aid in the enforcement of such regulations as the states

---

[26] Richardson, *Messages*, III, 175 *et seq*. On the contest in Congress see Savage, Chap. V.

[27] *Register of Debates*, 24 Cong., 1 sess., I, 26 *et seq*.

[28] Crallé, *Works of Calhoun*, II, 509–533; V, 190–208. The states, he maintained, were obligated by the *law of nations* to prevent their citizens from disturbing the peace and security of other states. If they failed to do so, the slaveholding states were privileged to resort to the same means to protect themselves that might be employed by separate and independent communities.

might adopt. Transmission of matter banned by the states was an intolerable interference with state's rights. The power to regulate the post office was entrusted to the federal government for the public good, and carrying abolition publications was not for the public good.

Calhoun's main speech in support of his proposed measure was delivered on April 12. It is notable because it asserted the paramountcy of the state's police power over powers unmistakably granted to Congress by the Constitution. The power of the United States over the mails was, he admitted, expressly delegated, but the power of the state over slavery was unquestionably reserved. Theoretically there was no conflict between the delegated and reserved powers, but actually it was possible for *laws* based on the two classes of powers to come into conflict. In that case, he urged, "the low must yield to the high; the convenient to the necessary; mere accommodation to safety and security. . . . Will any rational being say that the laws of eleven States of this Union, which are necessary to their peace, security and very existence, ought to yield to the laws of the General Government regulating the post-office, which at the best is a mere accommodation and convenience—and this when the government was formed *by the States* mainly with a view to secure more perfectly their peace and safety?" [29] If the laws of the states must yield in case of conflict, "there is not one of the reserved powers which may not be annulled by Congress under pretext of passing laws to carry into effect the delegated powers." [30] His concluding words were: "Let it be riveted in every Southern mind, that the laws of the slave-holding States for the protection of their domestic institutions are paramount to the laws of the general government in regulation of commerce and the mail;—that the latter must yield . . . in the event of conflict; that if the government should refuse to yield, the States have a right to interpose, and we are safe." [31]

[29] *Ibid.*, I, 526–527. *Cf.* these views with the sentiments of Taney, McLean, and other judges, tending in the same direction, especially McLean's *dictum* in Groves *v.* Slaughter.

[30] *Ibid.*, 528.

[31] *Ibid.*, 533. The challenging tone of Calhoun's speech is even more evident from these words: "If you refuse cooperation with our laws, and conflict should ensue between your law and our law, the southern States will never yield to the

Against the bill it was urged that the constitution of Massachusetts would be adjudged inflammatory by the reasoning used in respect to abolition literature, because it declares that all men are born free and equal. The Declaration of Independence would be excluded from the mails for like reasons. Mail addressed to a person became the property of that person, and he could not be deprived of it without due process of law. Besides, the bill transferred the regulation of the mails and the post office to the states. It required postmasters to examine the contents of the mails, gave them judicial powers, violated the right of the people to be secure against searches and seizures, and authorized the impairment of contracts.[32]

Henry Clay, with considerable insight as to the location of the line separating the state police power from the federal control of the post office, and with his usual disposition to compromise, tried to find the common ground between the disputants by suggesting that the evil lay, not in the transmission of the objectionable matter, but in its circulation after delivery. Let the states prevent the recipient from making a misuse of it, and the difficulty would be solved. Calhoun's bill failed, the vote standing 25 to 19.[33] In July Congress passed a bill *forbidding* postmasters to detain "any letter, package, pamphlet or newspaper with intent to prevent the arrival and delivery of the same." [34]

superiority of yours. We have a remedy in our hands, which, in such event, we shall not fail to apply. We have high authority for asserting that, in such cases, 'State interposition is the rightful remedy'—a doctrine first announced by Jefferson—adopted by the patriotic and republican State of Kentucky by a solemn resolution, in 1798, and finally carried out into successful practice on a recent occasion, ever to be remembered, by the gallant State which I, in part, have the honor to represent."—*Reg. of Deb.*, 24 Cong., 1 sess., 1144–1145.

[32] See speech of John Davis of Massachusetts, a member of the select committee. *Ibid.*, 24 Cong., 1 sess., 1106.

[33] McMaster, VI, 288–291.

[34] *U. S. Stat. at Large*, V, 80–90. This act was by no means the last word on the question of regulating the mails. In 1857 Attorney-General Cushing, discussing the act, gave it as his opinion that "a deputy postmaster, or other officer of the United States, is not required by law to become, knowingly, the enforced agent or instrument of enemies of the public peace, to disseminate, in their behalf, within the limits of any one of the States of the Union, printed matter, the design and tendency of which are to promote insurrections in such States." —*Official Opinions of the Attorneys General*, VIII, 501. In 1892 the Supreme Court held, in *In re* Rapier (143 U. S. 110) that Congress may establish an *Index Expurgatorius* and that post office officials may exclude, without trial by jury,

THE RIGHT OF PETITION

As early as 1829 a petition was sent to Congress praying that body to pass a law abolishing slavery in the District of Columbia.[35] Following the agitation over abolition literature such petitions became numerous. Most of them referred to the District of Columbia, and asked for the abolition of slavery or the slave trade, or both, in the district.

Upon the presentation of one such petition in the House of Representatives on December 18, 1835, John Henry Hammond of South Carolina moved that it be not received. "He could not sit there," he said, "and see the rights of the southern people assaulted day after day, by the ignorant fanatics from whom these memorials proceed."[36] In spite of the fact that many members from both sections thought it desirable to avoid a discussion which might excite the public mind, Hammond's motion started a debate over procedure which ran for weeks. Some members wished to refuse to receive the petitions, others to lay them on the table without debate, still others to refer them to the appropriate committee and treat them with respect.

Out of the discussion by the House came at last three resolutions which were adopted in May, 1836. Briefly stated they were as follows: (1) Congress has no constitutional authority to interfere with slavery in any state in any way; (2) Congress ought not to in-

any newspaper which contains matter regarded by Congress "as injurious to the people." The power to prescribe what may be carried in the mails is limited by the provision against unreasonable searches and seizures; hence letters are safeguarded in a way not applicable to newspapers and other printed matter which is not sealed. See discussion of *Ex parte* Jackson, 96 U. S. 727 (1877). The exclusion of periodicals from the mails does not forbid their circulation by other methods. Yet under the commerce power Congress may prohibit the carrying of lottery tickets from one state to another by an express company. See Champion *v.* Ames, 188 U. S. 321 (1903). Other cognate decisions are Lewis Pub. Co. *v.* Morgan, 229 U. S. 288 (1913); Milwaukee Pub. Co. *v.* Burleson, 255 U. S. 407 (1921).

In 1913 Congress passed the Webb-Kenyon act, forbidding the transportation of liquor into dry states, and the Supreme Court upheld it. This law rested on the power to regulate interstate commerce, but it would seem that an act such as Calhoun desired in 1836 would have been valid as resting on the parallel power of Congress over the mails.

[35] Ames, *State Docs.*, 221 et seq.
[36] *Reg. of Deb.*, 24 Cong., 1 sess., 1967.

terfere with slavery in the District of Columbia; and (3) all petitions, memorials, etc., relating to the subject of slavery shall, without printing or reference, be laid on the table and no further action taken upon them.[37]   The final resolution led John Quincy Adams, now in the midst of his remarkable post-presidential career in the House, to exclaim: "I hold the resolution to be a direct violation of the constitution of the United States, the rules of this House, and the rights of my constituents."

Some of the southern members were dissatisfied even with these pronouncements; for example, the second seemed to admit the right of Congress to abolish slavery in the district and to rest inaction on grounds of mere policy.   Northern members were also dissatisfied because many of them regarded the third resolution, called the "gag rule," as a violation of the right of petition guaranteed by the first amendment, and as an exercise of the power, prohibited by it, to abridge the freedom of speech.   The right of petition, they said, means more than the right to draw up petitions; it includes the right to have them received and considered by the body to which they are directed.

On January 28, 1840, the "gag rule" was adopted as a standing rule of the House, with the following wording: "That no petition, memorial, resolution, or other paper praying the abolition of slavery in the District of Columbia, or any State or Territory, or the slave trade between the States or Territories of the United States in which it now exists, shall be received by this House, or entertained in any way whatever." [38]   Not until December, 1844, was this rule repealed.

The Senate did not adopt the equivalent of the "gag rule" but it laid petitions on the table and debated the whole matter of the right of petition quite as hotly as the House and with equal effect upon the public.   In that branch Calhoun was the outstanding champion of the southern demand that the institution of slavery should not be discussed.   On January 7, 1836, he moved that the Senate should not receive two petitions asking for the abolition of

[37] A. B. Hart, *Slavery and Abolition*, 260, citing Tremain, *Slavery in Dist. of Col.*, 76.

[38] *Cong. Globe*, 26 Cong., 1 sess., 151.

slavery in the District of Columbia.[39] The debate which followed
lasted for more than two months, during which Calhoun was denounced by northern and southern Senators alike. The former
accused him of attempting to abolish the right of petition, while
the latter charged him with trying to arouse the North and South
against each other.

In a speech on March 9 he replied to these criticisms. He declared that he had always been devotedly attached to the Union
and to the institutions of the country, and that he was anxious to
perpetuate them to the latest generation. In asking that the petitions be not received, he had sought the welfare both of the South
and the Union, for the petitions were blows on the wedge that
would ultimately break the Union to pieces. They were a foul
slander on half of the states of the Union, because they denounced
slavery in the district as immoral and sinful, and as a national disgrace, and what was true of slavery in the district must be true
of it elsewhere. If Congress should legislate against slavery in the
district, the spirit of the Constitution would be violated, for that
document not only recognized the institution but gave the states
exclusive control over it within their respective borders. He believed that the abolitionists were attempting to undermine the institution, and that the South should unite to repel their attacks at
the very outset by refusing to receive their petitions to Congress.
The abolitionists waged war, he said, not with arms, but with the
more effective weapon of religious and political fanaticism. "How
can it be successfully met? . . . There is but one way: we must
meet the enemy on the frontier, on the question of receiving; we
must secure that important pass—it is our Thermopylae." [40]

[39] H. E. Von Holst, *John C. Calhoun*, 124–134.

[40] *Reg. of Deb.*, 24 Cong., 2 sess., 774–775. Calhoun made a frank defense of
slavery in a speech on February 6, 1837: "I hold that in the present state of
civilization, where two races of different origin, and distinguished by color, and
other physical differences, as well as intellectual, are brought together, the relation now existing in the slaveholding States between the two, is, instead of an
evil, a good—a positive good." ". . . I fearlessly assert that the existing relation
between the two races in the South . . . forms the most solid and durable foundation on which to rear free and stable political institutions. It is useless to disguise
the fact. There is and always has been in an advanced stage of wealth and
civilization, a conflict between labor and capital. The condition of society in the
South exempts us from the disorders and dangers resulting from this conflict;

Calhoun's efforts were unavailing, as the Senate voted to receive the petitions, although it rejected them after a short debate. By this course northern Senators wished to reassure the South, as the procedure would serve as a precedent in dealing with such petitions in the future.

Believing that the demands of petitioners touching the district were but the prelude to more radical ones, Calhoun did not share in this feeling of assurance; and his fears seemed to be justified when Senator Benjamin Swift of Vermont presented in December. 1837, a memorial from the legislature of his state declaring that Congress had power to abolish slavery and the slave trade in the district and also in the territories. The occasion of this memorial was the proposal to annex Texas, which had recently won its independence from Mexico. The first and second resolutions in the memorial protested against annexation, and the third opposed the admission of any more slaveholding states.[41]

Calhoun spent several days in formulating a reply to this memorial, setting forth his views on behalf of the South in six resolutions. When he introduced them on December 27, he explained that his purpose was to test the Senate. By adopting them it would show its intention to protect the rights of the South and preserve the Constitution as it really was. By rejecting them the Senate would virtually say: "Come here no longer for protection." Rejection would encourage the abolitionists to attack the South; adoption would curb their zeal. The resolutions, he thought, were self-explanatory. They were based on the two great principles of "non-interference" and "non-discrimination." These were the two great fundamental constitutional bases on which the salvation of the South rested. By the former term was meant non-interference with slavery in the states, and by the latter, equal rights in the territories and the District of Columbia.[42] In substance, the six resolutions were as follows:

First. In adopting the Constitution, each state acted as a sov-

and which explains why it is that the political condition of the slaveholding States has been so much more stable and quiet than that of the North."—Quoted by McLaughlin, *Con. Hist.*, 489–490.

[41] Ames, *State Docs.*, 225.

[42] Crallé, *Works of Calhoun*, III, 189.

ereign, free and independent state, entering the Union voluntarily to gain increased security against all dangers, domestic and foreign, and the more perfect enjoyment of its advantages, natural, political, and social.

Second. The states retained severally the sole control over their domestic institutions and police. Any intermeddling by one or more states or their citizens with the domestic institutions of others on any pretext whatever, political, moral, or religious, was not warranted by the Constitution and was dangerous to their peace.

Third. The federal government is a common agent of the states to carry out the powers delegated for the common security; it is the duty of the government so to use those powers as to give security to domestic institutions of each state and to resist all attempts to use them as instruments in attacks by one portion of the Union on the domestic institutions of another.

Fourth. Slavery is an important part of the domestic institutions of the southern and western states, recognized by the Constitution as an essential element in the distribution of powers among the states. No change of feeling elsewhere can justify attacks upon it. All such attacks are manifest violations of the constitutional compact.

Fifth. The intermeddling of any state or its citizens to abolish slavery in the District of Columbia or the territories, on the ground that it is immoral or sinful, or any act of Congress with that view, would be a dangerous attack on the institutions of all slaveholding states.

Sixth. The Union rests on equality of rights and advantages. Whatever destroys equality tends to destroy the Union. Hence it is a solemn duty of this body to resist all attempts to discriminate against any of the states. To refuse to extend to the South any advantages which might arise from the annexation of new states or territory, on the pretext that slavery is an immoral institution, would be contrary to the equality of rights which the Constitution was intended to secure.[43]

Again Clay sought to end discussion by formulating resolutions which would put Congress on record as to its powers over slavery

[43] *Ibid.*, III, 140.

in words which would win general approval. With this in view he submitted the following proposals:

First. Domestic slavery is subject to the exclusive control of the states in which it exists. Neither the people elsewhere nor Congress can rightfully exercise any power to interfere with it in any way.

Second. If any citizen of the United States should present to the Senate a petition touching the abolition of slavery in any state, it should be rejected without debate.

Third. Since both Maryland and Virginia were slave states when the District of Columbia was ceded to the United States, and still were, slavery could not be abolished in the district without violation of the good faith implied in the cession and acceptance; nor without infringement of the Constitution unless compensation were made to the owners; nor in any event without exciting the just alarm of the slave states. Therefore it ought not to be abolished in the district; but petitions for such action should be received, treated respectfully, and referred to the appropriate committee.

Fourth. To abolish slavery in Florida, the only territory where it existed, would be inexpedient because it would alarm the slave states; because the people of the territory had not asked for its abolition; because when the territory became a state the people would be entitled to decide for themselves; and because it would violate the Missouri Compromise.[44]

The historian must point out that the last statement was not correct, because the Missouri Compromise applied literally only to the lands purchased from France, and was not even by implication an agreement that all territories acquired later, lying south of the compromise line, should be open to slavery. At most it could only be regarded as a precedent for the division of new territory along that line. This fourth resolution invites a comment also because it foreshadows the popular sovereignty doctrine in the weight it attaches to the desires of the people of Florida Territory. This regard for the wishes of the inhabitants of the territories, harking back to the compact philosophy, was the soil from which the doctrine grew.

[44] *Cong. Globe,* 25 Cong., 2 sess., 55.

Of Calhoun's resolutions the first four were adopted, the first two without change, the third and fourth with some changes of phraseology to which the author did not object.   The substance of Clay's third and fourth resolutions were substituted for Calhoun's fifth.   The sixth was tabled.[45]   This action, of course, afforded some protection for the right of petition and led to further discussion of it.   Calhoun's most notable exposition of his view on this right was given in a speech delivered on February 13, 1840, in which he maintained that its importance had been much exaggerated, and that, under a popular form of government, it was the least important of political rights.   It belongs, he declared, to despotic governments, and was incorporated in the Constitution because of the grievances suffered by the unrepresented colonies prior to the Revolution.   In free America the need of the right had been almost destroyed by general suffrage and the practice of instructing representatives.   Hence its exercise had degenerated into a means of attacking others; it had become a menace rather than a protection.   The federal government was the agent, the servant, of the people.   "Who ever heard of a principal petitioning his agent, the master his servant, or the sovereign his subject?" [46]

As to the constitutional aspects of the regulation of the post office and the question of petitions, the debates of the thirties were inconclusive; but that they increased the sectional antagonism is certain.   From the point of view of constitutional interpretation their chief significance is that they brought out sharply the platform on which the South was to take its stand.   The doctrine of the paramountcy of the state police power (resting on the assumption of state sovereignty) and the principles of "non-interference" and "non-discrimination," were thenceforward increasingly the bases of southern argument.

[45] Crallé, *Works of Calhoun*, III, 168, 188, 202.
[46] *Ibid.*, III, 439 *et seq.*

X

ISSUES RAISED BY SLAVERY (*Concluded*)

FUGITIVE SLAVES

AS NORTHERN dislike of slavery increased, more and more obstacles were placed in the way of the recovery of fugitives. Individuals connived at their escape, private agencies in aid of runaways took on the organized form known as the "underground railway," and even states interposed "personal liberty" laws securing for alleged fugitives the privilege of the writ of habeas corpus and the right of a jury trial. As has been noted, the legislature of New York, in consequence of the controversy between Governor Seward and the Virginia executive, passed such an act at the end of the thirties.

The main purpose of the personal liberty laws in the beginning was to bring out the truth of the claimant's contention and to prevent the kidnapping of free Negroes. The fugitive slave law passed by Congress in 1793 provided merely that in case of the escape out of any state or territory of any person held to service or labor under the laws thereof, the person to whom such service was due, or his agent, might seize the fugitive and carry him before any United States judge, or before any magistrate of the city, town, or county in which the arrest was made; and such judge or magistrate, on proof to his satisfaction, either oral or by affidavit, that the person seized was really a fugitive, was authorized to grant a certificate which should serve as sufficient warrant for his removal to the state or territory whence he had fled.[1] This act, it would appear, was not passed in response to the demands of slave owners for legislation to carry out the guarantee which the Constitution gave them concerning the recovery of runaways. On the contrary, it was

---

[1] *U. S. Stat. at Large*, I, 302. The distinction between the constitutional provisions relating to fugitives from justice and service respectively should be noted here. In the former case the fugitive is to be surrendered on demand of the executive of the claimant state, duly supported by evidence of judicial proceedings; in the latter, the slave is to be delivered upon claim of the private party to whom the labor is due.

intended, by requiring a magistrate's warrant, to prevent the seizure and removal of free blacks.[2] Magistrates, however, proved to be easy to convince of the validity of claims to the ownership of black men, and kidnapping was almost as easy under the law as before its passage.

Dissatisfaction with the working of the act appeared first along the border.[3] The slave states soon manifested discontent for the reason that escapes were numerous in spite of the law, and began to ask for more effective legislation by Congress; on the other hand, the tendency appeared in the free states to interfere with the administration even of such legislation as existed for the protection of slave owners. Indiana led off along this path in 1824, followed by other states, for example, Pennsylvania in 1826, Connecticut in 1838, and Vermont and New York in 1840.[4]

By this last date antislavery leaders were questioning the validity of the provisions of the federal law of 1793 for proving slave property before state magistrates. It was doubted whether the government could impose any function in enforcement of the fugitive slave law upon state officials unless the state consented, and it seemed to be within the power of the state to forbid its agents to participate in the rendition of runaways. Acting on this belief, the Vermont legislature in a law of 1840 forbade any state court of record, or judge, or justice of the peace, or any other state magistrate, to take cognizance of any certificate in any case arising under the federal act; it likewise forbade any executive officer of any court, or any other officer, or citizen, to seize, arrest or detain, or to aid in the seizure, arrest, or detention, of any person claimed as a fugitive slave, or to transport or aid in the transportation of such person, under penalty, for any infraction of the act, of a fine of one thousand dollars, or imprisonment for not more than five years.[5]

[2] C. W. A. David, "The Fugitive Slave Law of 1793." The act protected master's by providing for the collection of damages from persons proved guilty of aiding slaves to escape.

[3] Allen Johnson, "The Constitutionality of the Fugitive Slave Acts," 166.

[4] Marion G. McDougall, *Fugitive Slaves.*

[5] Johnson, "Fugitive Slave Acts," 168. During the first decades under the Constitution, state's rights men succeeded in having Congress pass numerous acts vesting in state courts jurisdiction over federal questions of various kinds. A

The laws of the free states not only tended to prevent kidnapping but hindered the recovery of bona fide fugitives, and were regarded by the people of the slave states as deliberate attempts to nullify the constitutional safeguards of their rights. Much mutual recrimination occurred before the constitutionality of both the acts of Congress and the states was brought to the test, and the obligations of the states and federal government respectively determined, in the case of Prigg *v*. Pennsylvania, which came before the Supreme Court in 1842.[6]

Prigg was the agent of Margaret Ashmore, a citizen of Maryland, who claimed the services of a Negro woman who had escaped into Pennsylvania in 1832. He had entered the state in 1837 and had caused the woman to be apprehended by a state constable under warrant of a Pennsylvania magistrate. When he presented the fugitive before the magistrate and asked for a certificate authorizing her removal to Maryland, the official refused to take further cognizance of the case. Prigg thereupon carried the woman and her children across the state line without further ceremony, and delivered them to their owner. By the Pennsylvania act of 1826 the removal of an alleged fugitive without a magistrate's certificate was denounced as kidnapping and declared to be a felony. Under this statute Prigg was indicted and convicted, and by agreement between the two states concerned the case was carried to the Supreme Court on writ of error.

The decision, delivered by Justice Story, declared the Pennsylvania statute null and void on the ground that the power and obligation to enforce the constitutional guarantee relative to fugitive slaves rested with the federal government exclusively. The owner of a slave, Story declared, had the right under the Constitution to seize his property wherever he could do so without a breach of the

reaction set in when the state courts began to feel that Congress was imposing burdensome jurisdiction upon them; then they began to rule that the national legislature had no power to lay such duties upon the states. The Prigg case was the turning point; it put an end to attempts to put into practice the doctrine that Congress had the power to vest federal jurisdiction in state courts or state officers.—Charles Warren, "New Light on the History of the Federal Judiciary Act of 1789," 70–71.

[6] 16 Peters 539. Extract in Johnson, *Readings*, 416–421, and Commager, 292–295. See Swisher, *Taney*, 421–425, 477.

peace, and no state could interfere in any way. "But the right to seize and retake fugitive slaves, and the duty to deliver them up . . . derive their whole validity and obligation exclusively from the constitution of the United States, and . . . the natural inference is, in the absence of any positive delegation of power to the state Legislatures, that it belongs to the legislative department of the national government" exclusively, and is not a power which the state legislatures possess concurrently. "As to the authority . . . conferred upon state magistrates [by the federal law of 1793], while a difference of opinion has existed, and may still exist, on the point in the different states, whether the state magistrates are bound to act under it, none is entertained by this court that state magistrates may, if they choose, exercise the authority, unless prohibited by the state legislatures." Interpreted as a permissive measure, that is, the decision regarded the act as undoubtedly constitutional, but pointedly suggested that the state legislature might forbid state officials to exercise the functions which the law assigned to them.

This decision reflects Story's characteristic ways of thinking, and is as well reminiscent of the Court of Marshall's day. Indeed, the basis of his reasoning was the rule laid down by Marshall in Sturges *v.* Crowninshield: "Wherever the terms in which a power is granted to Congress or the nature of the power require, that it should be exercised exclusively by Congress, the subject is as completely taken from the State Legislatures as if they had been forbidden to act." [7] By the same sort of reasoning Marshall and Story had arrived at their view that Congress possessed exclusive power over interstate and foreign commerce. Story's conclusion denied to the states even the power to pass laws to *promote* the administration of federal legislation relating to fugitive slaves. [8]

[7] 4 Wheaton 122 (1819).

[8] Justice Harlan summarized the argument for Pennsylvania in the Prigg case as follows: "Her Attorney-General pressed the argument that the obligation to surrender fugitive slaves was on the States and for the States, subject to the restriction that they should not pass laws or establish regulations liberating such fugitives; that the Constitution did not take from the States the right to determine the status of all persons within their respective jurisdictions; that it was for the State in which the alleged fugitive was found to determine, through her courts or in such mode as she prescribed, whether the person arrested was, in fact, a freeman or a fugitive slave; that the sole power of the General Government in the premises was, by judicial instrumentality, to restrain and correct, not to forbid

At this point Taney took issue with Story, as might have been expected. He held that the states were not prohibited from *aiding* in the recovery of fugitives, but only from passing laws *impairing* the slave owners' right of recovery. The right to "support and enforce" federal acts was "necessarily implied."

Although Story regarded the establishment of the exclusiveness of the federal obligation as a great relief to the free states and a distinct point gained for liberty, the decision aroused much criticism both North [9] and South, and introduced a train of events which greatly aggravated the already serious sectional antagonism. Not long after the decision a Negro named Latimer was seized in Boston without a warrant. Friends of liberty sought to obtain a jury trial for the Negro, under the state liberty law, but the justice declined to issue a writ of habeas corpus against the captor on the ground that the Prigg judgment had proved that the Massachusetts law was unconstitutional. A great popular demonstration followed, but it was presently perceived that the decision had virtually sanctioned state legislation of the type enacted by Vermont in 1840. If the free states could not interfere actively with the recapture of fugitives, they might do so passively by refusing the use of jails and forbidding the aid of sheriffs, judges, and all other state officials.

On the heels of the Latimer case, therefore, came a new law of Massachusetts by which judges, sheriffs, constables, jailers, and all other state officers, were forbidden to take any part in the enforcement of the act of 1793. To the great irritation of the South, the legislature also renewed the old appeal to Congress to propose an amendment apportioning representation and direct taxation according to free inhabitants. When soon afterwards the opposite party came into control of the legislature, the resolutions were repassed in order to show the country that the demand was not that of a portion only of the people of the state. Copies of the resolves were sent to the other states, and, of course, drew forth the hearty con-

and prevent in the absence of hostile state action; and that for the General Government to assume primary authority to legislate on the subject of fugitive slaves, would be a dangerous encroachment on state sovereignty." Discussion of the Civil Rights Cases, 1875, quoted by Louis B. Boudin, *Government by Judiciary*, II, 143.

[9] See, for example, letter of Salmon P. Chase to Charles Sumner, April 24, 1847. *Diary and Correspondence of . . . Chase*, 114.

demnation of the southern legislatures. Georgia, for example, retorted that such an amendment would be a gross violation of the faith pledged when the Constitution was adopted.[10]

Other states soon followed Massachusetts in enacting new personal liberty laws, and within a half dozen years they were quite general throughout the North. It cannot be said that the legislatures were careful to keep their enactments within the limits indicated by the Supreme Court; on the contrary, they presently began to reintroduce provisions designed to afford the fugitives the protection which the federal law did not give. In the South the sense of injury grew apace. Sectional bitterness increased because the laws demonstrated that the people of the North were hostile to the peculiar institution of the South, and willing to carry this hostility even to the point of violating the Constitution. As a sort of southern manifesto, the legislature of Virginia adopted and published a report, in 1849, reviewing the situation and severely arraigning the northern states:

"The South is wholly without the benefit of that solemn constitutional guaranty which was so sacredly pledged to it at the formation of this Union. . . . No citizen of the South can pass the frontier of a non-slaveholding state and there exercise his undoubted constitutional right of seizing his fugitive slave, with a view to take him before a judicial officer and there prove his right of ownership, without imminent danger of being prosecuted criminally as a kidnapper, or being sued in a civil action for false imprisonment—imprisoned himself for want of bail, and subjected in his defense to an expense exceeding the whole value of the property claimed, or finally of being mobbed or being put to death in a street fight by insane fanatics or brutal ruffians. In short, the condition of things is, that at this day very few of the owners of fugitive slaves have the hardihood to pass the frontier of a non-slaveholding state and exercise their undoubted, adjudicated constitutional right of seizing the fugitive." [11]

The immediate object of Virginia's report, in which she expressed a sentiment general in the South, was to urge the enactment

[10] Ames, *State Docs.*, 239–240.
[11] *Ibid.*, 250–252.

of a new federal law which would more adequately secure the rights of slave owners. As early as 1817 Maryland had besought Congress to pass a new fugitive slave law, and other states had subsequently made similar appeals. In response to resolutions adopted by Kentucky in 1847, a Senate committee reported a bill, but it reached only the second reading.[12] The agitation for a new law became one of the factors which led eventually to the adoption of the compromise measures of 1850.

Among these compromise measures was included a fugitive slave law. Accepting the sole responsibility for making effective the constitutional right of recovery of fugitive slaves by their owners which the Prigg decision had laid upon the federal government, Congress by the new act created the machinery necessary for a national system of apprehending and returning runaways. The states as such, and state officials, were relieved of all participation in the task. Citizens of the states in their private capacity might, however, be called upon by federal agents to assist in the capture of fugitives, and were subject to penalties for refusal.[13]

The last provision rested on the doctrine of dual citizenship. This doctrine was a sound implication of the federal system from the beginning, but it had not yet gained general acceptance. It was to be embodied explicitly in the Constitution eighteen years later through the adoption of the fourteenth amendment. Un-doubtedly every citizen of the United States, a term which included every citizen of a state, owed obedience to the constitutional laws of Congress. But the requirement that every citizen should, upon demand of a federal official, turn slave catcher outraged northern sentiment, and led to conduct which almost completely disregarded the principles of constitutional law. Radical antislavery men justi-fied their acts by placing conscience above the Constitution, or by appealing to the police power of the state, which the contemporary decisions of the Supreme Court had done so much to exalt.

The personal liberty laws adopted after the passage of the new federal act were more than ever designed to obstruct the measures

---

[12] *Ibid.*, 249.

[13] *U. S. Stat. at Large*, IX, 462–465. Extract in William MacDonald, *Select Docs.*, 385–389, and Commager, *Docs.*, 321–323.

of Congress. Besides prohibiting the use of state jails and forbidding state judges and other officers to issue writs or aid claimants in any other way, they provided severe punishment for the seizure of free persons with intent to reduce them to slavery, and sought to maintain for alleged fugitives all the securities afforded by regular legal trial.[14] Despite the Compromise of 1850, which it was hoped would end the sectional struggle, these laws made the early fifties a time of turmoil. The forcible rescue of slaves retaken by their owners or agents became a common occurrence, and in several instances the conflicting national and state legislation led to serious clashes of authority. The most famous of these conflicts involved the courts of Wisconsin and those of the United States. A man named Booth, arrested for violating the federal fugitive slave law, was discharged from the custody of a United States marshal named Ableman on writ of habeas corpus issued by the state supreme court on the ground that the federal act was unconstitutional. Adopting the doctrines of 1798, the legislature proclaimed that "a *positive defiance* of [by] those sovereignties [the states], of all unauthorized acts done or attempted to be done under color of [the Constitution], is the rightful remedy."[15] In January, 1855, Booth was convicted in the United States district court, but again released on writ issued by the state court. It was not until 1859 that the case of Ableman *v.* Booth was brought before the Supreme Court on writ of error, and Marshall himself could not have exceeded the vigor with which Chief Justice Taney then expounded the supremacy of the federal judiciary.[16]

[14] McDougall, *Fugitive Slaves*, 67. The standard work on these laws is still the old book by Joel Parker, *Personal Liberty Laws* (1861). In September, 1850, Attorney-General John J. Crittenden gave an opinion to the effect that the fugitive slave laws did not affect the right to the writ of habeas corpus; in other words, neither act interfered with the use of the writ to prevent an attempt to seize a Negro fraudulently. Extract in Johnson, 423–425. The Massachusetts personal liberty act of 1855, a good example, is in Commager, 335–336. There is an interesting analytical summary of the personal liberty laws as they stood at the close of the fifties, in *De Bow's Review*, IV, 370 (Sept., 1860).

[15] Ames, *State Docs.*, 303–305. See James L. Sellers, "Republicanism and States Rights in Wisconsin."

[16] 21 Howard 506. Reprinted in Commager, 358–361. See discussion by Warren, II, 258–261, 332–333, 337–338, and Swisher, *Taney*, 526 *et seq*. In Ohio, Oberlin was a center of abolitionism and obstruction of the enforcement of the fugitive slave legislation. See W. G. Burroughs, "Oberlin's Part in the Slavery

In other cases federal officials were arrested or sued under state laws for pursuing their duties under the congressional act. In one of these a United States marshal was imprisoned on warrant from the Ohio court because he had rearrested a fugitive released from his custody on writ of the state court. In this case the marshal was himself released by Justice McLean, an Ohio man, upon application to the United States circuit court for a writ of habeas corpus.[17] Such actions on the part of the states led to the introduction of a bill in 1855 by Senator Isaac Toucey of Connecticut, providing for the removal to federal courts of suits against federal officers begun in state courts on account of their acts done under federal law. Twenty years later, the Republicans found it necessary to pass just such an act in order to carry through their program of reconstruction of the southern states. In 1855, however, the proposed measure appeared to antislavery men to be a device for the enforcement of the obnoxious fugitive slave law, and was denounced by them accordingly. *The New York Tribune* said that the bill should be headed "For the Better Protection of Negro-Hunters," and Chase, Seward, Fessenden, Sumner, and Wade, all later conspicuous leaders of the Republican Party, joined in the condemnation of the bill. The northern press in general upheld the nullifying measures of the states, reiterating the doctrines advanced by South Carolina during the struggle of 1828–1833, and counseling disobedience to the federal courts and laws.[18]

THE CONSTITUTION, SLAVERY, AND INTERNATIONAL LAW

Chattel slavery never had an existence in England. Even serfdom disappeared with the opening of the modern era. Yet in Britain's tropical colonies, as in continental America, slavery gained a foothold during the seventeenth and eighteenth centuries, and it was not until 1834 that it was abolished throughout the empire by act of Parliament. Nevertheless a feeling of antipathy towards the

Conflict"; W. C. Cochran, "The Western Reserve and the Fugitive Slave Laws"; B. F. Prince, "The Rescue Case of 1857"; G. T. Stewart, "The Ohio Fugitive Slave Law"; Lewis Tappan, "The Fugitive Slave Bill." On McLean's enforcement of the federal act see Weisenburger, *Life of McLean*, 194–195.

[17] Warren, II, 262.
[18] *Ibid.*, II, 259, 264–266.

institution gained considerable strength during the eighteenth century, and found partial expression in decisions of the courts. In the famous Somerset case in 1772 Lord Mansfield decided that a slave owner from a British colony who visited England bringing a slave with him could not compel the Negro to return to bondage. He declared that slavery was so odious that nothing short of positive law could support it. A half century later (1826) Lord Stowell held, in the case of the slave Grace, who had accompanied her mistress from Antigua to England and returned, that the freedom acquired while in England was conditional and was forfeited under the law of Antigua in consequence of the return.[19] These English precedents influenced courts in the United States to no small degree.

Canada, like the mother country, was a land of freedom. Escaped slaves occasionally succeeded in hiding in the free states, but in general Canada was for them the Land of Promise. So numerous were the fugitives who succeeded in crossing the State of Ohio, where the distance between the empire of slavery and the border was least, that Kentucky several times, in the years following 1820, requested the government to seek an agreement with Great Britain for their return. Negotiations were undertaken but no concessions were ever obtained.[20]

England's dislike of slavery led her to champion freedom so ardently that in her zeal she trespassed upon the rights of other nations. When vessels carrying slaves were wrecked upon the Bahamas and Bermudas or driven into their ports by stress of weather, the English authorties held that they were freed. The State Department complied with the demands which the slave states believed the Constitution entitled them to make, and insisted that slaves thus thrown by mischance on British soil did not become subject to British laws. The soundness of this position was confirmed by the award eventually made by the arbiters to whom the dispute with England was referred.

In 1831 the American brig *Comet*, with slaves on board, was wrecked on the Bahamas. The slaves, who were the property of American citizens, were rescued and carried to New Providence,

[19] Helen T. Catterall, "Some Antecedents of the Dred Scott Case."
[20] McDougall, *Fugitive Slaves*, 25.

where the governor refused to surrender them to their owners, on the ground that the laws of Great Britain did not recognize slavery on the high seas, and that since the Negroes were on British soil, it was his duty to give them the full protection of English law.

On appeal of the owners to the government of the United States, the State Department instructed Martin Van Buren, then minister to England, to take the matter up with the British Foreign Office. Van Buren presented it to Lord Palmerston on February 25, 1832, asking for the return of the slaves and the payment of a reasonable indemnity for their detention. Palmerston referred the case to the legal advisers of the crown, who recommended compliance with the demand, but the government failed to act or even to reply to Van Buren's note.[21]

Another case arose very soon. In February, 1833, the brig *Encomium*, while on a voyage from Charleston to New Orleans with slaves on board, was wrecked near the spot which had been the scene of the *Comet* disaster, and the rescued slaves were taken to Nassau. Again the local magistrate liberated the blacks, in spite of the protests of the resident United States consul. This case too was presented to the British Government with a request for a reply to the former note concerning the *Comet*.[22]

While the reply was still awaited, another vessel, the *Enterprise*, bound from the British West Indies to Charleston, was driven by stress of weather into the port of Hamilton. Here an organization known as The Friendly Society of People of Color sued out a writ of habeas corpus which was issued by the chief justice of the island, to bring the blacks on board the vessel before the justice to answer for themselves whether they would be free. The writ required the master of the vessel to produce the slaves on board; and upon this being done, they were taken from the ship by local officials and set at liberty.[23]

Mr. Vail, the American chargé in London after Van Buren left, was instructed to present this new case and to press for an answer to the previous representations of the United States. In doing so

[21] John Bassett Moore, *History and Digest of International Arbitrations to which the United States has been a Party*, I, 408; McMaster, VI, 241 *et seq.*
[22] Moore, *op. cit.*
[23] *Ibid.*, 409.

the chargé reminded the British Government that the case of the *Enterprise* was the third instance "of an American vessel, pursuing a voyage recognized as lawful by the legislation of the United States, and by all the principles of public law, forced, by act of God, to seek, in a British port, a refuge from the tempest, relief from starvation for her crew and passengers," which had been interfered with by local authorities.[24]

Six months later, on November 13, 1835, Lord Palmerston informed Mr. Vail that his government had decided to refer the whole subject to the judicial committee of the Privy Council, and that he would reply as soon as that body determined the proper course to be pursued. Mr. Vail was succeeded in 1836 by Mr. Stevenson, but two efforts on the part of the latter to obtain a decision from the British failed even to elicit a reply.[25]

The question now entered the debates of Congress. On February 7, 1837, the Senate requested the President to submit the correspondence in relation to the island outrages. He complied promptly, and after a careful examination of it the Senate passed resolutions asserting that "where a vessel on the high seas, in time of peace, engaged in a lawful voyage, was forced by stress of weather or other unavoidable circumstances into a port of a friendly power, the country to which she belonged lost 'none of the rights appertaining to her on the high seas, either over the vessel or the personal relations of those on board.' "[26] Calhoun would have the rights of slave owners asserted even more emphatically. On March 4 he introduced resolutions which declared that, since slavery was recognized by the law of nations, England had no right, in dealing with the citizens of other countries, to make a distinction between their slave property and property of other kinds, when vessels came temporarily within her jurisdiction. This resolution was adopted *nem. con.*, and while nineteen Senators did not vote, Calhoun chose to regard the action as unanimous.[27]

Since the cases of the *Comet* and *Encomium* occurred before August 1, 1834, on which date the act of Parliament abolishing

[24] *Ibid.*
[25] *Ibid.*
[26] *Ibid.*, 409–410.
[27] Von Holst, *Calhoun*, 202–209.

slavery in the colonies became effective, the British government finally, in 1840, agreed to pay the sum of $116,179.62 for the slaves set free from those vessels, at the same time refusing to pay an indemnity for those on the *Enterprise*, freed after the abolition act went into effect. The government admitted that the freeing of these was also a violation of international law, but held that no redress was obtainable.[28]

In this very year the schooner *Hermosa* was wrecked on the key of Abaco, while en route from Richmond to New Orleans, and again slaves were taken off, and after some judicial proceedings in Nassau, were liberated in spite of the objections of the master of the schooner and the United States consul.[29] This action naturally heightened the already intense feeling of the proslavery group against Great Britain. Then, as a climax to this series of high-handed deeds, came the *Creole* affair.

On October 27, 1841, the *Creole*, with about one hundred thirty-five slaves aboard, sailed from Hampton Roads for New Orleans. Among the slaves was one named Madison Washington, who after escaping from Virginia to Canada had returned in the hope of rescuing his wife and had been recaptured. Maddened by the prospect of renewed subjection in the lower South, he succeeded, while the vessel was at sea, in arousing some of the other slaves to make a stroke for freedom. In the uprising the blacks killed a passenger who owned several of them, wounded the master, chief mate, and two members of the crew, and forced the sailors under pain of death to take the ship to the British port of Nassau.

Upon its arrival, the United States consul requested the governor of the island to send soldiers on board to detain the slaves, and preferred charges against them. The authorities, however, announced that the alleged offenses were beyond the jurisdiction of the island courts, since international relations were involved; that the charges of murder would therefore be investigated, and those implicated would be detained pending instructions from the British government, while all of the other slaves would be released. Nineteen of them were found to be implicated in the murder and

[28] Moore, 411.
[29] *Ibid.*, 410.

violence.   The remainder were told that they were at liberty to go whither they pleased, and over the protest of the master and consul were assisted ashore by the island officials.[30]

The excitement of the South at this juncture was shown by resolutions passed by the legislature of Mississippi, denouncing the conduct of Great Britain and calling for a return of the slaves at all hazards.   Although the southern leaders were ever ready to insist upon non-interference by Congress or northern reformers with slavery as a "domestic" institution, they were equally ready to invoke the aid of the government as the agent of the states, in enforcing all of the constitutional guarantees of the institution, even in foreign relations.   They now insisted that the United States should demand the return of the slaves, and the Senate led by Calhoun called upon the President for information.[31]

Daniel Webster, as secretary of state, accepted the southern point of view, and stated his position in correspondence with Edward Everett, who had become the American representative in England. "We do not demand the restitution of fugitive slaves," nor, in the absence of any treaty stipulation, "do we demand the surrender of criminals fleeing from justice.   But all this we firmly believe is quite remote from what we hold to be our rights according to the laws and usages of nations in such cases as that of the *Creole;* that is to say, in cases of vessels carried into British ports by violence or stress of weather, we shall insist that there shall be no interference from the land with the relations or personal conditions of those on board, according to the laws of their own country.   That under such circumstances they shall enjoy the common law of hospitality, be subjected to no force, be entitled to have their immediate wants and necessities relieved, and to pursue their journey without mo- lestation." [32]

To Lord Ashburton, the British minister at Washington, Web- ster asserted that "a ship under international law on the high seas is a part of the territory of the nation to which she belongs," and "a ship though at anchor in a foreign harbor under such circum-

---

[30] *Ibid.*, 410–411.
[31] McMaster, VII, 54–55.
[32] George T. Curtis, *Life of Daniel Webster*, II, 106.

stances preserves its jurisdiction and its laws." "Jurisdiction over a foreign ship brought into port against its will does not extend to the divestment of property rights on board. On the general principle of international comity vigorous procedure under such circumstances as those that brought the *Creole* into port was barbarous and destructive of all hope of amicable relations."[33] Rehearsing the history of the *Creole* episode, he urged that the vessel was "taken into a British port, not voluntarily by those who had the lawful authority over her, but forcibly and violently against the master's will, and with the consent of nobody but the mutineers and murderers. Under these circumstances," he concluded, "it would seem to have been the plain and obvious duty of the authorities at Nassau, a port of a friendly power, to assist the American consul in putting an end to the captivity of the master and crew, restoring to them the control of the vessel, and enabling them to resume their voyage and to take the mutineers and murderers to their own country to answer for their crimes before the proper tribunal.[34]

Webster, in thus pleading the rights of the slave owners under international law, put aside all personal feelings, and, looking simply at the law of the matter, accepted a duty which devolved upon him under the Constitution. The antislavery leaders were not willing to admit the correctness of his reasoning. Charles Sumner, idealistic advocate of civil and political equality for all men, regardless of race, color, or birth, declared that the slaves on the *Creole* became free when they were taken, by the voluntary action of the owners, beyond the jurisdiction of the slave states, and upheld the action of the English authorities in giving them freedom.[35] Joshua R. Giddings, the antislavery firebrand from the Western Reserve, going far beyond Sumner, offered a set of resolutions which asserted that slavery, being an abridgement of the natural rights of man, can exist only by virtue of positive municipal law, and is necessarily confined to the territorial jurisdiction of the power creating it; that when a ship bearing slaves enters upon high seas, it ceases to be governed by the laws of the slave state from which it sailed, and

[33] William A. Dunning, *The British Empire and the United States*, 119.
[34] Joshua R. Giddings, *History of the Rebellion*, 178–179.
[35] Carter G. Woodson, *The Negro in Our History*, 347, 590–591.

the persons aboard, in their relations with one another, are amenable only to the laws of the United States; that the persons on board the *Creole,* in resuming their natural rights of personal liberty, violated no law of the United States, incurred no legal penalty, and are justly liable to no punishment; that all attempts to regain possession of or to remove said persons are unauthorized by the Constitution or laws of the United States, and are incompatible with our national honor.[36]

These resolutions raised a storm in the House. Upon a motion offered by John M. Botts of Virginia, a resolution was adopted censuring Giddings, whereupon he resigned his seat and appealed to his constituents in the sixteenth congressional district of Ohio, who immediately returned him to Congress.[37]

As the outcome of Webster's efforts, England at length agreed by treaty to submit the cases of the *Enterprise, Hermosa,* and *Creole* to arbitration. The award, made in 1853, set forth that:

All that the municipal authorities had a right to do in the *Creole* case was to keep the mutineers in custody until conveyance could be provided for their return to the United States.

As to the other slaves, the authorities should have seen that the owners' rights were protected by the law of nations, and that their rights under it cannot be abrogated or varied either by the emancipation act or by any other act of the British Parliament.

"We need not refer to authorities to show that slavery, however odious and contrary to the principles of justice and humanity, may be established by law in any country; and, having been so established in many countries, it cannot be contrary to the law of nations.

"The *Creole* was on a voyage, sanctioned and protected by the laws of the United States, and by the law of nations. Her right to

---

[36] Giddings, *Rebellion,* 180. *Cf.* case of U. S. *v.* Schooner *Amistad,* 15 Peters 518 (1841). The *Amistad* was a Spanish vessel carrying slaves to the United States contrary to law. The slaves murdered the officers and had control of the vessel when a war ship of the United States captured it and brought it into port. The court, Story handing down the decision, held that the Negroes should be freed and returned to Africa.

[37] *Ibid.,* Chap. XII. The vote censuring Giddings fell just short of the two thirds required to expel a member. See Byron R. Long, "Joshua Reed Giddings, a Champion of Political Freedom."

navigate the ocean could not be questioned, and as growing out of that right, the right to seek shelter or enter the ports of a friendly power in case of distress or any unavoidable necessity." [38]

"A vessel navigating the ocean carries with her the laws of her own country, so far as relates to the persons and property on board, and to a certain extent retains those rights even in the ports of the foreign nations she may visit."

Under this award Great Britain paid to the United States in 1854 an indemnity of $110,330. [39]

[38] Moore, II, 258. *Cf.* Swisher, *Taney*, 412–419, on the Supreme Court and the slave trade.

[39] For the history of the arbitration see Moore, IV, 4349–4378, and references.

XI

SLAVERY AND EXPANSION

THE ANNEXATION OF TEXAS

THE power to acquire foreign territory was not among those enumerated in the Constitution, nor was the question debated in the Constitutional Convention. The treaty for the purchase of Louisiana gave occasion for the first thorough discussion of the matter, and while the Federalists opposed the acquisition on grounds of policy, they agreed with the Republicans that the power was implied in those of making war and treaties.[1] This interpretation was confirmed by the decision of the Supreme Court in the case of the American Insurance Company *v.* Canter arising out of the purchase of Florida.[2] Despite these precedents, there were members of Congress who still believed that the annexation of foreign territory was unconstitutional, when the Texas question became a prominent issue in Tyler's presidency; and among those who favored annexation there was a great difference of opinion as to the proper method of procedure.

The chief debate followed the election of Polk in the autumn of 1844, a few months after the rejection by the Senate of Tyler's treaty for the annexation of Texas. It was precipitated by the proposal to annex Texas by joint resolution of the two houses.[3] The opponents of the proposal included those who insisted that the power of annexation did not exist, those who opposed annexation purely on antislavery grounds, and those who thought some other method preferable. As to the proper procedure, four different opinions were voiced by those who believed that acquisition was constitutional: (1) there were those who upheld the joint resolution; (2) there were others who believed that a new treaty was necessary; (3) there were some who thought that Texas must first be acquired as a territory (as provided by the rejected treaty)

[1] Hockett, *Con. Hist.*, I, 318.
[2] See discussion *post.*
[3] For the debate see *Cong. Globe*, 28 Cong., 2 sess., 16 *et passim.*

before she could be admitted as a state; while (4) others held that she could be annexed as a state. Those who agreed in the second opinion might differ on the third and fourth, so that the lines were badly crossed.[4]

The supporters of the joint resolution urged that the Constitution provides for the admission of new states by Congress, not the treaty-making organ, and that their method conformed to this requirement. The power to admit new states means any kind of state, whether erected from the territory already belonging to the United States or not. They cited the instances of Vermont, Rhode Island, North Carolina, Louisiana, Missouri, and Arkansas to show how varied were the types of state which had been admitted in the past, and alleged that Texas, like the last-mentioned three, was originally a part of the Louisiana Purchase Territory.

Those who urged the negotiation of a new treaty held that it was required by the necessity of obtaining the assent of Texas. An agreement with a foreign country through a joint resolution would be an unconstitutional substitution of a majority of the two houses for the President and Senate. They pointed out that the House of Representatives has no part in the making of treaties. Moreover, the joint resolution was a kind of legislation, and the legislative functions of Congress are confined to domestic affairs. Many of the anti-expansionists supported this reasoning, in order to defeat the joint resolution.

A third group held that Texas must first be acquired as a territory before she could be admitted as a state. Since Congress may admit new states, and may do anything which may be necessary and proper to admit them, it may annex new territory with a view to its admission to statehood. Texas might be annexed either by joint resolution or treaty, but only as territory, for admission to statehood would require an additional act of Congress. Senator Jabez W. Huntington of Connecticut expounded the constitutional principles involved in the admission of states from foreign territory by saying that "the power to annex foreign territory by treaty, and the power to admit New States into the Union by an act of Congress, are not concurrent, but distinct powers. Each is independent

[4] McMaster, VII, 396 et seq.

of the other, and neither [treaty-making organ nor Congress] can exercise both, nor can one exercise the authority conferred on the other. The one acquires territory; the other admits States." [5]

Some of the anti-expansionists revived the Federalist argument of 1803, and insisted that no foreign country could be annexed with a view to statehood, even by treaty, unless the Constitution were amended, for Congress may admit new states only from the original territory of the Union. In the end the joint resolution was adopted, leaving it optional with the President to negotiate a new treaty or offer Texas statehood, without further ado, upon indication of her desire. Tyler chose the latter alternative, but the question of annexation was submitted to a vote of the inhabitants of Texas. Their approval was promptly followed by recognition of Texas as a state.

THE PROBLEM OF SLAVERY IN ACQUIRED TERRITORY

The debates over the annexation were complicated by the objections of the antislavery element to the admission of a new slave state. When the war with Mexico followed, with the prospect of extensive conquests in the Southwest, a swarm of constitutional questions arose. Did Congress have unlimited power to govern the inhabitants of dependent territories? Or, in modern terms, Does the Constitution follow the flag? These are simple forms of putting questions which turned out to have many aspects and about which many different opinions developed. The most pressing problem concerned the status of slavery in the territory which might be acquired, and its solution proved to be not only difficult because of the conflicting interpretations of the Constitution, but dangerous because of the sectional strife which, already serious on account of the events which have been discussed, now threatened to go beyond all bounds.

On August 8, 1846, while the House of Representatives was considering a bill appropriating $2,000,000 to promote the peace negotiations, David Wilmot, a Pennsylvania free-soil Democrat, moved as an amendment to the bill, the proviso "that, as an express and fundamental condition to the acquisition of any territory from the Republic of Mexico by the United States, by virtue of any treaty

[5] *Cong. Globe,* 28 Cong., 2 sess., App., 399.

which may be negotiated between them, and to the use by the Executive of the moneys herein appropriated, neither slavery nor involuntary servitude shall ever exist in any part of said territory, except for crime, whereof the party shall first be duly convicted." [6]

Wilmot did not base his proposed prohibition on the general power of Congress over the territories, but on the fact that those in question were free under Mexican law. He declared that he was ready to defend the institutions of the South, but that lands which were free when acquired should remain free.[7] The proviso was adopted in the House. It failed in the Senate, but the attention of the public was attracted, and the legislatures of nine states passed resolutions either against the acquisition of territory or demanding the exclusion of slavery from any that might be acquired.[8] Early in 1847 the discussion of the proviso was renewed, and northern members, notably John Pettit of Indiana, urged its passage, basing the right of Congress to exclude slavery from the territories on the assumption that sovereignty over them was vested in the government of the United States.

The southern view was best presented in the House by Barnwell Rhett of South Carolina and in the Senate by Calhoun. The former denied that the government of the United States was sovereign over the territories. "Does the power 'to dispose of and make all needful rules and regulations' imply sovereignty? . . . Does not the clause relate to the territory only as property, and confer only powers necessary for its disposition and control as property? It speaks of the territories in connexion with the 'other property' of the United States. Congress can sell the lands lying within the territory, and, to secure purchasers and settlers in their persons and property, they can make 'all needful rules and regulations,' establish territorial governments and pass laws. . . . But the clause itself directly repudiates the idea that either Congress or the Government have any property, much less sovereignty over our territories. . . . It declares, that the territories belong to the United States. They are tenants in common, or joint proprietors, and co-sovereigns

---

[6] *Ibid.*, 29 Cong., 2 sess., 353. Reprinted in Johnson, 405.

[7] McMaster, VII, 473–505. See also Richard R. Stenberg, "The Motivation of the Wilmot Proviso." There is a life of Wilmot by Charles B. Going.

[8] McMaster, VII, 488. Ames, *State Docs.*, 243 *et seq.*

over them.   As co-sovereigns they have agreed, in their common compact, the Constitution, that their agent, the General Government, 'may dispose of, and make all needful rules and regulations,' with respect to them; but, beyond this, they are not limited or limitable in their rights. . . .   The only effect, and probably the only object of their reserved sovereignty, is, that it secures to each State the right to enter the territories with her citizens, and settle and occupy them with their property—with whatever is recognized as property by each State."   The citizen of any state "is not responsible to any of the co-sovereigns, for the nature of this property.   That is an affair between him and his State. . . .   Will not every foot of territory acquired be purchased by their common blood or treasure?   And do they not know that the Southern States must enter it with their slaves, or not at all? . . .   In exercising a common right over a common property, the southern States only do what the other States have also a right to do. . . .   It will be a strange injustice, if a portion of the States, whether free or slave, shall presume to set up their will as supreme over the territories, and through Congress, or any other instrumentality, shall attempt to exclude any of these co-States from possessing and colonizing them." [9]

Rhett's argument was hardly more than the expansion of the texts advanced by Calhoun in his resolutions of 1837.   A little more than a month after the above speech was delivered, Calhoun introduced a new set of resolutions, prefacing them with a speech in which he called attention to the relatively rapid growth of the free states and predicted the results which he thought must follow the destruction of the balance between the sections.   Just half of the existing twenty-eight states were free, said he, hence there was equality in the Senate, but nowhere else, since the House contained 138 representatives of the free states but only 90 representatives of the slave states, and in the electoral college they had respectively 168 and 118 members.   Iowa and Wisconsin were about to come in as states, and twelve more free states were possible from the terri-

[9] Speech of January 15, 1847. *Cong. Globe*, 29 Cong., 2 sess., App., 244–246, *passim*. Extract in Johnson, 406–408. *Cf.* views of Monroe *et al.* during the Missouri debate, *supra*, Chap. VIII. There is a life of Rhett by Laura A. White.

tory already belonging to the Union. Hence there was a prospect
of 28 free and 14 slave states. When this prospect became reality
the former would have the slave states completely at their mercy
in the Senate as well as in all other branches of the government.
Then, he predicted, grave consequences must follow. "The day
that the balance between the two sections of the country . . . is
destroyed, is a day that will not be far removed from political
revolution, anarchy, civil war, and widespread disaster." To prevent this the rights of the South must be protected by 'a returning
regard for the original spirit of the Constitution.[10]

The policy of excluding the southern states from equal privileges
with the northern states in the territories, he then asserted, was
entirely opposed to the Constitution. "Ours is a Federal Constitution. . . . It was so formed, that every state . . . should enjoy
all its advantages. . . . The whole system is based on justice and
equality—perfect equality between the members of this Republic.
Now, can that be consistent with equality which will make this
public domain a monopoly on one side—which, in its consequences
would place the whole power in one section of the Union to be
wielded against the other section?" The territory of the United
States, he urged, is the property of the "States United," and is held
jointly for their common use.[11]

In offering his resolutions, Calhoun said that he wished the Senate
by voting on them to give its opinion on two great principles, viz.,
the right of all states to share in the territories, and the right of the
people of a territory to decide what their constitution shall contain
when they became a state, with no right in Congress to interfere
except to guarantee to the state a republican form of government.[12]

The resolutions declared that the territories were common property; that Congress could not deprive any state of its equal right in
any territory acquired or to be acquired; that a law depriving citizens of any state of the right to emigrate to any territory with their
property would be a violation of the Constitution and established
rights, and would tend directly to subvert the Union itself; that

[10] Speech of Feb. 19, 1847, *Cong. Globe*, 29 Cong., 2 sess., 453 *et seq.*
[11] *Ibid.*
[12] *Ibid.*

Congress could impose on the states at the time of their admission no condition except that their constitutions be republican in form.[13]

During the debate on these resolutions, Calhoun was called on several times to explain and defend them. In one of these explanatory speeches he denied that the exclusion of slavery from the Northwest Territory should be regarded as a precedent to be followed. The territory, he pointed out, had been given to the United States by Virginia, a slave state, but as, under the Articles, the free states held a majority in Congress, they were able to exclude slavery notwithstanding the fact that the delegates from the slave states opposed the action almost to a man.[14] In a later speech he added that the southern members allowed the antislavery clause to be included in the Ordinance of 1787 only because the northern delegates agreed to insert the article providing for the rendition of fugitive slaves. As the two clauses constituted a compromise, and as a compromise involves only a waiver and not a surrender of a right, the ordinance could not be cited as a precedent.[15] The ordinance was contrary to the spirit of the Articles; and now the states carved out of the Northwest Territory were violating that part of the Constitution which provides for the return of fugitive slaves.

Moderate men, both North and South, were unwilling to take so extreme a stand as either Wilmot or Calhoun. President Polk believed that both sides should be content with the extension of the Missouri Compromise line.[16] By dividing the territories in this way, substantial recognition would be given to the equality of rights which Calhoun and Rhett so strongly demanded. This view had a number of supporters. But the ranks of the moderates were divided, for many of them adopted the doctrine of "popular sovereignty" as the proper solution of the whole question of slavery in the territories.

The most conspicuous advocate of popular sovereignty (or

[13] *Ibid.*

[14] Crallé, IV, 355–360.

[15] *Ibid.*, IV, 488. In both of these statements Calhoun's historical information was defective. Only one member of the Confederation Congress voted against the Ordinance of 1787, and he was from New York. As to the alleged compromise, see Way's article, cited *supra*, Chap. VIII.

[16] R. L. Schuyler, "Polk and the Oregon Compromise."

"squatter" sovereignty, as it was called in derision), was Senator Lewis Cass of Michigan, who was about to be named by the Democrats as their presidential candidate. On the day before Christmas, 1847, he wrote to A. O. P. Nicholson of Nashville an exposition of his views which promptly went to the newspapers as his personal platform.[17] He approached the problem from the standpoint of the relations between federal authority and the local police power. Although he did not use the words, he raised the question, in effect, Where is vested the power over the internal police affairs of the territories? As to the states, the theory of the Union presupposed that they had "reserved to themselves the regulation of all subjects relating to what may be termed their internal police. . . . Local institutions . . . whether they have reference to slavery or to any other relations, domestic or public, are left to local authority."

This principle Cass then took as the clue to the proper administration of the territories. How does the theory of local control of local police apply to the internal affairs of the territories? Admitting that the territories do not possess "the peculiar attributes of sovereignty" which the states have, Cass nevertheless insisted that the only grant of power over them in the Constitution, the clause empowering Congress "to dispose of and make all needful rules and regulations respecting the territory and other property," was intended to enable the general government to perform its functions as a property-holder. "The lives and persons of our citizens, with the vast variety of objects connected with them, cannot be controlled by an authority which is merely called into existence for the purpose of making *rules and regulations for the disposition and management of property*."

Owing to the fact that the relations of the territories to the general government were so imperfectly defined in the Constitution, Congress had at various times, said Cass, exercised a larger power than that of property-manager. "How far an existing necessity may have operated in producing this legislation, and thus extending, by rather a violent implication powers not directly given, I know not. But certain it is that the principle of interference should not be

[17] *Niles' Register*, LXXIII, 293–294. Reprinted in Johnson, 411–414.

carried beyond the necessary implication, which produces it. It should be limited to the creation of proper governments for the new countries, acquired or settled, and to the necessary provisions for their eventual admission into the Union; leaving, in the meantime, to the people inhabiting them to regulate their internal concerns in their own way. They are just as capable of doing so as the people of the States; and they can do so, at any rate as soon as their political independence is recognized by admission into the Union. During this temporary condition, it is hardly expedient to call into exercise a doubtful and invidious authority which questions the intelligence of a respectable portion of our citizens, and whose limitation, whatever it may be, will be rapidly approaching its termination—an authority which would give Congress despotic power, uncontrolled by the Constitution, over most important sections of our common country."

The doctrine thus invoked as a solution of the slavery issue in the territories was by no means original with Cass, although its specific application was new. The territorial system of the United States, first outlined in the Ordinance of 1787, was, whether consciously or not, patterned after the British colonial system. In providing a system of government of the settlers by agents appointed by the general government, it disregarded the principle of local self-government which lay at the basis of American federalism, and adopted in its stead the unitary system of the English. Although it did so tacitly, the ordinance asserted as truly as did the Declaratory Act of 1766,[18] that the control over the local police of dependencies was vested in the central government. Although necessity seemed to require such control for at least a temporary period, it is not surprising that from the first the system was distasteful to many Americans. It is true that some of the Federalists, like Gouverneur Morris, believed that colonies might be held in per-

[18] See Hockett, *Con. Hist.*, I, 86 *et seq.* Note the kinship, also, of the popular sovereignty doctrine with the colonial creed of autonomy in matters of internal police.—*Ibid., passim.* The question (discussed *post*) whether the Constitution extended *ex proprio vigore* to the new territories recalls the old one of the force of English law in the colonies. *Cf. ibid.*, 37 *et seq. Cf.* also Stephen A. Douglas, "The Dividing Line between Federal and Local Authority," for the mid-century argument.

manent subjection, but they were influenced by European practice to the point of losing sight of the logic of American political philosophy. The early Republicans spoke of the territorial status as one of degradation, under which a part of the population of the nation was deprived of some of the essential liberties of Americans.[19] In a country in which all government derived its authority from the people, the claim that Congress possessed sovereign power over the inhabitants of territories was illogical and discordant. As a matter of fact, the logic of events has proved to be stronger than the logic of eighteenth century philosophy.

As applied by Cass to the slavery issue, popular sovereignty was rejected both by the antislavery radicals and by the southern extremists. Many, however, seized upon it as promising to quiet the sectional struggle. It appealed because it was in harmony with the philosophy of popular government and because, as a do-nothing policy, it opened a path for Congress to withdraw from a difficult situation. On December 15 Senator Daniel S. Dickinson of New York offered a resolution that as soon as a territory was organized under a local government all questions of domestic policy should be left to a legislature chosen by the people. Leave the domestic legislation for territories to the local legislatures, he urged, and the sectional struggles which have caused such bitterness will be banished from the halls of Congress, and the government left free to pursue its course unembarrassed by sectional issues.[20]

The conflict of opinion delayed action. Senator D. L. Yulee of Florida moved to substitute for Dickinson's resolution one declaring that territory, possessed or to be acquired, is the common property of the Union, and Congress has no delegated, and territorial communities no inherent, right to impair the equal rights of all citizens to acquire and enjoy the common property.[21] Senator Arthur P. Bagby of Alabama proposed to add that Congress could not abolish or forbid slavery in any state or territory; nor could the treaty-making power or Congress exclude slavery from acquired terri-

[19] See Madison's speech on the admission of Tennessee, *Ann. of Cong.*, 4 Cong., 1 sess., 1308–1309.
[20] McMaster, VII, 499–502.
[21] *Ibid.*

tory; therefore such territory was open to all citizens without restriction on slavery. Nor could Congress delegate to a territorial legislature a power to exclude slavery.[22]

While the two houses were contending over these various views, the situation was complicated by the injection of the Oregon question. After decades of disagreement, England and the United States had at last decided (1846) to divide the far northwestern country, and in May, 1848, a message of President Polk to Congress recommended the establishment of a territorial government there. Pending the settlement of the dispute with England, the American settlers had organized a provisional government. Accordingly, when the committee to which the President's message was referred brought in its bill, it contained a provision recognizing the laws or ordinances adopted by the temporary government. One of these, however, prohibited slavery, and while no one believed that Oregon could ever become a slaveholding region, the Texas question and the Mexican War had so inflamed the sections that southern men objected both to the tacit exclusion of the institution from the Northwest by the proposed bill and the express application to it of the antislavery provision of the Ordinance of 1787. Most of them were willing to pass the subject over in silence, to be settled by the residents of the territory after the organization of the government. But Calhoun objected even to this course, and denied that either Congress or a territorial legislature had the right to exclude slavery from any territory.

Calhoun defended his doctrines in a speech on the Oregon bill, on June 27, 1848.[23] Once more he insisted that the territories, including Oregon, were legally open to all the citizens of the United States and could not be closed to slavery except by the people of each particular territory when they framed their constitution preparatory to admission to statehood. Like Cass and Rhett, he denied that the Constitution gave Congress absolute power over the territories, holding that the territorial clause related to the public lands as property. Again he stressed the arguments based on the equality of the states in a common Union, the recognition of slave property

[22] *Ibid.*, 503.
[23] Crallé, IV, 484 *et seq.*

by the Constitution, and the acquisition of the territories by the common expense and effort.

It is particularly noteworthy that Calhoun, the great exponent of state control of internal police, rejected the idea that the people of the territories possessed similar rights. In this he ran far ahead of the prevalent sentiment of his section, which for the most part was contented with popular sovereignty until after the Dred Scott decision. Yulee and Bagby were, like Calhoun, spokesmen of a minority.

In the Oregon debate Calhoun admitted that he had favored the Missouri Compromise at the time of its adoption, thinking it a good way of settling a serious intersectional difficulty. But he had come, he said, to regard his former position as a great error, because it surrendered, for temporary reasons, the high principles of the Constitution on which he thought the states should stand.[24] A compromise was a mere act of Congress which a later session might revoke. It could therefore give no security. He was done with compromise, but saw a clear path in the Constitution, to which he asked the country to return. The Missouri Compromise was not to be followed as a precedent. The North had imposed it on the South by superior strength; the South had always opposed it but had acquiesced because she could not attack it without causing discord between the sections.[25]

Calhoun admitted that a limited power of Congress to legislate for the territories was implied by the right to acquire territory by war or treaty. In such legislation, however, Congress was subject to the limitations imposed by the Constitution. As the agent of the states, it could not discriminate, in territorial legislation, between those of the North and South. In addition to this, the South could not be excluded from the territories by antislavery legislation because, of all property rights, that of the slave owners was the only one specifically guaranteed by the Constitution. It was not true, he maintained, that the Mexican laws forbidding slavery in the

[24] *Ibid.*, IV, 346. Calhoun had changed his mind regarding the Missouri Compromise as early as the beginning of 1838. *Ibid.*, III, 185.

[25] Again Calhoun had his facts wrong, if he refers to the vote in Congress, for a majority of southern members in both houses voted for the compromise. See *supra*, Chap. VIII.

territory now belonging to the United States held good until Congress should change them. When the territory was transferred, the Mexican law was superseded by the Constitution of the United States, at least so far as the two were in conflict. However, local law in general, he conceded, should stand until changed, to prevent disorder.[26]

Calhoun thus gave slavery an exceptional position. Since it enjoyed a privileged status under the Constitution, it became established in acquired territory, he contended, by the mere act of cession.

EFFORTS AT COMPROMISE

One of the attempts to bring a majority of Congress into agreement on these perplexing questions became known as the Clayton Compromise. On motion of Senator John M. Clayton, of Delaware, in 1848, the question of the territories was referred to a committee of eight members, along with that part of the President's message which related to New Mexico, California, and Oregon. This committee reported a bill for the organization of a territorial government in each of these regions, but they were not all to be of the same type. Oregon was to be given complete territorial organization with a delegate in Congress. Her existing laws were to remain in force for three months after the first meeting of the legislature, to which was left, in this manner, the slavery question. California and New Mexico, the two territories into which at that time it was planned to divide the region ceded by Mexico, were to have a less advanced form of government. They were to have no congressional delegates, and the legislative power over them was to be vested in a governor, secretary, and judges, appointed by the President and Senate. These officials, in their legislative capacity, were *forbidden* to deal with the question of slavery. The right to introduce or prohibit slavery was to depend upon the interpretation of the Constitution by the judges.[27]

[26] Crallé, IV, 490 *et seq.*

[27] *Cong. Globe*, 30 Cong., 1 sess., 950. Clayton hoped that the adoption of his proposals might prevent further discussion by Congress. Some evidence of the desire of members to be rid of the question appears from the following words of Senator Thomas H. Benton, on May 31, 1848: "This Federal Government was

In the House of Representatives, Alexander H. Stephens, who later became the Vice-President of the Confederacy, debating the proposal to leave all questions relating to slavery to the courts, cited the American Insurance Company v. Canter to show what this provision would mean in practice.[28] In this case Chief Justice Marshall had said, referring to the effect of the acquisition of Florida upon the legal relations of its inhabitants: "The same act which transfers their country, transfers the allegiance of those who remain in it; and the law, which may be denominated political, is necessarily changed, although that which regulates the intercourse and general conduct of individuals, remains in force until altered by the newly created power of the state." [29]

The compromise bill, said Stephens, "merely prohibits the Territorial Government from passing any law upon the subject; and leaves the southern man, who may be inclined to go there with his slaves, to contest his rights to the best of his abilities with the Courts of the Territory in the first instance, and then, if he chooses, with the Supreme Court of the Union." From the decision just quoted and other authorities Stephens made it clear that "the law by which the courts would decide questions of slavery there is the law which was in force in New Mexico and California upon that subject at the time of the conquest. . . . What was the law . . . ? Upon this point, I suppose, there can be no doubt. Slavery was abolished there in 1829."

Stephens denied that the Constitution recognized slavery except where it existed under municipal law, and asserted that it "no more carries the local law of slavery of any State into a State or Territory where, by law, it is prohibited, than it carries any other law; no more than it carries the law of interest upon money, the statute of limitations, the laws of distribution, or the penal laws of a State. . . . My position," he concluded, "is this: That slavery is

made for something else than to have this pestiferous question constantly thrust upon us to the interruption of the most important business. . . . What I protest against is, to have the real business of the country, the pressing, urgent, crying business of the country stopped, prostrated, defeated, by thrusting this question upon us."—Ibid., App., 686.

[28] Speech of August 7, 1848. Ibid., 30 Cong., 1 sess., App. 1104–1106 et passim. Extract in Johnson, 408–411.

[29] 1 Peters 511 (1828). Reprint in Commager, 248–249.

an institution which depends solely upon the municipal law of the place where it exists; and if it was prohibited by law in these Territories at the time of the conquest, it cannot exist there until the laws of the place be altered by the competent law-making power for the Territory." [30]

It was Stephens's purpose to prove that the proposed bill afforded no protection for the owner of slaves who chose to remove to the Southwest. It appears that his argument, so difficult for the mind untrained in law to follow, aroused some suspicions as to his loyalty to southern rights, for at the end of August as he passed through the town of Clinton, in Georgia, he found in the local newspaper an open letter asking for a further explanation of his attitude towards the Clayton Compromise. In reply he repeated his argument in less technical language:

"In New Mexico and California slavery was abolished and prohibited by express law at the time of conquest. And according to the decisions of the Supreme Court of the United States, which no man can gainsay nor deny; (I mean the *fact* of the decisions; I do not now speak of their correctness), all the laws which were of force at the time of the conquest will continue in force until altered by competent authority, *except such as were inconsistent with the Constitution of the United States* or the stipulations of the treaty. Is the prohibition of slavery by the local law of any state or place inconsistent with the Constitution of the United States? If it is, those laws of New Mexico and California will become abrogated and necessarily cease to operate upon the final fulfillment of the treaty stipulations. But if the prohibition of slavery by local law . . . is not inconsistent with the Constitution according to the decisions of the Supreme Court, they will of course remain in force until altered by competent authority. My own opinion is, that neither the existence of slavery or non-existence of it by the local law of any place is inconsistent with any provision of the Constitution. . . . Slavery depends upon the law of the place, which may be either *written or unwritten*. And where it exists the Constitution protects it, but it does not establish it where it is prohibited. . . .

[30] Speech of August 7, 1848, *loc. cit.*

"These are the principles I hold: Congress has no right to exclude the South from an equal share, and it is the duty of Congress to see that the rights of the South are as amply protected as the rights of the North. And it was this right of legal protection for the property of the South that was surrendered in that [Clayton] bill. If Congress has the power to declare exactly how far the interests of the North shall be protected, if they have the power to extend the Missouri Compromise line, they certainly have the power to say in clear and distinct words that up to that line on the South the rights of the South shall be protected—and not after prohibiting us from going North of that line leave us to contest with the Courts our rights on the South of it. This is what the Compromise bill did. It excluded us from the whole of Oregon, and left us to the Courts to decide whether we should be allowed to carry and hold our property in New Mexico and California. For such a Compromise I shall never vote." [31]

Clearly Stephens and Calhoun were far apart. The former's argument completely refuted the contention that the Constitution carried slavery into acquired territory *ex proprio vigore*, and in spite of his guarded language, Stephens seemed not ready to deny the power of Congress to legislate for the territories, so long as that power was fairly used to the equal advantage of both sections. Although he may not have intended it, his words implied that the extension of the Missouri Compromise line of 1820, with the South assured of the right to carry slaves into the region below it, was the most practicable solution of the problem. A few years later he had come to believe that the Missouri Compromise was unconstitutional. Such objections as he had offered to the Clayton Compromise wrecked that proposal; it passed the Senate on July 27 by a vote of 33 to 22, but was tabled in the House, and Congress again floundered about almost hopelessly in quest of a solution on which enough members could unite to effect legislation.

A bill was finally passed erecting a territorial government in Oregon, with an antislavery provision borrowed from the Ordinance of 1787. President Polk signed this bill because the territory concerned lay north of the Missouri Compromise line. The de-

[31] Am. Hist. Assn. *Report* for 1911, II, 120–122.

bate over the territories in the Southwest continued, simplified somewhat by the elimination of the Oregon factor.

Meantime the campaign of 1848 brought General Taylor to the presidential chair. So far as the slavery issue was concerned, the election was wholly indecisive, since each of the major parties evaded the question in order to maintain intact its intersectional organization. The triumph of Taylor over Cass therefore contributed little or nothing to the solution of the problems which were disturbing the nation. Sentiment in Congress, however, reflected the division without, and the paralysis of the law-making body continued, every new effort to find a way out seemingly only revealing a new difficulty.

One of these efforts was made by Senator Isaac P. Walker of Wisconsin, who in February, 1849, while the general appropriation bill was pending, precipitated a new debate by moving an amendment extending the Constitution to the territories.[32] Webster objected that Walker was proposing the impossible. He maintained that the Constitution cannot be extended over anything but the states. A territory, he explained, is not a part of the Union of states, and to the Union alone the Constitution applies. Not even the guarantees of personal liberty apply *ex proprio vigore* to the people of a territory, an act of Congress being required to extend them.[33]

This utterance had as its basis the legislation of Congress, especially for the Province of Louisiana, in 1803 and 1804,[34] but it drew a reply from the ever-alert Calhoun, who saw in this interpretation a denial of his pet idea that the Constitution carried slavery automatically into the territories. "The simple question is," he exclaimed, "does the constitution extend to the territories, or does it not extend to them? Why, the constitution interprets itself. It pronounces itself to be the 'supreme law of the land.' The land; —the territories of the United States are a part of the land. It is the supreme law, not within the limits of the States of this Union merely, but wherever the flag waves. Wherever our authority goes, the constitution, in short, goes;—not all its provisions cer-

[32] Miller, *Great Debates*, IV, 170–180.
[33] *Ibid.*
[34] See Hockett, *Con. Hist.*, I, 320–322.

tainly, but all its suitable provisions. Why, can we have any authority beyond the constitution? I put the question solemnly to
gentlemen: If the constitution does not go there, how are we to
have any authority or jurisdiction whatever? Is not Congress the
creature of the constitution?" [35]

Calhoun then remarked that he was surprised to hear that the
courts of the United States had decided that the Constitution does
not extend to the territories without an act of Congress. He was
incredulous, he said, that any tribunal pretending to have a knowledge of our system of government could pronounce such a mon-
strous judgment. He was inclined to believe that an error had
been made in ascribing such views to the court, but if such a decision had been given, he, for one, would say that it ought not to
be, and could not be respected. While the Constitution could not
become effective in the territories without the intervention of legislation, it was nevertheless the law of the land in obedience and conformity to which all laws must be made. Even the Senator from
Massachusetts would agree that Congress cannot create a nobility
or an established church in the territories—that these prohibitions
in the Constitution apply to acts relating to the territories as well as
to the states. If so then the positive provisions must apply there
also.[36]

Webster in his turn remarked: "The Senator denies the constitutionality of federal internal improvements within States but
votes for them in the territories under the conception that they are
no parts of the Union." [37]

This passage at arms hardly clarified the public thought; indeed,
it serves to show the historian that even these great intellects were
badly muddled in their ideas of the constitutional law of these novel
problems. Walker's amendment was adopted but later recon-
sidered and lost.

While Congress was making vain efforts to define a consistent
theory of constitutional law for territorial questions, the Supreme
Court, in consequence of cases arising out of the war, was establish-

[35] Crallé, IV, 536.
[36] *Ibid.*, 536–540.
[37] Miller, *op. cit.*

ing some principles of permanent value. One of these cases, Fleming v. Page, concerned the applicability of the tariff laws to Mexican territory temporarily held by military force.[38] Tampico had been in the hands of troops, and the question developed whether imports thence to the United States were subject to the same duties as imports from foreign countries. The court held that military occupation does "not enlarge the boundaries of this Union, nor extend the operation of the institutions and laws beyond the limits before assigned to them by the legislative power." Tampico, as regards all other nations, "was a part of the United States and belonged to them, as exclusively as the territory included in our established boundaries. But yet it was not a part of the Union. . . . The inhabitants were still foes and enemies and owed to the United States nothing more than the submission and obedience, sometimes called temporary allegiance which is due from a conquered enemy, when he surrenders to a force which he is unable to resist." Tampico was returned to Mexico at the peace, and the government of the United States exercised no rights or powers therein at any time except those of war. The decision was therefore that the tariff on imports to the United States from Tampico was not affected by the temporary military occupation.

The situation was different where imports were brought into territory acquired by the United States by the treaty which closed the war. The case of Cross v. Harrison raised the question whether imports into California in the interim between the ratification of the treaty and the action of Congress providing for the acquired territory, were dutiable under the laws of the United States. The court now held that California ceased to be foreign and became a part of the United States upon the ratification of the treaty, and that the duties were payable even though Congress had not extended the laws to the acquired lands.[39]

[38] 6 Howard, 603 (1850).
[39] 16 Howard 164 (1853).

XII

COMPROMISE AND CONFLICT

THE COMPROMISE OF 1850

WHILE Calhoun was insisting that Congress had no power to exclude slavery from any territory, the South was preparing to be content with less than he demanded. Calhoun himself admitted that if the territories were left free and open to the immigration of the world, "climate, soil, and circumstances would fix the line between the slaveholding and nonslaveholding States at about 36° 30'." It might zigzag a little, he said, but that would not matter, and would tend less to alienate the two great sections "than a rigid, straight, artificial line, prescribed by Congress." [1] Calhoun's doctrinaire insistence upon the legal right of slavery to go where nature forbade awoke no great response in his section, where a practical spirit suggested the wisdom of taking the kernel and letting the shell go.

In June, 1850, an expression of opinion outside of political circles came in the form of resolutions adopted by a southern convention meeting at Nashville, for the alleged purpose of considering the economic situation of the South. The sectional feeling had run so high by this time that apprehension was felt lest the convention indulge in plans of secession, as the notorious gathering at Hartford in 1814 was supposed to have done. The resolutions asserted: that the territories of the United States belong to the people of the several states of this Union as their common property; that Congress has no power to exclude from the territories any property lawfully held in any state; that it is the duty of the federal government to make early provision for the enactment of those laws which may be expedient and necessary to secure to the inhabitants of and immigrants to such territories the full benefit of the constitutional rights asserted; that the slaveholding states cannot and will not submit to the enactment by Congress of any law imposing onerous conditions

---

[1] Crallé, IV, 506.

or restraints upon the rights of masters to remove with their property into the territories.[2]

Up to this point the resolutions have the genuine Calhoun ring, but the remaining ones made it evident that the rights claimed were not to be demanded as an ultimatum. On the contrary the convention displayed a conciliatory disposition and suggested compromise in the twelfth resolution, which read: "It is the opinion of this Convention that this controversy should be ended, either by a recognition of the constitutional rights of the Southern people, or by an equitable partition of the territories." Thus was indicated approval of extending the Missouri Compromise line.

By this time the situation in the Southwest had changed. On account of the gold discoveries in California, the population of that region had increased so rapidly that a territorial government could no longer be thought of; the people, indeed, impatient at the delays of Congress, had taken matters into their own hands and adopted a free-state constitution, and were now knocking at the door of Congress requesting admission to the Union. In the Salt Lake Basin, moreover, the Mormon colony had created the necessity of organizing another territory.

The deadlock which had prevented legislation for the Southwest during a quadrennium was at last broken by the compromise measures adopted in 1850. The story of the compromise need not be retold, but, in so far as they related to the slavery issue, Clay's resolutions which paved the way for the compromise may be summarized as follows:

California should be admitted under her free-state constitution. Slavery does not exist by law, and is not likely to exist under natural conditions, in the country acquired from Mexico. Congress should therefore neither legalize it therein nor shut it out. Governments should be set up without any stipulations concerning slavery. Slavery ought not to be abolished in the District of Columbia while it exists in Maryland, unless Maryland consents and the owners are compensated. The trade in slaves brought in from other states to be sold in the district ought to be abolished. A more stringent

---

[2] Ames, *State Docs.*, 263–266; Commager, 324–325. See Farrar Newberry, "The Nashville Convention and Southern Sentiment."

fugitive slave law should be enacted, and Congress should declare that it has no power to interfere with the interstate slave trade.[3]

Although both Calhoun and the radical antislavery leaders were irreconcilable to the last, all of these proposals with the exception of the final one concerning the interstate slave trade, won a majority vote in both houses and became law. The leaders of the Whig and Democratic parties united their efforts to bring about this result, and both parties endorsed the compromise as a settlement of the sectional struggle. For a time it seemed probable that the public would acquiesce. The country was weary of strife. Most of the Free Soilers returned to their former party allegiance in 1852, and the southern irreconcilables were defeated in state contests.[4]

The sentiment which prevailed in the South at this time may be inferred from the so-called "Georgia platform." Upon the adjournment of the session of Congress which adopted the compromise, the governor of Georgia by proclamation called a convention representing the people of the state, to meet in December, 1850, for the purpose of determining whether to accept or reject the compromise. Led by Robert Toombs, Howell Cobb, and Alexander H. Stephens, all of them members of Congress, the convention decided to endorse it, but adopted resolutions explanatory of their action. These soon became known as the "Georgia platform" and influenced the decision of other southern states to a marked degree. The Georgia resolutions did not express entire approval of

---

[3] *Cong. Globe,* 31 Cong., 1 sess., 246–247. Jan. 28, 1850. Reprint in Commager, 319–320.

[4] Southern leaders were not happy over the compromise. When the Senate passed the bill for the admission of California as a free state, ten southern Senators protested that the action was fatal to the peace and equality of their states. Up to this time the only condition which the South had admitted might be imposed upon a new state was that it have a republican form of government. Now it would appear that Congress, under the rule of equality inculcated by Calhoun (who, of course, rejected this interpretation of the rule), could admit new states only in pairs, a free and a slave state together. Southern extremists were skillful in finding in the Constitution ample basis for all their demands. Said Robert Toombs of Georgia—one feels sure it would be correct to say *shouted* Toombs of Georgia—"We have the right to call on you to give your blood to maintain these thousands and all the rest of the slaves of the South in bondage. . . . This is a pro-slavery Government. Slavery is stamped upon its heart—the Constitution." *Cong. Globe,* 31 Cong., 1 sess., App., 199.

the compromise measures, but promised acceptance of them in a spirit of conciliation, as a "permanent adjustment of this sectional controversy." At the same time they threatened resistance "even (as a last resort) to a disruption of every tie which binds her to the Union," to any act of Congress encroaching further upon the rights of the slave states.[5]

Even the northern discontent caused by the new fugitive slave law tended to diminish after a few years. But suddenly the Kansas-Nebraska issue aroused again the dying embers of sectional conflict. This question brought the popular sovereignty doctrine to the front. The acts of 1850 erecting governments in Utah and New Mexico territories without prescription as to what should be done with slavery could be construed as endorsements of popular sovereignty, and in 1854 Senator Stephen A. Douglas of Illinois, interested in the promotion of railways across the great plains, and anxious to conciliate opposition in Missouri, where opinion was hostile to the opening of the plains to settlement as free territory, proposed the application of the same principle to the governments to be erected there.[6]

Out of Douglas's proposal came, in connection with the organization of the territories of Kansas and Nebraska, the outright repeal of the Missouri Compromise Act of 1820.[7] The North now

[5] Ames, *State Docs.,* 269–276; Commager, 323–324. See also R. P. Brooks, "Howell Cobb and the Crisis of 1850"; Cleo Hearon, "Struggle in Mississippi over Compromise of 1850"; H. V. Ames, "J. C. Calhoun's Connection with the Secession Movement of 1850"; St. G. L. Sioussat, "Tennessee, the Compromise of 1850 and the Nashville Convention"; Richard H. Shryock, *Georgia and the Union in 1850.*

[6] For a recent sympathetic account of Douglas's career see George Fort Milton, *The Eve of Conflict—Stephen A. Douglas and the Needless War.* Cf. Allen Johnson, *Stephen A. Douglas.*

[7] For the congressional history of the repeal see McLaughlin, *Con. Hist.,* 542 *et seq.* The repeal act provided that, the eighth section of the Missouri act of 1820 "being inconsistent with the principle of non-intervention by Congress with slavery in the States and Territories, as recognized by the legislation of eighteen hundred and fifty, . . . is hereby declared inoperative and void; it being the true intent and meaning of this act not to legislate slavery into any Territory or State, nor to exclude it therefrom, but to leave the people thereof perfectly free to form and regulate their domestic institutions in their own way, subject only to the Constitution of the United States."

The meaning of these latter words is not clear, and they were understood in different ways at the time. Many persons believed that the intent was to authorize the territorial legislature to deal with slavery as it saw fit, with the expectation that appeal would or could be taken to the courts on all questions of

learned, as Calhoun had said, that acts of Congress which could be repealed afforded no security for sectional interests. But both sides had long regarded the compromise as a sacred agreement, and the indignation of the antislavery element at the opening to slavery of the territory which they had regarded as forever consecrated to freedom led to the formation of the Republican Party, with the avowed purpose of excluding slavery from all territories and of refusing statehood to every territory that framed a proslavery constitution when it became populous enough to be admitted to the Union.

THE COURTS AND SLAVERY [8]

The leading decision of the Supreme Court touching slavery, prior to the fifties, was that in Prigg v. Pennsylvania, which has been discussed. In 1847, in the case of Jones v. Van Zandt, the Fugitive Slave Act of 1793 was again upheld.[9] Next the court passed on the case of Strader v. Graham, which came before it on writ of error from the Kentucky Court of Appeals.[10]

This case was popularly known as the case of the "Kentucky Minstrels," from the fact that Graham of Kentucky had several times sent three of his slaves to play at entertainments across the river in the State of Ohio. One day some of these minstrels crossed from Louisville to Cincinnati without their master's knowledge, and thence escaped to Canada. Graham sued Strader, the owner of the ferry, for conniving at the fugitives' escape, and he in his defense averred that he had not aided slaves to escape, since in consequence of the previous trips with the owner's consent, the Negroes had become free under the provisions of the Northwest Ordinance and the laws of Ohio. The Kentucky court had decided in Graham's favor, and the Supreme Court unanimously agreed that the status of the Negroes depended entirely on the laws of Ken-

the constitutionality of such laws. This was Douglas's explanation in 1859. See *Cong. Globe*, 35 Cong., 2 sess., 1245. For discussion of the whole topic see Milo M. Quaife, *The Doctrine of Non-Intervention with Slavery in the Territories.*

[8] An important collection bearing on this topic is Helen T. Catterall's *Judicial Cases Concerning American Slavery.*

[9] 5 Howard 215. See the account in McMaster, VII, 264–265.

[10] 10 Howard 82 (1850). On the topics of this chapter see Swisher, *Taney*, Chap. XXIII.

tucky. "It was exclusively in the power of Kentucky to determine for itself whether their employment in another State should make them freemen on their return." As the case presented no question of federal law, but only an issue of state law already decided by the state court, the Supreme Court held that it had no jurisdiction.

It is to be noted that in this case the Negroes' return was the determining factor. Representative Stephens, in his speech on the Clayton Compromise in 1848, admitted that "if I voluntarily take my slave into a State where slavery is by law prohibited, I have no right to retake him; he becomes free. No man will question this." The decision of both courts in the minstrels' case, as well as Stephens's opinion in the hypothetical one, ran back to the English precedents already cited. Stephens's hypothesis was analogous to the situation covered by Lord Mansfield's great decision in the Somerset case, while the Kentucky case reproduced that of the slave Grace, on which the British courts had passed in 1826, and strikingly illustrates the influence of English jurisprudence upon American legal development.

For American constitutional law, the decision in Strader v. Graham established the principle that each state made its own law determining the status of slaves who returned after temporary absences on free soil. The English precedents were of much weight in shaping the decisions of state courts, especially in the absence of exactly applicable statutes and prior to the Supreme Court decisions. In Missouri, for example, the courts applied the principle that free soil makes free men even in the event of the return of slaves to the state, in the erroneous belief that they were following the decision in the Somerset case. In several instances between 1825 and 1850 slaves were freed by the courts of that state because their masters had taken them for a period of residence in the Northwest Territory or the State of Illinois. Even unnecessary delay in a free state on the part of owners migrating from slave states to Missouri was regarded as sufficient ground for holding that the immigrant forfeited his slave property.[11] These decisions rested upon state comity—the recognition of the laws of sister commonwealths—as well as upon English precedents; but the judgment in Strader v.

[11] Catteral, "Antecedents of the Dred Scott Case," 66 et seq.

Graham brought into view the qualifying principle of the English decision of 1826, and proved to be the turning point in the history of Missouri court decisions.

Especially after the Van Zandt decision, the abolitionists and other antislavery radicals began to criticise the Supreme Court harshly. Judge McLean, who was inclined to participate in public discussions to an extent which would not now be thought seemly in a member of the Supreme Court, addressed a letter to a leading abolitionist at the close of the forties, in which he deplored the growing tendency to charge the court with prejudice, partisanship, and corrupt subservience to the proslavery interest.[12] His protest was unavailing. From the presidential campaign of 1848 forward, the Free Soil Party sought to undermine confidence in the tribunal. John P. Hale, the party candidate, declared about 1850 that the court would decide any slavery case in favor of the South, and in the campaign of 1856 called it "the citadel of slavery." [13] In this latter year two New Yorkers, William H. Seward in the Senate and Henry Bennett in the House, charged that a majority of the judges had been appointed in the interest of slavery.[14]

Webster is said to have referred to the judgment in Strader *v.* Graham as "not a respectable decision," [15] and in connection with that case the *New York Evening Post* remarked: "The courts need reorganizing, instead of the four members allotted to the free states they should have six." [16] In the middle of the fifties the court consisted of Chief Justice Taney, McLean of Ohio, and Wayne of Georgia, all of whom dated their service from the Jacksonian era; John Catron of Tennessee, Peter V. Daniel of Virginia, Samuel Nelson of New York, and Robert Grier of Pennsylvania, all of whom except Catron had been appointed between 1840 and 1846; and John A. Campbell of Alabama and Benjamin R. Curtis of Massachusetts, both of whom had been appointed

[12] Warren, II, 157.

[13] *Ibid.,* II, 222, 268.

[14] *Ibid.,* II, 268.

[15] Statement of *New York Evening Post,* quoted *ibid.,* II, 226.

[16] Quoted, *ibid.* In 1860, J. M. Ashley of Ohio declared in the House that the northern circuit embracing Ohio, Indiana, Illinois, and Michigan had more cases on docket in 1856 than all five of the southern circuits. *Cong. Globe,* 36 Cong., 1 sess., App., 365.

since 1850. Curtis had taken his seat in 1851 upon Woodbury's death, while Campbell had replaced McKinley upon his death in 1853.

The appointment of a Massachusetts man had not placated the antislavery element. Curtis had incurred the hatred of the abolitionists before his appointment by upholding the fugitive slave law, and they were soon denouncing him as a "slave-catching Judge, appointed as a reward for his professional support." [17] Impressed by the seriousness of the situation created about this time by the storm over such cases as Ableman v. Booth, the *American Law Register* appealed to the public pointing out the dire consequences which must follow if the court should be stripped of its powers. The popularity in the North, at the moment, of the doctrines of the Virginia and Kentucky Resolutions of 1798, the assertion that each state was the proper judge of its own reserved rights, threatened legislation to restrict the jurisdiction of the supreme tribunal. The success of the current views, the *Register* warned, would lead to "discord and confusion, statutes without obedience, courts without authority, an anarchy of principles, and a chaos of decisions, till all law at last shall be extinguished by an appeal to arms." [18]

In the South, of course, the court found more general support; and the *Southern Quarterly Review* regarded it as fortunate that the fixed terms of the judges gave the country a "perfectly independent judiciary." Nothing but this independence, in its opinion, was opposing the tempest raging in the North.[19] Strangely enough, the friends of the court believed that it could still the tempest by a further pronouncement of its opinion on the very issues which had raised the storm.

THE DRED SCOTT CASE

The first of the series of events which culminated in the Dred Scott decision was the proposal in the Clayton Compromise that all questions relating to slavery in the territories be left to the determination of the courts. The Free Soil campaign against the

[17] Warren, II, 272.
[18] *Ibid.*, II, 275–277.
[19] *Ibid.*, II, 277–278.

court probably got its impetus, at least in part, from this proposal; but in spite of the danger involved, the desire for a court decision survived the defeat of the Clayton Compromise, was stimulated by the repeal of the Missouri Compromise, and became active at a most unfortunate moment, when general confidence in the tribunal had been undermined by the attacks of the antislavery press and politicians.   The occasion for the reawakening of the desire was the argument of the Dred Scott case.[20]

In the autumn of 1846, a few weeks after Wilmot first proposed his proviso in Congress, Dred Scott began a suit against the widow of his former master, in the state circuit court in St. Louis, on the ground that the master, Dr. Emerson, an army surgeon, had taken him into the free state of Illinois and thence into the Louisiana Territory (the part which has since become Minnesota), and that consequently, under the Ordinance of 1787 and the Missouri Compromise Act, he became a free man and remained a free man when his master brought him back into the slave state of Missouri.   When Emerson died he left his property in trust for a child, and this fact made it impossible for the widow to emancipate the slave.   Mrs. Emerson hired Scott out on occasion for wages, but he was more a burden than a source of profit, and with his family became to some extent an object of charity on the part of a man named Taylor Blow, whose father had sold him to Dr. Emerson.

In this situation, it seems, is to be found the motive for the suit instituted in Scott's name at the expense of Blow, rather than in any design to use the case as a test of the laws governing slavery. The decisions of the state courts in similar preceding cases afforded reason for the expectation that the suit would succeed.   In January, 1850, Scott actually obtained a verdict; but the defendant appealed, and in 1852 the state supreme court reversed the decision of the lower court, although with one dissenting opinion.   The lower court had followed the precedents set by the state courts, but the supreme court now applied the rule established in Strader *v.* Graham, and held that Scott resumed his servile status upon his return.

[20] There are many accounts of the Dred Scott case (Dred Scott *v.* Sandford, 19 Howard 393).   One of the best, as well as one of the latest, is that of Warren, II, 279 *et seq.* See also F. H. Hodder, "Some Phases of the Dred Scott Case."

Meantime Mrs. Emerson had removed to Massachusetts and married Dr. C. C. Chaffee, of Springfield, who was a member of Congress and a strong abolitionist. Blow was not yet satisfied, and now arranged for a suit in the federal court. In order to keep the Chaffees out of the case, Mrs. Chaffee, by a fictitious sale, transferred the Negro to her brother, John F. A. Sanford, a resident of New York. Chaffee denied any control over Scott or the course of the suit, but his wife remained the real owner of the Negro.[21]

The suit against Sanford was brought in the United States circuit court for Missouri in November 1853, on the ground of the diverse citizenship of the two parties, a ground which assumed both the freedom and the citizenship of the plaintiff. Sanford's attorneys filed a plea in abatement, alleging that the court had no jurisdiction in the case, because Scott was born in slavery and therefore could not be a citizen with the right to sue in the federal courts. The plaintiff demurred to this plea and the court sustained the demurrer, but on May 15, 1854, rendered a decision affirming the finding of the Missouri Supreme Court. An appeal was then taken to the United States Supreme Court, Blow acting as Scott's bondsman.

Before the case came up for argument Congress repealed the Missouri Compromise. However, when first argued in February, 1856, the public was as yet scarcely aware that the case was on the docket. Henry S. Geyer, then Senator from Missouri, appeared for Sanford, assisted by Reverdy Johnson of Maryland, reputed to be one of the country's greatest lawyers. For Scott appeared Montgomery Blair of St. Louis. The arguments of counsel immediately revealed the potentialities of the case to the public. The case "involves questions of much political interest," said the press reports. "They are first, whether a free black man is a citizen of the United States, so as to be competent to sue in the Courts of the United States; second, whether a slave carried voluntarily by his master into a free State and returning voluntarily with his master

[21] McLaughlin's account of the relations between the various persons involved in the Scott case is quite different from the above statement. He says that he follows the statement agreed upon by the attorneys in the case. He believes also that the suit was "a genuine effort on the part of antislavery men to obtain freedom for a negro unlawfully, as they believed, held in bondage."—*Con. Hist.*, 553–554. *Cf.* Swisher, *Taney*, 486 *et seq.* The name is incorrectly spelled "Sandford" in the reports.

to his home, is a free man by virtue of such temporary residence; thirdly, whether the eighth Section of the Missouri Act of 1820, prohibiting slavery north of latitude 36° 30', is constitutional or not." [22]

That the court would affirm the decision of the circuit court was not a difficult inference for an intelligent man acquainted with the decision in Strader *v.* Graham. "There is a speculation abroad," wrote the Washington correspondent of the *New York Tribune*, "which amounts almost to a conviction that the decision of the Circuit Court will be affirmed, and principally upon the pretext that Scott voluntarily returned to the State of Missouri, by which act the authority of the owner was restored and the condition of slavery was resumed." [23]

It would appear to the lay mind that the status of the slave while on free soil would not be relevant to a discussion of his status after returning home, since the law of the place of his master's residence would then prevail in any event. However, in the Kentucky case, the court had thought proper to inquire into the effect of the Ordinance of 1787 upon the laws of the states created out of the Northwest Territory, and had held that it ceased to have binding force after the admission of the states. It could therefore not give freedom to a slave who visited one of these states with his master's consent. It was possibly the recollection of this discussion that now gave birth to the rumor that the court would pass upon the effect of the Missouri Compromise Act, although the same expectation was naturally aroused by the arguments of counsel. Gossip was busy with surmises as to what the court would do, but there seems to have been an impression that a decision sustaining the lower court would not necessarily involve a judgment upon the constitutionality of the compromise of 1820. In a second letter, written a few days after the one just quoted, the *Tribune* correspondent reported that there was some indication that a judgment on the compromise would be avoided, on the ground "that Scott, being a colored man, is not a citizen of Missouri in the legal point of view, and therefore cannot bring an action prop-

[22] Warren, II, 282.
[23] Quoted, *ibid.*, 283.

erly. This judgment would deny the jurisdiction of the Supreme Court." [24]

The judges were in fact puzzling over this very problem. All of them except McLean and Curtis agreed that the circuit court's decision on the merits should be sustained, and since that court had not found it necessary to consider whether a Negro born in slavery could be a citizen or not, McLean, Catron, Campbell, and Grier held that the plea as to citizenship was not properly before them. Taney, Wayne, Daniel, and Curtis held that it was. Nelson entertained doubts and requested a reargument, which was finally ordered. At this stage it seemed still less necessary to consider the Missouri Compromise. Shortly before the rehearing was ordered, Judge Curtis wrote to his uncle, George Ticknor, informing him confidentially that the court would not pass on the question of the Missouri Compromise, a majority of the judges being of the opinion that it was not necessary to a decision. [25]

The postponement of the decision was generally accepted by the public as evidence of a desire to avoid becoming entangled in partisan politics, in view of the impending presidential election; but the New York Tribune, an inveterate enemy of the court, could not miss the opportunity to fling a caustic remark in the direction of the judges. "The black gowns," it sneered, "have come to be artful dodgers." [26] As the time for the rehearing approached, in December, 1856, the Washington correspondent again reported that the court might deem it wise to rest its decision on some issue less likely to excite the public than would a judgment on the compromise. "Yet," he added, "the urgency of the slave-power is great." [27]

This last remark suggests that rumors were afloat indicating that pressure was being brought to bear upon the court. The extent to which such a surmise was warranted will be discussed presently. By this time the public was beginning to realize the immense effect which a decision on the compromise was likely to have upon future legislation relating to the territories, and men of prominence were

[24] Quoted, *ibid.*
[25] *Ibid.*, 284–285.
[26] *Ibid.*
[27] *Ibid.*, 288.

not silent as to the probable effects of a decision. In Congress, Benjamin Stanton of Ohio, while discussing a bill for the reorganization of the circuits, pointed to the disproportionate representation of the South in the judicial department, and hinted that the Union would be endangered by a decision against the power of Congress over slavery in the territories.[28] The readiness of men to adopt the principles which seemed at the moment to support their interests is well illustrated by Stanton's appeal on this occasion to the doctrines of the Virginia and Kentucky Resolutions. He contended that it was the right of the states to refuse obedience to any law which they deemed a "plain, palpable and deliberate violation of the Constitution," and likewise to disregard a decision of the court which they deemed unsound. If such words were surprising in the mouth of an Ohioan, it was no less strange to hear them controverted by a Virginia Democrat! [29]

After the reargument, the court's decision was again delayed by the illness of Judge Wayne and a fatal accident to the wife of Daniel. While the public waited the papers were filled with discussions and various rumors went abroad as to the probable outcome. It was the general opinion that Scott would lose, but there was no agreement as to the points which the judgment would cover. Alexander H. Stephens wrote to his brother that he urged the judges not to postpone "the case on the Missouri restriction." He evidently had not only spoken with them, but believed that they would deal with the compromise and that they would hold against it. "If they decide, as I have reason to believe they will, that the restriction was unconstitutional . . . the political question, as I think, will be ended as to the power of the people in their Territorial Legislatures. It will be in effect a re-adjudication." [30] In other words, a decision against the power of Congress would also effectually dispose of popular sovereignty.

In another letter Stephens wrote: "The decision will be a marked epoch in our history." "From what I hear, *sub rosa*, it will be according to my own opinions on every point as abstract political

[28] Quoted, *ibid.*, 290.
[29] *Ibid.*
[30] *Ibid.*, II, 286, note.

questions. . . . 'Squatter sovereignty speeches' will be on a par with 'liberty speeches.' " [31]   The sources of Stephens's *sub rosa* information do not appear, nor was the supposed information correct, but his comments show how keenly the pro-slavery element was interested in the outcome. When the justices met for conference on February 15, all but McLean and Curtis agreed that the court must decide the case on the ground that Scott's status after his return to Missouri depended upon the law of that state.

To Judge Nelson was assigned the duty of writing the opinion sustaining the lower court. Within a few days, however, it was learned that the two dissenting judges intended to write opinions discussing and sustaining the constitutionality of the Missouri Compromise Act. The majority therefore felt compelled to reconsider their own plan of omitting all discussion of it. If McLean and Curtis had refrained from bringing the compromise into the decision, the indications are that the majority would gladly have remained silent on that point. [32]

The ulterior motives of McLean and Curtis, if there were any, are matters of conjecture. McLean was a chronic aspirant for the presidency, and was suspected of seeking to make political capital out of his dissent. [33] Curtis has not escaped a similar suspicion of interested motives. Already he was probably contemplating resigning from the bench and resuming the practice of law in his home state, as he found the salary of a judge inadequate. His prospects of a sufficient practice were clouded by the unpopularity he had incurred by supporting the fugitive slave law, and to counteract this unpopularity he may have been tempted to render a dissenting opinion which would conform with the views of his antislavery neighbors. [34]

Judge Wayne was the member of the tribunal who most actively interested himself in persuading the majority members to agree

[31] *Ibid.*, 292–293.

[32] This conclusion is not accepted by some students. Professor McLaughlin, for one, thinks that outside pressure would have induced the court to give an inclusive decision.—*Con. Hist.*, 555 and note.

[33] For McLean's dissenting opinion and comment thereon see Weisenburger, *McLean*, Chap. XIII.

[34] *Cf.* Hodder, *loc. cit.* For effect of Curtis's dissenting opinion upon the northern estimate of him, see Warren, II, 320–321.

to an inclusive decision. According to a later statement by Curtis and Wayne's own admission, he became convinced that a broad decision by the court would quiet all agitation on the question of slavery in the territories. Believing thoroughly himself that Congress possessed no power to prohibit its introduction, he regarded it as expedient that the court should so declare, and was able to persuade Taney, Campbell, Daniel, and Catron that the chief justice should write an opinion covering all the points involved. Taney was probably favored on the ground that as chief justice his opinion would carry more weight than one delivered by an associate.

Critics of the court have charged that the decision finally rendered was the result of collusion between the proslavery leaders including the President. Lincoln himself hinted at such a conspiracy, in his "house divided" speech before the Republican state convention at Springfield, Ill., in June, 1858.[35] But there is no sufficient ground for the charge. It appears that Judge Grier hesitated to agree to the course recommended by Wayne, whereupon Catron wrote confidentially to Buchanan, the President-elect, telling him that the court would pass upon the constitutionality of the compromise, although he gave no hint as to whether it would be upheld or declared void. In view of the excellent opportunity to settle the agitation by a decision of the court, Catron urged Buchanan to "drop Grier a line" suggesting the importance of a decision one way or the other. Grier, he said, "has been persuaded to take the smooth handle for the sake of repose."[36]

Buchanan complied, and from Grier's answer the historian learns of the discussion in the conference of the justices. The first question to be considered was the right of a Negro to sue in the federal courts. The majority thought that this question did not arise on the pleadings, and that the opinion should be confined to the merits; also that the merits did not call for an opinion on the Missouri Compromise. Hence the commission to Nelson to write the opinion of the court sustaining the judgment of the circuit court.

[35] See extract in Commager, 345–347.
[36] Warren, II, 294–295. Catron's letter is printed in J. B. Moore, ed., *The Works of James Buchanan*, X, 106, note 1. It was elicited by an inquiry of the President-elect, and probably suggested the passage in Buchanan's inaugural. See discussion in Swisher, *Taney*, Chap. XXIV.

In view of the determination of McLean and Curtis to write dissenting opinions, however, it was later decided to include "both the troublesome points." "In our opinion both the points are *in* the case and may be legitimately considered." As to the *necessity* of considering them, continued Grier, Nelson and Catron refused to commit themselves. "I am anxious that it should not appear that the line of latitude should mark the line of division in the Court. I feel also that the opinion of the majority will fail of much of its effect if founded on clashing and inconsistent arguments. On conversation with the Chief Justice, I have agreed to concur with him. . . . There will . . . be six, if not seven . . . who will decide the Compromise law of 1820 to be of *non-effect*." [37]

At the time of this correspondence it was not unusual for members of the supreme bench to confide to friends the probable outcome of pending cases. Judge Curtis had told his uncle, nearly a year before, that the court would not pass upon the compromise of 1820, and other instances of such communications could easily be found.[38] Such a practice would undoubtedly now be regarded as reprehensible. The exchange between Buchanan and Grier disproves the conspiracy theory, but shows that the President was acquainted in advance with the nature of the decision. It was not hard for him to declare, in his inaugural address, after intimating that the court was the proper place for the settlement of the controversy over the territories, "to their decision, in common with all good citizens, I shall cheerfully submit, whatever it may be."

This utterance drew from the *New York Tribune* on the next day the caustic comment: "You may 'cheerfully submit,' of course, you will, to whatever the five slaveholders and two or three doughfaces on the bench of the Supreme Court may be ready to utter on this subject. But not one man who really desires the triumph of Freedom over Slavery in the Territories will do so. We may be constrained to obey, as law, whatever that tribunal shall put forth; but happily this is a country in which the People make both laws and Judges, and they will try their strength on the issue here presented." [39]

[37] *Ibid.*, 295–297.
[38] *Cf.* McLean's political letterwriting, Weisenburger, 140–141.
[39] Quoted by Warren, II, 299.

THE DECISION

On March 6, 1857, Chief Justice Taney finally read the opinion he had prepared.[40] Judges Nelson and Catron read separate opinions. The next day Judges McLean and Curtis delivered their dissenting views, and separate opinions were presented by Daniel, Grier, Campbell, and Wayne.[41] Taney dealt first with the plea in abatement; that is, he considered the argument that Scott, having been born in slavery, could not be a citizen entitled to sue in the federal courts, even admitting his contention that he was a free man in consequence of his residence in Illinois and Minnesota territory. If this plea was correct, it followed that the circuit court was without jurisdiction.

Reciting the constitutional provision which guarantees that "the Citizens of each State shall be entitled to all Privileges and Immunities of Citizens in the Several States," Taney held that the rights in question here are those pertaining to United States citizenship; those which belong to members of the political community brought into existence by the Constitution. Citizenship in a state does not necessarily mean United States citizenship. The rights pertaining to the two kinds of citizenship are different, and it does not follow that a man who has all the rights and privileges of a citizen of a state must be a citizen of the United States. The right to sue in the United States courts is a right of citizens of the latter class.

Taney's reading of the constitutional provision made it equivalent to some such wording as the following: The citizens of the United States resident in any state shall be entitled to all the privileges and immunities pertaining to United States citizenship in any state to which they may go.[42] "The question is simply this: Can a negro, whose ancestors were imported into this country, and

[40] 19 Howard 393. Extracts from Taney's decision and Curtis's dissenting opinion are given in Johnson, 436–445; Taney's decision is given also in Commager, 339–345.

[41] See E. I. McCormac, "Justice Campbell and the Dred Scott Decision"; Richard R. Stenberg, "Some Political Aspects of the Dred Scott Case."

[42] Compare this with Taney's words in the Passenger Cases: "We are all citizens of the United States; and . . . must have the right to pass and repass through every part of it without interruption, as freely as in our own states." Taney did not regard Negroes as citizens entitled to this privilege. He held this opinion concerning them as early as 1832. See Swisher, 154.

sold as slaves, become a member of the political community formed and brought into existence by the Constitution of the United States, and as such become entitled to all the rights, privileges, and immunities, guarantied by that instrument to the citizen?" For answer he appealed to history:

"It is true, every person, and every class and description of persons, who were at the time of the adoption of the Constitution recognized as citizens in the several States, became also citizens of this new political body; but none other. . . . In the opinion of the Court, the legislation and histories of the times, and the language used in the Declaration of Independence, show, that neither the class of persons who had been imported as slaves, nor their descendants, whether they had become free or not, were then acknowledged as part of the people, or intended to be included in the general words used in that memorable instrument. . . .

"They had for more than a century before been regarded as beings of an inferior order, and altogether unfit to associate with the white race, either in social or political relations; and so far inferior, that they had no rights which the white man was bound to respect. . . .

"Upon a full and careful consideration of the subject, the Court is of opinion, that, upon the facts stated in the plea in abatement, Dred Scott was not a citizen of Missouri within the meaning of the Constitution of the United States, and not entitled as such to sue in its courts; and, consequently, that the Circuit Court had no jurisdiction of the case, and that the judgment on the plea in abatement is erroneous." [43]

From Grier we have learned that the majority of the court believed that this examination of the plea in abatement was unnecessary to the review of the circuit court's decision, although it came legitimately within their purview. Since Taney's conclusion adverse to Negro citizenship meant that the lower court had erred in taking jurisdiction, to the lay mind it would seem that this con-

[43] See Swisher's concise summary of Taney's opinion, in *Taney*, 505–506. For references to the authorities on citizenship, see *supra*, Chap. VIII, note 50. *Cf.* George Livermore, *Opinions of the Founders of the Republic on Negroes as Slaves, as Citizens, and as Soldiers;* and T. V. Smith, "Slavery and the American Doctrine of Equality."

clusion was as far as the Supreme Court could consistently go.   But Taney held that although the circuit court had been without jurisdiction, the Supreme Court had the right to review its judgment. Hence the Supreme Court now proceeded to review this judgment on the merits.   Here again the layman would think that the precedent set in Strader *v.* Graham was all-sufficient.   Unless that decision was to be reversed, the discussion of the constitutionality of the Missouri Compromise could not affect the result.   Nevertheless the chief justice proceeded to examine the compromise act.

Arguing the question of congressional authority over the territories, Taney declared that the power conferred by the Constitution to "dispose of and make all needful rules and regulations respecting the territory or other property belonging to the United States" did not apply to the territory ceded by France in 1803, which "was acquired by the General Government, as the representative and trustee of the people of the United States, and must therefore be held in that character for their common use and equal benefit . . . and the Government holds it for their common use until it shall be associated with the other States as a member of the Union. . . . But until that time arrives . . . it was its duty to pass such laws and establish such a government as would enable those by whose authority they acted to reap the advantages they anticipated from its acquisition, and to gather there a population which would enable it to assume the position to which it was destined among the States of the Union."

Under the fifth amendment to the Constitution, "an act of Congress which deprived a citizen of the United States of his liberty or property merely because he came himself or brought his property into a particular Territory of the United States, and who had committed no offence against the laws, could hardly be dignified with the name of due process of law. . . .   The right of property in a slave is distinctly and expressly affirmed in the Constitution. . . . And no word can be found in the Constitution which gives Congress greater power over slave property, or which entitles property of that kind to less protection than property of any other description.   The only power conferred is the power coupled with the duty of guarding and protecting the owner in his rights.

"Upon these considerations, it is the opinion of the court that the act of Congress which prohibited a citizen from holding or owning property of this kind in the territory of the United States north of the line therein mentioned, is not warranted by the Constitution, and is therefore void; and that neither Dred Scott himself, nor any of his family, were made free by being carried into this territory; even if they had been carried there by the owner, with the intention of becoming a permanent resident."

As to the contention that residence in the free state of Illinois made Scott free, Taney's opinion was that "the principle on which it depends was decided in this court, upon much consideration, in the case of Strader *v.* Graham. . . . And this court held that their status or condition, as free or slave, depended upon the laws of Kentucky, when they were brought back into that State, and not of Ohio; and that this court had no jurisdiction to revise the judgment of a State court upon its own laws. . . . So in this case.

"Upon the whole, therefore, it is the judgment of this court, that it appears by the record before us, that the plaintiff in error is not a citizen of Missouri, in the sense in which that word is used in the Constitution; and that the Circuit Court of the United States, for that reason, had no jurisdiction in the case, and could give no judgment in it. Its judgment for the defendant must consequently, be reversed, and a mandate issued, directing the suit to be dismissed for want of jurisdiction."

CRITICISM OF TANEY'S OPINION: CURTIS'S DISSENTING OPINION

Taney's opinion covered all of the points which had been raised, but the numerous separate opinions, as Grier had feared would be the case, discredited the conclusions. Daniel, Grier, Campbell, Wayne, and Catron, in separate opinions, concurred in holding that a Negro could not be a citizen of the United States, and that Congress could not exclude slavery from the territories, but these conclusions were reached by three or four distinct processes of reasoning. As a present-day critic has said, we may surmise that the result desired induced the processes.[44]

[44] E. S. Corwin, "The Dred Scott Decision."

As to the *obiter* character of the opinion on the constitutionality of the Missouri Compromise, the same critic has pointed out that there are two theories as to what constitutes an *obiter dictum*. By the one theory everything in an opinion save only such part as is necessary to the determination of the rights of the parties to the case is to be considered as a mere utterance by the wayside, instructive for future reference but without the weight of legal precedent. By the other theory all of the opinion is decision which represents a deliberate application of the judicial mind to questions legitimately raised in argument. He cites the *American and English Law Encyclopedia* upon which he bases the statement as to the character of a dictum, and quotes as follows: "Where the record presents two or more points, any one of which, if sustained, would decide the case, and the court decides them all, decision upon any one of the points cannot be regarded as *obiter*." [45]

If the second of these theories be accepted, perhaps no part of Taney's opinion should be regarded as *obiter dictum*. In the last analysis, the question is one of legal definition and practice and the court did not deserve condemnation for the choice it made if its motives were correct. Of these technical points the American public, of course, knew nothing; and if it had, in the highly inflamed state of opinion it would have chosen the view which suited its mood. That the North adhered to the narrower idea of the nature of a dictum was due in part, moreover, to the court's own teaching and practice, for it should not be forgotten that twenty years before, upon first coming to the bench, Taney had announced that the court would "avoid volunteering any opinion on any question, involving the construction of the Constitution, where the case itself does not bring the question directly before them, and make it their duty to decide upon it." This policy was quite in contrast with the practice of the court under Marshall, and was more congenial to the temper of the public. In departing from it in the Dred Scott decision, Taney and his colleagues invited the criticism of a public which was by no means in a judicial frame of mind.

Even some of the members of the court animadverted on the

[45] *Ibid.*

departure from a wise rule. The opinion delivered by Justice
Catron contained a rebuke of the discussion of the merits of the
case after the jurisdiction of the federal courts had been denied.
Before publication, however, the opinion was revised and these
reflections were omitted.[46] Justice Nelson tacitly demurred to the
majority's procedure by presenting as his opinion the one which
he had prepared at the direction of the court; it was restricted to
an affirmation of the correctness of the lower court's decision.
Justice Curtis severely denounced "such an exertion of power"
by the majority as transcending "the limits of the authority of the
court."

Curtis's dissenting opinion gained a fame rarely attained by such
opinions. He attempted to show that Negroes were citizens of
some of the states when the Constitution was adopted; and these,
he held, became thereupon citizens of the United States. "Citizens
of the United States at the time of the adoption of the Constitution
can have been no other than the citizens of the United States under
the Confederation." Even "at the time of the ratification of the
Articles of Confederation, all free native-born inhabitants of the
states of New Hampshire, Massachusetts, New York, New Jersey
and North Carolina, though descended from African slaves, were
not only citizens of those States, but such of them as had the other
necessary qualifications possessed the franchise of electors, on equal
terms with other citizens."

He held that it continued to be true that the citizen of a state was
ipso facto a United States citizen. "I can find nothing in the Constitution which, *proprio vigore*, deprives of their citizenship any
class of persons who were citizens of the United States at the time
of its adoption, or who should be native-born citizens of any State
after its adoption; nor any power enabling Congress to disfranchise
persons born on the soil of any State, and entitled to citizenship of
such State by its constitution and laws. And my opinion is, that,
under the Constitution of the United States, every free person born
on the soil of a State, who is a citizen of that State by force of its
constitution or laws, is also a citizen of the United States." Curtis
maintained his argument by making his own definitions. He

[46] Warren, II, 320–321, note.

held that citizenship "is not dependent on any political or civil right and any attempt so to define it must lead to error."

If so, even by Taney's argument, "every such citizen, residing in any State, has the right to sue and is liable to be sued in the federal courts, as a citizen of that State in which he resides. . . . As the plea to the jurisdiction in this case shows no facts, except that the plaintiff was of African descent, and his ancestors were sold as slaves, and as these facts are not inconsistent with his citizenship of the United States, and his residence in the State of Missouri, the plea to the jurisdiction was bad, and the judgment of the Circuit Court overruling it was correct."

In urging that every citizen of a state was a citizen also of the United States, Curtis voiced an opinion which had been advanced from time to time since the days of the framing of the Constitution, and which was to be incorporated into the Constitution by the fourteenth amendment. It may be easier to understand Taney's attempt to separate the two kinds of citizenship if we recall the marked tendency, during two decades of his chief justiceship, to emphasize the police power of the states in controlling such matters as interstate migration. As the right to pass freely from one state to another was regarded by nationalists as guaranteed to citizens by the privileges and immunities clause, the contrary view, that the police power was superior to this right, was developed by the champions of state's rights.

In holding that the rights which the citizen enjoys by virtue of his dual citizenship are distinguishable—that those which he holds from his state are distinct from those which he holds under the Constitution of the United States—Taney anticipated the findings of the court in the Slaughter House Cases, in 1873.[47] He was correct, as judged by historical development, in distinguishing two classes of *rights* and two of citizenship, but *not* two classes of *citizens*. The modern view is that both classes of rights are vested in the same individuals, since they are at the same time citizens of their states and of the United States.[48]

[47] See *infra*, Chap. XVIII.
[48] There is a helpful discussion of this much-neglected question by Duane D. Smith, *The Development of the Concept of Citizenship in American Constitutional Law.*

But to resume the analysis of Curtis's opinion: Taking up the other parts of Taney's argument, he held that the decision against the validity of the Missouri Compromise was *obiter* and not binding, and, as we have noted, charged that the court was departing from its usual procedure. "I do not consider it to be within the judicial power of the court to pass upon any question respecting the plaintiff's citizenship in Missouri save that raised by the plea to the jurisdiction, and I do not hold an opinion of this court, or of any court, binding when expressed on a question not legitimately before it."

However, having concluded that Scott's Negro blood did not of itself decide the question of his citizenship, Curtis proceeded to examine the merit of his plea as to the effect of residence in free territory. This required an inquiry into the competence of Congress to pass the compromise act of 1820 excluding slavery from a part of the Louisiana Purchase. The constitutional power to make all needful rules for the territories, he held, included the power to provide a body of municipal law for settlers, and slavery had been consistently recognized as a subject for regulation under municipal law. Coming finally to the effect of residence upon Scott's status after his return to Missouri, Curtis accepted as a sound statement of the law of that state, the view of the one judge who, in the state case of Scott *v.* Emerson, following the precedent of earlier decisions, had held that the Negro was entitled to his freedom.

PUBLIC DISCUSSION

Curtis's opinion was regarded by those who agreed with him as a complete refutation of Taney's reasoning. It supplied the platform for the further activity of the Republican Party and saved that party from the destruction which acceptance of the majority finding would have entailed.

If the majority members of the court had foreseen the storm which followed the announcement of Taney's decision, more of them might have taken the "smooth handle for the sake of repose," and stuck to their original intention of letting the unnecessary points go, in accordance with the opinion prepared by Nelson. They seem to have shared the illusion of the Democrats in general regarding the court's power to settle the slavery issue.

The most serious of the attacks on the court took the form of a perversion of a sentence in Taney's opinion, so that he was misrepresented as himself saying that the "negro had no rights which the white man was bound to respect." The antislavery papers by continual repetition spread this charge throughout the land, studiously ignoring the explanation that the chief justice was merely summarizing the sentiments which he believed to have been generally held in the eighteenth century.[49] Regarding the utterance on the compromise as *obiter*, the *New York Tribune* struck a responsive chord in the hearts of many of its readers when it declared that "the Court has rushed into politics, voluntarily and without other purpose than to subserve the cause of slavery." It accounted the decision as "entitled to just so much moral weight as would be the judgment of a majority of those congregated in any Washington bar-room."[50]

Taney's religion did not fail to become the target of fanatics, one of whom, a newspaper correspondent, described his opinion as "long, elaborate, able, and Jesuitical." The intemperate comment of the radical press was deplored by the *New York Advertiser*, which, while expressing its own dissent from the decision, urged that "no one had a right to impugn the motives of the Court, and to do so is alike unjust and unwise. . . . Such a course, though it may be congenial with our temper at the moment, is sadly perilous to the common weal, the interests of freedom and free government being always best upheld by maintaining respect for the officers of the government, especially those of the Judiciary."[51]

But even the sober second thought of the more moderate classes failed to exonerate the court. Said the *New York Times:* "The circumstances attending the present decision have done much to divest it of moral influence and to impair the confidence of the country. . . . Among jurists, it is not considered to settle anything

[49] Taney was in fact by no means an ardent friend of the institution of slavery, and was actively interested in promoting the welfare of colored people. See Swisher, *R. B. Taney*, 92–94, *et passim*.

[50] Quoted by Warren, II, 304–305.

[51] Quoted, *ibid.*, 310.

more than the denial of jurisdiction. . . . It exhibited the eagerness of the majority of that tribunal to force an opinion upon the country and to thrust itself into the political contests." [52] The prediction of a writer in the *North American Review* of October, 1857, proved, unfortunately, to be quite accurate: "The country will feel the consequences of the decision more deeply and more permanently, in the loss of confidence in the sound judicial integrity and strictly legal character of their tribunals, than in anything beside; and this, perhaps, may well be accounted the greatest political calamity which this country, under our forms of government could sustain." [53]

The consequences of the decision for the country and for the court's prestige would have been unfortunate enough if it had been received calmly and considered soberly by the public. But malignancy did not permit the facts to speak for themselves. Instead falsehood and ridicule were used with skill by those who wished to discredit the court. An illustration appears in the "clever but venomous" description of its members by the *Tribune's* correspondent ten days after the decision: Wayne: "before he got old, the ladies used to be enamoured of his flowing locks and general beauty of appearance, to which he was himself not wholly insensible." Daniel: "old, and long, and lean, and sharp in the visage." Catron: "whose erroneous opinions would, as a general rule, more often result from obtuseness than from original sin." Campbell: "middle-aged, middle sized, . . . and possessed of middling talent." Grier: "succumbs under touch, and returns into shape on its removal. . . . Let Grier associate with none but honest men . . . and he would not disgrace himself." [54] By such ridicule, even more effectively than by loud denunciation, was the supreme tribunal of the nation brought into contempt.[55]

[52] Quoted, *ibid.*, 309.
[53] Quoted, *ibid.*, 316.
[54] Quoted, *ibid.*, 317–319.
[55] Sanford was said to have opposed the appeal to the Supreme Court, and to have planned to free Dred Scott, however the suit terminated. Sanford became insane during the trial. In May, 1857, within three months after the announcement of the court's decision, the Chaffees conveyed Scott to Taylor Blow, who immediately gave him his freedom. Scott himself was "tickled" to be the object of so much public interest, and laughed about "de fuss dey made dar in Washington 'bout de ole nigger.'" Warren, II, 301, note.

PART FOUR

WAR AND RECONSTRUCTION

XIII

CIVIL WAR PROBLEMS

SECESSION AND COERCION

AFTER the Dred Scott decision events moved rapidly. The leaders of the Republican Party refused to recognize the opinion of the Supreme Court denying the power of Congress to prohibit slavery in the territories. To have admitted its binding force would have been to cut the ground from under their feet and to leave the party without a program. Rejecting it as an *obiter dictum*, they asserted that the people were the court of last resort and appealed to public opinion. Lincoln predicted that a reconstituted court would some day reverse the decision.[1]

Meantime the attempt to allow the people of Kansas to exercise their "squatter sovereignty" brought the territorial situation to a crisis. The effort of the friends of a free state to "steal" Kansas by encouraging northern emigration thither was met by fraudulent voting in the territorial elections on the part of antislavery residents of Missouri. The election by such means of a proslavery legislature was followed by the calling of a convention which framed a constitution for a slave state. This constitution as a whole was not submitted to the vote of the inhabitants. Instead, they were allowed to vote for the constitution with slavery or for the constitution without slavery. The free-state party refused, under such circumstances, to vote at all, and proceeded to hold their own convention and frame another constitution. The rivalry of the two parties led to conditions approaching civil war.

In spite of the disorders, Buchanan's administration, carrying the doctrine of non-intervention to an extreme, maintained a "hands-off" policy until interference could no longer be avoided. Then, instead of taking a neutral position and providing an opportunity for a genuine expression of the will of the Kansas popu-

---

[1] The reader who feels the need of a fuller review of events from the Dred Scott decision to the election of Lincoln is referred to McLaughlin, *Con. Hist.*, 565–597.

lation, the administration in effect gave its support to the southern faction in the contest.

At this point Senator Douglas broke with the President. Professing that he did not care whether slavery was voted up or voted down, he insisted that the principle of popular sovereignty should be honestly observed, and that the voters of the territory should be allowed to choose their own institutions, not only in the matter of slavery, but in all respects whatsoever. As a result of this refusal to follow the lead of the President, Douglas was read out of the Democratic Party. Thus at last, that party, like the Whig Party before it, began to disintegrate over the slavery issue. Up to this time it had maintained its unity through its policy of choosing for federal offices northern men with southern principles.

This cleavage in the Democratic ranks was widened by the skill of Lincoln in his famous debates with Douglas in 1858. The southern wing of the Democracy had espoused popular sovereignty in the early fifties, and had embodied that doctrine in the party platform in the campaign of 1856. It had been no less popular with northern Democrats, many of whom acknowledged Douglas as their leader and loyally followed him after his breach with Buchanan. Not so the southerners. Since the Dred Scott decision had proclaimed the legal right of slavery to go into all territories, they were no longer content with a program which, as the Kansas situation showed, gave them only a fighting chance. On the contrary they were disposed to insist that Congress pass laws to protect their rights under the decision.

The divergence in the views of the northern and southern wings foreshadowed a split in the next presidential campaign. If Douglas adhered to popular sovereignty, the northern wing would demand a platform in 1860 identical with that which the party had adopted in 1856. But the southern wing would insist upon a platform revised in the light of the Dred Scott dictum, and it seemed quite unlikely, in that event, that the two factions would be able to unite either upon platform or candidates.

It was this split in the ranks of the opposition that Lincoln wished to bring about. Nothing else could make a Republican success so probable. Such was the larger strategy in his mind when he called upon Douglas to explain what became of popular sovereignty under the doctrine which the Supreme Court had expounded. By his reply Douglas persuaded himself and his northern friends that there was no such incompatibility between the two doctrines as Stephens had perceived even before the enunciation of the court's opinion.

But Douglas's "Freeport heresy," the argument which he advanced to prove that the people of a territory, merely by withholding the "friendly legislation" which was necessary for the existence of slavery anywhere, could keep it out of a locality where it had the right to go, failed to satisfy the demands of logic or to safeguard the interests of the slaveholders. The Democracy did split over the platform and candidate in 1860, and Lincoln, the Republican candidate, was elected to the presidency by a minority of the total popular vote, in consequence of the inability of the opposing groups to find a common ground.

The possibility of the success of a party which avowed the intention to exclude slavery from the territories and to refuse admission to slave states in future, led many southern leaders to decide that in such an event the Union should be dissolved. There had been threats of disunion at various critical times in the past, but the theory by which secession might be justified was now for the first time worked out with elaborate care. It rested upon the assumption that the Union was a league or confederation of sovereign states.

This assumption was not new, but it is difficult to tell when it originated. It may well have been carried over in the minds of the people from the pre-constitutional era. When the state conventions were considering the Constitution in 1787 and 1788, the fear was apparent that if a state ratified its step would be irrevocable. From this it might be inferred that at that time it was perceived that the nature of the proposed Union precluded any right of withdrawal. On the other hand, it might be pointed out that Virginia, New York, and other states, in their ratifying ordinances, declared that the powers granted by the Constitution might be resumed by those who made the grant. The Virginia ordinance contained the following statement: "We the delegates of the People of Virginia . . . declare . . . that the powers granted under the Constitution being derived from the people of the United States, may be resumed by them whensoever the same shall be perverted." [2]

If these words and the similar statements in the ordinances of other states were intended to assert the right of a single state to withdraw from the Union at will, it was singularly unfortunate to refer to the people of the *United States* as the source of federal power. It may be questioned whether the belief in state sovereignty was anything more than a hazy mental bias of the populace before Jefferson and Madison formulated it in the Kentucky and Virginia Resolutions of 1798. These documents made the theory a familiar and convenient weapon to which states thereafter resorted whenever their rights seemed to be endangered by the conduct of the federal government.

Although some of the New England Federalists contemplated or threatened secession during the first decade and a half of the nineteenth century, the dogma of state sovereignty was more often the basis of attempts to nullify federal measures by state action. Calhoun was careful to explain that nullification was not the same thing as secession, although both rested upon the same foundation. Likening the Union to a partnership, he pointed out that nullification was merely a disavowal by the principals of unauthorized acts of an agent (the federal government), while secession was a dissolution of the partnership.[3] Secession, although a right which the state possessed by virtue of its sovereignty, was an ultimate remedy not to be contemplated except as a last resort.

When the leaders of the South decided that the Union was destructive of the vital interests of their states, and that they must resort to this ultimate remedy, they elaborated the implications of the theory that the Union was the result of a voluntary compact entered into by sovereign states.[4] The Constitution was the "su-

[2] James G. Randall, *Constitutional Problems under Lincoln*, 15, note. *Cf.* Dwight L. Dumond, *The Secession Movement*, and *Southern Editorials on Secession*.

[3] "Fort Hill Letter," in Crallé, VI, 147–169, *et passim*. Reprinted in Johnson, *Readings*, 323–325.

[4] The states which seceded expressly affirmed this theory of union in the constitution which they framed for the Confederacy. How it worked is the theme of Frank L. Owsley's *State Rights in the Confederacy*.

preme law" of the United States, but only so long as the sovereign communities, each for itself, saw fit not to withdraw the delegated powers. The right of secession, they urged, was expressly reserved by Virginia and other states in their ratifying ordinances, and the other states, by accepting their acts, tacitly accepted the doctrine.[5]

This brief sketch of the history of the theory of secession must be paralleled by a review of the history of coercive action on the part of the federal government. Under the Articles of Confederation Congress possessed no right of compulsive operation, unless, indeed, such a right was implied, as Madison and others urged, as the indispensable means of performing its functions. In practice, at any rate, Congress dared not attempt to enforce its measures except through the agency of the state governments. The result was, in Hamilton's phrase, that the United States presented to the world the "awful spectacle" of a country without a government.

The members of the Constitutional Convention were unanimously agreed that the federal government must be given the power of compulsive operation. A practicable means of attaining this object was not easily found, however, since an express delegation of power to coerce a state found delinquent in the performance of its duties as a member of the Union threatened to result in a

[5] "THE RIGHT OF SECESSION," said Jefferson Davis, "is not something . . . outside of and antagonistic to the Constitution. . . . So far from being against the Constitution or incompatible with it, we contend that, if the right to secede is not prohibited to the States, and no power to prevent it expressly delegated to the United States, it remains as reserved to the States or the people, from whom all the powers of the General Government were derived."—*Rise and Fall of the Confederate Government*, I, 168.

The theory of secession is best set forth in the work by Davis just cited, and by Alexander H. Stephens, in *Constitutional View of the [Late] War between the States*. See also Dunbar Rowland, ed., Jefferson Davis, *Constitutionalist;* and the several essays in Dunning, *Studies in Southern History and Politics*. B. L. Gildersleeve, *The Creed of the Old South*, is helpful in getting the point of view of that section. Daniel W. Howe, *Political History of Secession*, should be consulted.

Dumond concludes that the great majority of southerners based their action in withdrawing from the Union upon the philosophy of the Declaration of Independence rather than the doctrine that there was a constitutional right of secession. —*Secession Movement*, 121. *Cf.* Arthur C. Cole, *The Whig Party in the South*, 194–195, and "The South and the Right of Secession in the Early Fifties." Whig leaders especially were shy of the secession doctrine. Even Stephens wrote to Howell Cobb in 1851 that it was only "a right to change the Govt., a right of revolution."—"Correspondence of Robert Toombs, Alexander H. Stephens and Howell Cobb," 238.

virtual condition of civil war whenever it should be attempted. The solution eventually worked out gave to the federal government the right to act directly upon individual citizens of all of the states. They could be taxed, drafted into the army, or punished for infraction of the laws of Congress. In case of combinations or conspiracies too powerful to be suppressed by the courts, Congress was authorized to provide by law for calling out the militia to suppress insurrections and enforce the laws. Moreover, the laws of Congress passed in pursuance of its constitutional powers were declared to be the supreme law of the land, and in case of conflict with state enactments, the courts were bound to give them precedence. These provisions were supplemented by congressional legislation, notably by the much disputed twenty-fifth section of the Judiciary Act of 1789, and by acts authorizing the use of other forces, land and naval, in addition to the militia.

The coercive power of the federal government had been put to the test repeatedly before the crisis of secession in 1861. Under an act of Congress providing for the use of the militia to suppress insurrection and enforce the laws of the United States, President Washington had enforced the revenue laws against the "Whiskey rebels" of western Pennsylvania. Under a new coercive act Jefferson had used the naval forces in administering the embargo. Most notably, Jackson had asked and received from Congress, in 1833, authority to use force in collecting the customs in South Carolina which that state's ordinance of nullification in 1832 had sought to prevent.

In general, conflict between state and federal authorities had been avoided because under the Constitution powers had been so carefully distributed that in theory the governments of state and nation operated in different spheres. This fact was closely associated with the theory that sovereignty had been divided, and that the state and federal governments were both sovereign within their respective spheres. This was John Marshall's view, although his interpretation of the Constitution restricted the sphere of the state as narrowly as possible. Jefferson and his followers accepted the same theory, but developed on their part the doctrine that disputes between the states and the national government were "political" in their nature, and should not be passed upon by the Supreme Court. To allow such jurisdiction was equivalent, they held, to allowing one party to the dispute to act also as judge. Each state had as good a right to judge for itself as the court had to judge for it.

By such reasoning Jefferson would have avoided the trend towards federal supremacy in disputes over the powers of states. But in practice his plan found no acceptance, although the Supreme Court under Taney accorded liberal recognition to the authority of the States in relation to the police power.

All of these attempts to avoid clashes between federal and state authority counted for little when the country faced the actuality of secession. There was no possibility of reconciling the theory of secession with the federal power of coercion. So long as the administration was headed by a vigorous executive who regarded it as his duty to enforce the laws of Congress in every state, it was certain that combinations of individuals to resist those laws, or to take themselves from under their operation while remaining within the geographical limits of the United States, would be dealt with as insurrection.

SECESSION IN PRACTICE

As we have seen, some of the southern states seriously contemplated secession in 1850, but finally accepted the compromise of that year, with the intimation, expressed in the "Georgia platform," that any further aggressions upon their rights would be resisted even to the point of severing the ties which bound them to the northern states; and the events of the years just preceding 1860 led the more forward of their leaders to determine that the election of a Republican President should be taken as the signal for withdrawing. South Carolina was the first state actually to take the step. Her legislature, assembled in the autumn to cast the electoral vote, lingered to take such action as might be deemed necessary in case of the election of Lincoln. When his success became evident, the legislature issued a call for a convention to which should be submitted the question of secession. This convention met, and on December 20, 1860, adopted an ordinance of secession.

In form, the process of secession merely reversed that by which the state entered the Union. It had become a member of the Union by ratifying the Constitution through the action of a delegate convention; it ceased to be a member (according to the secessionists) by means of a new ordinance passed by a similar delegate convention representing the sovereign people of the state. The ordinance read as follows:

"We, the people of the State of South Carolina in convention assembled, do declare and ordain, and it is hereby declared and ordained, that the ordinance adopted by us in convention on the twenty-third day of May, in the year of our Lord one thousand seven hundred and eighty-eight, whereby the Constitution of the United States of America was ratified, and also all acts and parts of acts of the general assembly of this State ratifying amendments of the said Constitution, are hereby repealed; and that the union now subsisting between South Carolina and other States, under the name of the 'United States of America,' is hereby dissolved." [6]

Four days later the convention issued another document entitled A Declaration of Causes which Induced her Secession from the Federal Union.[7] As a prelude to the exposition contained therein, the declaration recited that the people of the state, assembled in convention in April, 1852, had declared that the violations of the Constitution by the federal government justified withdrawal from the Union. At that time, however, South Carolina had foreborne. Having now "resumed her separate and equal place among nations," she deemed it due to herself, the remaining states, and the nations of the world, to declare the causes of her action.

The declaration then asserted that the Revolution of 1776 established "the right of a State to govern itself; and the right of a people to abolish a Government when it becomes destructive of the ends for which it was instituted." Moreover, the Revolution established the separate sovereignty of the states, as the Articles of Confederation expressly declared. "The parties to whom the

[6] Reprinted in MacDonald, *Select Docs.*, 441–442; Commager, 372. See C. S. Boucher, "South Carolina and the South on the Eve of Secession, 1852–1860," and "The Secession and Co-Operation Movements in South Carolina, 1848–1852"; also P. M. Hamer, *The Secession Movement in South Carolina.*

[7] Reprinted in Johnson, 459–462; Commager, 372.

Constitution was submitted were the several sovereign States; . . . Thus was established, by compact between the States, a Government with defined objects and powers limited to the express words of the grant. . . . We hold that the Government thus established is subject to the two great principles asserted in the Declaration of Independence; and we hold further, that the mode of its formation subjects it to a third fundamental principle, namely, the law of compact. We maintain that in every compact between two or more parties, the obligation is mutual; that the failure of one of the contracting parties to perform a material part of the agreement, entirely releases the obligation of the other; and that where no arbiter is provided, each party is remitted to his own judgment to determine the fact of failure, with all its consequences."

Having laid down these premises, the declaration proceeds to say that fourteen of the states have for years deliberately refused to fulfill their constitutional obligations with reference to the rendition of fugitive slaves, and affirms that the ends for which the federal government was instituted have been in this way defeated, and the government itself rendered destructive of them by the action of the non-slaveholding states. The charges against these states are enumerated as follows. They have:

Assumed the right of deciding upon the propriety of our domestic institutions;

Denied the rights of property established in fifteen states and recognized by the Constitution;

Denounced the institution of slavery as sinful;

Permitted the organization of societies with the avowed purpose of disturbing the peace;

Encouraged and assisted slaves to escape;

Secured the aid of the common government in promotion of these unconstitutional purposes.

Finally, a sectional party, observing the forms of the Constitution, has found means in the article establishing the executive department, of subverting the Constitution itself. "A geographical line has been drawn across the Union, and all the States north of that line have united in the election of a man . . . whose opinions and purposes are hostile to slavery. He is to be entrusted with the administration of the Common Government, because he has de-clared that that 'Government cannot endure permanently half slave, half free,' and that the public mind must rest in the belief that Slavery is in the course of ultimate extinction. . . . The Guarantees of the Constitution will then no longer exist; the equal rights of the States will be lost. The slaveholding States will no longer have the power of self-government, or self-protec-tion, and the Federal Government will have become their en-emy." All hope of remedy is rendered vain by the fact that public opinion in the North has invested a great political error with the sanctions of a more erroneous religious belief.

As the Gulf states one after another followed the example of South Carolina, they voiced similar views, although at less length. The preamble of the Texas act of secession, for example, read as follows: "Whereas the Federal Government has failed to accom-plish the purposes of the compact of union between these States, . . . and whereas, the action of the Northern States is violative of the compact between the States and the guarantes of the Constitu-tion; and whereas, the recent developments in Federal affairs make it evident that the power of the Federal Government is sought to be made a weapon with which to strike down the interests and property of the people of Texas and her sister slaveholding States, instead of permitting it to be, as was intended—our shield against outrage and aggression—therefore," etc. The remainder of the act declared the bonds of union severed.[8]

BUCHANAN FACES THE CRISIS

On November 17, with the crisis impending in South Carolina, President Buchanan addressed several questions to his attorney-general relating to the coercive powers of the federal government. In somewhat abbreviated form these inquiries were as follows:

[8] Texas was especially aggrieved by the failure, as she considered it, of the fed-eral government to provide for the protection of her frontiers against the In-dians. See Charles W. Ramsdell, "The Frontier and Secession."

Statements of other Gulf states are reprinted in Ames, *State Docs.*, 311–313, 318–320. Special studies of importance are the following: J. W. Garner, "First Strug-gle over Secession in Mississippi"; Percy L. Rainwater, *Mississippi: Storm Center of Secession, 1856–1861*; M. J. White, "Louisiana and the Secession Movement of the Early Fifties."

1. In case of conflict between state and federal authorities, is there any doubt of the supremacy of the constitutional laws of the latter?

2. What is the extent of my power to collect duties at a port where the revenue laws are resisted by a force which drives a collector from the custom house?

3. What right have I to defend public property if assaulted?

4. Can a military force be used for any purpose under the acts of 1795 and 1807, within the limits of a state, where there are no judges, marshal, or other civil officers?[9]

The President's last query had reference to the fact that the acts in question provided for use by the chief executive of military or naval force upon information from the appropriate civil officers that disturbances existed with which they were unable to cope. Attorney-General Black replied to Buchanan's questions in effect as follows:

1. Within their respective spheres, the federal government and the state government are both independent and supreme, and each is utterly powerless beyond its constitutional limits. In general, it is the duty of the President to see that the laws are faithfully executed. For this reason he nominates his own subordinates and removes them at his pleasure; the land and naval forces are under him as commander-in-chief. But power must be used only in the manner prescribed by the legislative department.

2. The functions of the collector may be exercised anywhere within the port. The law of 1833 permitted the President to establish the custom house at any place within the collection district. This was a temporary law.

3. The right to protect the public property is clear. The Constitution gives the United States exclusive right of legislation over all places purchased by consent of the legislature of a state for forts, etc. The right to protect such property is the owner's right to repel intrusion. It includes the right to recapture when unlawfully taken.

4 and 5. The militia can be used—also the land and naval forces

[9] George Ticknor Curtis, *James Buchanan*, II, Chap. XVI. The standard edition of Buchanan's works is that by John Bassett Moore.

—whenever the laws are opposed by combinations too powerful to be suppressed by ordinary judicial proceedings, or by the power vested in the marshals. Such a force can do no more than a civil posse—that is, it must be kept in strict subordination to the civil power, and if there are no civil officers, the use of troops would be illegal. If they are sent to aid the courts and marshals, there must be courts and marshals to be aided. Existing laws put the federal government on the defensive. You can use force only to repel an assault on the public property and aid the courts in the performance of their duty. If one of the states should declare her independence, your action cannot depend upon the rightfulness of the cause for such declaration. You can only execute the laws to the extent of the defensive means placed in your hands.[10]

Black ruled that Congress could not declare war on a state or carry on general hostilities against it. But he held that the right of the general government to preserve itself in its whole constitutional vigor by repelling a direct and positive aggression upon its property or officers could not be denied. This in his opinion was a very different thing from an offensive war to punish the people for the political misdeeds of the state government, or to enforce an acknowledgment that the government of the United States is supreme. "The Union must utterly perish at the moment when Congress shall arm one part of the people against another for any purpose beyond that of merely protecting the general government in the exercise of its proper constitutional functions." [11]

[10] Edward McPherson, *Political History of the United States during the Great Rebellion,* 51–52. Reprinted in Johnson, 454–455. McPherson was a clerk in the House of Representatives; his book is a collection of documents. Black's answer is to be found also in Curtis, *Buchanan,* II, 319–324, and Moore, *Works of Buchanan,* XI, 21, 22.

[11] Black held that the constitutional provisions concerning war referred only to a war with a foreign enemy. The militia, he thought, might be used only 1) to suppress insurrections against a state, in case the state asked for assistance; 2) to repel invasion of a state by a foreign foe; and 3) "to execute the Laws of the Union" (Art. I, sec. 8, par. 15). But force could be employed in executing federal law, he held, only to aid federal officers in performing their regular duties. His conclusion that the use of troops would be illegal where there were no courts and marshals to be aided meant, as one critic remarked, that where combinations in opposition to the government were "too powerful to be suppressed by the ordinary course of judicial proceedings, [they] could not be suppressed at all."

Black was an important character during these years. He presented the government's case to the Supreme Court in Ableman .v. Booth, and was nominated by

In December in his message to Congress Buchanan discussed the whole situation.[12] He deplored the long-continued agitation against slavery by the people of the North as the cause of the crisis, but he refuted the claim that the constitutional election of a President was a valid cause for dissolving the Union, and denied that any act of Congress, save possibly the Missouri Compromise, had ever impaired the rights of the South in slaves. The only violations of constitutional duty which he was able to find were the acts of the states directed against the Fugitive Slave Law, and for these neither Congress nor any President was responsible. The South, he conceded, had a right to demand justice in this respect.

As to the right of secession, Buchanan maintained that it could be justified as a constitutional remedy only on the supposition that the federal Union was a voluntary association of states, terminable at pleasure. This he denied as wholly inconsistent with the history and character of the Constitution. During the ratifying period, he alleged, it had not occurred to anyone, opponent or advocate, to assert or even intimate that their efforts were all vain labor, because the moment that any state felt itself aggrieved it might secede. Not until many years after the origin of the federal government was such a proposition advanced. Then it was met and refuted by President Jackson, on January 16, 1833.[13]

The Union, Buchanan went on, was intended to be perpetual. The old Articles declared that it was to be perpetual, and the preamble of the Constitution recites that it is established "in order to form a more perfect union." Yet the secessionists contend that this "more perfect union" does not include the essential attribute of perpetuity. The powers conferred upon the federal government also show that the Union is to be perpetual. The Constitution and laws of Congress are made the supreme law of the land,

Buchanan as successor of Justice Daniels upon the latter's death in 1861. The Senate took no action. There is a life of Black by William N. Brigance. See "Jeremiah Black and Andrew Johnson," by the same writer; also P. G. Auchampaugh, ed., "Black, Thompson, and Stanton in 1864."

[12] Richardson, *Messages*, V, 626–637. Reprinted, Johnson, 455–459. *Cf.* P. G. Auchampaugh, *James Buchanan and His Cabinet*, Chap. IV.

[13] Buchanan's indebtedness to Jackson, in dealing with nullification, seems evident from this discussion of the nature of the Union and of the federal government. But see Auchampaugh, *Buchanan and His Cabinet*, 147, note 31.

and the judges in the states are bound thereby. Members of the state governments are sworn to support the Constitution, and that instrument establishes a perfect and complete government with power to act on individuals.

The President reached in truth a high level of eloquence in his plea for the constitutional Union. "The Government . . . is a great and powerful government, invested with all the attributes of sovereignty over the special subjects to which its authority extends. Its framers never intended to implant in its bosom the seeds of its own destruction, nor were they at its creation guilty of the absurdity of providing for its own dissolution. It was not intended by its framers to be the baseless fabric of a vision, which, at the touch of the enchanter, would vanish into thin air, but a substantial and mighty fabric, capable of resisting the slow decay of time, and of defying the storms of ages."

What, then, is the remedy of the people of a state against tyranny? It is that right of resisting oppression which exists independently of all constitutions. Secession is nothing more nor less than revolution.

And what of the duty of the executive in case of an attempt to secede? He is bound, Buchanan continued, by his oath, to take care that the laws be faithfully executed. But what if that becomes impracticable, as in South Carolina, where all of the federal officers through whom the laws for the administration of justice can be executed, have resigned? Following Black, Buchanan concluded that, since force could be used by the executive only to aid the courts, it was not usable as matters stood. Congress alone could determine whether more power could be given to the executive for law enforcement.

Following Black again, as to the right to defend public property, Buchanan informed Congress that if any attempt should be made to expel the United States from the forts or other property belonging to the government, the officer in command had orders to act strictly upon the defensive. Then the responsibility for the consequences would rightfully rest upon the assailants. Finally, discussing the power of Congress to coerce a state which has withdrawn or is attempting to withdraw from the Union, Buchanan concluded that neither Congress nor any other branch of the federal government possessed such power. It had been withheld after discussion, he pointed out, by the federal Convention, and if conferred it would be useless. The Union rests upon public opinion, and can never be cemented by the blood of its citizens. If it cannot live in the affections of the people, it must one day perish.

The message concluded with an exhortation by the President to his dissatisfied countrymen, to pause and consider the alternatives of dissolution of the Union, among which is the possibility of amending the Constitution so as to safeguard slavery more effectively.

In this analysis of the situation by Black and Buchanan the right of the government to defend its property and repossess it if wrongfully seized stands out distinctly. It is surprising, therefore, to find that the President allowed the federal arsenals and their contents, as well as certain military posts, located in the seceding states, to fall into the hands of the seceders without resistance and without an effort put forth to recover them. In December he winked at the firing upon the *Star of the West* as it entered Charleston harbor with supplies for Fort Sumter. Northern writers have heaped abuse upon the head of the ill-starred executive. But it is only fair to say that the clue to his conduct is given in the closing words of his message. If the Union could not live in the affections of its people, it must one day perish! To have resisted forcibly these aggressions would have precipitated a conflict which, he was convinced, would have insured the destruction of the Union. Not until every effort at compromise had failed was force to be thought of.[14]

LINCOLN COMES TO OFFICE

If Lincoln had been in Buchanan's place during the winter of 1860–1861 it seems altogether likely that he would have pursued an almost identical policy. By the time of his inauguration the period of temporizing had passed. Proposals for safeguarding slavery by

[14] While Buchanan was drafting his message to Congress, Black abandoned his previous position and advised the President that he had the right to use military force to execute the laws of the Union against individuals in every state. Buchanan, bent on finding the path to peace, and supported by the arguments of the southern members of the cabinet, rejected this advice.—Auchampaugh, *Buchanan and His Cabinet*, 137 et seq.

constitutional amendment, the discussions of the Peace Convention —all the possibilities of compromise or conciliation had been considered and for one reason or another had failed.[15]   The time for action had come, and Lincoln's starting point was just where Buchanan stopped—the resolve to defend Fort Sumter if attacked.

In his first utterance as President, Lincoln explained his view of the doctrine of secession.[16]   It was not only essentially the same as Buchanan's in its reasoning, but even in its English it betrays indebtedness to the retiring President.   Said Lincoln: "I hold that in contemplation of universal law and of the Constitution, the Union of these States is perpetual.   Perpetuity is implied, if not expressed, in the fundamental law of all national governments.   It is safe to assert that no government proper ever had a provision in its organic law for its own termination.   Continue to execute all the express provisions of our national Constitution, and the Union will endure forever—it being impossible to destroy it except by some action not provided for in the instrument itself.

"Again, if the United States be not a government proper, but an association of States in the nature of a contract merely, can it, as a contract, be peaceably unmade by less than all the parties who made?"

Lincoln traced the beginnings of the Union to the Articles of Association of 1774.   It was carried a step further, he explained, by the Declaration of Independence and again advanced by the Articles of Confederation, in which thirteen states expressly plighted and engaged that it should be perpetual.   In 1787 one object in framing the Constitution was to form a more perfect Union.   "But if the destruction of the Union by one or a part only of the States be lawfully possible, the Union is less perfect than before the Constitution, having lost the vital element of perpetuity."

"It follows from these views that no State upon its own mere motion can lawfully get out of the Union; that resolves and ordinances to that effect are legally void; and that acts of violence,

[15] On the efforts at compromise see Frederic Bancroft, "Efforts at Compromise"; L. E. Chittenden, *Report of the Debates and Proceedings of the Peace Convention;* and W. E. Tilberg, "Responsibility for the Failure of Compromise."

[16] Inaugural address; Richardson, *Messages,* VI, 7, *et seq.;* Johnson, 464–466; Commager, 385–388.

within any State or States, against the authority of the United States, are insurrectionary or revolutionary, according to circumstances.

"I therefore consider that, in view of the Constitution and the laws, the Union is unbroken; and to the extent of my ability I shall take care, as the Constitution itself expressly enjoins upon me, that the laws of the Union be faithfully executed in all the States. . . .

"In doing this there needs to be no bloodshed or violence. . . . The power confided to me will be used to hold, occupy, and possess the property and places belonging to the government, and to collect the duties and imposts; but beyond what may be necessary for these objects there will be no invasion, no using of force against or among the people anywhere," no attempt to force obnoxious strangers as officeholders upon localities where hostility to the United States prevents competent resident citizens from holding federal offices. "You can have no conflict," he concluded, addressing the seceders, "without being yourselves the aggressors."

In a message to Congress in July, 1861, Lincoln carried further his argument against the theory of secession: The leaders of the secession movement "invented an ingenious sophism . . . that any State of the Union may consistently with the National Constitution, and therefore lawfully and peacefully, withdraw from the Union without the consent of the Union or of any other State. . . . With rebellion thus sugar-coated they have been drugging the public mind of their section for more than thirty years. . . . This sophism derives much . . . of its currency from the assumption that there is some omnipotent and sacred supremacy pertaining to a State—to each State of our Federal Union. Our States have neither more nor less power than that reserved to them in the Union by the Constitution—no one of them ever having been a State out of the Union. The original ones passed into the Union even before they cast off their British colonial dependence; and the new ones each came into the Union directly from a condition of dependence, excepting Texas.

"And even Texas, in its temporary independence, was never designated a State. . . . What is [a] 'sovereignty' in the political sense of the term? Would it be far wrong to define it as 'a political community without a political superior'? Tested by this, no one of our States, except Texas, ever was a sovereignty. And even Texas gave up the character on coming into the Union; by which act she acknowledged the Constitution of the United States, and the laws and treaties of the United States made in pursuance of the Constitution, to be for her the supreme law of the land. The States have their status in the Union, and they have no other legal status. If they break from this, they can only do so against law and by revolution. The Union, and not themselves separately, procured their independence and their liberty. By conquest or purchase the Union gave each of them whatever of independence or liberty it has. The Union is older than any of the States, and in fact it created them as States. . . .

"What is now combatted is the position that secession is consistent with the Constitution—is lawful and peaceful. . . . If all the States save one should assert the power to drive that one out of the Union, it is presumed the whole class of seceder politicians would at once deny the power and denounce the act as the greatest outrage upon State rights. But suppose that precisely the same act, instead of being called 'driving the one out,' should be called 'the seceding of the others from that one,' it would be exactly what the seceders claim to do, unless, indeed, they make the point that the one, because it is a minority, may do what the majority may not rightfully do. These politicians are subtle and profound on the rights of minorities. They are not partial to the power which made the Constitution and speaks from the preamble calling itself 'We, the People.' " [17]

[17] Richardson, *Messages*, VI, 24 *et seq*. Reprinted, Johnson, 468–471; Commager, 393–395.

XIV

WAR POWERS

PRESIDENTIAL AUTHORITY

AT the beginning of his presidency, Lincoln found the functions of the federal government, with the exception of the post office, virtually suspended in South Carolina, Georgia, Alabama, Florida, Mississippi, and Louisiana. Forts, arsenals, dockyards, custom houses, and movable property had been seized, and the remaining forts were menaced. As a measure of policy, he resolved to hold Fort Sumter until its abandonment became a military necessity. Provisions were therefore prepared for the garrison, and the governor of South Carolina was notified that unless delivery was resisted, no attempt would be made to send men, arms, or ammunition. This notice was followed by the bombardment and reduction of Sumter by the southern forces.[1]

The South thus became the aggressor, as Lincoln had anticipated would be the case. The attack was met by a call for militia, on April 15, in the following terms:

"Whereas the laws of the United States have been for some time past, and now are opposed, and the execution thereof obstructed, in the States of . . . by combinations too powerful to be suppressed by the ordinary course of judicial proceedings, or by the powers vested in the marshals by law:

"Now, therefore, I, Abraham Lincoln, President of the United States, in virtue of the power in me vested by the Constitution and laws, have thought fit to call forth, and hereby do call forth, the militia of the several States of the Union to the aggregate number of 75,000, in order to suppress said combinations and to cause the laws to be duly executed. . . .

[1] James G. Randall's volume, on *Constitutional Problems under Lincoln*, is excellent on all the questions of this period. The same author has recently issued *The Civil War and Reconstruction*. The new volume is general in scope, but contains much of interest to the student of constitutional history, discussed in its proper relations with other topics. See especially Chap. XV. The book includes extensive bibliographies.

"I deem it proper to say that the first service assigned to the forces hereby called forth will probably be to repossess the forts, places, and property which have been seized from the Union; and in every event the utmost care will be observed, consistently with the objects aforesaid, to avoid any devastation, any destruction of, or interference with property, or any disturbance of peaceful citizens of any part of the country." [2]

The Constitution makes the President the commander-in-chief of the army and navy of the United States, and of the militia of the several states when called into the service of the United States. It also makes it his duty to see that the laws are faithfully executed. Since the lawmaking power is vested in Congress, together with that of making rules for the government and regulation of the land and naval forces, and rules concerning captures on land and water, it would appear that it is the laws of Congress which the President is to execute. In other words, both as chief executive and as commander-in-chief his function waits upon that of the legislature. [3]

The sudden crisis of April, 1861, however, called for immediate action, and as Congress was not in session the safety of the nation would not admit of delay until it assembled. On the same day that the militia call was issued, Lincoln summoned Congress to assemble in special session on July 4. Then he took such steps as conditions seemed to require pending its coming together.

The call for militia was based upon authority given by the law of 1795, passed by Congress during the troubles in western Pennsylvania, [4] and in the proclamation the President was careful to define the purpose of the call in such a way as to keep well within the limits prescribed by Attorney-General Black's opinion. Notwithstanding this caution, the measure was construed by some of the slave states which had not yet seceded as an attempt to coerce sovereign states, and consequently North Carolina, Virginia, Ten-

[2] Richardson, *Messages*, VI, 13. Reprinted in MacDonald, *Select Statutes*, 1–2; Johnson, 466.

[3] See Clarence A. Berdahl, *War Powers of the Executive in the United States;* and Barton A. Ulrich, *Abraham Lincoln and Constitutional Government.* A near-contemporary work is William Whiting, *War Powers under the Constitution* (1871).

[4] See Hockett, *Con. Hist.,* I, 274–276.

nessee, and Arkansas followed the example of the states of the lower South in passing ordinances of secession.[5]

On April 19, four days later than the call for militia, Lincoln issued another proclamation, drafted by Secretary of State Seward, establishing a blockade of the ports of the seceded states, and denouncing the penalties of the laws of the United States for the prevention and punishment of piracy against any person who, "under the pretended authority of the said States or under any other pretense, shall molest a vessel of the United States or the persons or cargo on board of her."[6]   On May 3 the President issued a call for volunteers, thus increasing the size of the army without the authorization of Congress. Finally, early in the summer, he authorized the suspension of the writ of habeas corpus along the military line between Philadelphia and Washington.

All of these measures, except the call for the militia, were doubtful exercises of power on the part of the President, and gave rise to the charge of "military dictatorship," a charge which seemed to gain weight by the postponement of the special session until July. John Sherman, writing in August, said: "I never met any one who claimed that the President could, by proclamation, increase the regular army."[7]   Many critics maintained that the proclamation of the blockade was equivalent to a declaration of war, and thus an infringement upon the powers of Congress. It was also urged that the power to suspend the writ of habeas corpus belonged to the legislature alone.

When Congress convened in July, the President reviewed and justified his whole course.[8]   The call for the militia and the proclamation of the blockade he believed to be strictly within his legal

[5] Important studies of particular states are: William K. Boyd, "North Carolina on the Eve of Secession"; J. D. Eggleston, "The Attitude of Virginia Leaders toward Slavery and Secession"; James W. Fertig, *The Secession and Reconstruction of Tennessee;* Beverley B. Mumford, *Virginia's Attitude toward Slavery and Secession;* Henry T. Shanks, *The Secession Movement in Virginia;* James E. Walmsley, ed., "The Change of Secession Sentiment in Virginia in 1861."

[6] Richardson, *Messages,* VI, 15. Reprinted in Johnson, 467; MacDonald, *Select Statutes,* 3–4.

[7] Letter to *Cincinnati Commercial Gazette,* Aug. 12, 1861, quoted by Randall, *Constitutional Problems,* 38, note 17.

[8] Message of July 4, 1861, Richardson, VI, 24–28. Extracts in Johnson, 468–471; Commager, 393–395.

powers. As to the call for volunteers and the large additions to the regular army and navy, he said: "These measures, whether strictly legal or not, were ventured upon under what appeared to be a popular demand and a public necessity, trusting then, as now, that Congress would readily ratify them. It is believed that nothing has been done beyond the constitutional competency of Congress."

Lincoln's justification was two-fold. He urged (1) that the national safety imperatively demanded the measures he had taken, and (2) that as he had not exceeded the powers of Congress, legislative approval of his conduct would correct any defect in its legality. Congress responded to this rather remarkable appeal by passing an act, on August 6, 1861, which read:

". . . Be it . . . enacted, That all the acts, proclamations, and orders of the President . . . respecting the army and navy of the United States, and calling out or relating to the militia or volunteers from the States, are hereby approved and in all respects made valid . . . as if they had been issued and done under the previous express authority and direction of the Congress of the United States." [9]

A few months later the Supreme Court ruled that the presidential acts to which this statute referred were valid in themselves and required no such legislative sanction.[10] It can hardly be said, therefore, that the action of Lincoln and Congress created a precedent to the effect that in a crisis the executive can do acts which pertain to the legislative authority and procure their retroactive legalization. This is perhaps fortunate; it doubtless has its bearing on the fact that the vigorous measures taken by our government during the World War were worked out by Congress and the President, the latter taking care not to repeat Lincoln's experiment of acting in advance of the legislature. In 1862, however, Thaddeus Stevens, in the House of Representatives, upheld the doctrine that under such circumstances as prevailed during the early months of the Civil War, the President becomes by virtue of the Constitution to all intents and purposes a dictator.[11]

"The Constitution makes it the duty of the President to see that

[9] *U. S. Stat. at Large*, XII, 326.
[10] In the Prize Cases. See discussion *post*.
[11] There are lives of Stevens by E. B. Callender, S. W. McCall, and James A. Woodburn. Just published is Alphonse B. Miller, *Thaddeus Stevens*.

all laws be executed. If any unforeseen and uncontrollable emergency should arise endangering the existence of the Republic, and there were no legal provision or process by which the danger could be averted, the section of the Constitution which says that 'the President shall take care that the laws shall be faithfully executed' creates him, for the time being, as much a dictator as a decree of the Roman senate that the consul 'should take care that the commonwealth should receive no detriment' made him a dictator, and gave him all power necessary for the public safety, whether the means were inscribed on their tables or not. Of course such power would be limited by the necessity, and ought to exist only until Congress could be convened." [12]

Then, thought Stevens, Congress might create a dictator at any time if there were no other means left to save the Republic from destruction. Unamerican as these views seem, they doubtless had an influence in placating public opinion with regard to the conduct of the President, and in preparing the people for the extreme course pursued by Congress itself during the era of reconstruction.

As throwing further light upon contemporary opinion concerning the war powers of President and Congress respectively, it is worth while to note a debate which took place in June, 1862, between Charles Sumner and Orville H. Browning of Illinois, Douglas's successor in the Senate.[13] The latter contended that the war powers of the government were executive rather than legislative. Because of their very nature questions of military necessity were to be decided by the military commanders acting under the authority of the President as commander-in-chief. The full powers of a belligerent with which the government became clothed in war time under international law were, Browning insisted, confided to the President, who was answerable to the people. Sumner held that the war powers belonged to Congress, and his view has received the support of the courts. It is Congress which has the power to provide for the carrying on of war as well as the declaring of it,

[12] Speech of January 22. *Cong. Globe*, 37 Cong., 2 sess., 440 *et seq*. Extract in Johnson, 491–492. On presidential dictatorship see W. A. Dunning, "The Constitution in the Civil War," 175; J. G. Randall, "Lincoln in the Rôle of Dictator"; and Charles Warren, "Lincoln's 'Despotism' as Seen by Critics of 1861."

[13] *Cong. Globe*, 37 Cong., 2 sess., 2917 *et seq*.

and the limits of its war powers are fixed by the international law of belligerency, which supersedes, in the treatment of enemies, the guarantees of the fifth, sixth and other amendments.

THE PRIZE CASES

The Supreme Court took pains, nevertheless, to sustain the course of the President in issuing the proclamation establishing the blockade. Its validity was tested in the Prize Cases, which involved the *Amy Warwick* and certain other vessels from neutral countries which had been captured while attempting to enter the blockaded ports.[14] The problem presented to the judges by these cases was a difficult one. A blockade is an act of war, and if a state of public war existed, the Confederates would be entitled to treatment as belligerents. Such treatment was promptly accorded them by the leading European governments. But the power to declare war belongs to Congress, and Congress had not declared war. Moreover, Seward had taken the position officially that a state of war did not exist. In the eyes of the members of the administration, the southerners were in insurrection, amenable to the law of treason for warring against the United States, and to the law against piracy in molesting federal shipping. The proclamation, although an act of war, rested on the theory that the Confederates were insurgents and denied them the rights of belligerents. How could a presidential blockade be reconciled with the insurgency theory, and how could the court uphold the theory of insurgency without denying that the principles of international law governed the rights of neutrals in the present conflict?

The situation was enough to cause uneasiness. If the President lacked the power to establish the blockade, or if a state of war did not exist when the captures were made, the captures were illegal. Richard H. Dana, author of *Two Years before the Mast,* a famous book in its day, who acted as one of the attorneys for the government in the case, wrote to an acquaintance: "Contemplate, my dear sir, the possibility of a Supreme Court, deciding that this blockade is illegal! What a position it would put us in before the world whose commerce we have been illegally prohibiting, whom we have

[14] 2 Black 635 (1863). Extract in Johnson, 472–473.

unlawfully subjected to a cotton famine, and domestic dangers and distress for two years! It would end the war, and how it would leave us with neutral powers, it is fearful to contemplate! Yet such an event is legally possible—I do not think it probable. . . . The bare contemplation of such a possibility makes us pause in our boastful assertion that our written Constitution is clearly the best adapted to all exigencies, the last, best gift to man." [15]

The argument of the cases covered several days in February, 1863. Dana's presentation especially appealed to Judge Grier, upon whom it devolved to deliver the decision. At the close of Dana's argument, "in a burst of unjudicial enthusiasm," Grier exclaimed to a spectator who wrote an account of the incident, "Well, your little Two Years before the Mast has settled that question; there is nothing more to say about it!" [16]

In the decision sustaining the President's proclamation Grier wrote: "A civil war always begins by insurrection against the lawful authority of the government. A civil war is never solemnly declared; it becomes such by its accidents. . . . The laws of war, as established among nations, have their foundation in reason, and all tend to mitigate the cruelties and misery produced by the scourge of war. Hence the parties to a civil war usually concede to each other belligerent rights. . . .

"This greatest of civil wars was not gradually developed by popular commotion, tumultuous assemblies, or local unorganized insurrections. However long may have been its previous conception, it nevertheless sprang forth suddenly from the parent brain, a Minerva in the full panoply of war. The President was bound to meet it in the shape it presented itself, without waiting for Congress to baptize it with a name; and no name given to it by him or them could change the fact.

"It is not the less a civil war, with belligerent parties in hostile array, because it may be called an 'insurrection' by one side, and the insurgents be considered as rebels or traitors. . . . Whether the President, in fulfilling his duties as Commander-in-chief in suppressing an insurrection, has met with such armed hostile resistance,

[15] Quoted by Warren, II, 380.
[16] Ibid. For the influence of great advocates see Hockett, Con. Hist., I, 373.

and a civil war of such alarming proportions, as will compel him
to accord to them the character of belligerents, is a question to be
decided by him, and this Court must be governed by the decisions
and acts of the political department of the Government to which
this power was intrusted.[17] 'He must determine what degree of
force the crisis demands.' The proclamation of blockade is itself
official and conclusive evidence to the Court that a state of war
existed which demanded and authorized a recourse to such a
measure.''

In the point of view here given Grier was sustained by only one
justice whose appointment antedated Lincoln's election. This was
Wayne. Taney, Nelson, Catron, and Clifford dissented. Three
new men, appointed by Lincoln—Swayne, Miller, and Davis—with
Wayne and Grier made up the majority. In the letter above referred to, Dana expressed a doubt whether the court as constituted
before the changes under Lincoln would have upheld the proclamation. The gist of the dissenting opinions is that the President's
power to deal with insurrection cannot bring about a state of war.
His power is derived from domestic, or municipal, law, and not
the law of nations. Congress alone can declare war, or give such
recognition to its existence as will constitute in law a state of war.

The minority opinions bring out the fact that the date of the
legal as distinguished from the actual beginning of the war is important, because of the effect upon private property rights. Holding that congressional recognition was necessary to constitute legally the state of war, the minority fixed upon the Non-Intercourse
Act of July 13, 1861, as marking the beginning. This law reenacted the main features of the Force Act of Jackson's presidency,
and provided that when insurgents failed to disperse as directed by
the President, and claimed to act under authority of a state or states,
such claim not being repudiated by the persons exercising the functions of government in such state or states, then the President by
proclamation might declare such inhabitants in a state of insurrection against the United States. Captures before the date of this
act the minority held to be invalid.

Similarly, since the majority upheld the validity of the blockade,

[17] On "political cases" see *ante*, Chap. VII.

they regarded the date of the proclamation, April 19, as marking the legal beginning of the war, so far as the states named in the proclamation were concerned. For the states which seceded later, the war was held to begin with the issuance of the similar proclamation directed against them. Still another date has been accepted by the historian William A. Dunning. The Non-Intercourse act authorized the President to proclaim, under the circumstances indicated, a state of insurrection. Such a proclamation Lincoln issued on August 16,[18] and it was from that time, Dunning held, that the condition of territorial civil war existed.[19]

THE NATURE OF THE WAR

The decision in the Prize Cases had an important bearing also upon the nature of the war, that is, as to whether, after the action of Congress, it was an insurrection or a public war. Much depended upon the answer, since the powers of the government in dealing with captures, property rights of the enemy, and other matters would be different in the two cases. In the case of a public war individuals are relieved of personal responsibility for acts which would otherwise be criminal. A nation does not claim the municipal power over its enemies in a public war, but in the case of insurrection or rebellion it may do so.

The theory of the administration at the outset of the hostilities was that the conflict was an insurrection, and its coercive efforts were directed against individuals who had combined to resist the laws. Accordingly great care was taken not to recognize the Confederacy even as a *de facto* government. Negotiations for the exchange of prisoners were conducted warily, and the persistent official view of the status of the Confederacy was that it was a "pretended government." [20]

It proved to be impracticable to treat southern soldiers as traitors and sailors as pirates, and in spite of the refusal of formal recognition of the belligerency of the Confederacy, belligerent rights were accorded in practice. The threat of retaliation alone was sufficient

[18] Richardson, *Messages*, VI, 37–38. Reprinted in Johnson, 471–472.
[19] *Essays on Reconstruction*, 23.
[20] Randall, *Con. Probs.*, 64.

to force this policy upon the administration if sentiments of humanity had been insufficient. Yet the southerners continued to be regarded technically as traitors amenable to the municipal power of the government for crimes committed just as were the participants in the Whiskey Insurrection. They were, besides, public enemies, and the territory which they held was regarded as enemy's territory. According to its own theory, then, the government possessed both belligerent and sovereign rights; it could exercise the belligerent right of blockading the southern ports and the sovereign right of prosecuting the southerners for treason.

The conflict was thus both war and rebellion, and the southerners both rebels and belligerents. Said Charles Sumner: "Our case is double, and you may call it a rebellion or war as you please, or you may call it both." [21] This dual view was affirmed by Justice Grier in the Prize Cases.

SUSPENSION OF THE WRIT OF HABEAS CORPUS

Let us now return to the message which Lincoln sent to the special session of Congress in July, 1861. Among the measures which he then undertook to defend was the suspension of the writ of habeas corpus.

Early in the summer of 1861 the secession movement in Maryland had threatened to bring about the withdrawal of the state from the Union, and the isolation of Washington from the loyal northern states.[22] To prevent this by seizure of the leaders of the movement, the President had authorized General Winfield Scott to suspend the writ anywhere along the military line between Philadelphia and the capital city. The provision of the Constitution on which Lincoln based this action reads: "The privilege of the writ of *habeas corpus* shall not be suspended unless when in cases of rebellion or invasion the public safety may require it." [23]

This sentence does not state in what branch of the government the power of suspension shall rest in the circumstances indicated. It occurs in the article which deals with the prohibitions on the

[21] Quoted, *ibid.*, 71.

[22] The critical situation in Maryland is the theme of Carl M. Frasure in "Union Sentiment in Maryland, 1859–1861."

[23] Art. I, sec. 9, par. 2.

legislature, and up to this time had been regarded as belonging to that body. However, if Lincoln had awaited the meeting of Congress action would probably have come too late to prevent the danger which he apprehended. In his opinion, the provision being for an emergency, it was natural to infer that the President should use his discretion rather than that the danger should not be met until Congress could convene and act.

As a result of the President's order, one John Merryman, a lieutenant in a secessionist drill company, was arrested by General Cadwallader, commander of the military department in which Baltimore was situated, and confined in Fort McHenry. He applied for a writ of habeas corpus to Chief Justice Taney, who heard the petition while on circuit, and rendered his decision not in open court, but in chambers. Taney issued a writ directing General Cadwallader to produce Merryman in court, but the officer, who was under instructions to hold in secure confinement all persons implicated in treasonable practices, and to disregard writs issued by any authority whatsoever, declined to obey. Taney thereupon issued a writ of attachment for contempt, but the marshal was refused entrance to the fort, and would have encountered superior force had he attempted by *posse comitatus* to compel the General's appearance. Hence Taney filed his opinion in *ex parte Merryman*, with the clerk of the federal circuit court for Maryland, to be placed on record, and caused a copy to be transmitted to the President.[24]

Although the chief justice, as he told his son, believed that he was subjecting himself to probable imprisonment by his course,[25] he did not hesitate to deny the right of the President to suspend the writ of habeas corpus. In the opinion which he prepared, he adduced evidence to show that in England the power of suspension rested with Parliament. The rule of context indicated that in the United States also the power rested with the legislature. He quoted Story's opinion that Congress is the exclusive judge of the exigency requiring the suspension, and cited Marshall in further support of the

[24] Swisher, *Taney*, 547 *et seq.*; McPherson, *History of the . . . Great Rebellion*, 155–156. Extract in Johnson, 474–478; Commager, 398–401.
[25] Warren, II, 369, note, citing Tyler, *Life of Taney*.

view. Any one suspected of treason, he maintained, should have been reported to the district attorney and dealt with by judicial process. The overriding of the judiciary he denominated military usurpation, and called upon the President to fulfill his constitutional obligations by taking measures to cause the civil process of the United States to be respected.

That Taney's opinion expressed the apprehensions of many persons who felt that the President's course endangered the liberty of citizens and threatened the subordination of the civil to the military power, is certain. "It does appear to us," commented the *Cincinnati Commercial*, that Merryman "could have been held and punished by the civil power," [26] while the *Baltimore American* suggested that it would "be well for the highest officer of the government to justify a plain violation of the Constitution, while calling out troops to maintain that same Constitution inviolate." [27]

The press was by no means of one mind, however, and the attacks upon the aged chief justice by some newspapers were quite as violent as the denunciations hurled at him at the time of the Dred Scott decision. His inveterate enemy, the *New York Tribune*, said that he "takes sides with traitors, throwing around them the sheltering protection of the ermine." [28] The *New York Evening Post* charged him with using "his authority and position to the advantage of those who are armed against the Union." [29]

The public clamor drew from the President a statement in the July message. Said he: "The attention of the country has been called to the proposition that one who is sworn to 'take care that the laws be faithfully executed' should not himself violate them. Of course some consideration was given to the questions of power and propriety before this matter was acted upon. The whole of the laws which were required to be faithfully executed were being resisted and failing of execution in nearly one-third of the States.

[26] Quoted by Warren, II, 371. Merryman was in fact soon turned over to the civil authorities and eventually the case against him was dropped.

[27] Quoted, *ibid*. For discussions of Lincoln's course see A. C. Cole, "Lincoln and the American Tradition of Civil Liberty"; W. A. Dunning, "The Constitution in the Civil War"; S. G. Fisher, "Suspension of the Writ of Habeas Corpus"; Randall, *Civil War*, Chap. XV.

[28] Quoted, Warren, II, 369.

[29] Quoted, *ibid*, 370.

Must they be allowed to finally fail of execution, even had it been perfectly clear that by use of the means necessary to their execution some single law, made in such extreme tenderness of the citizen's liberty that practically it relieves more of the guilty than of the innocent, should to a very limited extent be violated? To state the question more directly, Are all the laws *but one* to go unexecuted, and the Government itself to go to pieces lest that one be violated?"[30]

Of course, Lincoln did not intend to admit that he had violated either the Constitution or the laws, and the day after Congress assembled his view of his rights with reference to the writ was confirmed by an opinion prepared at his request by Attorney-General Bates. This legal adviser held that the President's oath to "protect and defend the Constitution" made it his particular duty to put down rebellion. The courts lacked the strength to do so, and the only adequate means of suppression were in the hands of the executive. The court had formerly held, in Martin *v.* Mott, that the President was the judge of the exigency requiring the use of force in an analogous situation, and his obligation implied such discretion in the choice of means as to warrant the suspension of the writ. The three branches of the government being coordinate, a judicial hearing on the suspension of the writ was like an appeal on a matter of Presidential discretion. Such an appeal could not be entertained by a judge in chambers.[31]

Owing to the circumstances under which it was given, Taney's opinion was not regarded as a judicial determination of the issue, but merely as the views of one man. Fortified by Bates's opinion, Lincoln extended the order authorizing the suspension of the writ to the military line between Philadelphia and New York. Congress was placed in an embarrassing position. In the act of the special session ratifying the orders of the President relating to the army, navy, and militia, it maintained silence as to the order suspending the writ. Besides, Lincoln continued to issue such orders even while Congress was sitting. Unwilling either to hamper the execu-

[30] Richardson, *Messages*, VI, 24–28.
[31] July 5, 1861. McPherson, *Great Rebellion*, 159–161, *et passim*. Extract in Johnson, 478–481.

tive or to admit the correctness of his claim that the power of suspension was his independently of congressional legislation, the lawmaking body wrestled with the question through several sessions before it enacted any legislation.

At one time the House passed a bill which contained the words: "It is and shall be lawful for the President . . . to suspend." [32] The ambiguous character of this bill was shown by the comments upon it. Said Charles John Biddle of Pennsylvania, in the House: "Congress now gives a general power to the President to suspend. . . . We may thence infer that he does not possess it of his own . . . prerogative." [33] Said Senator Timothy Otis Howe of Wisconsin: "You declare that it is the right of the President already . . . you do not propose to confer the right upon him." [34] Congress was not willing to pass an act of such uncertain meaning, and yet the circumstances precluded the adoption of any statement which would be too definite.

THE ESTABLISHMENT OF MILITARY TRIBUNALS

In September, 1862, Lincoln issued a proclamation in support of the draft then in progress, declaring that all persons resisting the draft or discouraging volunteer enlistments should be subject to martial law and trial by court-martial, and that no resort to the writ of habeas corpus should be allowed on behalf of persons placed under military arrest.[35] The only possible basis for this proclamation was the war power which the more conservative thinkers held belonged to Congress and not to the President, except as exercised by him in execution of the laws of Congress. Lincoln's course suspended the fourth, fifth, and sixth amendments, with their safe-guards against arbitrary arrest and imprisonment, a power which the Milligan decision denied even to Congress.[36] The President's action without congressional authorization bordered on military despotism.

Lincoln's course seemed to recognize no rule or restraint but his

[32] Randall, *Con. Probs.*, 129–130.
[33] *Ibid.*
[34] *Ibid.*
[35] Richardson, *Messages*, VI, 98.
[36] See *infra*, Chap. XV.

own judgment of what was necessary. In criticism of this attitude, ex-judge Benjamin R. Curtis wrote contemporaneously that the proclamation and the orders which followed to carry it into effect "are manifest assumptions, by the President, of powers delegated to the Congress and to the judicial department of the government. It is a clear and undoubted prerogative of Congress alone, to define all offences, and to affix to each some appropriate and not cruel or unusual punishment. But his proclamation and these orders create new offences, not known to any law of the United States. 'Discouraging enlistments,' and 'any disloyal practice,' are not offences known to any law of the United States. . . . This proclamation and these orders remove the accused from the jurisdiction of the judiciary; they substitute a report, made by some deputy provost marshal, for the presentment of a grand jury; they put a military commission in place of a judicial court and jury required by the Constitution; and they apply the discretion of the commission and the President, fixing the degree and kind of punishment, instead of the law of Congress fixing the penalty of the offence." [37]

As to the powers which the President possessed as commander-in-chief of the army and navy, Curtis explained: "In time of war, a military commander, whether he be the commander-in-chief, or one of his subordinates, must possess and exercise powers both over the persons and the property of citizens which do not exist in time of peace. But he possesses and exercises such powers, *not in spite of the Constitution and laws of the United States, or in derogation from their authority, but in virtue thereof and in strict subordination thereto.* The general . . . uses authority unknown to the Constitution and laws of the United States in time of *peace;* but not unknown to that Constitution and those laws in time of *war.* The power to declare war, includes the power to use the customary and necessary means effectually to carry it on. As Congress may institute a state of war, it may legislate into existence and place under executive control the means for its prosecution. And, in time of war, without any special legislation, not the commander-in-chief only, but every commander of an expedition, or of a military post, is lawfully empowered by the Constitution and laws of the United

[37] *The Executive Power* (1862), *passim.* Extract in Johnson, 492–495.

States to do whatever is necessary, and is sanctioned by the laws of war, to accomplish the lawful objects of his command. But it is obvious that his implied authority must find early limits somewhere. . . .

"What, then, is his authority over the persons and property of citizens? I answer, that, over all persons enlisted in his forces he has military power and command; that over all persons and property *within the sphere of his actual operations in the field*, he may lawfully exercise such restraint and control as the successful prosecution of his particular military enterprise may, in his honest judgment, absolutely require; and upon such persons as have committed offences against any article of war, he may, through appropriate military tribunals, inflict the punishment prescribed by law. *And there his lawful authority ends*."

Such public criticism of the President at last compelled Congress to act. Meantime the question of the right to suspend the writ had been complicated by the proclaimed intent to try civilians by courts-martial. Finally a bill, carefully nursed through a conference of the two houses by Senator Lyman Trumbull of Illinois, was pushed through the Senate, not without sharp practice, in the "wee sma' hours" of the morning of March 3, 1863, after an all night session.[38] This act was still ambiguous; it was a compromise with the administration which left the issue concerning the writ just about where it had been at the beginning.

The law authorized the President to suspend the writ of habeas corpus anywhere during rebellion, but provided for the discharge of persons arrested under denial of the privilege of the writ, unless they were indicted by a grand jury within twenty days. It also protected United States officers against suits for malicious imprisonment by making the plea of a presidential order an adequate defense. The act seemed to say that the President's suspension of the writ in the past had been legal, and at the same time that the power of suspension was now conferred upon him by Congress. As to trials by courts-martial, the provision requiring indictment within twenty days implied that the civil courts should hear the charges against persons arrested by military authority.

[38] Randall, *Con. Probs.*, 130.

The issue between Congress and President as to the location of the right to suspend the writ of habeas corpus remains open to this day. The Supreme Court has never passed upon it, and although the weight of contemporary opinion perhaps inclined towards the congressional power, the argument on the other side cannot be ignored. A contemporary pamphleteer named Horace Binney reviewed the history of the writ and arrived at the conclusion that Lincoln's position was well taken.[39]

One of the latest students of the question holds that there is "an essentially executive quality in the whole proceeding" when the writ is suspended. Even when authorized by Congress the actual suspension is ordered at the discretion of the executive. Throughout the Civil War the President suspended the writ whenever he deemed it necessary, and neither Congress nor the courts restrained him. The precedent of actual procedure in war time is on the side of the executive prerogative.[40] In view of the commotion which resulted from Lincoln's practice, however, it seems likely that in future presidents will, like Wilson, let their conduct wait upon congressional action, unless circumstances force them to act.

[39] *The Privilege of the Writ of Habeas Corpus under the Constitution.* The treatise was issued in three parts, at separate times.
[40] Randall, *Con. Probs.,* 137.

XV

WAR POWERS (*Continued*)

MILITARY ARRESTS AND TRIALS

THE first general suspension of the writ of habeas corpus, without reference to geographical limits, was that decreed by the President's proclamation of September, 1862, against the discouragement of enlistments. That proclamation contemplated the arrest by military authority of persons charged with such offenses, and trial by courts-martial or military commissions. The first legislation by Congress on the subject of the suspension of the writ was the act of March 3, 1863,[1] and this act pointed to the trial of suspects before the civil courts. It required the military authorities to supply to the courts lists of persons arrested, and if no indictments were found against such persons within twenty days, they were to be discharged by judicial orders, upon taking the oath of allegiance and giving assurances of good behavior. In case the required lists were not furnished, judges were authorized to discharge prisoners by writ of habeas corpus. These provisions prepared a way for the speedy release of all citizens against whom no accusation of violation of federal law could be plausibly brought. After the expiration of the twenty days prisoners not indicted could be released upon the petition of any citizen. On paper, the act was a two-fold vindication of the civil authority: military officers were placed under regulations prescribed by Congress instead of the President, and the control which the executive had taken from the judiciary was restored.

The issue thus raised presented one of the most important of the constitutional problems of the war period. The roots of the doctrines maintained by Congress and the courts run far back into English soil.[2] On the European continent, the status of military law is in distinct contrast with its position in England and the

---

[1] *U. S. Stat. at Large*, XII, 755.
[2] See historical sketch in Randall, *Con. Probs.*, 140 *et seq.*

United States. While Germany and France have regarded it as entitled to dominate in war times, the governments of the English-speaking nations have rested upon the principle of the supremacy at all times of the civil power.

The Constitution gives to Congress the power "To make Rules for the Government and Regulation of the land and naval Forces." [3] Even before the Constitution was framed, the Continental Congress had adopted, during the Revolution, articles of war based upon English statutes. Later enactments under the Constitution revised these first rules; such were the laws passed in 1789, 1806, and 1916.

The English "Mutiny Acts," the first of which was passed in 1689, gave courts-martial a limited jurisdiction over military persons both in war and peace. The ordinary civil relations even of such persons were reserved to the jurisdiction of the civil courts. Civilians also were subject to martial law when extraordinary circumstances required that an entire community be placed temporarily under military control. At such times the usual procedures were suspended, arrests could be made on mere suspicion, without warrants, hearings on habeas corpus petitions were denied, and the military chief became lawgiver, judge and executive.

Resort to martial law was rare in England and in early American history. Between 1689 and the outbreak of the World War it was not once proclaimed in England or Ireland. In the United States the Whiskey Insurrection was dealt with without employing it, the leaders being arrested under warrants and tried by the regular courts. During the War of 1812 General Andrew Jackson imprisoned a judge who issued a writ of habeas corpus on behalf of a prisoner arrested by military authority, but Jackson was held in contempt of court and suffered a fine therefor. Thus the supremacy of the civil power was upheld. Rhode Island established martial law during Dorr's Rebellion. In recent years it has become more common in connection with labor troubles.

Some English authorities contend that martial law never completely supersedes civil procedure; that a military commander's acts may be reviewed by the courts, and in case of infringement upon private rights beyond the point reasonably warranted by necessity,

[3] Art. I, sec. 8, par. 14.

he may be held liable in a civil or even criminal action. Thus the
civil courts are made the final judges of the validity of summary
procedure.

No such principle had gained clear-cut acceptance in the United
States, partly because of the form of government. The courts
have been cautious about inquiring into the adequacy of the causes
for proclaiming martial law, because the discretion in that matter
is confided to an independent branch of the government.

When hostilities began in 1861, the administration promptly
organized its machinery for dealing summarily with suspected persons, entrusting its operation to the state department. Under
Seward's control an elaborate secret service was developed and military arrests soon became numerous. Persons so arrested were not
given the reasons for the action, and, indeed, in many cases the
authorities acted merely on suspicion without sufficient investigation to provide a reasonable basis for any definite charges. The
primary purpose was precautionary; the chief concern was to seize
persons who might be agents of the Confederacy. In such cases
detention rather than trial was aimed at, and detention was the best
preventive of the dangers apprehended. In many instances, as
one biographer of Seward tells us, the department "never made up
its case." [4]

Early in 1862 the control of the system was transferred to the
war department and procedure was somewhat mitigated without
any fundamental change in policy and aims. In practice, most
prisoners were merely held until the emergency which led to their
arrest had passed. The suspension of the writ of habeas corpus was
not regarded as inaugurating martial law, either before or after
the proclamation of September, 1862. The plan actually pursued
was a milder way of proceeding than would have been possible
under martial law even if of more doubtful legality. It involved
interference with liberty, but this evil was offset by the increased
safety of the public. A few people were wronged but the general
security was promoted.

Most of the arrests were made for good reasons, and in making
them the administration exercised considerable circumspection.

[4] Frederick Bancroft, *Life of Seward*, cited by Randall, *Con. Probs.*, 150.

The President, other high officials and chief generals, restrained the zeal of subordinate officers, and arrests were forbidden except on orders from Washington or other high authority, such as that of the governors of states. Mere disloyal talk was to be overlooked. Some subordinate officers, nevertheless, supposed that the suspension of the writ of habeas corpus disposed of all law, and disregarding instructions, arrested "noisy secessionists" and even sellers of Confederate "mottoes and devices." [5]

The treatment of prisoners was not brutal; they were released in large numbers when the war department took over Seward's task. Spies were sometimes paroled, or even released upon taking the oath of allegiance.[6]

Nevertheless the government did make a considerable use of military tribunals in the trial of offenses not in the code and in regions remote from the scene of war. Such practices involved a two-fold extension of military justice beyond the sphere which conservative opinion regarded as normal. Generals in northern military departments under presidental orders arrested and tried persons who discouraged enlistment, or engaged in other disloyal practices. In Missouri, for example, numerous civilians were tried for burning bridges, destroying railway and telegraph lines, furnishing information to the enemy, and bushwhacking, and severely punished, although the death penalty was not enforced in any case without the President's confirmation of the sentence. In enemy territory or regions under martial law the use of military commissions for the trial of non-military persons charged with offenses of a military character was generally regarded as proper; but where martial law did not exist and the courts were in unimpeded operation, the public reacted against the use of military tribunals in dealing with civilians.

The courts sometimes tried to interfere with the operations of the military, either by issuing injunctions or writs of habeas corpus; but the military officers refused to let their hands be tied. Where writs were issued for the release of minors who had enlisted without their parents' consent, they were frequently honored; but the

---

[5] Randall, *Con. Probs.*, 155.
[6] *Ibid.*, 156.

provost marshals were instructed to decline to produce men in court where military orders were involved. Often no return was made to the court in such cases, or the return on the writ cited the presidental orders. The judge might then issue an attachment for contempt against the officer, or merely file an opinion denouncing the action of the military as a usurpation.[7]

The restraints which the congressional act of March 3, 1863, sought to impose upon the exercise of military authority made no noticeable difference in the practice of the executive department. The arrest, confinement, and release of prisoners continued to be governed by the former policy. An outstanding episode showing the dominance of the military power was the Vallandigham case. General A. E. Burnside, in command of the military department which included the State of Ohio, issued an order on April 19, 1863, declaring that persons committing acts for the benefit of the enemy would be executed as spies and traitors. "The habit of declaring sympathies for the enemy," it was announced by this order, "will no longer be tolerated."[8]

On the first of May Clement L. Vallandigham was arrested for utterances during a speech at Mt. Vernon, and brought before a military commission for trial. He denied the jurisdiction of the commission, and as he refused to plead, the judge advocate entered for him a plea of "not guilty," and the trial proceeded. Vallandigham was allowed to have counsel and to cross-examine witnesses. At the close of the trial, he read a "Protest," in which he maintained that he was not triable by such a commission, and that he was entitled to all the constitutional guarantees concerning arrest and trial by jury. His "alleged offense," he declared, was unknown to the Constitution and the laws.[9]

When the commission found him guilty, and application was made in his behalf to the United States circuit court at Cincinnati for a writ of habeas corpus. This step raised the question of the right of the court to review the proceedings of the military commission, and the matter finally came before the Supreme Court

[7] *Ibid.*, 158–163. See account on pages 162–163 of a case similar to that of Merryman.
[8] *Ibid.*, 176–177. The order was known as "General Order No. 38."
[9] *Ibid.*, 177. There is a life of Vallandigham by J. L. Vallandigham.

on motion for a writ of certiorari to review the sentence.[10] On February 15, 1864, the court held, in *ex parte Vallandigham*,[11] that it had no power to issue such a writ to a military commission, which was not a court within the meaning of the Judiciary Act; under the act its appellate jurisdiction extended only to judicial courts.

In the preceding June Lincoln had explained the theory on which his whole policy of summary procedure was founded: "Thoroughly imbued with a reverence for the guaranteed rights of individuals, I was slow to adopt the strong measures which by degrees I have been forced to regard as being within the exceptions of the Constitution and as indispensable to the public safety. . . . I concede that the class of arrests complained of can be constitutional only when in cases of rebellion or invasion the public safety may require them; and I insist that in such cases they are constitutional wherever the public safety does require them, as well in places in which they may prevent the rebellion extending as in those where it may already be prevailing."[12]

Chief Justice Taney lost hope, during 1863, that the Supreme Court would "ever be again restored to the authority and rank which the Constitution intended to confer upon it. The supremacy of the military power over the civil seems to be established," he wrote, "and the public mind has acquiesced in it and sanctioned it."[13] Historians have drawn a moving picture of this heroic old man, in jeopardy of his own liberty as he believed, fighting his losing battle in behalf of civil liberty. "There is nothing more sublime in the acts of great magistrates that give dignity to Governments," wrote one, than the attempt of Chief Justice Taney in the Merryman opinion "to uphold the supremacy of the Constitution

---

[10] Randall, *Con. Probs.*, 178.

[11] 1 Wallace 243.

[12] Letter to Erastus Corning, June 12, 1863. John G. Nicolay and John Hay, eds., *Complete Works of Abraham Lincoln*, VIII. Cited by Warren, II, 373. A review of Lincoln's acts by a contemporary adverse critic is John A. Marshall's *The American Bastile*. During the World War, profiting by Lincoln's experience, President Wilson was careful to obtain congressional support for all of his acts involving civil rights: J. G. Randall, "Lincoln's Task and Wilson's"; W. A. Dunning, "Disloyalty in Two Wars"; and James P. Hall, "Freedom of Speech in War Time."

[13] Quoted by Warren, 374.

and civil authority in the midst of arms." [14]   Another exclaims: "There is no sublimer picture in our history than this of the aged Chief Justice, the fires of Civil War kindling around him, the President usurping the powers of Congress and Congress itself, a seething furnace of sectional animosities, serene and unafraid, while for a third time in his career, the storm of partisan fury broke over his devoted head, interposing the shield of the law in the defense of the liberty of the citizen." [15]

EX PARTE MILLIGAN

Taney was not destined to live until the rights for which he fought were vindicated by a bench composed largely of Republicans.[16]   One Milligan had been arrested not long after the Vallandigham decision, on order of the general commanding the military district of Indiana, and tried in October, 1864, by a military commission.   He was proved to be a member of two disloyal societies known as the "Order of the American Knights," and the "Sons of Liberty," and was convicted of conspiracy to release "rebel" prisoners and to march into Kentucky and Missouri in cooperation with "rebel" forces in an expedition directed against the authority of the United States.[17]

He was sentenced to be hung on May 19, 1865, but on May 10 a petition for a writ of habeas corpus was addressed to the United States circuit court in Indiana in his behalf.   The judges disagreed, but certified the question of law to the Supreme Court.   There the case was argued during March, 1866.   This time the court did not hold, as in the Vallandigham case, that it could not review a trial by a military commission.[18]   The war was now over, and Justice Davis, in giving the opinion of the court, said that during the rebellion the temper of the times had not allowed "that calmness . . .

[14] Mikell, "Roger B. Taney," 188. Quoted, *ibid.*, 372.

[15] Tyler, *Life of Taney*, 420 *et seq.* Quoted *ibid.*

[16] Taney died on October 12, 1864, and Salmon P. Chase was appointed his successor in December.

[17] Randall, *Con. Probs.*, 180. See also account in Warren, II, 418 *et seq.* The most elaborate account is Samuel Klaus, ed., *The Milligan Case.*

[18] *Ex parte Milligan*, 4 Wallace 2. Extract in Johnson, 495–499. The decision was announced in April, 1866, but the opinions of the judges were not delivered in full until the following term of court, beginning in December.

necessary to a correct conclusion of a purely judicial question." If there was no law to justify this military trial, "it is our duty to declare the nullity of the whole proceedings." The judges thereupon unanimously decided, in words penned by Davis, Lincoln's personal friend, that the military commission which he had authorized was unlawful.[19]

A majority of the court, consisting of Justices Davis, Field, Nelson, Grier, and Clifford, stated the further opinion that Congress as well as the President lacked power to institute a military tribunal outside of the actual theater of war, where the civil courts were open. In the words of Judge Davis: "No graver question was ever considered by this Court, nor one which more nearly concerns the rights of every American citizen when charged with crime, to be tried and punished according to law. The Constitution of the United States is a law for rulers and people, equally in war and in peace, and covers with the shield of its protection all classes of men, at all times and under all circumstances." Its provisions cannot be "suspended during any of the great exigencies of government. Such a doctrine leads directly to anarchy or despotism. . . . Martial rule can never exist where the Courts are open and in the proper and unobstructed exercise of their jurisdiction."

This expression injected into the case a question which did not arise on the facts, and led Justices Chase, Miller, Swayne, and Wayne to file a dissenting opinion. In this Chief Justice Chase wrote: "We cannot doubt that, in such a time of public danger, Congress had power, under the Constitution" to make provision for military trials outside of the war zone and where the courts were open. The civil courts "might be open and undisturbed in the execution of their functions, and yet wholly incompetent to avert threatened danger, or to punish with adequate promptitude and certainty, the guilty conspirators. . . . The power of Congress to authorize trials for crimes against the security and safety of the National forces may be derived from its constitutional authority to raise and support armies and to declare war, if not from its constitutional authority to provide for governing the National forces."

[19] There is a sketch of Davis by Harry E. Pratt.

Contemporary press comments for the most part reveal the intensity of partisan feeling rather than any calm judgment upon the action of the court. Said the *Independent:* "We regard it as the most dangerous opinion ever pronounced by that tribunal. . . . So far as it bears upon the actual points in issue and is a determination of the case under review, it will be yielded to. Beyond this, it will be treated as a mere partisan harangue, unseemly, because of the source whence it emanated . . . a sorry attempt of five not very distinguished persons to exhibit themselves as profound jurists, whereas they have only succeeded in proving themselves to be very poor politicians. We regret this decision on many grounds. The Supreme Court had begun to recover the prestige tarnished by the Dred Scott decision. . . . The recent decision restores the Court to the bad eminence it occupied when Taney dictated its decrees." [20]

The most vicious assaults were those of John W. Forney, in the *Washington Chronicle,* the semi-official organ of the Republicans in the Senate: "The hearts of traitors will be glad by the announcement that treason, vanquished upon the battlefield and hunted from every other retreat, has at last found a secure shelter in the bosom of the Supreme Court." [21]

The *National Intelligencer* pointed out the true issue when it said: "It is not Milligan, the alleged conspirator, who is set free; but Milligan, citizen, tried by an illegal tribunal. . . . It is not the crime of treason which is shielded by this memorable decision, but the sacred rights of the citizen that are vindicated against the arbitrary decisions of military authority. Above the might of the sword, the majesty of the law is thus raised supreme." [22]   The *Springfield Republican* indicated the permanent significance of the decision: it was "simply a reaffirmation of the sacred right of trial by jury. No good citizen can regret that the Constitution and laws are again declared supreme." [23]

The majority opinion as to the powers of Congress was more open to question. Writing in 1890 Professor John W. Burgess

[20] Quoted by Warren, II, 430–431.
[21] Quoted, *ibid.*, 433.
[22] Quoted, *ibid.*, 435.
[23] Quoted, *ibid.*, 437.

questioned whether it could ever stand the strain of actual war. "We may safely predict that it will necessarily be disregarded. In time of war and public danger, the whole power of the State must be vested in the General Government, and the constitutional liberty of the individual must be sacrificed, so far as the Government finds it necessary for the preservation of the life and security of the State." [24]

The expression of this opinion by the majority when it was not required by the facts presented drew upon the court the criticism of the contemporary bar. Pointing out that the judges disagreed on a point not before them, the *American Law Review* for April, 1867, commented: "Instead of approaching the subject of the powers of the coordinate branches of the government as one of great delicacy, which they were loath to consider, but which they felt bound to pass upon because it was involved in the righteous decision of the cause before them, yet concerning which they had nothing to do, and would have nothing to say, except so far as it was necessary to the determination of that cause, they seemed eager to go beyond the record, and not only to state the reason of their present judgment, but to lay down the principles on which they would decide other questions, not now before them involving the gravest and highest powers of Congress. They have seemed to forget how all-important it is for the preservation of their influence that they should confine themselves to their duties as Judges between the parties in a particular case; how certainly the jealousy of the coordinate departments of the government and of the people would be excited by any attempt on their part to exceed their constitutional functions; and how, the more a case before the Supreme Court assumes a political aspect, the more cautious should the Judges be to confine themselves within their proper limits." [25]

This writer found his chief reason for alarm, however, not in the decision, but in the attitude of the public toward the court. If the people were indignant it was not because the judges had shown political prepossessions, but because they were held blameworthy

[24] *Political Science and Comparative Constitutional Law* I, 250–252. Quoted *ibid.*, 440.
[25] I, 572, quoted *ibid.*, 441.

if they did not.   The people had "a feeling that a Judge of the
Supreme Court of the United States who gives judgment contrary
to the wishes, for the time being, of a majority of the people, or, at
any rate, contrary to the wishes of an Administration which raised
him to the Bench, is liable to the same just censure that waits upon
a politician who has left the party to which he has pledged himself, and votes with the opposition; that a Judge is in fact, a representative to carry out the wishes of a political party." [26]

The Milligan decision had a very significant bearing upon the
contest already going on between President Johnson and Congress
over the question of reconstruction.   Johnson, who was at the time
bent upon ending military government in the South, regarded the
decision as an endorsement of his policy, and issued orders dis-
missing all trials of civilians by military commissions pending in
southern states.   Supreme Court justices, moreover, refused to sit
in the circuit courts in the southern states while these states were
under military government.[27]   The Republicans, who claimed that
the war was not yet over, were much disturbed by the action of
the President and judges, which implied that the trial of Lincoln's assassins was illegal.   The Milligan decision, declared Thaddeus Stevens, "places the knife of the rebel at the throat of
every . . . loyal union man in the South." [28]   Fearing that the
court might discharge the "assassins" by writ of habeas corpus,
radical congressmen discussed legislation to abridge its appellate
jurisdiction, to require unanimous decisions in constitutional cases,
and even to nullify the decisions in the Milligan case, Cummings v.
Missouri, and ex parte Garland.   An act was in fact passed which
deprived the court of jurisdiction in the case of ex parte Mc-
Cardle.[29]

[26] *Ibid.*, 442.
[27] *Ibid.*, 421.   The refusal of the judges to hold the circuit court sessions in the
South delayed the trial of Jefferson Davis for treason.   On Davis's trial see Roy
F. Nichols, "United States v. Jefferson Davis"; and D. K. Watson, "The Trial of
Jefferson Davis; an Interesting Constitutional Question."   Warren's account is
good: see II, 485–487.
[28] *Cong. Globe*, 39 Cong., 2 sess., I, 125.
[29] *Ibid.*, 249, 252, 286, 502, 616, *et passim.*   For congressional action in relation
to the McCardle case, see *ibid.*, 40 Cong., 2 sess., I, 478 *et seq.*   All of the cases
mentioned in text are discussed *infra*, Chap. XVIII.

IMMUNITY OF FEDERAL OFFICERS

While Milligan's case was before the Supreme Court, he was confined in the Ohio penitentiary under orders of General Alvin P. Hovey. After the decision of the court, he was released, and later brought an action against General Hovey for false imprisonment, in the federal circuit court, where a jury awarded him nominal damages. Pending the outcome of this suit, the *Cincinnati Enquirer* expressed the hope that Milligan would win. "It would be a healthy, political sign to show that there was a limit to military usurpation; and that even the President of the United States cannot give an order, or enforce a decree, against the law of the land, and that his illegal orders are no protection to his subordinates." [30]

American law borrowed from England the principle that officers of government are liable for their official conduct if it results in injury of private persons. During the war, many officers would have suffered from suits for acts which were not really theirs, but those of the government itself, unless they had been given some degree of immunity for such acts. The war had not been long in progress before federal officers began to be attacked. Pierce Butler, whom Simon Cameron, the secretary of war, had placed in confinement on suspicion of holding a Confederate commission, sued Cameron just as he was about to sail as minister to Russia, charging assault and false imprisonment. In 1863 Seward was likewise sued on a charge of false imprisonment, by G. W. Jones, who had once been the minister of the United States in Bogata; and on one occasion Governor Seymour, of New York, tried to prosecute General Dix for suppressing the *New York World*.[31] Secretary Edwin M. Stanton, after serving for some time as war secretary, said that if such suits held, he would be liable to imprisonment for a thousand years! [32]

It was this situation that called for the provision in the act of March 3, 1863, making the plea of a presidential order a sufficient defense for a military officer's acts.[33] Section 4 of that statute con-

[30] Quoted by Warren, II, 427, note.
[31] See *post*.
[32] See Randall's discussion of this topic, *Con. Probs.*, 187 *et seq*.
[33] See *ante*.

tained the indemnifying words: "Any order of the President, or under his authority, made at any time during the . . . present rebellion, shall be a defence in all courts to any action or prosecution, civilian or criminal, pending or to be commenced, for any search, seizure, arrest, or imprisonment . . . under and by virtue of such order, or under color or any law of Congress."

When suits against officers were brought in state courts, the act provided for their removal to federal tribunals unless judgment was found for the defendant.

In spite of the statute many suits were brought in state tribunals at the close of the war, especially in Kentucky, and efforts were made to prevent them from being transferred to the courts of the United States. In that commonwealth an officer who impressed horses while pursuing guerillas was prosecuted for horse stealing. Others who gave passes to Negroes were indicted for aiding in the escape of slaves. Firing on guerillas under arrest, to prevent their escape, led to the charge of murder. Conviction on such charges was severely punished, and state courts rejected the defense pleas based on the indemnity act on the ground that it was unconstitutional. Transfer to the federal courts was also denied on the ground that no federal question was involved, and an act was passed to give an appeal to the highest state court in case any lower court granted a transfer to the federal tribunals.[34] Many individuals held on suspicion of disloyalty sued federal officials for false imprisonment.

Congress attempted to meet such difficulties by supplementary legislation making state judges liable if they proceeded with cases after efforts to transfer them. This and other features of both the original and supplementary acts were open to serious objections, but the worst feature of the legislation was the failure to provide any means of relieving those who were despoiled by the acts of the indemnified officers. A proposal was made to allow them to recover damages, which the United States would assume, but it failed of adoption.[35]

[34] Randall, *Con. Probs.*, 195 *et seq.*
[35] George A. Finch, "Superior Orders and War Crimes." The two leading cases arising out of this legislation were The Justices *v.* Murray, 9 Wallace 247 (1870), and Mitchell *v.* Clarke, 110 U. S. 647 (1884).

REGULATION OF NEWSPAPERS

In connection with this discussion of the status of the personal rights of citizens during the war a few words should be said concerning the liberty of the press. In most cases where individuals were subjected to military arrest they were suspected of committing or contemplating acts dangerous to the public safety. Mere licentiousness in speech was not often the basis of action, the case of Vallandigham being the one conspicuous instance.

The freedom of the press presents a somewhat different although closely related problem.[36] At the beginning of the war practically the only statutes relating to the control of the press were state libel laws. These were designed chiefly to afford a remedy for individuals who suffered personal injuries, such as defamation of character, and did not recognize injuries which might be inflicted upon the public through criticisms tending to undermine the government. The regulation of the press, moreover, was regarded as a state function, since the first amendment specifically forbids Congress to pass any law abridging the liberty of the press. The one attempt of Congress to prevent or punish utterances designed to injure the government—the Sedition Act of 1798—had been so completely repudiated by public opinion that it served as a warning against the repetition of so doubtful an experiment even in actual wartime.[37] At no time during the Civil War did the government attempt a general censorship and such measures as it did take were inadequate and ineffective. The policy followed was nevertheless due to deliberate choice rather than weakness.

The government took over the control of telegraph lines leading out of Washington, in April, 1861, and stopped all messages giving military information or unapproved news concerning governmental activities. The following February the control was extended to all telegraph lines, and they were closed to all communications relating to military affairs except such as were authorized by the secretary of war or district commanders. In the summer of 1861 (August), an attempt was made to reach a "gentlemen's

[36] See Randall's discussion, *Con. Probs.*, 480 *et seq.*
[37] See Hockett, *Con. Hist.*, I, 288 *et seq.*

agreement" with the newspapers. In return for the promise of facilities for the transmission of intelligence especially regarding battles, the editors agreed to abstain from printing anything that could give aid or comfort to the enemy. Some papers refused to accept such limitations.[38]

The war period coincided with an era of unprecedented enterprise on the part of the greater newspapers. Many of them spent huge sums in perfecting their organizations for obtaining war news, maintaining numbers of special correspondents in the camps, and pursuing their objects with remarkable ingenuity and persistence. In February, 1862, Stanton sent out an order to prevent unauthorized publicity: "All newspaper editors and publishers have been forbidden to publish any intelligence received by telegram or otherwise respecting military operations by the United States forces. Please see . . . that this order is observed. If violated . . . seize the edition and give notice to this department, that arrests may be ordered."[39] The correspondents were under military law, and subject to punishment even by death if "convicted of holding correspondence with or giving intelligence to, the enemy, either directly or indirectly."[40] Sherman, while on the march to the sea, announced that correspondents with his expedition who sent out unauthorized communications would be dealt with as spies.[41]

The increasing severity of these paper regulations indicates that none of them was effective. The "gentlemen's agreement" soon broke down. The editors used their own judgment as to what news would be detrimental to the public welfare, and their opinion differed from that of the government officials. During the early months when the telegraph was regulated only at Washington, news went out from Philadelphia, New York, and other cities. When the government took over all of the telegraph lines, the news was transmitted by mail. Many of the correspondents at the front or elsewhere held clerkships and made it their primary business to get "copy." "The location of Grant's guns secretly

[38] Randall, *Con. Probs.*, 482.
[39] *Ibid.*, 503.
[40] *Ibid.*, 490.
[41] *Ibid.*, 491.

placed against Vicksburg in 1863 was published; his proposed con-
centration upon City Point in July, 1864, was revealed; Sherman's
objectives in his Georgia march and the disposition of his various
corps were proclaimed; full details concerning the land and sea
expedition against Wilmington, N. C., in December, 1864, were
supplied. Northern papers practically functioned as Confederate
spies in Union camps, for copies of these journals were easily obtained by Southern generals. General Lee, with a practical eye
for detecting military information, regularly scanned the enemy's
papers; and his confidential dispatches to President Davis show
that he gained many bits of valuable information concerning the
army of the Potomac at times when the Union generals were quite
mystified as to his own forces." [42]

Although Sherman's attempt to stigmatize the reporters as spies
was ill-advised, since the term could only apply where it could be
shown that the individual was in the employ of the enemy, it was
a natural result of exasperation over the leakage of military secrets
and the ineffectiveness of remedies. The right of Congress to place
correspondents under military control seemed clear enough. The
denial to them of confidential information, the censoring of their
dispatches at military headquarters, the punishment by court-
martial of such as conveyed useful intelligence to the enemy, were
never attacked as inconsistent with the provisions of the first
amendment, and the act of Congress providing for the punishment
of communication with the enemy plainly rested upon the constitutional power to make rules for the government of the land
and naval forces. The usual punishment accorded to offenders
was exclusion from the lines of a command. Sherman initiated
proceedings against one reporter who had revealed operations at
Vicksburg, but the court ruled that it must be shown that the
identical communication had been sent to the enemy. In no case
was the death penalty employed, and the instances of trial by
court-martial are rare. [43]

The war power over the press was less clear. The provocation

---

[42] *Ibid.*, 486–487. This quotation is printed with the permission of D. Appleton
and Company.

[43] *Ibid.*, 490 *et passim.*

given both by the publication of military news and by vicious attacks upon the administration, was extreme. The *New York
World* had this to say regarding the policy of emancipation: "The
administration shines, like the moon, by reflected light. It borrows
its ideas and its policy so far as it has any, from these crazy radicals. . . . By surrendering itself to their wild and reckless guidance it is ruining the country; and it is important that the people
should see, even at the expense of a good deal of disgust and loath-
ing, what has been substituted in the public counsels for statesman-
like sagacity and far-seeing wisdom." [44]   Another example of
this hypercritical attitude, which was nevertheless not at all unusual, is the utterance of the *Chicago Times* anent the second inaugural address of President Lincoln:

"The inaugural addresses of the past presidents of the United
States are among the best of our state papers. . . . Contrast with
these the inaugural address of Abraham Lincoln. . . . Was there
ever a nation, once great, so belittled? Is such another descent of
record in the history of any people? We had looked for something
thoroughly Lincolnian, but we did not foresee a thing so much
more Lincolnian than anything that has gone before it. We did not
conceive it possible that even Mr. Lincoln could produce a paper
so slipshod, so loose-jointed, so puerile, not alone in literary construction, but in its ideas, its sentiments, its grasp. . . . By the side
of it, mediocrity is superb." [45]

This very journal had been within two years the beneficiary of
Lincoln's moderation. As the consequence of an attack upon the
administration on account of the Vallandigham affair, it had been
suppressed by General Burnside, in June, 1863. The publishers
had obtained a temporary injunction from the federal circuit court
restraining Captain Putnam from executing Burnside's order, but
Putnam, disregarding the injunction, seized the newspaper office
and a mass meeting held in the court house in Chicago to protest
this action showed that public feeling was aroused.

Lincoln's disposition in such matters had already been indicated
in a letter to a subordinate of Burnside, disapproving his action

[44] Quoted, *ibid.*, 487.
[45] Quoted, *ibid.*, 488.

against certain Indiana newspapers. This letter had not been delivered when the *Times* was suppressed, but when the news of the latter action reached Washington, Stanton wrote to Burnside that the President advised an early revocation of his order. "The irritation produced by such acts is in his opinion likely to do more harm than the publication would do." [46] A day or two later, with the approval of the cabinet, Lincoln revoked the order himself.

The next May the *New York World* was guilty of publishing a bogus proclamation attributed to the President. It recalled the disasters of the war, set a day of public humiliation and prayer, and called for 400,000 men. On the very day of publication, Stanton obtained from Lincoln an order to General Dix, in command at New York, to arrest and imprison the editors, proprietors, publishers, and all others who reprinted the proclamation after notice had been given of its falsity. The persons arrested were to be tried by military commission, and Dix was to hold the newspaper plant and allow no issues until further notice. Dix obeyed reluctantly, but after three days the arrested men were released and the publication of the paper was resumed.[47]

The workings of the federal system during the war were illustrated by the action of the New York authorities which followed. Governor Seymour called the attention of the grand jury to General Dix's conduct, and when the jury took no action, he directed the district attorney for New York County to prosecute the General. Dix was thereupon tried upon a charge of "kidnaping" and inciting riot. The prosecution argued that his conduct was illegal because the city was not under martial law. The plea of the defense that the indemnity act gave him immunity from prosecution was met by the claim that the act itself was unconstitutional. This view the court accepted, although the counsel for the defense urged that the country was in a state of war, that the President held the war power, and that Congress had authorized imprisonment with the writ of habeas corpus suspended, so that Dix could have had no criminal intent such as was necessary to constitute the crime of kidnapping.[48]

[46] Quoted, *ibid.*, 495.
[47] *Ibid.*, 496–497.
[48] *Ibid.*, 497–499.

On the whole the control over the press during the war was slight. Civil actions brought no results. Indictments were found in a few cases but no convictions followed. For example, the publisher of one New York paper was prosecuted on the charge of encouraging resistance to the draft, but discharged on the ground that the draft was not in actual operation at the time of his utterance. In announcing this opinion the federal commissioner took pains to uphold the right of citizens to criticise the measures of government. The resort to military control was rare, and usually confined to cases where there was a strong presumption of disloyalty. Thus the editor of a Missouri newspaper was arrested in February, 1862, charged with publishing information for the benefit of the enemy. Although he denied the jurisdiction of the military commission, he was tried, found guilty, and banished from the state.[49]

The weakness of the government's position lay in the fact that the suppressions of papers and arrests and trials of editors were acts done where there was no martial law. In principle such arrests were not different from those condemned in the Milligan decision, and the cases of the *Times* and *World* will probably go down in history as instances of the resort to military power in a "sphere where the supremacy of the civil authorities should have been conceded."

One other phase of press control may be mentioned. In the latter part of 1861 the postmaster-general ordered the exclusion from the mails of certain papers which had been condemned as disloyal by a federal grand jury. The judiciary committee of the House of Representatives required the postmaster-general to state by what authority he acted in this matter, and in reply that official convinced the committee that a course of precedents running through twenty-five years, and knowingly acquiesced in by Congress, justified his procedure.[50]

The continuous stream of abuse which opposition papers emitted throughout the war is proof that liberty of the press existed, to the point of license. Quite apart from the doubtfulness of the Presi-

[49] *Ibid.*, 490–491, 504–505.
[50] *Ibid.*, 501–502.

dent's right to adopt regulatory measures, he was probably right in believing that where newspaper utterances were supported by public opinion, repressive measures would increase the sentiment adverse to administration policies. As for the more violent sheets, their very abusiveness cost them the respect of the public. It was wise to let them "strut their uneasy hour and be forgotten."

XVI

WAR POWERS (*Concluded*)

ENEMY'S PROPERTY

THE view that the Civil War was both a public war and a rebellion greatly complicated the problem of dealing with the property of the southerners. Which aspect of the war should govern in dealing with such property? If the policy of the government in this particular was to rest upon the view that the conflict was a war between belligerents, then the enemy's property would be subject to the rules of international law. If, on the other hand, the Confederates were to be dealt with as traitors, their property rights were defined and the power of the government limited by certain provisions of the Constitution, notably that which declares that "no Attainder of Treason shall work . . . Forfeiture except during the Life of the Person attainted." [1]

Most of the members of Congress, intent upon their objects, cared little for consistency. Whenever minority members, usually War Democrats or border-state men, raised questions concerning the war powers of Congress, the legal character of the war, the status of the Confederates, or the law of belligerency *versus* municipal law, the defense of majority measures betrayed a deplorable lack of legal and constitutional logic. It is difficult if not impossible to reconcile some of the acts of Congress with the principles either of international or constitutional law. Eventually the task devolved upon the Supreme Court, and it is not surprising to find that its best efforts sometimes fail to satisfy the judgment of history.

The first act of the war period relating to enemy's property was a statute of the Confederacy under date of May 21, 1861, which confiscated debts due residents of the loyal states. Another act of August 30 of the same year sequestered the property of all adherents of the Union cause.[2]

[1] Art. III, sec. 3, par. 2. On the topics treated in this chapter see Randall, *Civil War*, Chaps. XX–XXI.
[2] Randall, *Con. Probs.*, 275 *et seq.*

On the federal side, an act of August 6, 1861, made it the duty of the President to seize and confiscate all property used in promoting insurrection, including slaves.[3] Congress had constitutional power to pass this act under the provision authorizing it to make "rules concerning captures on land and water." This provision is to be regarded as restricting Congress to such rules as are sanctioned by international law, and this first act did not transgress the rights of the southerners as belligerents. As the war went on, however, the desire developed to confiscate all of the property of "rebels." As "rebels" and "traitors," however, the southerners were protected by the clause of the Constitution quoted above.

The dilemma involved in this situation was pointed out by members of Congress who opposed wholesale confiscation, but was practically ignored by those who desired it.[4] In international law, the property of an enemy could be proceeded against by an action *in rem.* Such procedure did not require the presence of the owner or claimant, who, indeed, was regarded as having no standing in court. The liability of the property to seizure or capture and confiscation depended entirely upon the fact of its belonging to the enemy. If the intent of Congress was to provide, however, for the confiscation of the property of rebellious citizens, as a punitive measure, constitutional law applied instead of international law. In that case it would be necessary to prove in the individual instance that the owner or claimant was guilty of treason, since the forfeiture was a part of the punishment for that crime; and trial for treason involved the right of the accused to be brought into court and to plead in his own defense.

THE SECOND CONFISCATION ACT

Congress sought to evade this dilemma by passing a bill based upon both international and constitutional law. This act, passed on July 17, 1862, was intended as a punitive measure against rebels, whose property was to be confiscated as a penalty.[5] But

[3] *U. S. Stat. at Large,* XII, 319. Reprinted in MacDonald, *Select Statutes,* 21–22.
[4] See, *e.g.,* speech of Senator Collamer, on April 24, 1862. *Cong. Globe,* 37 Cong., 2 sess., 1809–1810, *et passim.* Extract in Johnson, 482–486.
[5] *U. S. Stat. at Large,* XII, 589–592. Reprinted in MacDonald, *Select Stats.,* 49–53.

it made no provision for the trial and conviction of the persons accused of rebellion; instead it borrowed a procedure from the practice of prize courts in dealing with captures by providing for a *civil suit against the property of enemies*. Even here the law was illogical, for the rules to be applied were those of the common law, instead of those of admiralty law in proceedings *in rem*. This strange mixture of municipal and international law was defended on the ground that the southerners were both public enemies and traitors. Said Senator Lyman Trumbull of Illinois: "We may treat them as traitors, and we may treat them as enemies, and we have the right of both belligerent and sovereign, so far as they are concerned." [6] It was strange logic by which Trumbull and others added together the rights of belligerent and sovereign and obtained a result which released Congress from all of the restrictions of both. Yet "in the struggle between those who upheld the restraints of the Constitution and those who considered only the limits of international law," writes Professor Dunning, "the government practically escaped all restrictions whatsoever." [7]

In the debate the advocates of the bill deduced the right to enact it from the power of Congress to declare war, to make rules concerning captures, to provide for calling forth the militia to suppress insurrections, and from the necessary and proper clause. The opponents cited the parts of the Constitution forbidding the passage of bills of attainder, providing that no person shall be deprived of property without due process of law, that private property shall not be taken for public use without just compensation, and that no attainder of treason shall work forfeiture except during the life of the person attainted. In rebuttal, the supporters could only contend that these constitutional limitations were not framed for such a state of affairs as existed. The bill which they passed was a virtual assertion that the war power of Congress is unlimited, in dealing with "rebels." [8]

Sections 5 and 6 of this Second Confiscation Act as finally passed subjected the property of certain classes of southerners to for-

[6] Quoted by Dunning, *Essays*, 34.
[7] *Ibid.*, 36–37. Quoted by permission of The Macmillan Company.
[8] *Ibid.*, 31.

feiture. That belonging to officers of the government, civil, military, and naval, was seizable without qualification. In the case of other supporters of the rebellion, a warning by proclamation was to give them sixty days in which to return to their allegiance. In case of failure to heed this warning, their property was subject to confiscation under proceedings to be brought in the federal district courts or the courts of territories. If the property was found to belong to a person who had engaged in rebellion, it was to be condemned as enemy's property and to be forfeited to the United States.

When this act was presented to President Lincoln he was inclined to veto it. In his opinion it violated the limitation in the attainder clause by providing for the final and complete extinction of title to real estate. Moreover, by proceedings *in·rem* the act attempted to work forfeiture without convicting the owner of his supposed crime. Congress met these objections by hurriedly passing a joint resolution explaining that the law was not to be construed as applying to acts done before its passage, nor as working forfeiture of real estate beyond the life of the offender. Considering this resolution as essentially a part of the bill, Lincoln signed both, although his objections were only partly satisfied.[9]

To escape from the constitutional difficulties involved in upholding the Confiscation Act as a measure of municipal (domestic) law, the Supreme Court finally took the position that it rested upon the war power. It drew a distinction between the first sections of the act, which dealt with crime against the sovereign, and the later sections "which have in view a public war," and in the Confiscation Cases [10] ruled that the reference to persons served only to identify the property concerned in the proceedings. The decision in the leading case was not rendered until 1871 after a number of minor decisions had partially cleared the way. This case, Miller *v.* U. S.,[11] originated as an action under both confiscation acts to cause forfeiture of shares of stock in a Michigan concern, which were alleged to be the property of Samuel Miller, a

[9] Randall, *Con. Probs.*, 279–280.
[10] 87 U. S. 92–117 (1873).
[11] 11 Wallace 268 (1871).

"rebel" residing in Virginia. The central question involved was, Were the confiscation acts an exercise of the war power, or did they impose a penalty under the municipal authority of Congress? A second issue was the question, Did the acts violate the fifth and sixth amendments?

The court held that the act of 1861 and the 5th, 6th, and 7th sections of the act of 1862 were exercises of the war power and declared that the power of confiscation has "always been an undoubted belligerent right." The opinion disregarded the contention that the tone of the entire second act marked it as a measure to punish rebels, although the court admitted that if such were the case, there was force in the objection that Congress had disregarded constitutional restrictions. As an exercise of the war power, the court held that Congress was not bound by the constitutional provisions.[12]

Three of the justices dissented, on the ground that the forfeitures decreed were punitive, and could not be imposed unless the guilt of the owner were shown. These justices, in other words, took the opposite horn of the dilemma and viewed the act of Congress as an exercise of municipal authority, subject to the limitations of the Constitution. This view raised the question of the property owner's right to a hearing.

In November, 1863, a resident of Alabama whose property had been proceeded against filed an answer in the federal court of which the judge refused to take notice, holding that the state as in insurrection and all of its inhabitants alien enemies, and therefore without the right to plead in the courts of the United States. Later, in the circuit court, Justice Nelson held that the defendant should have been allowed to plead. After the war this same question came before the Supreme Court in the case of McVeigh v. United States.[13] In the lower court McVeigh had appeared by counsel, but his appearance had been disregarded on the ground of residence within the Confederacy. The Supreme Court, however, held that the allegation of criminality was at the bottom of the whole proceeding against his property, and that the order of

---

[12] See Randall's discussion, *Con. Probs.*, 312–315.
[13] 78 U. S. 259 (1870).

the lower court to strike his claim and answer from the record on the ground that he was a rebel was a prejudgment of the very point at issue.[14]

Proceedings *in rem* seemed to justify the presumption that in case of the owner's failure to appear, the court should enter a decree of condemnation without a hearing. In Miller *v.* U. S. the court ruled that after such default it was not necessary even to conduct an *ex parte* hearing. But in thus admitting that the condemnation proceedings could be affected in any degree by the owner's plea or default, the court involved itself in the bad logic which Congress had used in passing the law. To take its stand upon the war power, and then to admit that an effect could be produced by the owner's default in exercising a right to plead which existed only under municipal law, was inconsistent. The dissenting judges were more logical in adhering to the view that, as the act rested upon municipal law, a judgment on default was a denial of "due process."

In holding that the right to confiscate had "always been an undoubted belligerent right," the court was not on certain ground. Some of the early authorities had questioned the right of a belligerent in a public war to confiscate private property within its jurisdiction belonging to individuals in the enemy nation, while others had held that such confiscation was reasonable. Congress, in passing the confiscation acts, departed from humane usage, although according to Marshall, Story, and Kent, it was within the rights accorded by international law.[15] The total amount realized

---

[14] Randall, *Con. Probs.*, 308–312.

[15] England had for centuries protected the property of foreign merchants with whose governments she was at war. During the War of 1812 Marshall had said: "it may be considered as the opinion of all who have written on the *jus belli* that war gives the right to confiscate, but does not itself confiscate." (Brown *v.* U. S., 8 Cranch 110. 1814.) Story in the same case maintained that war vested the power to confiscate in the executive without express statutory authority. Following this decision, Chancellor Kent regarded the legal point as settled but held that modern practice was against the exercise of the right. Wheaton, basing his statement on practice, held that enemy's property found in the territory of a belligerent was not liable to confiscation. This rule, he said, was not inflexible. Among recent authorities Hall calls confiscation a "dying right," and Lawrence says that the majority of continental publicists agree that international law does not permit its exercise. See Randall's discussion, *Con. Probs.*, 293 *et seq.*, 301–303.

Many difficulties were encountered in administering the confiscation acts. In

by the government as the result of sales of confiscated property was almost negligible. The chief effect of the legislation was to produce a feeling of irritation and injury on the part of a few despoiled persons. The final administration of all the confiscation measures of the war period was lenient. Court decisions held that pardon gave the victims of the First Confiscation Act a claim to the proceeds which the government had received, but that the second act, under which the seizure of property was not regarded as a penalty, was not affected by pardon. Many landed estates were restored; indeed, so few were confiscated that the plan of small allotments to freedmen collapsed for want of land.[16]

EMANCIPATION

The general confiscation measures shade off almost imperceptibly into the question of slave property, and Lincoln's Emancipation Proclamation, if defensible at all, rests upon the war powers of

Bigelow v. Forrest (9 Wallace 339. 1869) the Supreme Court held that under the act of 1862 no title to confiscated property could be passed which would outlast the life of the original offender. Thus was upheld the forfeiture clause of the Constitution as a limitation upon a power which the court later held rested upon the right of a belligerent under international law. Another inconsistency appeared in the judgments relating to the reversionary title, which would accrue to the offender's heirs, the courts held, but not to his assigns. After the war, when the disabilities of the Confederates had been removed by pardon and amnesty acts, the courts swung around to the position that the offender could convey an assurance of permanent future title which would hold good even against his legal heirs.—*Ibid.*, 286–288.

[16] *Ibid.*, 291, 330, 337, 340, *et passim*. Besides the First and Second Confiscation Acts, two other statutes were in effect acts of confiscation. The first of these laid a direct tax which was duly apportioned among the states, including those of the Confederacy. (*U. S. Stat. at Large*, XII, 422–426. Reprinted in MacDonald, *Select Stats.*, 39–42). In default of payment, the lands were to be forfeited and sold to the highest bidder, with title in fee simple. The administration of this act involved many odious practices: for example, payment in person was sometimes insisted upon. On the validity of this last requirement depended the claim of the Lees to the Arlington estate. Mrs. Robert E. Lee had tendered the amount of the tax through an agent, and the commissioner had refused it. This refusal was the basis of the Supreme Court's decision against the government in United States v. Lee (106 U. S. 196. 1882). The government thereupon acquired title by purchase. In 1891 Congress appropriated money for the reimbursement of the victims of the direct tax legislation of the war period.—Randall, *Con. Probs.*, 317 *et seq.*

The other statute was the Captured Property Act of March 12, 1863 (*U. S. Stat. at Large*, XII, 820). The law was used chiefly as a warrant for seizing cotton, most of which had been or was likely to be acquired by the Confederate government.—*Ibid.*, 323 *et seq.*

a military commander as defined by international law. "The law of nations," declared Charles B. Sedgwick of New York in the House of Representatives, "clearly sanctions the emancipation of the enemy's slaves by military force and authority. It is an understood and received doctrine." [17] But if the right of confiscation of private enemy property on land in general was doubtful, even when exercised by Congress, much more doubtful was the right of the commander-in-chief to confiscate slave property without legislative authority.

In their relations with other countries, Americans had previous to the Civil War always denied the right of the military authorities to liberate slaves. Lord Dunmore's effort to free them in Virginia at the opening of the Revolution had been denounced, and at the close of two wars the United States had claimed compensation for the deportation of slaves who had taken refuge within the British lines. John Quincy Adams, while secretary of state, had expounded the American point of view in instructions to our minister in Russia, when the Czar had undertaken to arbitrate the claim of the United States against Great Britain for slaves carried away from America at the close of the War of 1812.[18]

The statesmen of the old South had vigorously asserted the complete control of each state over the subject of slavery as a matter pertaining to the internal police power; and the statesmen of the free states had never disputed the general truth of the proposition. In the course of a debate in the late thirties, however, John Quincy Adams was led to place the relation of the war power to slavery in a new light. In 1837, when the proslavery leaders in Congress were attempting to commit that body to the doctrine that the federal government could never under any circumstances molest the institution in those states which saw fit to maintain it, Adams, speaking in defense of the right of petition, declared in the House that the proposed resolutions did not state the truth. At this time and again in 1842 he argued that in case of war an invaded country would be subject to martial law, and the commander of the invading armies would have power to emancipate

[17] Quoted *ibid.*, 347.
[18] *Ibid.*, 344 *et passim.*

all slaves in the territory occupied. "From the instant your slave State becomes a theater of war, servile, civil or foreign," he declared in 1842, "the war powers of Congress extend to interference with slavery in every way."[19]

Neither President nor Congress, however, at the beginning of the war, contemplated the employment of any such power.[20] Although radicals like Thaddeus Stevens soon began to urge action against slavery, with little reference to the constitutional authority of the government, a series of events running through some fifteen months were required to bring about a change in the government's policy. Before Lincoln's proclamation was finally determined upon, these events had gradually prepared the way by impairing the system of slavery at several points.

During this earlier period Lincoln found it necessary more than once to restrain the antislavery zeal of military commanders. Frémont, in Missouri, had publicly decreed the confiscation of the property of all persons in the state who took up arms against the Union, and the freeing of their slaves.[21] Lincoln ordered Frémont to modify this decree to bring it into conformity with the Confiscation Act of 1861. In May, 1862, Hunter declared that the slaves in Georgia, Florida, and South Carolina were free on the ground that their servile status was incompatible with martial law. This order Lincoln also revoked. Both of these generals had issued orders of political import which no immediate military necessity demanded.[22]

Meantime, a situation developed in Virginia which led to the first steps towards a new policy. When General Benjamin F. Butler took command of Fortress Monroe, his predecessor turned over to him three runaway slaves who had fled to the Union lines. Butler needed workmen, and was informed that the Confederates were employing slaves in the construction of military fortifications and otherwise. In an interview with the Confederate Major Carey, therefore, Butler refused to return the fugitives, for two reasons.

[19] C. F. Adams, "John Quincy Adams and Martial Law."
[20] See resolutions on objects of the war in Richardson, *Messages*, VI, 430; reprinted in Commager, 395–396.
[21] Commager, 397–398.
[22] Randall, *Con. Probs.*, 354.

As Virginia now claimed to be a foreign country, she could no longer ask for the return of fugitives under the Fugitive Slave Law; and as slaves were being used by the Confederates on war works, he called them "contraband." [23]

Although some generals refused to receive fugitive slaves within their lines, others followed Butler's example, and Congress presently, by act of March 13, 1862, forbade the use of federal forces for the return of fugitives.[24]   On July 17, 1862, Congress passed another act providing that no fugitive slave escaping from one state into another should be given up unless charged with crime, except in cases where the owner was loyal to the Union.   By the same law slaves of rebel owners coming into the Union lines were declared to be free.[25]

Thus the state of war rendered the operation of the Fugitive Slave Law impracticable.[26]   The First Confiscation Act declared that the owners of slaves should forfeit the labor of such as were employed in making arms, fortifications, or in other military operations.   The implication was that such slaves were entitled to freedom, because of "contraband" employment, but no means were specified for carrying the provision into effect and it had little practical significance.[27]

The Second Confiscation Act carefully distinguished between slave property and property of other kinds.   It provided for proceedings *in rem* for property in general; but decreed that the slaves of traitors should be freed if the masters were executed; also, that slaves belonging to persons engaged in rebellion, if they escaped or were captured or found in any place taken from the enemy by the forces of the United States, should be forever freed from their servitude.   Again there is no evidence of actual enforcement of the provisions, but Congress continued to pass laws pointing to the emancipation of certain classes of slaves under particular circumstances.   Thus the Militia Act of July 17, 1862, gave freedom

[23] *Ibid.*, 355. See documents in Commager, 396–397, and Johnson, 500–502.
[24] *U. S. Stat. at Large*, XII, 354.
[25] *Ibid.*, 589. See Randall, *Con. Probs.*, 356.
[26] The acts of 1793 and 1850 were repealed on June 28, 1864. *U. S. Stat. at Large*, XIII, 200. Reprint in MacDonald, 113.
[27] Randall, *Con. Probs.*, 356–357.

to the slave of an enemy if he rendered military service to the Union, and to his wife, mother, and children as well unless they belonged to loyal owners.[28]   The law added nothing to the Second Confiscation Act except that the record of military service might prove useful in establishing the claim of the Negro and his family to freedom.   In April, 1862, Congress abolished slavery in the District of Columbia, with compensation for loyal owners; and in June abolished slavery in the territories without compensating masters.   Finally, on February 24, 1864, freedom was given to the slave-soldiers of loyal masters, with compensation to the latter.[29]

This last act, however, came long after the presidential proclamations of emancipation.   The first of these, the preliminary proclamation issued in September, 1862, was determined upon in a cabinet consultation some weeks before.   It had come to be thought by the President and his official family that the Union cause would be strengthened by some measure directed against slavery.   Northern sentiment was more and more outspokenly demanding that the war be directed against slavery, and it appeared that foreign sympathy might be won in larger degree by a change of policy.   In order that the new policy might appear as the demand of a government whose arms were prevailing in the field, it was decided that the proclamation should not be issued until the Union armies achieved a conspicuous victory.   Antietam was regarded as a sufficient success, and on September 22 the President announced by proclamation "That, on the first day of January, in the year of our Lord one thousand eight hundred and sixty-three, all persons held as slaves within any state or designated part of a state, the people whereof shall then be in rebellion against the United States, shall be then, thenceforward and forever, free; and the Executive Government of the United States, including the military and naval authority thereof, will recognize and maintain the freedom of such persons, and will do no act or acts to repress such persons, or any of them, in any efforts they may make for their actual freedom." [30]

This threat was, of course, unheeded by the Confederates, and

[28] *U. S. Stat. at Large*, XII, 597–600.   Extract in MacDonald, 54–56.
[29] Randall, *Con. Probs.*, 358–365.   See *U. S. Stat. at Large*, XII, 376–378; *ibid.*, 432; XIII, 6–11.   Extracts in MacDonald, Nos. 18, 20, 36.
[30] Nicolay and Hay, *Works of Lincoln*, VIII, 36–41.

on the first day of January, 1863, Lincoln issued the definitive proclamation, designating the states and parts of states which were still
in rebellion, and declaring "that all persons held as slaves within the
said designated states and parts of states are, and henceforward
shall be, free; and that the Executive Government of the United
States, including the military and naval authorities thereof, will
recognize and maintain the freedom of said persons. . . .

"And I further declare and make known that such persons, of
suitable condition, will be received into the armed service of the
United States to garrison forts, positions, stations, and other places,
and to man vessels of all sorts in said service.

"And upon this act, sincerely believed to be an act of justice,
warranted by the Constitution upon military necessity, I invoke
the considerate judgment of mankind and the gracious favor of
Almighty God." [31]

The supporters of this action on the part of the President elaborated the whole doctrine of military power and necessity. The
Constitution, they reasoned, authorizes the government to wage
war; international law is always a part of the government's legal
resources; the Supreme Court had declared that the United States
possessed the rights of a belligerent in dealing with the Confederacy;
all of the inhabitants of the Confederacy were enemies, and seizure
of the enemy's property was a necessary result of war; emancipation
was humane, striking at a kind of property which modern nations
had ceased to recognize; finally the military importance of slavery
made it a legal target. The President's proclamation was justified
as the act of a commander-in-chief whose powers in wielding the
rights of a belligerent under international law had been upheld in
the case of the blockade. The arguments which John Quincy
Adams had used nearly a generation before were frequently cited,
and were probably quite influential in inciting the demand for such
action as the President had taken. [32]

One practical effect of the final proclamation was the flocking

[31] *U. S. Stat. at Large*, XII, 1268–1269. Reprinted in Commager, 420–421; Johnson, 504–506; MacDonald, 59–61.

[32] See Johnson, 503–504, quoting Whiting, *War Powers of the President* (1862),
66–68, *passim*. Commager, 421–422, gives the resolutions of the Illinois legislature
as an example of opposition opinion.

of Negroes to the Union armies. Thousands became soldiers, many were put to work for wages, and women, children, and infirm in great numbers became wards of the government. Hastily improvised organizations were effected to superintend the interests of these needy Negroes; for example, in the neighborhood of Washington the Society of Friends volunteered their services, and for a time was utilized by the President as an agency. The generals of the army did what they could also, and out of the beginnings made by them was evolved the plan of the Freedman's Bureau, which Congress created by law in 1865.

The vast majority of the slaves remained quietly with their masters, and those who looked at the proclamation's terms were inclined to think it a very ineffective measure. Lord Russell, in England, commented on January 17: "The Proclamation . . . professes to emancipate all slaves in places where the United States authorities cannot exercise any jurisdiction . . . but it does not decree emancipation . . . in any States, or parts of States, occupied by federal troops. . . . There seems to be no declaration of a principle adverse to slavery in this proclamation. It is a measure of war of a very questionable kind." [33]

Lincoln himself honestly believed that the law of war gave him the right to take enemy's property "whenever taking it helps us or hurts the enemy." "I felt," he said, with reference to emancipation, "that measures otherwise unconstitutional might become lawful by becoming indispensable to the preservation of the Constitution through the preservation of the nation." [34] Nevertheless he had doubts as to whether the Supreme Court would sustain the edict. He perceived also that awkward questions might be raised as to its validity and scope. "A question might be raised," he once wrote, "whether the proclamation was legally valid. It might be urged that it only aided those that came into our lines, and that it was inoperative as to those who did not give themselves up; or that it would have no effect upon the children of slaves born hereafter; in fact it would be urged that it did not meet the evil." [35]

[33] Quoted by Randall, 379–380.
[34] Quoted ibid., 378.
[35] Nicolay and Hay, *Works of Lincoln*, X, 353.

Several proposals were made in Congress to give statutory force to the proclamation, but all failed. Sumner wished "to see emancipation . . . placed under the guarantee of an act of Congress . . . not . . . left to float on a presidential proclamation." Such utterances served chiefly to lead the President's opponents to say that even his friends confessed that his acts were illegal.[36]

Slavery in the loyal states was, of course, not touched by the proclamation, and Confederate territory already within control of the Union forces was excepted from its terms, since no military necessity could require its application there. If the people of the seceded states had met the terms of the preliminary proclamation, nothing would have prevented the war from ending with slavery intact. As to the force of the proclamation in the region to which it applied, it has been well written: "It would seem that, being a military measure by a commander-in-chief . . . it could not operate further than as a military order. From that time, all slaves coming under the control of the forces . . . in the manner recognized by the law of belligerent occupation, were to be free. If this is the correct view, . . . it became therefore a question of fact, as to each slave and each region of the country, whether the forces of the Union had such possession as to give effect to the proclamation." [37]

Lincoln felt that the policy embodied in the proclamation was required by the exigencies of the situation in the closing months of 1862, but that it was far from being a solution of the whole slavery problem. For months before he issued the preliminary proclamation he had been contemplating a policy by which gradual emancipation might be effected through the voluntary action of the states, assisted by the federal government. In April Congress passed a resolution recommended by him, pledging financial aid to any state which would undertake emancipation. The presidential message of December 1, 1862, laid before Congress the details of a plan of cooperation between the government and the states. It proposed the delivery of United States bonds to every state which

[36] Randall, 383, note 31.
[37] R. H. Dana, Jr., in annotations on Wheaton's *International Law*, quoted by Randall, 384, note 32.

should abolish slavery before 1900. All slaves freed during the war should be forever free, but loyal owners were to be compensated. An amendment to the Constitution was suggested to set at rest all questions as to the legality of the plan.[38]

As late as February, 1865, Lincoln cherished the hope of compensated emancipation, and even included the Confederate States in the scope of the plan. Congress, however, beyond passing the resolution of April, 1862, took no action. West Virginia, Tennessee, Maryland, and Missouri by different methods abolished slavery, and the Maryland legislature created a commission to present to the federal government a claim for the aid promised by the resolution. Missouri and Kentucky contemplated similar action, but the promise of Congress proved to be a momentary whim, and objections were raised that the action of the states had not been prompt enough. As to compensation for the South, the death of Lincoln put an end to all such thoughts. Congress felt no obligation except to the loyal border states, and even their claims were easily forgotten.[39]

THE THIRTEENTH AMENDMENT

Nevertheless the unsatisfactory status of slavery under the various acts of Congress and the presidential proclamation, plus considerable friction in the border states between federal and state officials who interpreted these measures differently, made evident the necessity of some definitive action. Out of these conditions sprang the movement for the thirteenth amendment. Senator Trumbull, arguing in favor of the abolition of slavery everywhere by amendment, pointed out that the piecemeal legislation of Congress was ineffectual and that the effect of the President's proclamation was in controversy; that opponents denied the competence of the President to issue such a proclamation, and denied that it effected emancipation anywhere; that it excepted half of the slave states, and that Congress could not pass an effectual law, because it could not interfere with slavery in any state. A constitutional

[38] Richardson, *Messages*, VI, 126 *et seq.*; extract in Commager, 403–405. See Randall's discussion, 365–369.
[39] *Ibid., passim.*

amendment, then, was the only way of "ridding the country of slavery . . . so that it cannot be resuscitated." "This amendment adopted, not only does slavery cease, but it can never be reestablished by State authority, or in any other way than by again amending the Constitution." [40]

Lincoln favored the amendment for the reasons already indicated. The amendment, he said, is "a king's cure for all evils. It winds the whole thing up." [41] But members of Congress were found who objected to this program. Never before had the amending power been resorted to to narrow the scope of the reserved police power of the states, and the proposal now seemed questionable. It was even denied that such an amendment could be made constitutionally. Senator Willard Saulsbury of Delaware, like the early Federalists when they opposed the creation of states from the Louisiana Territory, likened the situation to the case where several parties form a contract for given purposes, and then three fourths of them add another item, telling the dissenters "we will bind you because you have entered in." [42] George H. Pendleton of Ohio declared: "Neither three fourths of the States nor all of the States save one, can abolish slavery in that dissenting State; because it lies within the domain reserved entirely to each State for itself, and upon it the other States cannot enter." [43]

It may be remarked in passing that, with the exception of the right of the states to equal suffrage in the Senate, and the right of each not to be divided or joined with others without its consent, the Constitution contains no provision which is beyond the reach of an amendment; yet reasoning similar to that of Pendleton was to reappear, especially in connection with the contest over the eighteenth amendment.

The thirteenth amendment, forbidding slavery and involuntary servitude, except as a punishment for crime, throughout the United States and in every place subject to their jurisdiction, and empower-

[40] Quoted *ibid.*, 391.
[41] Quoted *ibid.*, 383, note 30.
[42] *Cong. Globe*, 38 Cong., 1 sess., 1441. Quoted by Randall, 393. Words in quotation marks are Randall's paraphrase. The debate on the amendment ran from early January to the end of March, 1864.
[43] *Annual Cyclopedia*, 1865, p. 207, quoted *ibid.*

ing Congress by appropriate legislation to enforce it, was duly passed by the two houses and sent to the states.[44] It was proclaimed as in effect on December 18, 1865. When such an amendment was first considered, Trumbull himself doubted whether it would be possible, during the war, to obtain the necessary number of ratifications. This was in 1863. The next year, however, when passed and sent to the states, the prospect was better. The total number of states, including those which had seceded, was 36, so that the number required for ratification was 27. The free states numbered 23, the loyal slave states 2, and the Confederate states 11. Since Kentucky and Delaware rejected the amendment, the votes of four Confederate states were needed, in addition to those of all the loyal states, to make up the required three fourths.

As a matter of fact, eight Confederate states ratified before the last four of the free states did so. Foes of the amendment then raised objections to the validity of the ratification on the ground that the Confederate states were not competent to vote on it. President Johnson had advised Congress in the same month in which ratification was completed, that loyal governments had been established in the southern states. Congress refused to recognize the governments set up under Johnson's plan of reconstruction, however, and it was the resolutions of ratification by these provisional governments which were challenged. But Congress chose to consider that the provisional governments were competent to ratify. Radicals like Stevens, who declared that the southern states had ceased to exist, would have omitted them in the count of states. The majority preferred a less consistent course; but the confusion of thought and action drew from Edward Bates a comment, entered in his diary, which awakens the sympathy of the reader: "In debate in H. of R. old Thad amidst other ravings declared that 'The State of Tennessee is not known to this House or to Congress!' . . . And so it seems that they are not states in the Union, yet they can enact a Constitution for the United States!" [45]

[44] *Revised Statutes of the U. S.*, 30. Reprinted in Johnson, 506; MacDonald, 138–139.

[45] MS. Diary of Edward Bates, under date of Dec. 12 and 21, 1865, quoted by Randall, 400, note 59.

XVII

PROBLEMS OF RECONSTRUCTION

THE PRESIDENTIAL THEORY

THE central doctrine in the presidential theory of reconstruction, held by Lincoln and after him, in all essentials, by Johnson, is that a state is indestructible. According to this doctrine, a state which had attempted to secede was still a state in the Union, but was in defective relations with the government of the United States. "All the officers as well as the constituents of the rebel organizations were insurgents, and hence incapable of political recognition by the United States authorities. With the removal of this disability, the *ante-bellum* status returned. But until such removal the vitality of the state was suspended through the incapacity of its organs to fulfill their functions. The President's pardon was the healing agent. Restored by it to normal relations with the general government, the people of the states became immediately invested with the *right* to establish their own will in organized form, and with the *right* to assume the former relation with the Union." [1]

Furthermore, as commander-in-chief, it rested with the President to determine when the insurrection had been put down in any state, and this military power coupled with the power to pardon enabled him to set forth the terms on which amnesty would be extended to those lately in arms against the Union. On December 8, 1863, Lincoln issued a proclamation of amnesty offering pardon to those persons (with certain exceptions) who had participated in the rebellion, with restoration of property rights except in slaves and in cases where rights of third parties had intervened, on condition that they take an oath pledging loyalty and

---

[1] Dunning, *Essays*, 104. Quoted by permission of The Macmillan Company. There is a monograph by C. H. McCarthy on *Lincoln's Plan of Reconstruction.* For the reconstruction era in general, see Edward McPherson, *The Political History of the United States . . . during . . . Reconstruction*, and E. G. Scott, *Reconstruction during the Civil War.*

support of all acts of Congress dealing with slaves, as well as presidential proclamations referring to the same, except in so far as either might be modified or held void by the Supreme Court.[2]

Proceeding to the next step, the proclamation provided that whenever, in the states enumerated, "a number of persons, not less than one-tenth in number of the votes cast in such State at the Presidential election of the year A. D. 1860, each having taken the oath aforesaid, and not having since violated it, and being a qualified voter by the election law of the State existing immediately before the so-called act of secession, and excluding all others, shall re-establish a State government which shall be republican and in nowise contravening said oath, such shall be recognized as the true government of the State, and the State shall receive thereunder the benefits of the constitutional provision which declares that 'the United States shall guarantee to every State in this Union a republican form of government and shall protect each of them against invasion, and, on application of the legislature, or the executive (when the legislature can not be convened), against domestic violence.' "[3]

As to the freedmen, the President promised not to object to any provisions which might be made by the new state governments, provided that such measures recognized and declared their permanent freedom, and provided for their education, making temporary provision for them as a landless and homeless laboring class.

So far only could the executive go. "To avoid misunderstanding," the proclamation added, "it may be proper to say that whether members sent to Congress from any State shall be admitted to seats constitutionally rests exclusively with the respective Houses, and not to any extent with the Executive." And finally, it was pointed out that the mode of restoration indicated in the proclamation was the "best the Executive can suggest," but "it must not be understood that no other possible mode would be acceptable."

[2] Richardson, *Messages*, VI, 213–215.   Reprinted in Johnson, 509–512; MacDonald, 85–88.
[3] *Ibid.*

The fact that the two houses were respectively, under the Constitution, the judges of the qualifications of their members, as intimated by Lincoln in this proclamation, gave Congress the whip hand in the reconstruction process, which could never become complete until the houses were satisfied and ready to accept the senators and representatives from the southern states. The congressional leaders believed that Congress was the proper agent in reconstruction, not only because of the power of seating or unseating members, but also because the guarantee of a republican form of government, which rested upon the United States as an obligation to the states severally, could be performed only through congressional legislation to carry the guarantee into effect.[4]

THEORIES OF THE CONGRESSIONAL LEADERS

Republican leaders were dissatisfied with Lincoln's plans because an oath of loyalty from so small a proportion of the former voters did not provide a sufficient guarantee of the loyal disposition of the population of the state when restored to its former relations with the Union. They predicted that the war-time leaders would speedily reassert their control after the process of restoration had been completed and wished to exact "penalties for the past and pledges for the future." Similarly, they feared for the future of the freedmen, whom Lincoln's plan seemed virtually to abandon to the mercy of their former masters. Some of the more radical leaders were already contemplating suffrage for the blacks, partly in order to place in their hands a weapon for the defense of their rights in future, and partly, perhaps, as a means of maintaining the supremacy of the Union party in the South.

As the antagonism between Congress and the executive developed, these radical leaders formed rival theories. As early as February 11, 1862, Charles Sumner advanced what came to be known as the "State-Suicide Theory."[5] The next year he discussed the problem further: "With the State governments already *vacated* by rebellion, the Constitution becomes, for the time, the supreme

---

[4] *Cf.* Luther *v.* Borden, *supra,* Chap. VII.

[5] McPherson, *Hist. of the . . . Rebellion, 322.* Reprinted in Commager, 406–407.

and only law, binding alike on President and Congress, so that neither can establish any law or institution incompatible with it. And the whole Rebel region, deprived of all local government, lapses under the exclusive jurisdiction of Congress, precisely as any other territory; or, in other words, the lifting of the local government leaves the whole vast region without any other government than Congress, unless the President should undertake to govern it by military power." [6]

According to Senator Sumner, then, a territory became a state by entering the Union, and by secession from the Union became a territory, under the control of Congress except in so far as constitutional restrictions applied. Representative Thaddeus Stevens went even further in his "Conquered Province Theory:" "They [the seceded states] have torn their constitutional States into atoms, and built on their foundations fabrics of a totally different character. Dead men cannot raise themselves. Dead States cannot restore their existence 'as it was.' Whose especial duty is it to do it? In whom does the Constitution place the power? Not in the judicial branch of Government, for it only adjudicates and does not prescribe laws. Not in the Executive, for he only executes and cannot make laws. Not in the Commander-in-Chief of the armies, for he can only hold them under military rule until the sovereign legislative power of the conquerer shall give them law. Unless the law of nations is a dead letter, the late war between two acknowledged belligerents severed their original compacts and broke all the ties that bound them together. The future condition of the conquered power depends on the will of the conqueror. They must come in as new states or remain as conquered provinces. Congress . . . is the only power that can act in the matter." [7]

Both of these theories involved the belief that the states as corporate bodies were destroyed by the war. While the majority of congressmen were not satisfied with the presidential theory, they were hardly more ready to accept any theory which held that the states had ceased to exist. At the same time they desired some

[6] "How to Treat the Rebel States," *Atlantic Monthly*, XII, 518–526 (October, 1863), quoted in Johnson, 528.
[7] *Cong. Globe*, 39 Cong., 1 sess., 72. Reprinted in Johnson, 530.

theoretical basis for action of the most free and drastic nature. Hence it was that they accepted the theory of "Forfeited Rights," which will be discussed presently.

However, while the thirteenth amendment was pending the Wade-Davis bill was matured as a relatively mild substitute for the presidential plan. It provided that the provisional governors, who had been appointed from time to time as the northern arms recovered control of southern states, should be continued until the war ended. Then civil government might be restored when *one-half* of the white male citizens took an oath of loyalty. The work of restoration was to be done by a state convention in which no man should sit who had voluntarily fought against the Union. This convention, moreover, must amend the state constitution in such a way as to disqualify the leaders of the rebellion for the office of governor and for membership in the legislature, prohibit slavery, and repudiate the debts made in carrying on the war. When these amendments had been ratified by a majority of the qualified voters, the representatives of the state would be allowed their seats in Congress.[8]

This bill reached Lincoln in July, 1864, within ten days of the close of the session. The clauses relative to the amendments to be made to state constitutions seemed to him like dictation. He had consistently maintained that Congress could not intrude upon the states' police control over slavery, but, unwilling to antagonize Congress by a veto, he held the bill until the session expired, announcing later that he saw no objection to the plan set out therein as a method of voluntary procedure on the part of any of the southern states.[9]

PRESIDENTIAL RECONSTRUCTION COMPLETED

Before any further developments of consequence took place, Lincoln's death brought Johnson to the presidency.[10] The new

[8] *Cong. Globe*, 38 Cong., 1 sess., 3449. Bill reprinted in Commager, 436–439.
[9] Richardson, *Messages*, VI, 222; reprint in Commager, 439.
[10] Johnson's career has been the subject of considerable attention in recent years, and there has been a distinct reaction against the unfavorable appraisal originated during the struggles of the reconstruction era. The chief books written from the new viewpoint are: George F. Milton, *The Age of Hate: Andrew Johnson and the Radicals;* Lloyd P. Stryker, *Andrew Johnson: A Study in Cour-*

President had attracted Lincoln's attention in the course of the war by his sturdy loyalty when his state (Tennessee) seceded. Although he was a Democrat, Lincoln appointed him military governor of Tennessee, and in 1864, believing that a southern War Democrat of such qualities would strengthen the Republican cause, had used his influence to bring about his nomination as Vice-President on a ticket which in the national crisis sought to appeal to loyal men of all parties by assuming the name of "Union Party." Although Johnson had previously shown a vindictive spirit towards the South, it now developed that his views on reconstruction were substantially the same as Lincoln's. This was demonstrated when he issued a new amnesty proclamation, following the same general lines as that of his predecessor. The list of southerners excluded from the privilege of amnesty was somewhat longer, however, and the assertion of the right of each state to take its own steps in dealing with the freedmen and "rebel" leaders was made in more explicit terms: The state convention "or the legislature thereafter assembled, will prescribe the qualifications of electors, and the eligibility of persons to hold office under the constitution and laws of the state, a power the people of the several states composing the Federal Union have rightfully exercised from the origin of the government to the present time." [11]

During the recess of Congress in the summer and autumn of 1865, although well aware that its leaders were restive under executive plans, Johnson pushed his program of restoration wellnigh to completion. In his message of December 4, 1865, he informed Congress that "gradually and quietly, and by almost imperceptible steps, I have sought to restore the rightful energy of the General Government and of the States. To that end provisional governors have been appointed for the States, conventions called,

age; and Robert W. Winston, *Andrew Johnson, Plebian and Patriot.* Somewhat more general in scope are: Howard K. Beale, *The Critical Year: A Study of Andrew Johnson and Reconstruction;* and Claude G. Bowers, *The Tragic Era: The Revolution after Lincoln.* A useful book is C. E. Chadsey, *The Struggle between President Johnson and Congress over Reconstruction.* See also Lawrence H. Gipson, "The Statesmanship of President Johnson," and Curtis Nettels, "Andrew Johnson and the South."

[11] Richardson, *Messages,* VI, 310–312. Reprinted in Commager, II, 7–8; MacDonald, 133–135.

governors elected, legislatures assembled, and Senators and Representatives chosen to the Congress of the United States. At the same time the courts of the United States, as far as could be done, have been reopened, so that the laws of the United States may be enforced through their agency. The blockade has been removed and the custom-houses reestablished in the ports of entry, so that the revenue of the United States may be collected. The Post-Office Department renews its ceaseless activity, and the General Government is thereby enabled to communicate promptly with its officers and agents. The courts bring security to persons and property; the opening of the ports invites the restoration of industry and commerce; the post-office renews the facilities of social intercourse and of business." [12]

Johnson admitted that this policy was attended with some risk as to the loyalty of the states after they resumed their functions as states of the Union, but this was a risk, he thought, that must be taken. He reported that he had invited the states to ratify the thirteenth amendment, and closed the message with an appeal, in cautious language, to Congress, to accept the results of his efforts:

"The amendment to the Constitution being adopted, it would remain for the States whose powers have been so long in abeyance to resume their places in the two branches of the National Legislature, and thereby complete the work of restoration. Here it is for you, fellow-citizens of the Senate, and for you, fellow-citizens of the House of Representatives, to judge, each of you for yourselves, of the elections, returns, and qualifications of your own members." [13]

PRESIDENT *versus* CONGRESS

Plainly, the President considered the war over, the work of reconstruction done, and the seating of the southern members a formality which the houses should go through without delay. His policy was a policy of restoration rather than one of reconstruction. The houses, however, were not to be stampeded into action. Not only were they irritated by the President's apparent determina-

[12] Richardson, VI, 353–358. Extracts in Johnson, 515–517.
[13] Richardson, VI, 558.

tion to be beforehanded with them, but they were not satisfied that adequate guarantees had been exacted from the southern states. The treatment of the blacks under the new codes which Johnson's restored governments had adopted looked from the North much like attempts to reestablish slavery is disguised form. The response of Congress to the suggestion of the President was, therefore, the appointment of a joint committee of the two houses, on reconstruction. This committee was charged with inquiring into the condition of the states lately in rebellion, and reporting whether any of them was entitled to representation. The whole procedure intimated that Congress would not recognize the new state governments until additional guarantees, to be prescribed by itself, should be given.

While the committee was at work, Congress began to pass bills which were intended to safeguard the rights of the freedmen, supposed to be jeopardized by the "black codes." These bills aroused the President, who soon became involved in a conflict with Congress. Before it came to an end, presidential reconstruction was thrown overboard bodily and replaced by a much more drastic program worked out by the congressional radicals.

Following the emancipation proclamation, a freedmen's bureau had been established to care for black refugees.[14] This was a temporary measure; but the new southern codes seemed to require its continuation and extension. A new freedmen's bureau bill of 1866 provided for officials to have oversight and supervision over freedmen and refugees in all parts of the United States. The powers of these officials were vague and amounted almost to an unlimited discretion. The chief features of the bill were the provisions of the seventh and eighth sections, which made it the duty of the President to extend the military protection of the bureau to all cases where the civil rights and immunities of whites were denied to Negroes who had been slaves. Any person who should under color of a state law or custom deprive a Negro of his equal rights should be deemed guilty of a misdemeanor. Where the ordinary courts were suspended by the rebellion, bureau officials were to have jurisdiction over such cases, such jurisdiction to cease

[14] Paul S. Peirce, *The Freedmen's Bureau.*

whenever the normal relations of the state with the United States were restored.[15]

The defenders of this bill considered it a war measure. As such the President might have accepted it, but he disliked to admit that the United States was still in a state of war, when his message had announced the contrary. Believing that the only proper basis for the bill, a state of war, did not exist, he vetoed it.

Meantime the thirteenth amendment had been ratified, in December, 1865, and another bill was now framed with the purpose of giving citizenship to the freedmen and placing them under the permanent protection of the civil authorities of the United States. This civil rights bill contained the first definition of citizenship that had appeared in the history of American legislation. "All persons born in the United States, and not subject to any foreign power, excluding Indians not taxed," were declared to be citizens. All citizens as thus defined were by the terms of the bill secured in the enjoyment of equal rights in holding property, entering into contracts, appearing in court, etc., and it was declared to be a misdemeanor to deprive any citizen of such equal rights, or to discriminate against a citizen. Breaches of these provisions were placed under the jurisdiction of the courts of the United States.[16]

By the time this bill was passed, the actions of the southern states had made it manifest that they would not, of their own volition, accord equal rights to the freedmen, whom they deemed incapable as yet of full status as citizens, and in need of guardianship. The point of view of the South was not easy of comprehension by northern idealists who had little real understanding of the situation which existed in the former slave states. Nevertheless they attempted to control a remote situation by unprecedented legislation. "At first glance," says Professor Dunning, "the provisions of the bill appeared out of all relation to our constitutional system. Never before had Congress been known to arrogate to itself the power to regulate the civil status of the inhabitants of a state. The proposition that United States courts should assume jurisdiction of disputes

---

[15] See documents and references in Commager, II, 1–7, 10–14.

[16] *U. S. Stat. at Large*, XIV, 27–29. Extract in Commager, II, 14–15; MacDonald, 141–146.

relating to property and contracts, and even of criminal actions down to common assault and battery, seemed like a complete revelation of that diabolical spirit of centralization, of which only the cloven hoof had been manifested heretofore." [17]

The supporters of the legislation found an alleged warrant in the second section of the thirteenth amendment, giving Congress power to enforce the prohibition of slavery. They now declared that *any deprivation of equal rights* subjected the person suffering the deprivation to a degree of servitude. By this logic, it became the duty of Congress to counteract by its own legislation the effects of such discriminating laws. Thus the United States was to become the champion of "equality," the protector of the individual against oppression by the state in the exercise of its internal police power!

Opponents argued that the freedman was subject to the laws of his state like any other inhabitant, and that the true meaning of the enforcement clause of the thirteenth amendment was that Congress should have power to provide for the enjoyment of the writ of habeas corpus by any Negro whose master might persist in holding him in slavery. The idea that the amendment carried any great centralization of power was unheard of, they declared, while it was pending in Congress.

A veto of such an act by a President who had a keen regard for the rights of states was, of course, inevitable.[18] Already the breach between President and Congress had grown wider. If Johnson could have brought himself to accept the freedmen's bureau bill, it is conceivable that he might have gained the support of a group in Congress large enough to prevent radical legislation, provided his own course continued to be moderate and tactful. His veto, however, tended to throw the moderates into the ranks of the radicals, for his temper seemed uncompromising. With the strength added by this group, the radicals now passed the civil rights bill over the veto, and it was actually upheld by the courts, following the fashion adopted by the federal judiciary during the war of

[17] *Essays*, 93. Quoted by permission of The Macmillan Company.
[18] The veto message is in Richardson, *Messages*, VI, 405 *et seq.* Reprint in Commager, II, 15–18.

refraining from interference with the action of the "political" branches of the government.[19]

Notwithstanding the acceptance of the congressional interpretation by the federal courts, there was some uneasiness as to the soundness of the act, and its friends felt that its aims would be more securely attained by embodying its provisions in another amendment. If another amendment was to be passed, it soon appeared that certain other stipulations should be added to the above. One effect of the thirteenth amendment threatened to be an enlarged representation in Congress from the former slave states, since the freeing of the slaves abrogated the three-fifths clause and *all* Negroes would be counted in the apportionment. The northern radicals desired that the freedmen should enjoy the suffrage, and felt that if it were denied them, they must not be counted in apportioning representation. Even some of these radicals doubted the power of Congress to prescribe the qualifications of voters in the states, and believed that nothing short of a constitutional amendment could impose the desired restrictions upon state action. All of these matters were therefore dealt with by the joint committee on reconstruction, which on April 30, 1866 proposed a fourteenth amendment.[20]

The first section of the new amendment forbade any state to make or enforce any law which should abridge the privileges or immunities of citizens of the United States; to deprive any person of life, liberty, or property without due process of law; or to deny to any

[19] In U. S. *v.* Rhodes (1 Abbot 56. *Fed. Cases,* XXVII, No. 16151, U. S. Circuit Court for Kentucky, 1866), it was held that the thirteenth amendment had "reversed and annulled the original policy of the constitution." Chase, in Turner's case (1 Abbot 84. *Fed. Cases,* XXVI, No. 14247, U. S. C. C. for Maryland, 1867), on similar grounds, held Maryland's laws discriminating against black apprentices to be a violation of the amendment.

[20] The journal of the joint committee was published by the 63 Cong., 3 sess., as Sen. Doc. No. 711. See also Benjamin B. Kendrick, *The Journal of the Joint Committee,* and the story of the framing of the amendment as told in Randall, *Civil War,* 735–739; also Horace E. Flack, *The Adoption of the Fourteenth Amendment.* Charles W. Collins, *The Fourteenth Amendment and the States,* gives attention chiefly to the later interpretations of the amendment as related to the retained powers of the states. *Cf.* William D. Guthrie, *Fourteenth Article of Amendment to the Constitution of the United States.*

person within its jurisdiction the equal protection of the laws. This section was formulated by John A. Bingham, of Ohio. During the debate in the Senate a definition of citizenship was affixed to these clauses which somewhat amended the definition in the civil rights bill: "All persons born or naturalized in the United States, and subject to the jurisdiction thereof, are citizens of the United States and of the State wherein they reside." Thus, after three quarters of a century, and after infinite confusion and embarrassment, a point was cleared up which should have been determined by the express wording of the original Constitution. At that time the presence of the class of free Negroes made it impossible.

The second section of the amendment provided for representation in the lower house of Congress in proportion to population, with a reduction in proportion to the number of adult male inhabitants who might be disfranchised by state action. The third section disqualified the southern leaders as federal office holders until Congress should by a two-thirds vote remove such disability. The fourth guaranteed the federal debt and repudiated the Confederate debt, on behalf of both states and nation. The fifth gave Congress power to enforce the provisions of the amendment.[21]

The purpose of the amendment, in the thought of its framers, was expressed by Representative Bingham: "to protect by *national* law the privileges and immunities of all the citizens of the Republic and the inborn rights of every person within its jurisdiction whenever the same shall be abridged or denied by the unconstitutional acts of any State."[22]

To the state governments reconstructed by Johnson this new amendment was now sent. To the southerners, however, acceptance of such limitations upon what had always been regarded as the rights of states was well-nigh unthinkable, and one after another their legislatures rejected it. To the radicals in Congress in turn, this action seemed to be proof that the President's policy had not laid the foundation for stable and unvexed future relations between

[21] *Revised Statutes of the U. S.*, 31 (edn. 1878). Reprinted in Johnson, 526–527; MacDonald, 208–210.

[22] *Cong. Globe*, 39 Cong., 1 sess., 2542–2543. May 10, 1866. Extract in Johnson, 520. For further information consult White's *Lyman Trumbull* and Dyer's *William M. Evarts*.

the restored states and the Union. Rejection seemed to prove that his policy was a failure and that more drastic action was necessary. Now Congress cast aside the President's work and turned to action based on more radical theories of the relations of the states and nation. Some scholars believe that Congress would have taken its drastic measures even if the southern states had accepted the amendment.

The report of the joint committee, made in June, 1866, held that the President could go no further in dealing with the states than to provide temporary military government, leaving the final adjustment, with restoration of civil government, to Congress. "As commander-in-chief of a victorious army, it was his duty, under the law of nations and the army regulations, to restore order, to preserve property, and to protect the people against violence from any quarter until provision should be made by law for their government. He might, as President, assemble Congress and submit the whole matter to the law-making power; or he might continue military supervision and control until Congress should assemble on its regular appointed day. Selecting the latter alternative, he proceeded, by virtue of his power as commander-in-chief, to appoint provisional governors over the revolted States. . . . But it was not for him to decide upon the nature or effect of any system of government which the people of these States might see fit to adopt. This power is lodged by the Constitution in the Congress of the United States, that branch of the government in which is vested the authority to fix the political relations of the States to the Union, whose duty it is to guarantee to each State a republican form of government, and to protect each and all of them against foreign or domestic violence, and against each other. We cannot, therefore, regard the various acts of the President in relation to the formation of local governments in the insurrectionary States, and the conditions imposed by him upon their action, in any other light than as intimations to the people that, as commander-in-chief of the army, he would consent to withdraw military rule just in proportion as they should, by their acts, manifest a disposition to preserve order among themselves, establish governments denoting loyalty to the Union, and exhibit a settled determination to return to their allegiance, leaving with the law-making power to fix the terms of their final restoration to all their rights and privileges as States of the Union." [23]

The view that, "inasmuch as the lately insurgent States had no legal right to separate themselves from the Union, they still retain their positions as States, and consequently the people thereof have a right to immediate representation in Congress without the imposition of any conditions whatever," is combatted as untenable. "Whether legally and constitutionally or not, they did, in fact, withdraw from the Union and made themselves subjects of another government of their own creation. And they only yielded when . . . compelled by utter exhaustion . . . not willingly, but . . . because they could no longer resist, affording no evidence whatever of repentance for their crime, and expressing no regret, except that they had no longer the power to continue the desperate struggle. . . ." "It is more than idle, it is mockery, to contend that a people who have thrown off their allegiance, destroyed the local government which bound their States to the Union as members thereof, defied its authority, refused to execute its laws, and abrogated every provision which gave them political rights within the Union, still retain, through all, the perfect and entire right to resume, at their own will and pleasure, all their privileges within the Union, and especially to participate in its government, and to control the conduct of its affairs. . . . On the contrary, we assert that no portion of the people of this country, whether in State or Territory, have the right, while remaining on its soil, to withdraw from or reject the authority of the United States. They must obey its laws as paramount, and acknowledge its jurisdiction. They have no right to secede; and while they can destroy their State governments, and place themselves beyond the pale of the Union, so far as the exercise of state privileges is concerned, they cannot escape the obligations imposed upon them by the Constitution, and the laws, nor impair the exercise of national authority. The Constitution, it will be observed, does not act upon States, as such, but upon the people;

[23] *Report of the Joint Committee on Reconstruction,* 39 Cong., 1 sess., Doc. No. 30, xiii–xxi *et passim. Cf.* Commager, II, 18–20, and references. The majority report was made by Stevens on June 8; a minority report was presented on the 19th.

while, therefore, the people cannot escape its authority, the States may, through the act of their people, cease to exist in an organized form, and thus dissolve their political relations with the United States." [24]

MILITARY RECONSTRUCTION

The end of the rebellion was proclaimed by President Johnson on April 2, 1866,[25] and the courts acted accordingly.

But Congress ignored the executive's action and proceeded with as much disregard of southern rights as if it had accepted the views of Sumner or Stevens. Its policy of "thorough" was embodied in the Reconstruction Act of March 2, 1867, which called for the division of the South into military districts, each under a commander whose functions should continue until the process of reconstruction was completed: "When the people of any one of said rebel States shall have formed a constitution of government in conformity with the Constitution of the United States in all respects, framed by a convention of delegates elected by the male citizens of said State, twenty-one years old and upward, of whatever race, color, or previous condition, who have been resident in said State for one year previous to the day of such election, except such as may be disfranchised for participation in the rebellion or for felony at

[24] In the case of Texas v. White (7 Wallace 700. 1868), the Supreme Court substantially upheld the doctrine advanced by the joint committee. The issue in this case was whether Texas, having seceded, was nevertheless a state in the sense necessary to enable it to be a party to a suit in the federal courts. Said the court: "Considered . . . as transacted under the Constitution, the ordinance of secession, adopted by the convention and ratified by a majority of the citizens of Texas, and all the acts of her legislature intended to give effect to that ordinance, were absolutely null. They were utterly without operation in law. The obligations of the State, as a member of the Union, and of every citizen of the State, as a citizen of the United States, remained perfect and unimpaired. It certainly follows that the State did not cease to be a State, nor her citizens to be citizens of the Union. . . .

"It is by no means a logical conclusion . . . that the governmental relations of Texas to the Union remained unaltered. . . . All admit that, during this condition of civil war, the rights of the State as a member, and of her people as citizens of the Union, were suspended. The government and the citizens of the State, refusing to recognize their constitutional obligations, assumed the character of enemies, and incurred the consequences of rebellion." Extracts from the decision are in Commager, II, 59–63, and Johnson, 550–552. See R. Earl McClendon, "Status of the Ex-Confederate States as Seen in the Readmission of United States Senators."

[25] U. S. Stat. at Large, XIV, 811–813. Extract in MacDonald, Select Stat., 139–141.

common law, and when such constitution shall provide that the elective franchise shall be enjoyed by all such persons as have the qualifications herein stated for electors of delegates, and when such constitution shall be ratified by a majority of persons voting on the question of ratification who are qualified as electors for delegates, and when such constitution shall have been submitted to Congress for examination and approval, and Congress shall have approved the same, and when said State, by a vote of its legislature elected under said constitution, shall have adopted the amendment to the Constitution of the United States, proposed by the Thirty-ninth Congress, and known as article fourteen, and when said article shall have become a part of the Constitution of the United States said State shall be declared entitled to representation in Congress, and senators and representatives shall be admitted therefrom on their taking the oath prescribed by law, and then and thereafter the preceding sections of this act shall be inoperative in said State." [26]

This legislation left no initiative with the states. The military commanders registered citizens (as defined by the civil rights bill) to act as voters in choosing members of the state conventions. The conventions were required to frame constitutions containing the dictated provisions, and including Negro suffrage, and to submit the constitutions to the voters for ratification. The legislatures, when set up, were required to ratify the fourteenth amendment before the states were to be given representation. The act was based on the theory that the war had not yet ceased, and was justifiable only on that ground. The procedure of Congress can be harmonized with the President's proclamation only on the theory that the conditions existing in 1867 amounted to a new case of rebellion; but this theory is hardly consistent with the fact that the courts were open.

The defenders of the act attempted to justify it by citing the obligation of the United States to guarantee to every state a republican form of government. Such a position assumes that a state would lack a republican form of government if any class of citizens was disfranchised. This, however, was an entirely novel view of

[26] *U. S. Stat. at Large*, XIV, 428–429. Reprinted in Commager, II, 30–31; MacDonald, 158–160.

the meaning of "republican form of government." The precedents, especially in the case of the Dorr Rebellion, were quite against the view. Webster had said, in 1848, "The law and the Constitution go on the idea that the states are all republican, that they are all representative in their forms, and that these popular governments in each state, the annually created creatures of the people, will give all proper facilities and necessary aids to bring about changes which the people may judge necessary in their constitutions." [27]

President Johnson vetoed the bill. "The military rule which it establishes," he said, "is plainly to be used . . . solely as a means of coercing the people into the adoption of principles and measures to which it is known that they are opposed and upon which they have an undeniable right to exercise their own judgment." Then he reasoned with great force against the propriety and constitutionality of the proposal:

"This is a bill passed by Congress in time of peace. There is not in any one of the States brought under its operation either war or insurrection. The laws of the States and of the Federal Government are all in undisturbed and harmonious operation. The courts, State and Federal, are open and in the full exercise of their proper authority. Over every State comprised in these five military districts, life, liberty, and property are secured by State laws and Federal laws, and the National Constitution is everywhere in force and everywhere obeyed. What, then, is the ground on which this bill proceeds? The title of the bill announces that it is intended 'for the more efficient government' of these ten States. It is recited by way of preamble that no legal State governments 'nor adequate protection for life or property' exist in those States, and that peace and good order should be thus enforced. The first thing which arrests attention upon these recitals, which prepare the way for martial law, is this, that the only foundation upon which martial law can exist under our form of government is not stated or so much as pretended. Actual war, foreign invasion, domestic insurrection—none of these appear; and none of these, in fact, exist. It is not even recited that any sort of war or insurrection is threatened.

[27] Everett, *Works of Webster*, VI, 231. Quoted by Dunning, 132.

"The purpose and object of the bill—the general intent which pervades it from beginning to end—is to change the entire structure and character of the State governments and to compel them by force to the adoption of organic laws and regulations which they are unwilling to accept if left to themselves. The negroes have not asked for the privilege of voting; the vast majority of them have no idea what it means. This bill not only thrusts it into their hands, but compels them, as well as the whites, to use it in a particular way. If they do not form a constitution with prescribed articles in it and afterwards elect a legislature which will act upon certain measures in a prescribed way, neither blacks nor whites can be relieved from the slavery which the bill imposes upon them. Without pausing here to consider the policy or impolicy of Africanizing the southern part of our territory, I would simply ask the attention of Congress to that manifest, well-known, and universally acknowledged rule of constitutional law which declares that the Federal Government has no jurisdiction, authority, or power to regulate such subjects for any State. To force the right of suffrage out of the hands of the white people and into the hands of the negroes is an arbitrary violation of this principle. . . . That the measure proposed . . . does violate the Constitution . . . is too clear to admit of the least doubt." [28]

The congressional election in the autumn of 1866 had been fought on the issue of presidential *versus* congressional reconstruction; the outcome was an increased majority in Congress ready to support the radical leaders. This majority was sufficient to pass the Reconstruction Act over Johnson's veto. Thus overridden, he believed it to be his duty to carry its provisions into effect. Congress passed supplementary acts to provide for details and overcome difficulties not foreseen when the principal act was drafted, and some of these encountered the presidential veto. Congress, however, had a working majority sufficient to override the veto in all such cases, and the program of the radicals was carried steadily forward.[29]

[28] Richardson, *Messages*, VI, 498–507 *et passim*. Extracts in Commager, II, 31–35; Johnson, 538–541. The veto was probably drafted by J. S. Black.
[29] See acts of March 23 and July 19, 1867, and March 11, 1868 (Commager, II, 38, 41, 49; MacDonald, 170, 179, 198), and veto messages of March 23 and July 19, 1863 (Richardson, VI, 531–534, 537–544. Reprinted in Johnson, 541–546).

THE FIFTEENTH AMENDMENT

The required number of states had ratified the fourteenth amendment before the close of 1868. It became apparent in due time that its provisions would not result in the enfranchisement of the Negro by the southern states; or rather that when left to themselves they would promptly disfranchise them. To put the enjoyment of the right of suffrage by the freedmen beyond the power of the states, therefore, a new amendment was conceived and passed by Congress. This fifteenth amendment declared that "the right of citizens of the United States to vote shall not be denied or abridged by the United States or by any State on account of race, color, or previous condition of servitude." An additional section gave Congress power to enforce the article by appropriate legislation.[30]

Among the supporters of the amendment were the universal suffragists, who desired to have the ballot conferred not only upon the freedmen but upon women as well. In the course of the debate there were many who pointed out that the wording of the amendment not only would not enfranchise women, but would not even result in the enfranchisement of the Negroes, since educational and property qualifications, and others, could be devised which would reach the Negroes as a class while affecting the whites far less.

In the debate, the advocates of the measure tried to show that the framers of the Constitution had not intended that the regulation of the franchise should be left to the states. For example, Samuel Shellabarger of Ohio, in the House, quoted Hamilton's essay in the *Federalist*, in which he referred to the wisdom of withholding this power from the *legislative* discretion of the states, fallaciously ignoring the meaning of the passage, which recognizes the power as one reserved to the *people* of the states, and "not alterable by the state governments." [31]

The opponents of the amendment insisted upon the fundamental

[30] *Revised Statutes of the U. S.*, 32 (edn. of 1878). Reprinted in Johnson, 576; MacDonald, 226. See John M. Mathews, *Legislative and Judicial History of the Fifteenth Amendment;* William C. Coleman, "The Fifteenth Amendment."
[31] *Cong. Globe*, 40 Cong., 3 sess., App., 151. Reprinted in Johnson, 572–574.

right of a state to control the question of suffrage, and professed to see in it a proposal to empower the United States to regulate elections for the states. This they argued would be equivalent to *depriving* them of a republican form of government.[32]

The ratification of this amendment was added to the conditions required for the restoration of the states which had not yet been reconstructed. The last ratification was given in 1870, and the article became a part of the fundamental law.

The interpretation of the amendment by the Supreme Court is that it gives no one the right to vote—that it only gives to the citizen of the United States the right to be exempt from adverse discrimination in the exercise of the suffrage because of race, color, or previous condition of servitude, leaving the states free to impose restrictions on other grounds. "The right of suffrage is not a necessary attribute of national citizenship; but exemption from discrimination in the exercise of that right on account of race, etc., is." [33] The right to vote in a state comes from the state, but the right of exemption from discrimination on the grounds indicated is a right conferred by the Constitution of the United States.

SUPPLEMENTARY LEGISLATION

The aim of the nationalists, the politicians, and the humanitarians in Congress, in their program of reconstruction, so far as it related to the freedmen, was to secure equal rights for them including the suffrage. The steps which were to be necessary were not all foreseen at the time of the passage of the Reconstruction Act of March 1867. The fifteenth amendment was planned only when

[32] See for example the speech of Senator James R. Doolittle of Wisconsin, Feb. 6, 1869. *Cong. Globe*, 40 Cong., 3 sess., App., 151. Reprinted in Johnson, 574–576.

[33] "The privilege to vote in any state is not given by the Federal Constitution, or by any of its amendments. It is not a privilege springing from citizenship of the United States. It may not be refused on account of race, color, or previous condition of servitude, but it does not follow from mere citizenship of the United States. In other words, the privilege to vote in a state is within the jurisdiction of the state itself, to be exercised as the state may direct, and upon such terms as the state may deem proper, provided, of course, no discrimination is made between individuals, in violation of the Federal Constitution. The state might provide that persons of foreign birth could vote without being naturalized." Mr. Justice Peckham, in Pope v. Williams (193 U. S. 621. 1903).

experience showed the necessity of it; it was an afterthought. Even it proved insufficient to secure what the radicals desired, and a whole crop of laws followed designed to counteract the southern methods of "undoing" reconstruction and eliminating the Negroes from politics.[34]   Among the foremost of these methods was that comprehensively designated by the term "Ku Klux Klan."

The Enforcement Act of 1870 provided for the punishment of persons who hindered any citizen of the United States from exercising the right to vote.   It gave jurisdiction in such cases to the United States courts, and provided that, if necessary, military force might be used to aid the courts in the enforcement of the right of citizens to vote as guaranteed by the fifteenth amendment.[35]

A Supplementary Act, passed February 28, 1871, provided for the punishment of fraudulent registration, and for the appointment by the United States circuit courts of federal supervisors of elections in cities and large towns.[36]

The Act to Enforce the Fourteenth Amendment, passed April 20, 1871, and sometimes known as the "Ku Klux Act," provided for the punishment of such deeds as made the Ku Klux Klan notorious; for the use of military force where the Klan could not otherwise be dealt with; and for the suspension of the writ of habeas corpus in such cases.[37]

A Federal Election Law of June 10, 1872, made further provision for the supervision of elections where a member of Congress was to be chosen.[38]

This series of measures came to a climax with the Civil Rights Act of March 1, 1875.   Such an enactment had been a pet plan of Senator Sumner for many years, and it was finally passed after his death.[39]   Sumner was the chief of the northern idealists who demanded race equality in practice, on moral grounds and as a

[34] W. W. Davis, "Federal Enforcement Acts."
[35] *U. S. Stat. at Large*, XVI, 140–146.   May 31, 1870.   Reprinted in MacDonald, 227–235.
[36] *U. S. Stat. at Large*, XVI, 433–440.   Reprinted in MacDonald, 249–262.
[37] *U. S. Stat. at Large*, XVII, 13–15.   Reprinted in MacDonald, 262–268.
[38] *U. S. Stat. at Large*, XVII, 348–349.   Reprinted in MacDonald, 291–293.
[39] See Moorfield Storey, *Charles Sumner*, Chaps. XXIV, XXV; Carl M. Frasure, "Charles Sumner and the Rights of the Negro"; L. E. Murphy, "The Civil Rights Law of 1875."

human right. As passed, the bill was entitled "An Act to Protect All Citizens in Their Civil and Legal Rights." [40]

The first paragraph stated the principle on which the bill rested, a principle which was moral rather than legal: "Whereas, it is essential to just government we recognize the equality of all men before the law, and hold that it is the duty of government in its dealings with the people to mete out equal and exact justice to all, of whatever nativity, race, color, or persuasion, religious or political . . . therefore

"*Be it enacted* . . ., That all persons within the jurisdiction of the United States shall be entitled to the full and equal enjoyment of the accommodations, advantages, facilities, and privileges of inns, public conveyances on land or water, theaters, and other places of public amusement; subject only to the conditions and limitations established by law, and applicable alike to citizens of every race and color, regardless of any previous condition of servitude."

[40] *U. S. Stat. at Large*, XVIII, 335–337. Reprinted in MacDonald, *Select Statutes*, 303–306.

XVIII

RECONSTRUCTION COMPLETED

THE IMPEACHMENT OF PRESIDENT JOHNSON

URING the excitement and stress of the years immediately following the war Congress went to extremes in many directions. In its dealings with the South and its assumption of national sovereignty it ignored old constitutional landmarks; and in its relations with the other branches of the federal government it asserted a paramount authority which carried it to the very verge of constitutional catastrophe. The conflict with the executive in working out the policy of reconstruction led Congress to encroach upon that department quite as much as the executive had encroached upon the sphere of Congress during the crisis of the war, when Lincoln wielded almost the power of a dictator.

By an act of January 17, 1867, Congress repealed a clause of the Confiscation Act of 1862 authorizing the President to pardon by proclamation. The Reconstruction Act of July 19, 1867, declared that no right to vote should result from "any executive pardon or amnesty," and the fourteenth amendment conferred on Congress the power to remove the disabilities of rebels.[1] These limitations upon the President's pardoning power were matched by others restricting his authority as commander-in-chief. The Army Appropriation Act of March 2, 1867 provided that all orders of the President or the secretary of war, relating to military operations, should be issued through the general of the army, with headquarters at Washington. On the same day was passed a new Tenure of Office Act.[2] This provided that civil officers appointed by and with the advice and consent of the Senate should hold their offices until their successors should be appointed in like manner. This required, in effect, that removals as well as appointments, should have the assent of the Senate, since refusal of confirmation of new

[1] Commager, II, 41.
[2] *Ibid.*, 35.

347

nominees would leave the incumbent in office. Further stipulations were that when any officer so appointed should, during the recess of the Senate, be shown by evidence satisfactory to the President to be guilty of crime or misconduct in office, or incapable of performing his duties, the President might suspend him and designate another to perform his duties until the Senate should meet again. The President was required to submit the facts to the Senate within twenty days after the beginning of the ensuing session, and if the Senate did not concur in the removal the suspended officer was to resume his duties. Appointment to or acceptance of office contrary to the provisions of the act was declared to be a high misdemeanor. This bill, like so many others, Johnson vetoed as an encroachment upon his constitutional prerogative;[3] but, like so many others, it was repassed over his veto.

The question of the President's power to remove officials was an old one. The Constitution is specific as to how appointments shall be made, but is silent as to removals, except in the case of officers who are mentioned as removable by impeachment. The debate on this point in the first Congress, in 1789, turned on the nature of the power, whether it was an independent attribute of the executive or incidental to the power of appointment.[4] The former view prevailed at the time, and became a precedent against the new interpretation made by Congress in 1867.[5]

The phrasing of the act of 1867 was such as to bring any violation within the scope of the impeaching power, for the Constitu-

[3] *Ibid.*, 36. The entire cabinet concurred in Johnson's view; Stanton was emphatic in condemning the act. See Randall, *Civil War*, 763.

[4] See Hockett, *Con. Hist.*, I, 236 *et seq.*

[5] In 1839 the Supreme Court was asked to issue a mandamus ordering a district court to restore a clerk of court to office. The court held that in the absence of constitutional or statutory regulation, "it would seem to be a sound and necessary rule to consider the power of removal as incident to the power of appointment," and that "it was very easily adopted as the practical construction of the Constitution that the power was vested in the President alone" with reference to all presidential appointees. The court therefore refused to issue the mandamus, saying that "if the Judge is chargeable with any abuse of his power, this is not the tribunal to which he is amenable." Ex parte Hennen, 13 Peters 230. In Myers *v.* U. S. (272 U. S. 52), decided in 1926, involving a postmaster, the President's power of removal was upheld; but in Rathbun *v.* U. S. (55 *Sup. Ct. Reporter* 869) the court held (1935) that Congress could limit the President's power to remove a member of the federal trade commission.

tion provides for the impeachment and removal from office of the President, and other civil officers, upon conviction of bribery, treason, "or other high crimes and misdemeanors." Elsewhere the Constitution provides that the sole power of impeachment shall belong to the House, and the sole power of trying impeachments to the Senate, the chief justice presiding in case of impeachment of the President, and a vote of two thirds being required for conviction.[6]

From the beginning of the constitutional era, there had been two conflicting views of the meaning of the word "misdemeanor" as used in this clause. The conservative view was that the term was to be construed in its ordinary legal sense of an indictable offense. Since many acts of a reprehensible character could not be brought within this meaning, the more liberal view was that the term should be construed to include any misbehavior which in the judgment of the Senate unfitted the officer for his position.[7] Advocates of this view held that it was within the power of Congress to define the word "misdemeanor," and the Tenure of Office Act rested upon this alleged right.

Previous to 1867 there had been five cases of impeachment: In the first, involving a senator, it was somewhat ambiguously held that a senator is not a civil officer.[8] All the other cases involved judges, and in every instance the articles exhibited by the House had charged offenses which were not technical violations of law. There had been two convictions: Judge Pickering had been found guilty (1802) of drunkenness and profanity on the bench although insane, and Judge Humphreys had been found guilty (1861) of advocating secession, which was not at that time a violation of any statute of the United States. Both of these judges had been removed from office. Impeachment involved a dilemma: unless the term misdemeanor were liberally construed, it would be difficult or impossible to remove officers who were not actually criminal; but on the other hand a latitudinarian construction opened the door to impeachments on purely political grounds, and once admitted

[6]Art. I, sec. 2, par. 5; art. I, sec. 3, par. 6, 7; art. II, sec. 4; art. III, sec. 1.
[7] See Hockett, *Con. Hist.*, I, 310 *et seq.*
[8] *Ibid.*, 310, note. There is a Senate document on impeachment cases, 1796–1904.

it was difficult to see what checks existed to prevent abuse of the power of the Senate.

The first effort to impeach Johnson followed the congressional election of 1866.[9] The judiciary committee of the House made a diligent search for evidence which could furnish grounds for the action, and presented a report covering more than a thousand pages, without being able to charge any specific offense.[10] They did make the general accusation that Johnson had used his power to reconstruct government in the southern states in the interests of rebellion and the Democratic Party; but these grounds were altogether too vague to promise success, and the resolution to impeach was rejected by the vote of 108 to 57.[11] The passage of the Tenure of Office Act, and its violation by the President in the case of Stanton, gave the congressional party, as they thought, the opportunity which they had previously sought in vain.

Edwin M. Stanton, the secretary of war, was a hold-over from Lincoln's cabinet. He was in sympathy with the congressional plan of reconstruction, and Johnson believed that he used his position to obstruct the administration and to betray cabinet secrets to the President's political enemies. He declined to resign at Johnson's request, and was thereupon suspended and General Grant was appointed secretary of war *ad interim*. The Senate being at the time in recess, the President in a message to that chamber in December gave the reasons for his action, but the Senate refused to concur.

It had been Johnson's plan to persuade Grant to refuse to yield his post to Stanton, in order that the latter might be compelled to appeal to the court. In this way he hoped that the constitutionality of the Tenure of Office Act would be brought before the judiciary and passed upon. Grant, however, offered no opposition to the reinstatement of Stanton, thus frustrating the President's design. Johnson thereupon removed Stanton and appointed Adjutant-General Thomas secretary *ad interim*.

Stanton refused to vacate his office upon the demand of Thomas,

[9] *Cong. Globe*, 39 Cong., 2 sess., 320. See account in Randall, *Civil War*, 761 et seq.

[10] *Impeachment Investigation*, 40 Cong., 1 sess., *House Report No. 7*.

[11] *Cong. Globe*, 40 Cong., 2 sess., 68 (Dec. 7, 1867).

and the latter was arrested on the charge of violating the Tenure of Office Act. If Thomas had been brought to trial, Johnson's plan to bring the act before the court for adjudication would have succeeded. Thomas's lawyers were planning in his defense to attack the constitutionality of the act. But the congressional leaders, perceiving that the arrest of Thomas was a *faux pas*, suddenly dropped the case, and turned upon the President himself.

On February 24, 1868, by a vote of 126 to 47 the House adopted a resolution to impeach Andrew Johnson on the charge of having committed high crimes and misdemeanors. Those Republicans who had previously held back now believed that the President had given ground for the proceeding by violating the Tenure of Office Act. The House charges included eleven articles dealing with five matters: [12] the most important ones referred to the removal of Stanton; the appointment of Thomas; criticism of Congress in public speeches; and opposition to the execution of the reconstruction measures of Congress. The new and most serious were the first two, dealing with the President's conduct under the Tenure of Office Act.[13]

Johnson's reply to the charges alleged that the power of removal was a constitutional right of the President which could not be taken away by an act of Congress. The Tenure of Office Act he therefore held to be void. The appointment of Thomas was a temporary designation which it was argued did not require the consent of the Senate.

The only charges of the House which alleged acts contrary to law were those dealing with the removal of Stanton and the appointment of Thomas. To maintain the other charges, the managers of the trial had to hold that the meaning of misdemeanor was not confined to indictable offenses. They defined an impeachable

[12] Richardson, VI, 709 *et seq.* Reprinted in Commager, II, 43–47.
[13] The standard history of the Johnson impeachment is David M. DeWitt, *The Impeachment and Trial of Andrew Johnson.* See J. G. Randall, *The Civil War,* Chap. XXXIV and references; also lives of Johnson cited *supra*, and Dunning, *Essays,* 253–303. The subject has created a considerable literature. The following items may be mentioned: F. T. Hill, "Impeachment of Andrew Johnson"; H. G. Otis, "The Causes of [Johnson's] Impeachment" (strongly biased against Johnson); G. Hunt, "The Impeachment of Andrew Johnson. The President's Defense"; Gamaliel Bradford, "Edward M. Stanton."

crime or misdemeanor as "one in its nature or consequences sub-versive of some fundamental principle of government, or highly prejudicial to the public interest." It might be a violation of positive law, or "abuse of discretionary powers . . . for any improper motive." They also maintained that the Senate when sitting in impeachments is not a court bound by the usual rules of evidence and procedure. Each senator was free, they declared, to rest his opinion on any information that bore on the general question of fitness of the officeholder, and each must give the verdict which he thought was demanded by the welfare of the country. Having thus insisted that it was not necessary to prove that the accused was a criminal, the prosecution proceeded to treat him as such, using language designed to create prejudice rather than to bring out any real misconduct. Johnson had succeeded to the presidency "by murder most foul," cried Benjamin F. Butler, referring to Lincoln's assassination as if Johnson were guilty of it. He was the "elect of an assassin." "We have brought the criminal to your bar, and demand judgment at your hands for his so great crimes." [14]

The defense argued that the Senate was a court, and cited the use of words in the Constitution to uphold the view. The words "try," "conviction," "judgment," they said, implied the procedure of a court. Test votes indicated that the Senate regarded itself as a court. For example, a motion was adopted giving the chief justice power to decide questions of law, with an appeal to the Senate. This view bound the Senate to obey the rules of evidence.

As to the Tenure of Office Act, the prosecution, in attempting to prove that the removal of the secretary of war was a misdemeanor, argued that the original recognition by Congress of the removal power of the Executive did not bind later Congresses. Experience, they urged, had shown that the older view was an error, which the Tenure of Office Act was designed to correct. The President was bound to execute the laws, not to decide whether or not they were constitutional. The defense admitted that, generally speaking, the President is bound to execute the laws, but argued that he was not bound to do so in the case of one which deprived him of rights vested in him by the Constitution. In case

[14] *Cong. Globe,* 40 Cong., 2 sess., supplement, 29–51.

of doubt, they urged, he may certainly take steps to secure judicial action. Such steps are likely to necessitate a technical violation of law as a means of bringing the issue before the court. The prosecution, in effect, was calling on the Senate to remove a President for a technical violation of a law which, if in conflict with the Constitution, was no law at all.[15]

As the trial proceeded the strong arguments of the defense were reinforced by growing doubts as to the applicability of the Tenure of Office Act. The act contained a proviso that cabinet members should hold their offices during the term of the President who appointed them, and for one month thereafter. Stanton was Lincoln's appointee, and had not been reappointed by Johnson. Thus it was possible to take the view that his tenure under the act ended one month after Johnson became President. The prosecution maintained that Johnson was serving out Lincoln's term, and that Stanton was entitled to serve until a month after Johnson's tenure of office ceased, but the argument was not convincing. Evarts brought out, by the statements of senators, that it was not expected that the law would prevent Johnson from removing hold-over secretaries.

The prosecution also charged a misdemeanor in the appointment of Thomas as secretary of war *ad interim*. The question was thus raised whether the President had the power to evade the advisory right of the Senate by repeated *ad interim* appointments. It is probable that the President had not the right to make such *ad interim* appointments, but he did not claim such power, for he nominated Thomas Ewing for the office the day after Stanton's removal.

As the case of the prosecution had weakened as the trial progressed, it was thought best to take the first vote on the article of the charges most likely to result in conviction. This was the eleventh, which combined a charge of attempting to defeat the Tenure of Office Act with a charge of a general purpose of defeating congressional reconstruction. Thus it combined the charge of

[15] The ablest argument on Johnson's behalf was that of William M. Evarts. See *ibid.*, 322–323. Evarts's *Arguments and Speeches* have been edited by his son, Sherman Evarts. There is a life of Evarts by B. Dyer.

misdemeanor in the narrow legal sense with a charge of misdemeanor in the broadest sense. Hence it seemed likely to unite all
who thought that Johnson should be removed on any view of the
case whatsoever. The vote on the article stood 35 for conviction
and 19 for acquittal. As a vote of two thirds was necessary for
conviction, the impeachment had failed. The margin by which
conviction had been defeated, however, was probably not as narrow
as the figures seem to indicate, for it is believed that two senators
who voted for conviction would have cast their ballots for acquittal
if such action had been necessary to prevent conviction. Seven
of the senators who voted for acquittal were Republicans.

The acquittal was due to the feeling that it would be a mistake
to convict a President for merely differing from Congress in judgment and political opinions; and the feeling that the public would
not sustain such a verdict. Each senator was allowed to file his
opinion on the case, and that of Senator Trumbull was an able
statement of this view: "Once set the example of impeaching a
President for what, when the excitement of the hour shall have
subsided, will be regarded as insufficient causes . . . and no future
President will be safe who happens to differ with a majority of the
House and two-thirds of the Senate on any measure deemed by
them important, particularly if of a political character. Blinded by
partisan zeal, with such an example before them they will not
scruple to remove out of the way any obstacle to the accomplishment of their purposes, and what then becomes of the checks and
balances of the Constitution, so carefully devised, and so vital to its
perpetuity?" [16]

The acquittal of President Johnson thus became a precedent
against impeachment on political grounds. While the tendency to
give to the term "misdemeanor" a wider significance than its strict
legal meaning was not checked, and perhaps was even advanced, it
became more than ever evident that this wider significance would
be restricted by public opinion to offenses against ethical propriety.

[16] Quoted by Dunning, *Essays*, 300–301. Dunning adds the comment: "If
Andrew Johnson had been convicted on a direct presentation of the question here
raised, the co-ordination of the departments in the American system would have
been a thing of the past."—*Ibid.*, 290. Quoted by permission of The Macmillan
Company.

Later cases have confirmed this tendency, which may now be said to have crystallized into an accepted principle.[17]

JUDICIAL INTERPRETATIONS

Under Lincoln the Supreme Court underwent a rapid renewal of personnel. There had been two such periods previously; between 1804 and 1811 five new justices were appointed in a total of seven, while between 1829 and 1837 six were appointed newly in a total of nine. Lincoln appointed five new men.[18] Lincoln like Jackson appointed a chief justice. Under Jackson Roger B. Taney had been elevated to the position. When he died, in October, 1864, Lincoln appointed Salmon P. Chase, who had served in his cabinet as secretary of the treasury.

With the exception of Chase, Lincoln's new men were Republicans, and, of course, opposed to slavery. If the war and the thirteenth, fourteenth, and fifteenth amendments, had not in effect reversed the Dred Scott decision, the new court would undoubtedly have done so, as predicted by Lincoln himself after the famous decision of Taney. Chase was of Democratic antecedents, and tended to construe the fundamental law strictly, as well as to oppose slavery.

During the war itself several important cases arose which involved "political" issues. For the most part, the court sought to avoid any conflict in these matters either with Congress or the President. The *ex parte* Merryman case was a notable exception. The Prize Cases of 1863 afforded a typical example of the policy of the court to avoid interference with the coordinate branches of the government wherever these branches possessed discretionary power, and to construe this discretion very liberally. Thus, in February, 1864, the court refused to entertain the appeal to Vallandigham from a military commission, on the ground that there

---

[17] Hockett, *Con. Hist.*, I, 314. *Cf.* David Y. Thomas, "The Law of Impeachment in the United States."

[18] Daniel died May 30, 1860; McLean, April 4, 1861; Taney, Oct. 12, 1864; Catron, May 30, 1865. Campbell resigned when his state (Alabama) seceded in 1861. Lincoln's appointees were Samuel F. Miller (Iowa), Noah H. Swayne (Ohio), David Davis (Illinois), Salmon P. Chase (Ohio), and Stephen J. Field (California), all between 1862 and 1864.

was no legal method of effecting such an appeal—a purely technical ground.

The decision in the Milligan case, after Chase's accession, and some other decisions rendered at about the same time, seemed to indicate that the court, now that the war was over, might "put the brakes" on the process of congressional reconstruction. Such were the apparent tendencies in Cummings v. Missouri, and in re Garland. The Missouri constitution of 1864 excluded rebels and sympathizers from office and from the practice of the professions. These provisions the court held to be *ex post facto*.[19] The Garland case involved the question of the constitutionality of the test oath provided by Congress for attorneys practicing before the Supreme Court. Garland had been engaged in such practice before the war, and since the war had been pardoned by the President. The court held that the power of Congress to prescribe the qualifications of attorneys did not give it a means of punishing misdoers beyond the reach of the executive pardon.[20] The public expectation was aroused that the court would probably rule that the reconstruction acts were unconstitutional and void, if cases involving them were brought before it.

This opportunity was presented in the case of Mississippi v. Johnson. A motion was made on behalf of the State of Mississippi for leave to file a bill praying the court to enjoin perpetually Andrew Johnson and District Commander Ord from executing the reconstruction acts. The petition pleaded that the acts were unconstitutional. Instead of discussing whether this plea was correct or not, however, the court avoided all discussion of constitutionality and considered merely whether it had power to enjoin the President. It declared the application to be without precedent, although occasions had not been wanting, which fact indicated that it was the general judgment of the legal profession that no such application should be entertained.

"The Congress is the legislative department of the government; the President is the executive department. Neither can be restrained

---

[19] 4 Wallace 277 (1867). See Thomas Barclay, "The Test Oath for the Clergy in Missouri"; F. W. Lehman, "Edward Bates and the Test Oath."
[20] 4 Wallace 333 (1867).

in its action by the judicial department; though the acts of both, when performed, are, in proper cases, subject to its cognizance." The impropriety of such interference was clearly to be seen upon consideration of the possible consequences. If the injunction were allowed, and the President refused to obey it, the court would be without power to enforce process against him. If the President complied, on the other hand, and refused to execute the acts of Congress, he might be subjected to impeachment for obeying the court. "We are fully satisfied that this court has no jurisdiction of a bill to enjoin the President in the performance of his official duties." [21]

The reconstruction acts had been passed within three months after the Milligan decision. The setting up under these acts of military tribunals in the South was directly contrary to the decision, and seemed to be a defiance of the court on the part of Congress. The court had shown sensitiveness to public opinion, and the Milligan decision had been rendered just when the dislike of military courts was most pronounced. In spite of the challenge of Congress, the court took pains to avoid becoming involved in a dispute with the other departments, as the decision in Mississippi v. Johnson shows.

The game was not over, however, for the State of Georgia presently sought to restrain, through court action, Secretary of War Stanton from enforcing the reconstruction acts within its borders. The court now held, however, that as the secretary of war was the subordinate of the President, an injunction against him would be the equivalent of one against his chief.[22]

It is evident that the court avoided a discussion of the constitutionality of the reconstruction acts because it was not prepared to interfere with measures which such a discussion might have required it to hold unconstitutional. It did not follow that, if it believed in the constitutionality of the acts, it would have refrained from a decision to that effect, since in that event there would have been no need of interfering with their enforcement. In later times, indeed, the court entertained an application for an injunction

[21] 4 Wallace 475 (1867). Extract in Johnson, 547–550.
[22] Georgia v. Stanton, 6 Wallace 50 (1867).

against an official of the cabinet, because it was able to deny the application on the ground that the law which the official was enforcing was constitutional.[23]

The opponents of congressional reconstruction made nevertheless one more effort. For the protection of federal officials engaged in the reconstruction program, Congress, in 1867, had extended the appellate jurisdiction of the Supreme Court to all habeas corpus cases arising under United States law.[24] McCardle, a Mississippi editor, arrested under the reconstruction acts, sought under this provision to bring before the court the legality of his arrest, which involved the constitutionality of the acts.[25] It now seemed that the court would be compelled to face the issue; but friends of military reconstruction, fearing a ruling against the acts, especially when a motion to dismiss McCardle's appeal was denied, hurried through the House a repeal of the habeas corpus provision before the court could try the case and give a decision.[26] The Senate concurred, and the judges dismissed the cause for want of jurisdiction.

The case of Texas v. White, already discussed in part, did not require the expression of a direct opinion as to whether the reconstruction acts were constitutional or not. It did require the court to determine whether Texas, pending the readmission of her congressmen, was a state of the Union in the sense of the constitutional provision giving the Supreme Court original jurisdiction in suits in which a state is a party. The decision, nevertheless, was, as Professor Dunning says, "a substantial justification of the course through which Congress had reorganized the South. This discussion was probably better as politics than as law; its chief significance was in the evidence it gave that the court would recognize and not seek to interfere with the *faits accomplis* of congressional policy."[27]

The decision accepted the view of Congress that the governments

[23] Rhode Island v. Palmer, 253 U. S. 350 (1920).

[24] *U. S. Stat. at Large*, XIV, 385. See discussion in Warren, 464 *et seq.*, and Randall, *Civil War*, 804–805.

[25] 6 Wallace 318 (1867).

[26] *Cong. Globe*, 40 Cong., 2 sess., I, 478 *et seq.* On the attitude of Congress at this time, see *supra*, Chap. XV, note 29 and accompanying text.

[27] William A. Dunning, *Reconstruction, Political and Economic*, 258. Quoted by permission of Harper & Brothers.

established under authority of the President were provisional; that the obligation to "guarantee a republican form of government" to each state was primarily a duty of Congress; that "republican form of government" now meant one in which blacks were not disfranchised. "Nothing in the case before us," said the decision, "requires the court to pronounce judgment upon the constitutionality of any particular provision of these acts." [28]

LEGAL TENDER CASES

Among the measures indicating the centralizing and nationalizing tendencies of the period and affording evidence of the new consciousness of national sovereignty, most striking were the legal tender acts and the decisions growing out of them. The first legal tender act was passed in 1862. The income from war taxation was proving to be insufficient to meet the immediate need of large sums. The act therefore provided for the issue of bills of credit—government notes, later known as "greenbacks"—to be used as money, and they were made legal tender by the terms of the statute. They presently began to depreciate in value, and were far below par when the war ended. Hence the plans of the government for their retirement were met by a popular demand that they be continued as a permanent part of the national money system, and Congress was slow to provide for their retirement in the face of such opinion.

Chase, as secretary of the treasury, had advocated the issue of the notes, although he feared the evils of a depreciated currency, and regarded the plan as an expedient to be resorted to temporarily, and only from necessity. When the war was over, as chief justice he felt that the court should correct the policy of Congress and the tendency to perpetuate the paper as a part of the circulating medium. In the case of Bronson v. Rodes,[29] the court held that it would enforce a contract providing specifically for payment in coin, thus withdrawing the debtor's privilege of tendering the government notes in such cases. Then the case of Hepburn v. Griswold arose.[30]

[28] See W. W. Pierson, Jr., "Texas v. White."
[29] 7 Wallace 229 (1869).
[30] 8 Wallace 603.

The case came up first in 1867, but the decision was not announced until early in 1870. Chase and the majority held that Congress had not authorized the note issues to be used as legal tender in the case of debts contracted before the statute was passed. Chase argued that such an authorization would impair the obligation of contracts, and, employing his Democratic principles of strict construction, he held that no such power had been given to Congress. It had been specifically forbidden to the states, and no powers were to be inferred as resulting from the general nature of the government.

Chase's opinion was directly in line with Jeffersonian strict construction; but serious practical difficulties appeared at once. The railroads, for example, demanded to know how they were to pay interest on antebellum bonds in gold, while collecting their revenues in paper. Nor was it the capitalistic interests alone which suffered, for the same hardship was inflicted, for example, on widows who were unfortunate enough to be burdened with antebellum mortgages on their little properties.

Such conditions led to a rather general hope that the decision would be reversed, and the reversal came as the direct consequence of a partial change in the personnel of the court. Two new judges were appointed by President Grant soon after the decision was rendered in the Hepburn case. One of these took the place of a justice who had resigned, and the other filled a vacancy existing at the time of the decision. The two new judges, with the three who had dissented in the earlier decision, now made up a majority of the court, and the reversal came in the case of Knox *v.* Lee.[31]

The new decision recognized in Congress "that general power over currency which has always been an acknowledged attribute of sovereignty in every other civilized country than our own." It asserts the doctrine of resultant powers, first set forth by Hamilton in the bank opinion of 1790: "It is allowable to group together any number of [specific powers] and infer from them all that the power claimed has been conferred." Thus through legislation paper can

---

[31] 12 Wallace 457 (1871). Extract in Commager, II, 64–67. Grant's new appointments gave rise to the charge that he packed the court. See Boudin, *Govt. by Judiciary*, II, Chap. XXV.

be made legal tender even where the obligation of a contract is impaired. Presumably even a contract providing specifically for payment in gold may thus be set aside.

A few years later, in the case of Juilliard *v.* Greenman [32] the same doctrine was repeated and elaborated: "The exercise of this power not being prohibited to Congress by the Constitution, it is included in the power expressly granted to borrow money on the credit of the United States. . . . Congress as the legislature of a sovereign nation, being expressly empowered by the Constitution to lay and collect taxes, etc. . . . and the power to make the notes of the government a legal tender in the payment of private debts being one of the powers belonging to sovereignty in other civilized nations, and not expressly withheld from Congress by the Constitution; we are irresistibly impelled to the conclusion that the impressing upon the treasury notes of the United States the quality of being a legal tender in the payment of private debts is an appropriate means, conducive and plainly adapted to the execution of the undoubted powers of Congress."

This reasoning may be summarized by saying that the power to issue legal tender paper is implied in express powers, and the *validity* of the *implication* rests, in these decisions, on the nature of sovereignty as exemplified in the political world generally.

THE UNDOING OF RECONSTRUCTION [33]

In 1870 the triumph of the congressional policy seemed complete. It was confidently maintained by the nationalizing school that the war amendments had effected a complete revolution in our constitutional jurisprudence by transferring from the states to the United States the duty of protecting all of the fundamental rights of citizens. The enforcement acts rested on this theory. Yet soon after the decision in Texas *v.* White the court shattered the theory of the nationalists in its judgment in the Slaughter House Cases, and foreshadowed the judicial nullification of the laws to give effect to it.

The Slaughter House Cases were decided April 14, 1873.[34] By a

[32] 110 U. S. 421 (1884).
[33] William A. Dunning, "The Undoing of Reconstruction."
[34] 16 Wallace 36. Extract in Johnson, 562–571, and Commager, II, 71–75.

vote of five to four, the court declared that the war amendments narrowed the powers of the states in specific ways, but did not change the fundamental character of the Union as a dual system with powers distributed between the states and the United States. The privileges and immunities of citizens of the United States, referred to in the fourteenth amendment, were held to be certain particular rights arising under specific provisions of the fundamental law. These only were the *rights of citizens of the United States*, and these only could the United States protect. Civil rights in general remained under control of the states as had been the case from the beginning.[35]

In the case in question a law of Louisiana had created a monopoly of the business of slaughtering cattle in the City of New Orleans, and suit was brought by persons who claimed that the act violated the fourteenth amendment. John A. Campbell, who had resigned his seat on the Supreme Bench of the United States when his state seceded in 1861, was one of the attorneys for the slaughter house companies.[36] He argued that the state law imposed servitude on the plaintiffs through restrictions on the use of their property, abridged their privileges and immunities as citizens of the United States, denied them the equal protection of the laws, and deprived them of their property without due process of law. He

[35] To illustrate: in the later case of United States *v.* Cruikshank (*post*) the court ruled that the right to assemble existed long before the Constitution was adopted, hence was not a right pertaining to United States citizenship, *but* that the right to assemble *in order to petition Congress*, or for anything else connected with powers and duties of the national government, is a right pertaining to United States citizenship.

[36] John Archibald Campbell was a native of Georgia. He was appointed to a cadetship at West Point by John C. Calhoun while the latter was secretary of war, but resigned on account of the death of his father. He practiced law successfully in Alabama and served for a while in the legislature. He was appointed to the United States Supreme Bench in 1853, upon the death of McKinley. At that time the *New York Times* commented: "His professional learning is said to be vast and his industry very great. Outside his profession he is most liberally cultivated and, in this respect, ranks beside Story. . . . His mind is singularly analytical. . . . His character is of the best stamp, modest, amiable, gentle, strictly temperate, and inflexibly just."

Campbell was a staunch defender of state's rights, but not a secessionist. He despaired of preserving the Union after Lincoln's election, but did not believe that that event justified a dissolution of the Union. When his state seceded he believed it his duty to follow; hence he resigned from the bench on April 26, 1861. There is a life of Campbell by Henry G. Connor.

did not think that the state's police power warranted the creation of the monopoly. His argument rested upon the acceptance of the nationalist interpretation of the fourteenth amendment. Said he: The "national principle has been indefinitely enlarged. The tie between the United States and every citizen in every part of its jurisdiction has been made intimate and to the same extent the Confederate features of the Government have been obliterated. The States, with their connection with the citizens, are placed under the oversight and enforcing hand of Congress. The purpose is manifest to establish, through the whole jurisdiction of the United States, one people. . . .

"Those who deprive the first clause of its validity, and demand an interpretation which would leave the State governments in possession of their powers over persons and property unimpaired, place a stigma upon the authors of the article."

One's surprise at such an argument on the tongue of a loyal southerner is lessened when one bears in mind the fact that the law in question was a part of the legislative program of a corrupt carpetbag government against which Campbell sought to protect the people. For this purpose he seized the obvious weapon and argued that the power of the legislature was restricted by the amendment. He lived to rejoice over the rejection of his argument by the court, which at this crisis rendered a decision which did much to preserve the original concept of the nature of the Union as one of autonomous states.

The law rested, held Justice Miller, who delivered the opinion of the court, on the police power, one which was, from its very nature, incapable of any very exact definition or limitation. "The regulation of the place and manner of conducting the slaughtering of animals," however, "and the business of butchering within a city, and the inspection of the animals to be killed for meat, and of the meat afterwards, are among the most necessary and frequent exercises of this power." [37]

[37] Miller was born in Kentucky, but removed to Iowa because of anti-slavery principles. When appointed to the bench, his professional experience consisted of a decade of practice as a country physician and twelve years as a country lawyer. He was both a union man and a friend of the autonomous status of the states. There is a biography by Charles N. Gregory.

By the first section of the fourteenth amendment "the distinction between citizenship of the United States and the citizenship of a state is clearly recognized and established." This distinction is of great weight, because the next paragraph of the same section "speaks only of privileges and immunities of citizens of the United States, and does not speak of those of citizens of the several States. The argument, however, in favor of the plaintiffs rests wholly on the assumption that the citizenship is the same, and [that] the privileges and immunities guaranteed by the clause are the same. . . .

"If, then, there is a difference between the privileges and immunities belonging to a citizen of the United States as such, and those belonging to the citizen of the State as such, the latter must rest for their security and protection where they have heretofore rested; for they are not embraced by this paragraph of the amendment. With the exception of a few express limitations which the Federal Constitution imposed upon the States—such, for instance, as the prohibition against ex post facto laws, bills of attainder, and laws impairing the obligation of contracts . . . the entire domain of the privileges and immunities of citizens of the States . . . lay [originally] within the constitutional and legislative power of the States, and without that of the Federal Government. Was it the purpose of the fourteenth amendment, by the simple declaration that no State should make or enforce any law which shall abridge the privileges and immunities of citizens of the United States, to transfer the security and protection of all the civil rights . . . from the States to the Federal Government? And where it is declared that Congress shall have the power to enforce that article, was it intended to bring within the power of Congress the entire domain of civil rights heretofore belonging exclusively to the States? . . .

"We are convinced that no such results were intended by the Congress which proposed these amendments, nor by the legislatures of the States which ratified them."

Although Miller mentioned, by way of illustration, a few of the privileges pertaining to federal citizenship, he declined to attempt an enumeration, saying "we may hold ourselves excused from defining the privileges and immunities of citizens of the United

States which no State can abridge, until some case involving those privileges may make it necessary to do so."

As to due process of law, the justice said: "under no construction of that provision which we have ever seen, or any that we deem admissible, can the restraint imposed by the State of Louisiana . . . be held to be a deprivation.[38] Similarly, the "equal protection" clause was not infracted. "We doubt very much whether any action of a State not directed by way of discrimination against the negroes as a class, or on account of their race, will ever be held to come within the purview of" the provision that "no state shall deny to any person within its jurisdiction the equal protection of the laws." "It is so clearly a provision for that race and that emergency, that a strong case would be necessary for its application to any other. . . . We may safely leave that matter until Congress shall have exercised its power, or some case of State oppression, by denial of equal justice in its courts, shall have claimed a decision at our hands. We find no such case in the one before us." [39]

Justice Stephen J. Field wrote the principal dissenting opinion, contending that the monopoly created by the state law so far deprived free men in general of the liberty of pursuing the calling of their choice as to subject them to an unconstitutional degree of servitude.[40]

Following this decision many other cases arose calling for determination as to whether particular privileges were rights of United States citizens or not. Thus an Illinois woman sought in vain relief from a state law which excluded her from the practice of law. Another complained in vain because the law of her state denied

[38] See Edward S. Corwin, "The Doctrine of Due Process . . . before the Civil War."

[39] Miller was on dangerous ground in talking about the purpose of the framers of the fourteenth amendment. The "equal protection" clause was one of the new provisions upon which corporations learned to rely within the next few years. Cf. Marshall's rule of construction, supra, Chap. II. In United States v. Wong Kim Ark (169 U. S. 649. 1897) the court held, concerning the fourteenth amendment, "doubtless the intention of the Congress which framed and of the states which adopted this Amendment . . . must be sought in the words of the Amendment; and the debates in Congress are not admissible as evidence to control the meaning of those words." See W. L. Royall, "The Fourteenth Amendment and the Slaughter House Case."

[40] There is an excellent life of Field by Carl B. Swisher.

her the right to vote, the court assuring her that that right pertained to state citizenship, sex being a test not debarred by the Constitution of the United States.

In the case of United States v. Reese [41] decided in October, 1875, the court, now under Morrison R. Waite as chief justice, held that sections three and four of the Civil Rights Enforcement Act of May 31, 1870 were unconstitutional, because they did not strictly limit federal jurisdiction, in the protection of the right to vote, to cases where it had been denied by a state on grounds of race or color or previous condition of servitude. The objectionable provisions penalized inspectors in state elections for refusing to receive and count votes, and for obstructing any citizen in his attempt to vote. Thus again it was held that the fourteenth amendment did not authorize a general guardianship of citizens' rights. At statute extending so broadly to discriminations and obstructions of all types, the court held was not warranted by the enforcement clause of the fifteenth amendment. The care taken by the court in announcing this decision is indicated by the fact that it was not announced until fifteen months had elapsed after the hearing of the case. [42]

The case of the United States v. Cruikshank, [43] also decided in 1875, related to a massacre of Negroes in Louisiana. The court again held that some of the rights protected by the act of May 31, 1870 were not rights pertaining to United States citizenship, in particular, that it was not the duty or right of the government of the United States to protect its citizens against their fellow-citizens; this was the business of the state. The right to assemble and bear arms pertained to state citizenship, not to United States citizenship, and redress for violation must be sought in the courts of the state.

In Presser v. Illinois [44] the court held that while the second amendment concerning the bearing of arms is a limitation only on Congress, yet, since all citizens capable of bearing arms constitute the potential military force of the national government, states can-

[41] 92 U. S. 214 (1876).
[42] See discussion of these and other cases in Warren, II, *passim*.
[43] 92 U. S. 542.
[44] 116 U. S. 252 (1886).

not prohibit the people from keeping and bearing arms so as to deprive the United States of this resource.

In United States *v.* Harris [45] the conspiracy clause of the Ku Klux Act was held unconstitutional. A band of whites in Tennessee had taken a Negro from officers and abused him. The court held that under the amendments Congress was authorized to guarantee equality of civil rights against violation by a *state* or officers thereof, but not against violations by private individuals. In such cases redress must be sought in the state courts. The conspiracy clause of the Ku Klux Act was held to be void because it gave jurisdiction over such cases to the federal courts. The decision disposed of the theory that the *failure* of a state to protect Negroes in the enjoyment of equal rights was a *denial*, forbidden by the fourteenth amendment, and warranting interference on the part of the federal government.

The Civil Rights Cases arose under the act of 1875.[46] The court held that the rights mentioned in that act were not strictly civil rights, but social; in any case, that the federal government had no power concerning them, and that the legislation was unconstitutional. The enforcement clause of the fourteenth amendment, said Justice Bradley, "does not invest Congress with power to legislate upon subjects that are within the domain of state legislation, but to provide modes of relief against state legislation or state action" contrary to the amendment.

THE END OF AN ERA

These decisions left the fate of the Negro largely to the tender mercy of the state in which he resided. In time the southern states even found means of depriving him of the ballot without violating the fifteenth amendment. His chief protection on the part of the federal government, as it turned out, was to arise from the clauses which forbid states to deprive any person of life, liberty or property without due process of law, or to deny to any person the equal protection of the laws. Much could be written on the appli-

[45] 106 U. S. 629 (1882).
[46] United States *v.* Stanley, 109 U. S. 3 (1883). For references on the whole subject of citizens' rights see *supra*, Chap. VIII, note 48.

cation of these provisions to the Negro, but this discussion belongs in a later volume. The point with which we are now concerned is that the decisions of the Supreme Court in the seventies and early eighties largely undid the attempts of the radicals to make the federal government the special guardian of the rights and interests of the freedmen.

The decisions concerning the status and rights of freedmen and the powers of states were symbols, moreover, of the end of the effort to nationalize the Union and make Congress the supreme power. The radicals were thwarted in part by President Johnson's vigorous defense of state's rights and the executive prerogative and in part by the court's maintenance of the theory of distributed powers. Judicial decisions such as that in the Slaughter House Cases made it clear that the governmental system of the United States was still dual; that there were still two spheres, one of the state and one of the Union; and that while the former had been contracted and the latter enlarged, the old principle of distribution was intact. It had been the antebellum custom to speak of sovereignty as divided between the two sets of governments, and to regard the federal and state governments as sovereign each within its own sphere. The phraseology of divided sovereignty had become so habitual that the courts continued to use it; but with the war it ceased to be accurate, if it ever had been. States still have their rights, removed as always beyond the power of invasion by the federal government; but sovereignty is to be regarded as residing in the people of the nation. It remains correct, however, to speak of dual governments and distributed powers.

The congressional radicals represented the influence of the rising industrialism if the Northeast, which had inherited the philosophy of Alexander Hamilton. It had long contested the control of the agrarian element of the population, which had united South and West on various occasions, notably under Andrew Jackson, in opposition to its land and tariff policies. During and after the war it gained the support of the Northwest against disunion, slavery, and the danger of "rebel" rule if Johnson's mild reconstruction plans were carried out. Under cover of this alliance on issues growing out of the war, the industrial party sought to obtain protection for the future from vexatious regulation by state legislatures controlled by popular majorities.

As Roscoe Conkling explained later, the radicals aimed through the fourteenth amendment "to curb the many who would do to the few as they would not have the few do to them." Stripped of the language of the golden rule, this statement means that the amendment was intended to empower the federal government to protect corporations against the state governments. The protection was to be obtained through the due process and equal protection clauses.

The significance of these provisions was not perceived by either counsel or court in the Slaughter House Cases, in which the chief emphasis was placed on the privileges and immunities clause. The argument of Campbell did, indeed, rest partly upon the due process provision; he reasoned that the Louisiana statute deprived the monopoly company's competitors of liberty. But not for another dozen years did lawyers and judges begin seriously to develop the implications of the clause as applied to corporations as well as individuals.[47] The power which this provision gave to the federal courts in restraining states was rapidly unfolded by judicial decisions after about 1886, and in the perspective of a half-century appears to be the chief achievement of the radicals in their efforts to nationalize the United States and to centralize power in the federal government.

But this story belongs to a new era in which questions arising from the new industrialism became uppermost in men's minds. The respective powers of states and federal government continued truly to be significant, as well as the clash of sectional interests; but the new era is distinguished by the clash of capital and labor, and other questions far more national in scope than the old issues, affecting classes even more than sections. They were, moreover, confronted by a people with a changed psychology.

The close of the era of reconstruction is therefore a fitting point at which to terminate the present volume. In doing so it should

[47] Conkling's statement was made in 1882, when he was acting as attorney in San Mateo County v. S. P. R. R. (116 U. S. 138). He produced the unpublished journal of the joint committee on reconstruction, of which he had been a member, to support his assertion.

be noted, by way of summary, that during the first century of independence certain fundamental constitutional problems were
settled. The country began its life under the Constitution with the
nature of the Union an open question, and with no agreement as to
where final authority rested to maintain the scheme of distributed
powers. The lack of agreement at these two essential points was,
at bottom, the cause of most of the difficulties experienced in making the system work successfully. Perhaps it would have been impossible at the outset to reach agreement. That the system did
work was due primarily to the universal love for the Constitution
professed and undoubtedly felt by those who by no means agreed
as to its meaning. It worked consequently, but with great friction,
with incessant disputes and bitter feelings over constitutional theories behind which were the conflicting interests of states and sections: it even survived the supreme test of war.

Were the courts or the states the final judges of the distribution
of powers? The debate over this issue began with Hamilton and
Jefferson and did not cease during the whole of the antebellum
period. Did the United States form a sovereign nation, or a confederation of sovereignties? That question, akin to the preceding,
likewise found no answer which commanded general acceptance.
In practice Jefferson's idea that new powers should be conferred
upon the central government only by amendment was eclipsed by
Hamilton's principle of implied powers—a device which certainly
removed a popular check upon the development of centralized
government and facilitated the gaining of control by interested
minority groups. In practice, also, notwithstanding all adverse
criticism, the Supreme Court became established as the actual arbiter, short of force, of questions concerning the distribution of
powers. Even when composed of judges most sympathetic with
the claims of states, as under Taney, this rôle of ultimate arbiter was
not surrendered. Moreover, even in the period when it was most
responsive to popular, democratic opinion, and hence most disposed
to curb corporations in the public interest, the court was principally
responsible for interpretations of the law which led "big business"
to look to the general government as its friend, rather than to the
states.

The tendencies manifested in the antebellum period were brought to a head by the war. From the conflict the United States emerged a nation—no longer even in men's theorizing a confederation. States still possessed autonomy in purely local affairs, but of questions concerning their powers, as well as of the constitutionality of acts of Congress, the Supreme Court was accepted as judge, although some continued to begrudge it these functions. With these fundamentals settled and the fourteenth amendment added to the Constitution, the era which now opened was a new one. The country entered its second century of independent existence with a substantially different set of problems and a changed constitutional system.

LIST OF REFERENCES

Adams, Alice Dana, *The Neglected Period of Anti-Slavery in America, 1808–1831.* Radcliffe College *Monographs*, No. 14. Boston, 1908.

Adams, Charles Francis, "John Quincy Adams and Martial Law." Massachusetts Historical Society *Proceedings*, 2d ser., XV, 436–478 (1901–1902).

——, ed., *Memoirs of John Quincy Adams.* 12 v. Philadelphia, 1874–1877.

Adams, John Quincy, *Memoirs.* See Adams, Charles Francis, editor.

Alexander, D. S., "John W. Taylor, New York's Speaker of the House of Representatives." *Quarterly Journal* of the New York State Historical Association, I, 4–37 (January, 1920).

Altizer, P. J., "Jurisdiction of the Federal Courts Based upon Diversity of Citizenship. . . ." *American Law Review*, XLIII, 409–436 (June, 1909).

Ambler, Charles H., *Thomas Ritchie: A Study in Virginia Politics.* Richmond, 1913.

American Nation. See Hart, Albert Bushnell, editor.

Ames, Herman V., "J. C. Calhoun's Connection with the Secession Movement of 1850." American Antiquarian Society *Proceedings*, n. s., XXVIII, 19–50 (April, 1918).

——, *Proposed Amendments to the Constitution . . . during the First Century of Its History.* American Historical Association *Report* for 1896, II.

——, *State Documents on Federal Relations, 1789–1861.* New York, 1907.

Annals of the Congress of the United States. 42 v. Washington, 1834–1856.

Anonymous, *Defense of a Liberal Construction of the Powers of Congress as to Internal Improvements, etc.* Philadelphia, 1831.

Attorneys-General, *Official Opinions of the Attorneys-General of the United States advising the Presidents and Heads of Departments in relation to their Official Duties.* 38 v. (through 1937). Washington, 1852–.

Auchampaugh, Philip Gerald, ed., "Black, Thompson, and Stanton in 1864." *Tyler's Quarterly Historical and Genealogical Magazine*, X, 237–250 (April, 1929).

——, *James Buchanan and His Cabinet on the Eve of Secession.* Privately printed, 1926.

Bancroft, Frederic, *Calhoun and the South Carolina Nullification Movement*. Baltimore, 1928.

——, "The Final Efforts at Compromise, 1860–1861." *Political Science Quarterly*, VI, 401–423 (Sept., 1891).

——, *The Life of William H. Seward*. 2 v. New York, 1900.

Barclay, Thomas, "The Test Oath for the Clergy in Missouri." *Missouri Historical Review*, XVIII, 345–381 (April, 1924).

Beale, Howard K., *The Critical Year: A Study of Andrew Johnson and Reconstruction*. New York, 1930.

Beard, Charles A., *Economic Origins of Jeffersonian Democracy*. New York, 1915.

Benton, Thomas H., *Thirty Years View. . . .* 2 v. New York, 1854–1856.

Berdahl, Clarence A., "War Powers of the Executive in the United States." University of Illinois *Studies in the Social Sciences*, IX, Nos. 1 and 2. Urbana, 1921.

Biddle, George W., "Constitutional Development in the United States as influenced by Chief-Justice Taney," in *Constitutional History of the United States as Seen in the Development of American Law. (A Course of Lectures before the Political Science Association of the University of Michigan.)* New York, 1889.

Bigelow, John, ed., *The Complete Works of Benjamin Franklin*. 10 v. New York, 1905–1907.

Binney, Horace, *The Privilege of the Writ of Habeas Corpus under the Constitution*. Philadelphia, 1862–1865.

Boucher, Chauncey S., *The Nullification Controversy in South Carolina*. Chicago, 1916.

——, "The Secession and Co-Operation Movements in South Carolina, 1848 to 1852." Washington University *Studies, Humanistic Series*, V, 67–138 (April, 1918).

——, "South Carolina and the South on the Eve of Secession, 1852 to 1860." Washington University *Studies, Humanistic Series*, VI, 79–144 (April, 1919).

Boudin, Louis B., *Government by Judiciary*. 2 v. New York, 1932.

Bowers, Claude G., *The Tragic Era: The Revolution after Lincoln*. New York, 1929.

Boyd, William K., "North Carolina on the Eve of Secession." American Historical Association *Report* for 1910, 165–178.

Bradford, Gamaliel, "Edward M. Stanton." *Atlantic Monthly*, CXVI, 180–191 (Aug., 1915).

Brigance, William N., "Jeremiah Black and Andrew Johnson." *Mississippi Valley Historical Review*, XIX, 205–218 (Sept., 1932).

——, *Jeremiah Sullivan Black: a Defender of the Constitution and the Ten Commandments*. University of Pennsylvania, 1934.

Brooks, Robert Preston, "Howell Cobb and the Crisis of 1850." *Mississippi Valley Historical Review*, IV, 279–298 (Dec., 1917).

Brown, Everett S., ed., *The Missouri Compromises and Presidential Politics, 1820–1825, from the Letters of William Plumer, Jr.* Missouri Historical Society *Publications*, XI. St. Louis, 1926.

Buchanan, James, *Works of.* See Moore, John Bassett, editor.

Burgess, John W., *Political Science and Comparative Constitutional Law.* Boston, 1893.

Burns, Edward McNall, *James Madison, Philosopher of the Constitution.* New Brunswick, N. J., 1938.

Burroughs, W. G., "Oberlin's Part in the Slavery Conflict." Ohio State Archaeological and Historical Society *Publications*, XX, 269–334 (July, 1911).

Callender, E. B., *Thaddeus Stevens, Commoner.* Boston, 1882.

Carson, Hampton L., *History of The Supreme Court of the United States, with Biographies of all the Chief and Associate Justices, 1790–1902.* 2 v. Philadelphia, 1902.

Catterall, Helen T., ed., *Judicial Cases Concerning American Slavery and the Negro.* 5 v. Washington, 1926–1937.

——, "Some Antecedents of the Dred Scott Case." *American Historical Review*, XXX, 56–71 (Oct., 1924).

Chadsey, Charles E., *The Struggle between President Johnson and Congress over Reconstruction.* Columbia University *Studies in History, Economics, and Public Law*, VIII, No. 1. New York, 1896.

Chase, Salmon P., *Diary and Correspondence.* American Historical Association *Report* for 1902, II.

Chittenden, L. E., *A Report of the Debates and Proceedings in the Secret Sessions of the Conference Convention, for Proposing Amendments to the Constitution of the United States, Held at Washington, D. C., in February, 1861.* New York, 1864.

Cobb, Howell, "Correspondence." See Toombs, Robert.

Cochran, W. C., *The Western Reserve and the Fugitive Slave Law.* Western Reserve Historical Society *Collections*, CI. Cleveland, 1920.

Cole, Arthur C., "Lincoln and the American Tradition of Civil Liberty." Illinois State Historical Society *Journal*, XIX, 102–114 (Oct., 1926–Jan., 1927).

——, "The South and the Right of Secession in the Early Fifties." *Mississippi Valley Historical Review*, I, 376–399 (Dec., 1914).

——, *The Whig Party in the South.* Washington, 1913.

Coleman, William C., "The Fifteenth Amendment." *Columbia Law Review*, X, 416–450 (May, 1910).

Collins, Charles W., *The Fourteenth Amendment and the States.* Boston, 1912.

Commager, Henry S., *Documents of American History.* 2 v. in one. New York, 1934.

Conger, John L., "South Carolina and the Early Tariffs." *Mississippi Valley Historical Review,* V, 415–433 (March, 1919).

Congressional Debates. See *Register of Debates in Congress.*

Congressional Globe, containing the Debates and Proceedings. 108 v. Washington, 1834–1873.

Connor, Henry G., *John Archibald Campbell, Associate Justice of the United States Supreme Court, 1853–1861.* Boston, 1920.

Corwin, Edward S., "The Doctrine of Due Process . . . before the Civil War." *Harvard Law Review,* XXIV, 366–385, 460–479 (March-April, 1911).

——, "The Dred Scott Decision in the Light of Contemporary Legal Doctrines." *American Historical Review,* XVII, 52–69 (Oct., 1911).

——, *National Supremacy.* New York, 1913.

Crallé, Richard, ed., *Works of John C. Calhoun.* 6 v. New York, 1853–1855.

Curtis, Benjamin R., *The Executive Power.* Boston, 1862.

Curtis, Benjamin R., Jr., ed., *Memoir of Benjamin R. Curtis.* 2 v. Boston, 1879.

Curtis, George Ticknor, *Life of Daniel Webster.* 2 v. New York, 1870.

——, *Life of James Buchanan.* 2 v. New York, 1883.

David, C. W. A., "The Fugitive Slave Law of 1793." *Journal of Negro History,* IX, 18–23 (Jan., 1924).

Davis, Jefferson, *Rise and Fall of the Confederate Government.* 2 v. New York, 1881.

Davis, John P., *Corporations: A Study of the Origin and Development of Great Business Combinations and their Relation to the Authority of the State.* 2 v. New York, 1905.

Davis, William Watson, "Federal Enforcement Acts," in Dunning, William A., *Studies in Southern History and Politics,* 202–228.

Denham, R. N., Jr., "An Historical Development of the Contract Theory in the Dartmouth College Case." *Michigan Law Review,* VII, 201–225 (Jan., 1909).

Denman, Clarence P., *The Secession Movement in Alabama.* Montgomery, 1933.

DeWitt, David M., *The Impeachment and Trial of Andrew Johnson.* New York, 1903.

Dodd, William E., "Chief Justice Marshall and Virginia." *American Historical Review*, XII, 776–797 (July, 1907).

——, "John Taylor 'of Caroline.'" *The Nation*, XCII, 316 (March 30, 1911).

——, ed., "John Taylor, Prophet of Secession." *John P. Branch Historical Papers for 1908*, 214–252. Randolph-Macon College, Ashland, Va., 1908.

Douglas, Stephen A., "The Dividing Line between Federal and Local Authority." *Harper's Magazine*, XIX, 519–537 (Sept., 1859).

Drell, Bernard, "John Taylor of Caroline and the Preservation of an Old Social Order." *The Virginia Magazine of History and Biography*, XLVI, 285–298 (Oct., 1938).

Dumond, Dwight L., *The Secession Movement*. New York, 1931.

——, ed., *Southern Editorials on Secession*. New York, 1931.

Dunning, William A., *The British Empire and the United States*. New York, 1914.

——, "The Constitution of the United States in the Civil War." *Political Science Quarterly*, I, 163–198 (June, 1886).

——, "Disloyalty in Two Wars." *American Historical Review*, XXIV, 625–630 (July, 1919).

——, *Essays on Reconstruction*. New York, 1910.

——, *Reconstruction, Political and Economic*. The American Nation, XXII.

——, *Studies in Southern History and Politics, Inscribed to William Archibald Dunning*. New York, 1914.

——, "The Undoing of Reconstruction." *Atlantic Monthly*, LXXXVIII, 437–449 (Oct., 1901).

Dyer, Brainerd, *The Public Career of William M. Evarts*. Berkeley, 1933.

Eggleston, J. D., "The Attitude of Virginia Leaders toward Slavery and Secession." *The Virginia Teacher*, XIII, Nos. 6–7 (Sept., Oct., 1932).

Elder, Jeannette, *The Constitutional Views of Judge Spencer Roane*. Manuscript thesis submitted for the degree of Master of Arts at The Ohio State University, 1934.

Evarts, Sherman, ed., *The Arguments and Speeches of William Maxwell Evarts*. 3 v. New York, 1919.

Everett, Edward, ed., *The Works of Daniel Webster*. 6 v. Boston, 1851.

Farrand, Max, *Records of the Federal Convention of 1787*. 3 v. New Haven, 1911.

Fertig, James W., *The Secession and Reconstruction of Tennessee.* Chicago, 1898.

Field, O. P., "The Doctrine of Political Questions in the Federal Courts." *American Law Review*, LVIII, 711–746 (Oct., 1924).

Finch, George A., "Superior Orders and War Crimes." *American Journal of International Law*, XV, 440–445 (July, 1921).

Fisher, Sydney George, "Suspension of the Writ of Habeas Corpus." *Political Science Quarterly*, III, 454–488 (Sept., 1888).

Flack, Horace E., *The Adoption of the Fourteenth Amendment.* Johns Hopkins University *Studies in Historical and Political Science*, extra volume XXVI. Baltimore, 1908.

Ford, Paul Leicester, ed., *The Writings of Thomas Jefferson.* 10 v. New York, 1892–1899.

Ford, Worthington C., and Hunt, Gaillard, eds., *Journals of the Continental Congress, 1774–1789.* 33 v. Washington, 1904–1936.

Fox, Dixon Ryan, ed., *Sources of Culture in the Middle West.* New York, [c1934].

Franklin, Benjamin, *Works of.* See Bigelow, John, editor.

Frasure, Carl M., "Charles Sumner and the Rights of the Negro." *Journal of Negro History*, XIII, 1–24 (April, 1928).

——, "Union Sentiment in Maryland, 1859–1861." *Maryland Historical Magazine*, XXIV, 210–224 (Sept., 1929).

Fuess, Claude M., *Daniel Webster.* Boston, 1930.

Garner, James W., "First Struggle over Secession in Mississippi." Mississippi Historical Society *Publications*, IV, 89–104 (1901).

Giddings, Joshua R., *History of the Rebellion.* New York, 1864.

Gildersleeve, B. L., *The Creed of the Old South.* Baltimore, 1915.

Gipson, Lawrence H., "The Statesmanship of President Johnson: A Study of the Presidential Reconstruction Policy." *Mississippi Valley Historical Review*, II, 363–383 (Dec., 1915).

Going, Charles B., *David Wilmot, Free-Soiler.* New York, 1924.

Gold, A. E., "Jurisdiction of the Supreme Court over Political Questions: What is a Political Question?" *Cornell Law Quarterly*, IX, 50–54 (Dec., 1923).

Gordy, John P., *Political History of the United States.* 4 v. (Only two published.) New York, 1908.

Gregory, Charles N., *Samuel Freeman Miller.* Iowa State Historical Society *Biographical Series.* Iowa City, 1907.

Guthrie, William D., *Fourteenth Article of Amendment to the Constitution of the United States.* Boston, 1898.

Hall, James P., "Free Speech in War Time." *Columbia Law Review* XXI, 526–537 (June, 1921).

Hamer, P. M., *The Secession Movement in South Carolina.* Allentown, Pa., 1918.

Hart, Albert Bushnell, ed., *The American Nation: A History from Original Sources.* 28 v. New York, 1904–1918.

——, *Slavery and Abolition. The American Nation,* XVI.

Hearon, Cleo, "The Struggle in Mississippi over the Compromise of 1850." Mississippi Historical Society *Publications,* XIV, 7–229 (1914).

Hill, F. T., *Decisive Battles of the Law.* New York, 1906.

——, "Impeachment of Andrew Johnson," in his *Decisive Battles of the Law,* 135–174.

Hockett, Homer Carey, *Constitutional History of the United States, 1776–1826.* New York, 1939.

——, "Rufus King and the Missouri Compromise." *Missouri Historical Review,* II, 211–220 (April, 1908).

——, *Western Influences on Political Parties to 1825.* Ohio State University *Contributions in History and Political Science,* No. 4. Columbus, 1917.

Hodder, Frank H., "Side Lights on the Missouri Compromises." American Historical Association *Report* for 1909, 153–161.

——, "Some Phases of the Dred Scott Case." *Mississippi Valley Historical Review,* XVI, 3–22 (June, 1929).

Houston, David F., *Critical Study of Nullification in South Carolina. Harvard Historical Studies,* III. New York, 1896.

Howe, Daniel W., *Political History of Secession, to the Beginning of the American Civil War.* New York, 1914.

Howell, Roger, *The Privileges and Immunities of State Citizenship.* Johns Hopkins University *Studies in Historical and Political Science,* XXXVI. Baltimore, 1918.

Hunt, Gaillard, *John C. Calhoun.* Philadelphia, 1908.

——, "The Impeachment of Andrew Johnson: The President's Defense." *Century Magazine,* LXXXV, 422–434 (Feb., 1913).

——, ed., *Writings of James Madison.* 9 v. New York, 1900–1910.

——, and Scott, James B., eds., *Debates in the Federal Convention of 1787.* Washington, 1920.

Hunt, T. P., *The Book of Wealth, in which it is Proved from the Bible, that it is the Duty of Every Man, to become Rich.* New York, 1836.

Hunter, M. H., "Early Regulation of Public Service Corporations." *American Economic Review,* VII, 569–581 (Sept., 1917).

Hurd, John Codman, *The Law of Freedom and Bondage in the United States.* 2 v. Boston, 1858–1862.

Jameson, John Franklin, ed., *Correspondence of John C. Calhoun.* American Historical Association *Report* for 1899, II.

——, "Studies in the History of the Federal Convention of 1787." American Historical Association *Report* for 1902, I, 89–167.

Jefferson, Thomas, *Writings of.* See Ford, P. L., editor, and Washington, H. A., editor.

Jervey, Theodore D., *Robert Y. Hayne and His Times.* New York, 1909.

Johnson, Allen, "The Constitutionality of the Fugitive Slave Acts." *Yale Law Journal,* XXXI, 161–182 (Dec., 1921).

——, *Readings in American Constitutional History, 1776–1876.* Boston, 1912.

——, *Stephen A. Douglas.* New York, 1908.

Joint Committee on Reconstruction, *Journal.* 63 Cong., 3 sess., *Sen. Doc. No. 711.*

——, *Report.* 39 Cong., 1 sess., *House Report No. 30.*

Judiciary Committee of the House of Representatives, *Impeachment Investigation—Testimony Taken before the Judiciary Committee of the House . . . in the Investigation of the Charges against Andrew Johnson.* 40 Cong., 1 sess., *House Report No. 7.*

Kendrick, Benjamin B., *The Journal of the Joint Committee of Fifteen on Reconstruction.* Columbia University *Studies in History, Economics, and Public Law,* LXII. New York, 1914.

King, Charles R., ed., *Life and Correspondence of Rufus King.* 6 v. New York, 1894–1900.

King, Rufus, *Life and Correspondence.* See King, Charles R., editor.

Klaus, Samuel, ed., *The Milligan Case.* New York, 1929.

Lehman, F. W., "Edward Bates and the Test Oath." Missouri Historical Society *Collections,* IV, 389–401 (1912–1913).

Lewis, William D., ed., *Great American Lawyers.* 8 v. Philadelphia, 1907–1909.

Lien, A. J., "Privileges and Immunities of Citizens of the United States." Columbia University *Studies in History,* etc., LIV, No. 1. New York, 1913.

Lincoln, Abraham, *Complete Works.* See Nicolay and Hay, editors.

Livermore, George, *Opinions of the Founders of the Republic on Negroes as Slaves, as Citizens, and as Soldiers.* Boston, 1862.

Long, Byron R., "Joshua Reed Giddings, a Champion of Political Freedom." Ohio State Archaeological and Historical Society *Publications,* XXVIII, 1–47 (Jan., 1919).

McCall, S. W., *Thaddeus Stevens.* Boston, [1900].

McCarthy, Charles H., *Lincoln's Plan of Reconstruction.* New York, 1901.

McClendon, R. Earl, "Status of the Ex-Confederate States as Seen in the Readmission of United States Senators." *American Historical Review*, XLI, 703–709 (July, 1936).

McCormac, E. I., "Justice Campbell and the Dred Scott Decision." *Mississippi Valley Historical Review*, XIX, 565–571 (March, 1933).

MacDonald, William, *Jacksonian Democracy. The American Nation*, XIII.

——, *Select Documents Illustrative of the History of the United States, 1776–1861.* New York, 1903.

——, *Select Statutes and Other Documents . . . 1861–1898.* New York, 1903.

McDougall, Marion G., *Fugitive Slaves.* Boston, 1891.

McKee, Jay W., *State Exclusion Laws.* Manuscript dissertation submitted for the degree of Doctor of Philosophy at The Ohio State University, 1935.

McLaughlin, Andrew C., *Constitutional History of the United States.* New York, 1935.

McMaster, John Bach, *History of the People of the United States.* 8 v. New York, 1883–1913.

McPherson, Edward, *Political History of the United States during the Great Rebellion.* New York, 1864.

——, *The Political History of the United States . . . during . . . Reconstruction. . . .* 2 edn. Washington, 1875.

Madison, James, *Letters and Other Writings* (Congress edn.). 4 v. Philadelphia, 1865.

——, *Writings of.* See Hunt, Gaillard, ed.

Malone, Dumas, *The Public Life of Thomas Cooper.* Durham, N. C., 1926.

——, "Thomas Cooper and the State Rights Movement in South Carolina, 1823–1830." *North Carolina Historical Review*, III, 184–197 (April, 1926).

Marshall, John, "Marshall-Story Correspondence." Massachusetts Historical Society *Proceedings*, second series, XIV, 324–360. Boston, 1901.

Marshall, John A., *The American Bastile: A History of the Illegal Arrests and Imprisonments of American Citizens during the Late Civil War.* Philadelphia, 1870.

Mathews, John M., "Legislative and Judicial History of the Fifteenth

Amendment." Johns Hopkins University *Studies in Historical and Political Science*, XXVII, Nos. 6–7. Baltimore, 1909.

Merriam, Charles E., "The Political Philosophy of John C. Calhoun," in Dunning, *Studies in Southern History and Politics*, 319–338.

Meyers, W. J., "The Privileges and Immunities of Citizens in the Several States." *Michigan Law Review*, I, 286–308 (Jan., 1903); 364–383 (Feb., 1903).

Mikell, William E., "Roger Brooke Taney," in William D. Lewis, ed., *Great American Lawyers*, IV, 77–194.

Miller, Alphonse B., *Thaddeus Stevens*. New York, 1939.

Miller, Marion Mills, ed., *Great Debates in American History*. 14 v. New York, 1913.

Milton, George Fort, *The Age of Hate: Andrew Johnson and the Radicals*. New York, 1930.

——, *The Eve of Conflict—Stephen A. Douglas and the Needless War*. Boston, 1934.

Monroe, James, "Correspondence." *William and Mary College Quarterly*, first series, X, 5–24 (July, 1901).

Moore, Blaine Free, "The Supreme Court and Unconstitutional Legislation." Columbia University *Studies in History*, etc., LIV, No. 2. New York, 1913.

Moore, John Bassett, ed., *History and Digest of International Arbitrations to which the United States has been a Party*. 6 v. Washington, 1898.

——, ed., *The Works of James Buchanan, Comprising his Speeches, State Papers, and Private Correspondence*. 12 v. Philadelphia, 1908–1911.

Munford, Beverley B., *Virginia's Attitude toward Slavery and Secession*. New York, 1909.

Murphy, L. E., "The Civil Rights Law of 1875." *Journal of Negro History*, XII, 110–127 (April, 1927).

Nettels, Curtis, "Andrew Johnson and the South." *South Atlantic Quarterly*, XXV, 55–64 (Jan., 1926).

Newberry, Farrar, "The Nashville Convention and Southern Sentiment of 1850." *South Atlantic Quarterly*, XI, 259–273 (July, 1912).

Nicolay, John G., and Hay, John, eds., *Complete Works of Abraham Lincoln*. 12 v. New York, 1905.

Nichols, Roy F., "United States *v*. Jefferson Davis." *American Historical Review*, XXXI, 266–284 (Jan., 1926).

Niles Weekly Register. 75 v. Baltimore, 1811–1849. (Republished in 36 vols.)

Otis, Harrison G., "The Causes of [Johnson's] Impeachment." *Century Magazine*, LXXXVII, 187–195 (Dec., 1912).

Owsley, Frank L., *State Rights in the Confederacy*. Chicago, 1925.

Parker, Joel, *Personal Liberty Laws*. Boston, 1861.

Parrington, Vernon L., *Main Currents in American Thought*. 3 v. New York, 1927–1930. (One volume edition, 1939.)

Peirce, Paul S., "The Freedmen's Bureau: A Chapter in the History of Reconstruction." State University of Iowa *Studies*, III, No. 1. Iowa City, 1904.

"Personal Liberty Laws in the Free States." *De Bow's Review*, XXIX, 370–373 (Sept., 1860).

Pierson, W. W., "Texas *v.* White." *Southwestern Historical Quarterly*, XVIII, 341–367; XIX, 1–36; 142–158 (April, July, Oct., 1915).

Pratt, Harry E., "David Davis, 1815–1886." Illinois State Historical Society *Transactions*, 1930, 157–183.

Prince, B. F., "The Rescue Case of 1857." Ohio State Archaeological and Historical Society *Publications*, XVI, 292–309. Columbus, July, 1907.

Quaife, Milo M., *The Doctrine of Non-Intervention with Slavery in the Territories*. Chicago, 1910.

Rainwater, Percy L., *Mississippi: Storm Center of Secession, 1856–1861*. Baton Rouge, 1938.

Ramsdell, Charles W., "The Frontier and Secession," in Dunning, William A., *Studies in Southern History and Politics*, 63–79.

Randall, James G., *The Civil War and Reconstruction*. Boston, [c1937].

——, *Constitutional Problems under Lincoln*. New York, 1926.

——, "Lincoln in the Rôle of Dictator." *South Atlantic Quarterly*, XXVIII, 236–252 (July, 1929).

——, "Lincoln's Task and Wilson's." *South Atlantic Quarterly*, XXIX, 349–368 (Oct., 1930).

Register of Debates in Congress. 29 v. Washington, 1825–1837.

Revised Statutes of the United States. 2 edn. Washington, 1878.

Rhett, Robert Barnwell, "Letter to Richard Crallé, Oct. 25, 1854." *American Historical Review*, XIII, 311 (Jan., 1908).

Richardson, James D., comp., *A Compilation of the Messages of the Presidents*. . . . 10 v. Washington, 1896–1899.

Richman, Irving B., "Citizenship of the United States." *Political Science Quarterly*, V, 104–123 (March, 1890).

Roane, Spencer, "Correspondence," in *John P. Branch Historical Papers for 1905*, 123–142. Randolph-Macon College, Ashland, Virginia, 1905.

——, "Letters of," in New York Public Library *Bulletin*, X, 167–180 (1906).

——, Reprints of articles signed "Amphictyon" and "Hampden" from *Richmond Enquirer*, March 30, April 12, June 11, 15, 18, and 22, 1819, in *John P. Branch Historical Papers for 1905*, 51–122. Randolph-Macon College, Ashland, Va., 1906.

——, Reprints of articles signed "Algernon Sidney," from the *Richmond Enquirer*, May 25 and 29, June 1, 5, and 8, 1821, in *John P. Branch Historical Papers for 1906*, 78–183. Randolph-Macon College, Ashland, Va., 1906.

Rowland, Dunbar, ed., *Jefferson Davis, Constitutionalist.* . . . 10 v. Jackson, Miss., 1923.

Royall, William L., "The Fourteenth Amendment: the Slaughter-House Cases." *Southern Law Review*, n. s., IV, 558–584 (Oct., 1878).

Russell, Alfred, "Status and Tendencies of the Dartmouth College Case." *American Law Review*, XXX, 321–356 (May-June, 1896).

Savage, William S., *The Controversy over the Distribution of Abolition Literature, 1830–1860.* Association for the Study of Negro Life and History, Inc., 1938.

Schuyler, Robert L., "Polk and the Oregon Compromise." *Political Science Quarterly*, XXVI, 443–461 (Sept., 1911).

Scott, Eben Greenough, *Reconstruction during the Civil War.* Boston, 1895.

Scott, James B., see Hunt, Gaillard.

Sedgwick, Henry D., *Francis Parkman.* Boston, 1904.

Sellers, James L., "Republicanism and State Rights in Wisconsin." *Mississippi Valley Historical Review*, XVII, 213–229 (Sept., 1930).

Shanks, Henry T., *The Secession Movement in Virginia, 1847–1861.* Richmond, Va., 1934.

Shryock, Richard H., *Georgia and the Union in 1850.* Durham, N. C., 1926.

Simms, Henry H., *Life of John Taylor.* Richmond, Va., 1932.

Sioussat, St. George L., "Tennessee, the Compromise of 1850 and the Nashville Convention." *Mississippi Valley Historical Review*, II, 313–347 (Dec., 1915).

Smith, Charles W., Jr., *Roger B. Taney: Jacksonian Jurist.* Chapel Hill, N. C., 1936.

Smith, Duane D., *The Development of the Concept of Citizenship in American Constitutional Law.* Manuscript dissertation submitted for the degree of Doctor of Philosophy at The Ohio State University, 1936.

Smith, Edwin, "Spencer Roane," in *John P. Branch Historical Papers for 1905,* 1–33. Randolph-Macon College, Ashland, Virginia, 1905.

Smith, T. V., "Slavery and the American Doctrine of Equality." *Southwestern Political and Social Science Quarterly,* VII, 333–352 (March, 1927).

Steiner, Bernard C., *Life of Roger Brooke Taney.* Baltimore, 1922.

Stenberg, Richard R., "The Motivation of the Wilmot Proviso." *Mississippi Valley Historical Review,* XVIII, 535–541 (March, 1932).

——, "Some Political Aspects of the Dred Scott Case." *Mississippi Valley Historical Review,* XIX, 571–577 (March, 1933).

Stephens, Alexander H., *Constitutional View of the Late War between the States.* 2 v. Philadelphia, [c1868–1870].

——, "Correspondence." See Toombs, Robert.

——, "Letter," in American Historical Association *Report* for 1911, II, 120–122.

Stewart, G. T., "The Ohio Fugitive Slave Law." *Firelands Pioneer,* n. s., V, 60–82 (July, 1888).

Storey, Moorfield, *Charles Sumner.* Boston, 1900.

Story, Joseph, "Correspondence." See Marshall, John.

——, *Life and Letters.* See Story, William W., editor.

Story, William W., *Life and Letters of Joseph Story.* 2 v. Boston, 1851.

Stroud, George McDowell, *A Sketch of the Laws Relating to Slavery in the Several States of America.* 2 edn. Philadelphia, 1856.

Stryker, Lloyd P., *Andrew Johnson: a Study in Courage.* New York, 1929.

Sumner, Charles, "Our Domestic Relations." *Atlantic Monthly,* XII, 507–529 (Oct., 1863).

Swisher, Carl B., *Stephen J. Field, Craftsman of the Law.* Washington, 1930.

——, Roger B. Taney. New York, 1935.

Tappan, Lewis, *The Fugitive Slave Bill: Its History and Unconstitutionality.* New York, 1850.

Tawney, R. H., *Religion and the Rise of Capitalism.* New York, [c1926].

Thomas, David Y., "The Law of Impeachment in the United States." *American Political Science Review,* II, 378–395 (May, 1908).

Tilberg, W. E., "Responsibility for the Failure of Compromise in 1860." *Historical Outlook*, XIV, 85–93 (March, 1923).

Tocqueville, Alexis de, *Democracy in America.* 2 v. Boston, 1873.

Toombs, Robert, *Correspondence of Robert Toombs, Alexander H. Stephens and Howell Cobb.* American Historical Association *Report* for 1911, II.

Treiber, Jacob, "The Jurisdiction of the Federal Courts in Actions in which Corporations are Parties." *American Law Review*, XXXIX, 564–580 (May, 1905).

Turner, Frederick J., *The United States, 1830–1850: The Nation and Its Sections.* New York, 1935.

Tyler, Samuel, *Memoir of Roger Brooke Taney.* Baltimore, 1872.

Ulrich, Barton A., *Abraham Lincoln and Constitutional Government.* Chicago, 1916.

United States Statutes at Large. Boston, 1845–1873. Washington, 1875–.

Vallandigham, James L., *A Life of Clement L. Vallandigham.* Baltimore, 1872.

Van Buren, Martin, *Autobiography.* American Historical Association *Report* for 1918, II.

Van Dyne, Frederick, *Citizenship of the United States.* Rochester, N. Y., 1904.

Van Santvoord, George, *Sketches of the Lives and Judicial Services of the Chief-Justices of the Supreme Court of the United States.* New York, 1854.

Von Holst, H. E., *John C. Calhoun.* Boston, 1882.

Walmsley, James E., ed., "The Change of Secession Sentiment in Virginia in 1861." *American Historical Review*, XXXI, 82–101 (Oct., 1925).

Warren, Charles, *Congress, the Constitution, and the Supreme Court.* Boston, 1925.

——, "Lincoln's 'Despotism' as Seen by Critics of 1861." *New York Times*, May 12, 1918.

——, "New Light on the History of the Federal Judiciary Act of 1789." *Harvard Law Review*, XXXVII, 49–132 (Nov., 1923).

——, *The Supreme Court and the Sovereign States.* Princeton, 1924.

——, *The Supreme Court in United States History.* Rev. edn., 2 v. Boston, 1926.

Washington, H. A., ed., *The Writings of Thomas Jefferson, Being his Autobiography, Correspondence, . . . and Other Writings.* 9 v. Washington, 1853–1854. (Often called "Congress edition.")

Watson, D. K., "The Trial of Jefferson Davis, an Interesting Constitutional Question." *Yale Law Journal*, XXIV, 669–676 (June, 1915).

Way, Royal B., "Was the Fugitive Slave Clause of the Constitution Necessary?" *Iowa Journal of History and Politics*, V, 326–336 (July, 1907).

Weber, Max, *The Protestant Ethic and the Spirit of Capitalism.* London, [1930].

Webster, Daniel, *Works of.* See Everett, Edward, ed.

Weisenburger, Francis P., *The Life of John McLean.* Columbus, Ohio, 1937.

Weston, M. F., "Political Questions." *Harvard Law Review*, XXXVIII, 296–333 (Jan., 1925).

White, Horace, *The Life of Lyman Trumbull.* Boston, 1913.

White, Laura A., *Robert Barnwell Rhett, Father of Secession.* New York, 1931.

White, M. J., "Louisiana and the Secession Movement of the Early Fifties." Mississippi Valley Historical Association *Proceedings*, VIII, 278–288 (1914–1915).

Whiting, William, *War Powers under the Constitution.* Boston, 1871.

Willoughby, W. W., *Constitutional Law of the United States.* 2 v. New York, 1910.

Winston, Robert W., *Andrew Johnson, Plebian and Patriot.* New York, 1928.

Woodburn, James A., "The Historical Significance of the Missouri Compromise." American Historical Association *Report* for 1893, 249–298.

——, *The Life of Thaddeus Stevens: A Study in American Political History.* . . . Indianapolis, 1913.

Woodson, Carter G., *The Negro in our History.* Washington, 1922.

Wright, Benjamin F., Jr., "Political Institutions and the Frontier," in Fox, D. R., ed., *Sources of Culture in the Middle West*, 15–37.

Wright, T. R. B., "Judge Spencer Roane." *Virginia Law Register*, II, 473–481 (November, 1896).

INDEX

Ableman v. Booth, 196, 232.
Abolition, 177 f.
  See Mails.
Adams, John, 5, 67.
Adams, John Quincy,
  campaign of 1828, 83;
  edits journal of Convention, 69;
  on emancipation, 315;
  on Plumer's proposal, 69;
  on right of petition, 183.
Admiralty jurisdiction, 97, 136–138.
Agrarianism, 368.
Alabama,
  on foreign corporations, 124.
  See Comity Cases.
Amending process,
  Madison on, 4;
  Monroe on, 15;
  nullification and, 35.
Amendment,
  eleventh, 128;
  fifteenth, 343;
    interpretation, 344;
    ratification, 344;
    supplementary legislation, 345–346;
  fourteenth;
    application to corporations, 126, 129;
    enforcement, 471;
    interpretation, 361–366;
    provisions, 335–336;
    purpose, 336, 369;
    South rejects, 336;
    South required to ratify, 340;
  Jefferson on a., 370;
  limitations on power of, 323;
  proposals of, 146;
  thirteenth, 322 f.;
    adopted, 324;
    effect on representation, 335;
    objections to, 323;
    ratification challenged, 324.
American Antislavery Society, 177 f.
American Insurance Company v. Canter,
  144, 219;
  Calhoun on, 223;
  cited by Stephens, 219.
Amistad case, 204 n.
Amnesty,
  Johnson's proclamation of, 330;

Amnesty—Continued
  Lincoln's proclamation of, 325–326.
Amy Warwick, The. See Prize Cases.
Annexation,
  of foreign territory, 206 f.;
  of Texas, 185, 206 f.
Antislavery. See Abolition, American
  Antislavery Society, Petition, right
  of.
Aristocracy. See Capitalism, Middle
  class.
Arkansas,
  and popular sovereignty, 159 n.;
  secedes, 273;
  territory of, 151.
Arlington. See Lee, Robert E.
Ashburton, Lord, 202.

Bagby, Arthur P., 215.
Baldwin, Abraham,
  conversation with Stiles, 58;
  dispute with Dayton, 61;
  informs Congress on Convention, 58.
Baldwin, Henry,
  appointed associate justice, 93;
  death, 102 n.;
  opinions:
    on bills of credit, 135 f.;
    in Miln case, 103.
Bancroft, George, 71.
Bank of Augusta v. Earle, 121 f.
Bank of U. S. v. Deveaux, 127 n., 128 n.
Bank of the United States (Second).
  See United States Bank.
Barbour, James, 11, 157.
Barbour, Philip P.,
  appointed associate justice, 93;
  death, 102 n.;
  decision in Miln case, 99 f., 101.
Bayley, Thomas H., 176 f.
Bates, Edward, 283, 324.
Belligerents,
  rights of, 279, 308–314;
  treatment of Confederates, 279 f.
  See Civil War, Insurrection, Prize
  Cases.
Bennett, Henry, 231.
Benton, Thomas H.,
  and Missouri constitution, 160 n.;